I

MW00583726

Shakespeare and Feminist Criticism

First published in 1991, this book is the first annotated bibliography of feminist Shakespeare criticism from 1975 to 1988 — a period that saw a remarkable amount of ground-breaking work. While the primary focus is on feminist studies of Shakespeare, it also includes wide-ranging works on language, desire, role-playing, theatre conventions, marriage, and Elizabethan and Jacobean culture — shedding light on Shakespeare's views on and representation of women, sex and gender. Accompanying the 439 entries are extensive, informative annotations that strive to maintain the original author's perspective, supplying a careful and thorough account of the main points of an article.

Shakespeare and Feminist Criticism

An Annotated Bibliography and Commentary

Philip C. Kolin

Routledge
Taylor & Francis Group

First published in 1991
by Garland Publishing Inc.

This edition first published in 2017 by Routledge
2 Park Square, Milton Park, Abingdon, Oxon, OX14 4RN
and by Routledge
711 Third Avenue, New York, NY 10017

Routledge is an imprint of the Taylor & Francis Group. an informa business

A Library of Congress record exists under LC control number: 91027900

ISBN 13: 978-1-138-28151-6 (hbk)
ISBN 13: 978-1-315-27109-5 (ebk)
ISBN 13: 978-1-138-28153-0 (pbk)

SHAKESPEARE AND FEMINIST CRITICISM
An Annotated Bibliography and Commentary

Philip C. Kolin

Library of Congress Cataloging-in-Publication Data

Kolin, Philip C.
    Shakespeare and feminist criticism : an annotated bibliography and
commentary / Philip C. Kolin.
        p.   cm. — (Garland reference library of the humanities ; vol.
1345)
    Includes indexes.
    ISBN 0–8240–7386–X (alk. paper)
    1. Shakespeare, William, 1564–1616—Criticism and interpretation—
Bibliography. 2. Feminism and literature—England—History—16th
century—Bibliography. 3. Women and literature—England—
History—16th century—Bibliography. 4. Sex role in literature—
Bibliography. I. Title. II. Series.
Z8811.K76   1991
[PR2965]
822.3'3—dc20   91–27900
                                                                              CIP

Printed on acid-free, 250-year-life paper
Manufactured in the United States of America

FOR

MARY,

REGINA COELI

TABLE OF CONTENTS

Shakespeare and
Feminist Criticism

INTRODUCTION

For approximately the last two decades, feminist criticism has provided an invaluable discourse for understanding and appreciating Shakespeare's plays and poems. To be sure, pro-feminist interpretations of Shakespeare and other Renaissance texts can be found long before this. In 1589, Jane Angar's *Protection of Women* protested both "Euphemism (male-controlled discourse) and men's unfounded notions about women," according to Simon Shepard (1981, item 166). Since 1700, there have been numerous appreciations of Shakespeare's women, both for their imaginative and their intellectual powers. In his *Notes on Othello* (1765), Dr. Johnson observed: " ... the soft simplicity of *Desdemona*, confident of merit, and conscious of innocence, her artless perseverance in her suit, and her slowness to suspect that she can be suspected, are such proof of Shakespeare's skill in human nature, as I suppose, it is vain to seek in any modern writer." In our own century, George Bernard Shaw, who envisioned himself a feminist advocate, denounced Shakespeare's *Shrew* (see Lise Pedersen, 1977, item 50) and thought he could improve upon *Antony and Cleopatra*. A plethora of studies from the 1920s, 1930s, and 1940s have assessed the female character types that Shakespeare drew upon, as illustrated by Celeste Turner Wright's article on "The Amazons in Elizabethan Literature" (*Studies in Philology* 37 [1940]: 433-56).

Yet it is only since the mid-1970s that feminism as both theory and praxis has focused on Shakespeare. Writing in 1977, Carole McKewin entitled her work "Shakespeare Liberata: *Shakespeare and the Nature of Women*, and the New Feminist Criticism" (item 45). McKewin applauded Juliet Dusinberre's *Shakespeare and the Nature of Women*, published in 1975, as "the first full-length study of Renaissance drama in the mode of the new feminist criticism" and further commended Dusinberre's work for providing a "major step in an important and exciting area of Shakespeare studies." In 1977, feminist studies were just taking off. As McKewin pointed out, "In workshops at the Modern Language Association and at the Shakespeare Association of America, in various scholarly essays and in classrooms, the new feminist criticism of Shakespeare has moved from the status of fashionable topic to that of a tentative method of inquiry just outside the walls of the academy" (pgs. 157-58). Eleven years later, Ann Thompson reported that feminist interpretations of Shakespeare were becoming firmly established within the academy walls: "There has been an explosion of feminist criticism of Shakespeare during the 1980s. It is arguable that the feminist approach will turn out to have been one of the most lively, productive and influential aspects of Shakespeare criticism in this decade" (1988, item 437, p. 74). Given the importance of feminist studies of Shakespeare in the 1980s, Thompson could justifiably assert that feminist interpretations of Shakespeare were "not something that can be relegated to an all-woman ghetto, but [have become] a major new perspective that must eventually inform all readings" (p. 84).

Contributions of Feminist Criticism to the Study of Shakespeare

In his brief overview of feminist criticism of Shakespeare, Terence Hawkes (1986, item 337) limits the scope of feminist criticism to a study of Shakespeare's women and an investigation of the plays from a woman's perspective. Undeniably, feminists have made lasting contributions in both of these areas, but in more depth and with greater breadth than Hawkes seems willing to concede. Feminists have explored numerous topics besides those cited by Hawkes to provide a more balanced view of the plays and to recover and restore women's place in them. As Gayle Greene observes, feminist criticism of Shakespeare is more a matter of "reassessing than discovering a literary canon" (1981, item 158). While not claiming to be exhaustive, the following list of feminist (re)interpretations of Shakespeare suggests that these critics' insights are many and diverse.

(1) Thanks to feminist criticism, women characters in the plays (and the poems) are being explored in more productive and provocative

ways. At their most basic level, feminist interpretations of Shakespeare have called attention to and in many instances freed women characters from critical and cultural stereotypes that have marginalized, distorted, or negated women's contributions, creativity, and self-fashioning.

(2) Feminist readings have examined these female characters within the sometimes contradictory and anxious ideologies of sex, gender, power, and race of Elizabethan and Jacobean England. The result is that these women are rightfully seen as more complex, more central, and sometimes even subversive when they are situated within a more problematic and uncertain context than previous criticisms could or would be willing to admit.

(3) Feminists have successfully re-investigated the institutions and ideologies of patriarchy upon which much in the plays has been based. In the process, feminist interpretations have revealed that patriarchy, with its view of women as subservient to men, often promulgated a dangerous male code that is inconsistent and/or impossible to navigate agreements with, as Peter Erickson (1985, item 284) maintains. Carol Thomas Neely succinctly sums up the goals of many feminists in their confrontation with and challenge of patriarchy in Shakespeare: "feminists wished to undo hierarchies, interrogate binary oppositions, and divulge contradictions in phallocentric discourse and culture" (1988, item 427, p. 7).

(4) As a result of (3), feminists have challenged and problematized many male-centered critical approaches to Shakespeare's plays, to his women characters, and to male/female identities in the plays. Feminists have unearthed the prejudices that have masqueraded as givens in much traditional (and biased) criticism of Shakespeare. In doing so, feminist critics stress that patriarchy is not necessarily a hallowed construct that can explain everything in a play because it frequently explains away women's importance or ignores their (subversive) presence in the text. Feminism is both corrective and challenging.

(5) One of feminism's greatest contributions, as summarized by Susan Bassnett (1988, item 404), is that "Feminist criticism of Shakespeare has brought the whole question of sexuality in the plays to our attention...." Freed from the traditional binary and oppressive oppositions that classified women as evil/lecherous and men as noble/powerful, sexuality can be seen as a life force, a pattern to ensure creation and mutuality. Not distorted by convention, sexuality

constitutes and helps to explain major assumptions about all Shakespeare's characters, female as well as male.

(6) Feminist readings of Shakespeare have expanded the restricting notion of gender articulated by earlier critical schools and still adhered to by some contemporary approaches to the plays. It has been falsely assumed by many critical approaches that men behave in one way and women in another. Men act and women talk, to quote a Renaissance proverb. Feminist critics have rooted out "gender inequalities," as Jacqueline Rose (1985, item 307) terms them. The adage that one cannot change his/her sex but can change his/her gender elucidates many characters and situations in Shakespeare. Feminists usefully emphasize that gender roles are not imposed upon characters biologically but culturally. When society oppresses women, their roles are oppressed. Marilyn French aptly observed that "the most complete awareness" of ideas of gender "are found in the greatest artist Shakespeare" (1981, item 155). Perhaps most significantly, feminists have repeatedly shown how changes in gender can expand a character's opportunities instead of restricting them. As Carol Thomas Neely points out about *Antony and Cleopatra*: "feminist critics have ... found in the play the dissolution of gender boundaries, a dissolution variously interpreted ..." (1985, item 298, p. 136). Thanks to feminist criticism, gender is not indissolvably fixed in Shakespeare. Male characters can profitably incorporate female characteristics, and women characters can assume masculine ones.

(7) An expansive sense of gender has enabled feminists to re-evaluate the idea of genre. Gender has controlled genre and vice versa. Generic considerations have been responsible for severely restricting women's characterization and participation in a play because of gender. In particular, tragedy has focused on gender issues glorifying male valor at the expense of women's identity and accomplishments. Ann Thompson (1988, item 437) warns feminists not to privilege the tragedies at the expense of the other plays. Madelon Gohlke (1980, item 115, p. 180) insightfully urges that the tragedies should be seen "as a vast commentary on the absurdity and destructiveness of [the] defensive posture" men assume in protecting their male identity and oppressing women.

(8) Applying the insights of gender/sex studies to Shakespeare's theatre, feminists have increased our understanding of Shakespeare's androgynous heroines, unquestionably one of his greatest creations.

Feminist studies have provocatively explored the complex layers of role-playing that are only possible because of Shakespeare's representations of these characters. Boy actors playing women playing boys can test and disprove gender and societal assumptions. As one critic asks of an androgynous heroine, "Who is speaking?" And as Coppelia Kahn (1981, item 160) has insightfully pointed out, sexual identity can be different from personal identity.

(9) In its many achievements, and certain to be a part of its future accomplishments, feminist studies of Shakespeare have employed a variety of critical methods and discourses from collateral disciplines in art/iconography, psychology/psychiatry, Marxism, and linguistics/semiotics. For example, Marguerite Waller (1986, item 349) pleads for feminism and deconstructionism to work together; and Gayle Greene (1981, item 158) urges feminist critics of Shakespeare to adopt Marxist political zeal in their work. For Greene, both feminism and Marxism are necessarily "radical and radicalizing." Madelon Gohlke profitably offers a "feminist-psychoanalytic" reading of the tragedies (1980, item 115). As feminist criticism of Shakespeare abundantly proves, feminism is not a monolithic school but a vibrantly diverse discipline that profits from and does not shun disagreement. Yet even within that diversity feminist critics, as Gayle Greene stresses (1983, item 217), are engaged in a collaborative enterprise, sharing and building upon each other's work.

Essential reading for understanding the goals, problematics, and achievements of feminist studies of Shakespeare are a series of review essays published during the last 14 years. These review essays, listed chronologically, include: Carole McKewin (1977, item 45); Martha Andresen-Thom (1978, item 56); Carol Thomas Neely (1981, item 162); Gayle Greene (1983, item 217); Anne Parten (1984, item 267); Kathleen McLuskie (1985, item 295); Peter Erickson (1985, item 285); Jeanne Addison Roberts (1986, item 346); Peter Erickson (1987, item 366); Lynda Boose (1987, item 355); Gerald Rabkin (1988, item 429); Neely (1988, item 427); Ann Thompson (1988, item 437); and Claire McEachern (1988, item 425).

What follows is a bibliographic survey of some of the significant topics feminists have explored in their studies of Shakespeare.

Was Shakespeare a Feminist or Wasn't He?

Shakespeare's own (or perceived) views of women occupy an important place in much feminist criticism. But there is no swelling chorus of bardology among feminists. Shakespeare has been claimed as a feminist, a protofeminist, a cryptofeminist, and an antifeminist. Some representative opinions of Shakespeare as a feminist include the following. For Susan Shapiro (1978, item 75) Shakespeare was "the noblest feminist of them all"; and for Velma Richmond (1978, item 72) Shakespeare believed that the future of humanity lay in following the feminine way of life. He was way ahead of his time for many feminists (Diane Dreher, 1986, item 330, p. 116). Marilyn French charts a significant move toward the feminine as Shakespeare's career advanced: "Shakespeare began his career with profound respect for 'masculine' qualities and profound suspicion of 'feminine' ones. In a very short span–by the time he wrote *The Two Gentlemen of Verona*–he had come to admire 'feminine' qualities. By the end of his career, he had come to fear and deplore the power and capriciousness of the masculine principle, and to idealize certain aspects of the feminine" (1981, item 155, p. 17). While Linda Bamber admits that Shakespeare's plays are "governed by a male perspective," she emphasizes that the idea of the feminine is central to his work and that the comic heroines express Shakespeare's own prerogatives (1982, item 175). Gayle Greene (1982, item 187) honors Shakespeare for being more liberal than his contemporaries, even though his heroines (e.g., Portia, Rosalind) are assimilated into the patriarchy.

Inga-Stina Ewbank expressed a middle of the road opinion: "I do not think he was either a feminist or an antifeminist, though partisan readers could no doubt read antifeminism in *Macbeth*, the opposite into *Othello* and (somewhat disturbingly) both into *King Lear*" (1978, item 58, p. 223). Similarly moderate views come from Martha Andresen-Thom (1978, item 56) who, in reviewing Juliet Dusinberre's *Shakespeare and the Nature of Women*, observed:

> I like her ideal but I am not sure it is a given of Nature, for our ideas of nature–feminine, masculine, human–are necessarily time-bound, culture-bound. And though we may safely call Shakespeare's vision of the nature of women more

"modern" because like ours [it is] more complex and more liberal, we may less safely call him a "feminist" if we mean by that a propagandist of certain ultimate and unambiguous truth about *the* nature of women–or woman. (273)

Also reviewing Dusinberre, Carole McKewin cautioned that Shakespeare offers a "darker vision of women" than Dusinberre endorses (1977, item 45). And even less sanguine about Shakespeare's beliefs, some feminists have assaulted him as a "sexist" (e.g., Peter Berek, 1988, item 405), an arch-conservative. Admitting Shakespeare's dedication to patriarchy, Coppelia Kahn (1982, item 190) locates a plus in this for feminists trying to uncover the pernicious patriarchal myths: "Paradoxically, it is because he [Shakespeare] does not stand outside patriarchal ideology, does not wholly reject it, that he is able to render the dilemmas of manhood so compellingly" (p. 37). Jeanne Addison Roberts (1986, item 346) also cautions that Shakespeare knew no other type of political rule except patriarchy and while Peter Reynolds (1988, item 430) concedes that Shakespeare may have felt sympathy for the lovers in *A Midsummer Night's Dream*, "he nevertheless reflects the prevailing attitude of his day" (p. 89) about the subjugation of women to their fathers and husbands. Similarly, Joost Daalder (1988, item 412) claims that we must not forget that Shakespeare's world is male dominated and his views on sex highly complicated.

Contrary to Dusinberre and others, B.J. Pendlebury (1975, item 14), Anne Parten (1984, item 267), and Sarup Singh (1988, item 434) accuse Shakespeare of following a double standard. For Parten, Shakespeare "fostered a more conservative ideal of wifely inequality and obedience even when the husband committed adultery." For Murray Schwartz, Shakespeare's common theme is the mistrust of women (1980, item 135). Kahn (1982, item 190, p. 40) has similarly remarked: " ... at some point in every play Shakespeare wrote, we hear the cuckoo's note .... "

Some feminist critics oppose drawing any conclusions about Shakespeare's beliefs. Peter Erickson's article on "Shakespeare and the Author Function" (1985, item 285) is essential reading along these lines. Erickson contends that it is impossible to assess Shakespeare's views and that there is no definitive philosophy of gender running through the works. For James Hill (1986, item 338) Shakespeare's response to women is subject to much debate, since Shakespeare constructed the women's roles with the strengths and limitations of the boy actors in mind. This practice must clearly be a "limiting filter," argues Hill.

Shakespeare's views of women have been traced to his own family history and temperament. Virginia Woolf glowingly honored Shakespeare for being androgynous, a view endorsed by Myra Schotz (1980, item 134), Phyllis Rackin (1987, item 393), and Robert Kimbrough (1982, item 192). The latter two critics find that Shakespeare advocates and celebrates androgyny in the plays. Stevie Davies (1986, item 328) believes that Shakespeare's family history accounts for his interest in feminine sources of masculine identity. Other feminists see reasons for Shakespeare's glorification of women, particularly the daughters of the romances, in his own life as a man who had to depend on his daughter for the succession of his line. Marianne Novy (1984, item 262), for one, believes that Shakespeare's own changing views of gender can be attributable to his being a grandfather; the romances emphasize "generativity" for characters and playwright. Stephen Orgel (1986, item 345) likewise claims there are biographical parallels between Shakespeare's daughters and Miranda and Ariel. Shakespeare's relationship with his mother has not always been interpreted in positive ways. A psychological study by Alexander Wolf (1980, item 146) argues that Shakespeare suffered from diegophrenia, or a split personality, because of his mother; and Donald Silver (1983, item 239) maintains that Shakespeare's mother cast him off as a poor replacement for a child she lost.

For many scholars Shakespeare's feminism, or lack thereof, must be judged against the practices of his own time. Again, opinion is divided. In Sue-Ellen Case's words, for some Shakespeare "was ahead of his time or the best of his time" (1988, item 410, p. 22). Diane Dreher echoes Erick Stockton's view that "he was as much of a feminist as an Elizabethan can be" (qtd., 1986, item 330, p. 115). Shakespeare was far more liberal than any other dramatist for Dusinberre (1975, item 6), devoted to dissolving the "artificial distinctions between the sexes" (p. 153). Marianne Novy asserts that Shakespeare saw through "the limitations of conventional gender expectations" (1984, item 262, p. 200). Opposing such views are those of Joost Daalder (1988, item 412) that Shakespeare's world is male dominated or that, for Marilyn Williamson (1986, item 352), he mythologizes patriarchy. Certainly a good number of feminists (Carol Thomas Neely, Lynda Boose, etc.) take strong issue with new historicist critics because they situate at the center of

Shakespeare's concern the protection and perpetuation of male power and authority. While acknowledging that Shakespeare supports patriarchy, Peter Erickson maintains that it is a benevolent rule of the fathers into which even the brightest and toughest heroine could be assimilated (1985, item 284).

Shakespeare's views of women have logically for many (and inevitably for others) been traced to his characters. Feminist readers have tried to come to terms with Shakespeare's own beliefs within the text and subtext of his women and men. Of course, trying to piece out what Shakespeare thought from his characters' actions and words is nothing new. Dryden's famous remark in 1679 clearly placed Shakespeare on the side of the men. As Dryden averred, Shakespeare's "excellency [was] in the more manly passions; Fletcher with the softer; Shakespeare writ better betwixt man and man. Fletcher betwixt man and woman" (qtd. in Carol Carlisle, 1980, item 106). More critical still of Shakespeare's abilities to create a satisfactory portrait of a woman, John Upton in 1748 concluded that Shakespeare doubtless had never "known such a character as a fine lady" (qtd. in Carlisle). A century later, the Victorians' unmatched praise for Shakespeare's pristine heroines amounted to hagiography (see Russell Jackson, 1979, item 88).

Today the much more sophisticated, and balanced, views of feminist readers locate Shakespeare's respect for and sometimes subversion of femininity in his women, and men, too. For some, Desdemona or Cordelia is the ideal that women as well as men should strive to emulate; other critics dim the accolades for these traditionally enshrined women to concentrate on Shakespeare's more problematic characters in whom they see his views reflected. Clara Claiborne Park sounds a cautionary note against bardology when she admits that Shakespeare did indeed "glorify the young woman as never before," but he also took the threat out of her behavior to appease his male culture (1980, item 133). Mary Free more stringently warns that it is wrong to see the heroines of Shakespearean comedy as "independent iconoclasts"; instead, they are the product of a male playwright who is not the "woman's champion" (1986, item 334). More bitter still, Marcia Reifer accuses Shakespeare of draining the life out of Gertrude and Ophelia by not giving them the dramatic attention they merit (1984, item 269). And B.J. Pendlebury simply concludes that Shakespeare did not necessarily endorse what his characters did or thought (1975, item 14).

Pendlebury's sentiments are compatible with the skepticism voiced by many feminists about trying to pin down conclusively what Shakespeare thought about women. Martha Andresen-Thom points out that women in the drama do not necessarily reflect a liberal culture but can express the masculine desire for such women (1978, item 56). McKewin stresses that feminist criticism must distinguish between "Shakespeare's use of male fantasy and his sanctions of it" (1977, item 45, p. 162). According to Sue-Ellen Case, it is misleading for feminists to even talk about Shakespeare's women, since he did not write for women nor did he present them on stage, using boys instead who aroused "homoerotic" passions (1988, item 410). Jonathan Dollimore (1986, item 329) also stresses that the boy actors incited the audience to homoeroticism. Kathleen McLuskie (1985, item 295) criticizes any feminist for privileging Shakespeare's women characters. Not allowing us to forget that Shakespeare wrote for a "male entertainment industry," McLuskie insists that any attempt to paint him as "Shakespeare the Feminist" is just historically inaccurate.

Shakespeare and Renaissance Ideologies of Marriage and Women

Feminists have read widely and deeply in contemporary customs and beliefs about women and marriage to understand how these ideologies inform Shakespeare's plays or how the plays deconstruct (or subvert) these conventional views. General overviews of women in Elizabethan and Jacobean England by Linda Woodbridge (1984, item 272) and Lawrence Stone (1977, item 54) offer good starting points to embark on a study of wedding customs in Shakespeare's England. Dusinberre (1975, item 6) extensively investigates Shakespeare's plays in light of Puritan views of women, chastity, marriage, and adultery. Arguing that Renaissance dramatists were positively influenced by Puritan doctrines, Dusinberre concludes that Shakespeare's women were made in the Puritan image of enlightened and educated human beings who deserved respect and even spiritual equality with men. Dusinberre's views are not shared by all feminists, obviously, as the critiques of her work by McKewin (1977, item 45) and Andresen-Thom (1978, item 56) demonstrate. Thirteen years after the publication of Dusinberre's *Shakespeare and the Nature of Women*, Eve Horwitz (1988, item 417) announced that masculine rational control, celebrated by the Puritans, is denied by the feminine misrule that Paulina represents in *The Winter's Tale* and which is "salutary and healing, possessed of a purgative power" (p. 10). Women's moral strength offers a new, higher spiritual code of behavior than narrow masculine views of sexuality and procreation. The Puritans' influence on the changing views of women and marriage during the Renaissance is also discussed by Mary Beth Rose (1988, item 431), by Sarup Singh (1988, item 434), and by Diane Dreher in her Chapter Two (1986, item 330).

Needless to say, of all Renaissance rituals/customs affecting women, marriage has received the most attention from feminist critics. In particular, Linda Fitz (1980, item 112); Ann Jennalie Cook (1977, item 35); Judith Cook (1980, item 108); Joan Klein (1980, item 123, and 1982, item 193); Marjorie Garber (1981, item 156); Louis Montrose (1983, item 231); and Mary Beth Rose (1988, item 431) provide wide-ranging discussions of Renaissance marriages as they were interpreted through manuals, etiquette books, and legal commentaries. Klein surveys the ways in which women were dependent on male institutions (most notably matrimony) and comments on the severe restrictions and punishments placed upon women who countered the official orthodoxy. Marilyn French (1981, item 155) characterized Renaissance marriage as an agreement between two men–father and husband–and yet another example of oppressive male power. Perhaps the highest praise for Shakespeare comes from Judith Gardiner (1985, item 288) who claims that Shakespeare himself shaped the Renaissance ideologies of marriage. According to Fitz (1980, item 112), Shakespeare favored free choice in marriage rather than a marriage made through parental arrangement.

Adolescent marriages, frequent in Shakespeare, are the subject of studies by D'Orsay Pearson (1983, item 235) and Ann Jennalie Cook (1977, item 35). Juliet, Anne Page, Marina, and Miranda are some very young Shakespearean brides. Shakespeare's dramatic practice, however, flies in the face of Renaissance custom, assert Cook and Pearson. In fact, Juliet's early marriage actually "violated Elizabethan norms" (Pearson, 1983, item 235). Though Elizabethan marriages may have been contracted when the parties were quite young, the weddings were not consummated until much later, when the couple had grown into maturity. Shakespeare may have altered this practice in *Romeo and Juliet* to capitalize on Italy's reputation as a land of passion. Unions consummated before the benefit of wedlock are discussed in a number of works on *Measure for Measure* (e.g., Margaret Ranald, 1979, item 93; Meredith Skura, 1979, item 96; Jan Kott, 1980, item 124; David Sundelson, 1983, item 241; Marilyn Williamson, 1986, item 352) and *All's Well* (e.g., Neely, 1985, item 298 and Susan Snyder, 1988, item 436). Interpreting the bed tricks in these two plays, Zvi Jagendorf (1983, item 223) looks at them in light of the Biblical act of procreation and concludes that Shakespeare "reverses the Biblical archetype that a man can gain wisdom" in the dark. Studying Elizabethan marriage laws, Germaine Greer (1981, item 159) finds them "garbled," making matrimony easy to get into and just as easy to get out of.

Shakespeare frequently departed from conventional wedding rituals to emphasize disorder and deranged patriarchy. Hyman Muslin (1982, item 197) discusses the ways parents use marriage in *Romeo and Juliet* to threaten their children's selfhood. Three articles by Lynda Boose (1975, item 4; 1982, item 177; and 1986, item 324) investigate the ways in which brides and brides-to-be in *Merchant of Venice*, *As You Like It*, and *King Lear* are assisted or thwarted in their journeys into matrimony by fathers. Violating the wedding ritual of giving the bride to the groom, Lear frustrates the rites of marriage by wanting to keep Cordelia for himself (Boose, 1986). Harry Berger (1979, item 80) claims, too, that in wanting to keep Cordelia for himself Lear would make her his mother and "become his own grandson." Diane Dreher's Chapter Three, "The Paternal Role in Transition" (1986, item 330), also explores wedding rituals in light of patriarchal imperatives. Claire McEachern (1988, item 425) maintains that *Lear* reverses the traditional marriage ritual by wanting Cordelia to buy her right to marry. The thesis of Carol Thomas Neely's book (1985, item 298) is that broken nuptials give women the power to resist domination while marriage restores male control.

Married life in Shakespeare is far from bliss. Shakespeare presents happy couples when they are betrothed but does not show us a complete picture of a happily married woman (Mary C. Williams, 1980, item 145). Timothy G.A. Nelson (1975, item 12) makes a similar point. In her Chapter One, "The Comedies of Courtship: Men's Profit, Women's Power," Marilyn Williamson (1986, item 352, p. 25) observes: "The marriage, which usually represents monetary profit or social advancement for the men, means subordination for the women, who may have been spirited and powerful during the courtship." Harry Berger (1982, item 176) explores life after marriage in *Much Ado*, pointing out that it offers unnatural confinement for the women. Williamson (1986) reminds us that in Shakespeare's age, a married woman was "no person," someone without status. We have only to think of Adriana and Antipholus of Ephesus from the early *Comedy of Errors* to Leontes and Hermione in the late *Winter's Tale* to see how accurate these observations by feminists are. The first night of Desdemona's marriage is hardly blissful. Timothy G.A. Nelson and Charles Haines (1983, item 232) argue that because of the Iago-engineered fights on Cyprus, Othello's marriage was never consummated. Articles by Edward Snow (1980, item 138) and Lynda Boose (1975, item 4; 1986, item 324) pay special attention to Desdemona's wedding sheets and the Renaissance custom of displaying the blood-stained sheets after the wedding night to prove that the bride was a virgin. Boose (1975) and Neely (1977, item 49; 1985, item 298) carefully relate the sheets to the strawberry-embroidered handkerchief that Othello received from his mother. (Marjorie Garber [1986, item 336] believes that the bloody napkin Orlando shows Rosalind is also related to the blood-stained sheets of matrimony.) Well into marriage, the couples in *Merry Wives* experience distress. Anne Parten (1985, item 304) compares Ford's and Falstaff's punishment with the indignities reserved for the henpecked/cuckolded husband in the Elizabethan skimmington. David Bevington (1984, item 244) argues that unhappy Shakespearean marriages are based on sexual conflicts; and Irene Dash (1981, item 152) demonstrates how marriage imposes restraints on Othello. Richard Wheeler (1975, item 20) concentrates on the fragmentation of family relations in *All's Well*. And Timothy G. A. Nelson (1985, item 301) finds that childbearing and raising in the plays are fraught with danger and foreboding.

Representations of the female in art and iconography assist readers to interpret Shakespeare's women. Clark Hulse (1978, item 64) and Robin Bowers (1981, item 150) pursue similarities between iconography and Lucrece in *Rape of Lucrece*. Mary Hamer comments on Cleopatra in and through art (1988, item 416). Peter Stallybrass explores Renaissance views of women's bodies as grotesque (1986, item 348). In an extensive discussion of Ophelia, Elaine Showalter (1985, item 308) uncovers the layers of meaning that Hamlet's forlorn mistress had as the quintessential example of female madness in art, literature, and psychiatry. Ophelia is the subject of many studies that concentrate on Renaissance types and typology. Cherrell Guilfoyle (1980, item 117), for example, compares Ophelia to Mary Magdalen. Paulina in *Winter's Tale* likewise has a varied ancestry. For Carolyn Asp (1978, item 57), she keeps company with Lady Consolation and Beatrice as a figure in the *Consolatio* tradition; and for Stevie Davies (1986, item 328), Paulina is the woman magus. Quite differently, her character is indebted to the "urban witch/bawd" for D'Orsay Pearson (1979, item 92).

Of all Renaissance women, Queen Elizabeth unquestionably merits most attention from feminists attempting to discover contemporary beliefs about women, men, and the issues of power and identity. In her person Elizabeth summed up the paradoxes of the age and possibly explained some of the tensions in Shakespeare's plays. Kim Noling (1988, item 428) comments on the significance of the infant Elizabeth in *Henry VIII*. For Susan Bassnett (1988, item 404), Elizabeth as woman and ruler was a "split entity." She was the virgin queen with the masculine heart, as Louis Montrose points out (1986, item 344). Montrose deconstructs the "cult of Elizabeth" in Shakespeare's "distinctly phallocentric" sphere. She was a woman who paradoxically ruled a patriarchy and yet enhanced the role of women, according to Velma Richmond (1978, item 72). As portrayed in *Henry VIII*, Elizabeth was the "best model for the earthly role" for Hugh Richmond (1979, item 94). Stephen Orgel (1986, item 345) maintains that Elizabethan power was maternal and paternal, something like Caliban's inheritance. Finding another Shakespearean character to compare with Elizabeth, Velma Richmond (1978, item 72) believes that Cleopatra echoes the British queen; and for Angela Pitt (1981, item 165), Portia is modeled after the great queen. Gabriele Jackson (1988, item 420) even finds some elements of Elizabeth in Joan of Arc. Heather Dubrow (1987, item 364) links the sexual politics in *Venus and Adonis* to ambivalence about Queen Elizabeth, another aggressive woman. For Dianne Ferris (1981, item 154), Shakespeare was dissatisfied with a woman on the throne and expressed his displeasure through Richard II, a feminine ruler with whom Elizabeth compared herself. In contrast to Ferris's reading, Peter Erickson (1987, item 365) studies *Merry Wives of Windsor* in light of the cultural stresses found in a patriarchal country ruled by a queen who invites comparisons with the resourceful merry wives. Erickson points to one of the chief Elizabethan paradoxes–England had to affirm the queen to affirm the patriarchy she sustained.

Combating Stereotypes

Feminist critics have called attention to the ways in which cultural and sexual stereotypes have powerfully defined and oppressed women in Shakespeare's plays and poems. This happens, Kathleen McLuskie argues (1988, item 426), when woman is read as a sign, not a self. Focusing on traditional and non-traditional roles of women in Shakespeare, feminist critics have written many consciousness-raising studies. Conventionally, women have been portrayed as weak and men as strong. Carolyn Asp (1981, item 147) pursues the implications of sexual stereotyping in *Macbeth*, where manliness is equated with strength and weakness is associated with the feminine. Jan Blits (1981, item 149) does likewise in *Julius Caesar*. And Rob Wilson (1987, item 402) sees Desdemona as both poison and medicine. The bifurcation continues with women being characterized (or perceived) as half god/half fiend. Valerie Traub (1988, item 438), and Cherrell Guilfoyle (1980, item 117), for example, explore the whore/angel dichotomy into which women are often forced in the plays. Studies by S. N. Garner (1976, item 23); Carol Thomas Neely (1985, item 298); and R. S. White (1986, item 350) of the critical dichotomy surrounding Desdemona alert us to the severe limitations of either/or views in this play. Dusinberre (1975, item 6) traverses the twin (ideological) dangers of Petrarchan idolatry and antifeminist satire.

Discussing *Love's Labor's Lost*, Irene Dash (1981, item 152) points out how and why the Princess mocks Petrarchan conventions. Thomas Greenfield (1977, item 40) argues that idealizing Cordelia in Act 1 only compromises Lear's tragedy. Neely (1985, item 298) shows that Shakespeare exposes the limitations of Petrarchianism when his men idealize women. Similarly, Barbara Bono (1986, item 323) demonstrates how Rosalind transforms the Petrarchan views of women to make them companions–not just mistresses–to men; and Nancy Hayles (1979, item 86) reveals how Rosalind establishes herself not as a "Petrarchan abstraction" but a real woman. Peter Erickson (1985, item 284) attempts to prove that by idealizing women, men are turned into slaves. And, finally, Heather Dubrow (1987, item 364) maintains that though Shakespeare satirizes Petrarchan conventions in the sonnets, the poet's speaker could not break away from them.

Yet despite such idealizations, it is safe to say that the angelic side of woman in Shakespeare has received far less representation than her stereotypical weak and evil side. Distorted views of women, of course, come from a corrupt and corrupting masculine code (Barbara Mowat, 1977, item 47). Gayle Greene (1979, item 82) and Coppelia Kahn (1981, item 160) identify the damaging characteristics of this code–honor, violence, revenge, following the rule of the fathers blindly. Kahn uses this code to explain the conduct and tragedy of a number of Shakespeare's heroes, most notably Romeo and Macbeth; Greene focuses on Othello. While A.K. Nardo (1977, item 48) argues that Romeo is torn between such a male code and love for his lady Juliet, Marianne Novy (1984, item 262) concludes that Romeo accepts that code and the "manhood of violence" it imposes on him. Similarly pointing out the destructiveness of such a masculine code, Neely's Chapter Three (1985, item 298) assesses the etiology of revenge in *Othello* and concludes that a phallocentric society produces division and misrepresentation of women. Myra Schotz (1980, item 134) declares that in Shakespeare only Macduff escapes a distorted masculine heroism.

A major element of that code is that men regard and treat women like property. Stephen Hannaford (1984, item 255) offers a useful catalogue of themes and narratives of men's sexual possessiveness of women in Renaissance drama. Ironically, women–society's disenfranchised citizens–validated lineage and succession in a patrilineal society (see, for example, Kahn, 1976, item 25). Jean Kline (1975, item 10) and James Calderwood (1988, item 409), in quite different ways, concentrate on Othello's possessiveness of Desdemona. Kahn (1976, item 25) explores Lucrece's fate as a wife who is her husband's property in *Rape of Lucrece*. Kathleen McLuskie (1982, item 196) analyzes woman as commodity in *Taming of the Shrew,* and Nona Fienberg (1982, item 183) similarly explores woman as commodity in *Pericles*. Gayle Greene (1979, item 82) argues that given such treatment women cannot protect themselves in the male world of *Othello*. Marianne Novy (1984, item 262) labels *Troilus and Cressida* as "one of the most devastating pictures in the Shakespeare canon of gender relations ... consequent on the treatment of women primarily as property" (p. 110). Men want to control their wives (Cohen, 1987, item 360) and fathers their daughters in a number of Shakespearean plays. As A.K. Nardo (1977, item 48) observes, Juliet is imprisoned because of her gender. Denied her freedom, Miranda becomes Prospero's "sexual bait," according to Lorie Jerrell Leininger (1980, item 125). Stephen Orgel

(1987, item 389), too, explores the ways in which Miranda (and other daughters) were used as commodities to win economic advantages for their fathers. The ultimate control of woman in a patriarchal society for Kahn (1976, item 25) is found in Lucrece's rape. Suzanne Gossett (1984, item 253) points out that raped women often had to marry the rapist, marriage being the social cure for such a crime. Heather Dubrow (1987, item 364) delves into the patriarchal complicity in the *Rape of Lucrece*. Laura Bromley (1983, item 214) also discusses the malefactions in *Rape of Lucrece*. Catherine Stimpson (1980, item 139) and W.D. Adamson (1980, item 100) insightfully study the plight of rape victims in Shakespeare.

Women's sexuality was particularly threatening to men who often branded them as whores or witches (Barbara Mowat, 1977, item 47; Dianne Hunter, 1988, item 419), or associated women's loose moral behavior with mirth, as in *The Merry Wives of Windsor* (Anne Parten, 1985, item 304). Peter Stallybrass (1986, item 348) points out that when women are classified by gender, they are stereotyped as lustful daughters of Eve. Reviewing some feminist books on motherhood, Kahn (1982, item 190, p. 35) astutely perceives that "woman's body becomes 'the carnal scapegoat' for ... fears of the flesh and mortality." This distortion of the feminine is a reflection of and a comment on male anxiety. Threatened by women's sexuality, men equated the sex act with the loss of life, as Meredith Skura (1979, item 96) points out in *Measure for Measure*. James Calderwood (1984, item 246) contends that sex is equated with death in *Macbeth* where Macbeth's murderous deeds are described as lustful acts. Valerie Traub (1988, item 438) argues that once they are "sexualized," women are diseased in the male imagination and must be contained, thus explaining what happens to Gertrude, Ophelia, and Desdemona. Katherine Henderson and Barbara McManus (1985, item 292) study many examples of such female stereotyping in Shakespeare and link these stereotypes to contemporary satires and pamphlets about women with which they have much in common. Many discussions of women in specific plays emphasize this feminine fate; for example, David Sundelson (1983, item 241) claims that Vienna turns all women into whores in *Measure for Measure;* women are stigmatized as lecherous and evil in *King Lear* for Martha Fiske (1987, item 367); and Hermione and Desdemona are reduced to sex objects according to Derek Cohen (1987, item 360).

A number of the plays illustrate the pernicious double standard at work. Women fall easily, and once fallen, no possibility for redemption exists for them (see Dusinberre, 1975, item 6; Singh, 1988, item 434). Anne Parten (1984, item 267) and Chapter Five of Coppelia Kahn's *Man's Estate* (1981, item 160) discuss the double standard of finding women in adultery more guilty than men. Joyce Sexton's monograph deals exclusively with the slandered woman (1978, item 74). Randolph Splitter (1982, item 204) points out that different meanings are attached to the word *honest* when applied to a woman as opposed to when it refers to a man. The sexual stereotypes inundating *Othello* have received much attention, especially from John Drakakis (1988, item 413) and Kathleen McLuskie (1988, item 426). McLuskie asks us to compare and contrast the different stories about Desdemona to understand the subversive effects of cultural stereotyping.

Feminist readings, however, do more than identify and lament stereotyping. Many show how Shakespeare combatted the very idea of stereotyping in characterizing his women. Deborah Aquino (1986, item 320) points to the anti-stereotypical women in the early comedies, especially Kate, and holds that, in general, the women before *Much Ado* are the dominant forces in their plays. In her Chapter Six, Novy contends that *Romeo and Juliet* transcends the traditional stereotypes of men and women (1984, item 262). Diane Dreher (1986, item 330), most notably in her Chapter Five on "Defiant Daughters," describes the ways young women challenged patriarchy; Charles Frey (1980, item 113) concentrates on the daughters of romance who break the customary pattern of control.

Several of Shakespeare's powerful women break stereotypical bonds and thereby arouse male fears. Portia, Helena, and Hermione are among the most male-threatening women in the canon. Each of their achievements is linked to the education/punishment/ transformation of a man. Portia has been variously interpreted as a learned woman (Lisa Jardine, 1987, item 377), a "poet-lawmaker" (Monica Hamill, 1978, item 63), a castrating wife and "phallic mother" (Vera Jiji, 1976, item 24), and the only one strong enough to save her marriage to Bassanio (Seymour Kleinberg, 1983, item 227; Catherine Wildermuth, 1982, item 209; and Karen Newman, 1987, item 388). H.R. Coursen (1985, item 279) submits that Portia, like Lady Macbeth, belongs in the male category of extroverted thinker. For Kahn (1985, item 293), Portia challenges male stereotypes that use the threat of female betrayal as a defense for men's actions. And while W. Thomas MacCary believes that Portia caricatures male excesses (1981, item 161), Mary Mathis (1988, item 424) contends that she exemplifies the best manhood has to offer. Many of these roles take Portia far beyond the stereotypical confines imposed on her by previous critical schools–dutiful daughter tied to a father's will; romantic heroine.

In discussing the nature of woman, feminism has concomitantly probed the nature of man and masculinity. For example, Diane Dreher's (1986, item 330) study of dominant and defiant women in Shakespeare contains a valuable section on "Male Development and the Crisis of Middle Life." For Kahn (1982, item 190), "female perspectives" and the "male experience" should be seen as "complementary, and ideally, mutually reinforcing" (p. 32). A number of feminists have demonstrated that Shakespeare challenged male stereotypes as well as female ones. Jane Carducci (1987, item 356), for example, concentrates on the failure of male language and institutions in *Titus Andronicus*. David Willbern (1978, item 79) also draws attention to male flaws in *Titus*. And Marjorie Garber pays attention to failures in male rules and regulations in *Romeo and Juliet* (1981, item 156). Lisa Lowe argues that manhood is bestowed on Coriolanus only through an act of wounding and emasculation (1986, item 342). For R.S. White (1978, item 78) and David Leverenz (1980, item 128), Hamlet's only salvation is to reach into his mother's feelings. Karen Newman (1987, item 388) has shown that when Othello upholds the gender system of wife ownership, he is ironically endorsing Desdemona's so-called sexual appetite which ideologically is linked to his blackness. Two studies take a different approach to male/female stereotypes by obliterating differences between them. Sandra Clark (1987, item 359) maintains that the wives in *Merry Wives* are not subversive females but are as protective of property rights as their husbands are; and Roger Shiner (1987, item 397) concludes that both sexes alike struggle for power.

"In Defense of Cressida ... "

One of feminist criticism's most laudable contributions to the study of Shakespeare is its reappraisal of so-called threatening, or problematic, women characters. Feminist criticism thus challenges years of male-dominated (and biased) readings of such oft-branded women as Cressida, Joan of Arc, and Gertrude. (Examining Cleopatra, Linda

Fitz's article [1977, item 37] is a model of its kind in discussing such male bias.) Feminist studies raise new questions and possibilities about these women characters not conceivable or permitted by other critical discourses where women's function and even selfhood are not explained but explained away by appealing to misleading stereotypes. Consequently, women like Joan and Cressida have been propagandized as evil or lecherous and consigned to a static role.

A significant number of feminist studies have come to the rescue of the much maligned Cressida. The title of Carolyn Asp's article (1977, item 32), which I chose as the heading for this section, clearly issues the battle call. Gayle Greene (1980, item 116) and Mary Hurst (1983, item 221), in particular, emphasize that Cressida deserves better treatment and that critics have misread Shakespeare's intentions. Greene is especially concerned with the obstacles Cressida must face in developing her own self. Hurst claims that Shakespeare "vindicates" Cressida, and Greene similarly argues that Shakespeare "exonerates" Cressida. She has been victimized by masculine society (Trojan and Greek) that has turned her, as Asp claims, into a "pawn of male desire." Reduced to property, Cressida has been so brutally invaded by men that her selfhood is endangered. As Alan Sinfield puts it, "Throughout the play she is jostled and harassed into successive positions, trying futilely to manipulate love codes designed to advantage the male. She is hardly allowed to exist as an independent person" (1982, item 203, p. 34). Greene concurs (1980, item 116).

Grant Voth and Oliver Evans (1975, item 19) and Mary Hurst (1983, item 221) emphasize that Cressida is a much more complex character than her detractors have given her credit for being. Judith Cook maintains that Cressida is not evil but, instead, a shrewd realist (1980, item 108). She effectively uses her wit and her language in a man's world that sells and barters (Hurst), and she knows far more about "legitimate" love than the callow Troilus (Voth and Evans). For Rene Girard (1985, item 289), Cressida is more "likable" than Troilus, and even when she betrays him, she is only imitating what he did to her. Discussing her wit, Stephen Lynch (1984, item 259) praises Cressida for her self-awareness; she is the only character in *Troilus and Cressida* who "perceives her own weakness" (p. 366). Cressida may invite the disdain of some feminists because she trades in male desire (Douglas Wilson, 1983, item 243), yet her actions shed revealing light on the presence and absence of desire (Girard, 1985, item 289). Marilyn

French expresses a frequently held observation about Cressida–"no other Shakespearean heroine is as knowledgeable about sex as Cressida is" (1981, item 155). Other ages were kinder to Cressida. Eighteenth-century director John Philip Kemble presented her and Troilus not as cynical but as romantic lovers (Jeanne Newlin, 1975, item 13). Undeniably, she is a "barometer" of changing views of female sexuality (Nikki Stiller, 1981, item 168), and thanks to the reinterpretation of feminist critics, her stock has gone up.

Joan of Arc is another maligned woman whom feminists have asked readers to re-examine and reappraise. Joan is the "epitome of female sexuality" for Patricia Silber (1979, item 95) and a figure of sexual ambiguity for Marilyn Williamson (1987, item 401). However, as Williamson points out, Joan's vices mirror Talbot's (the great English hero) weaknesses, too. And Gabriele Jackson (1988, item 420) astutely claims that Joan is linked in image and action to both the witches and Queen Elizabeth herself, reflecting the contradictory ideologies of the age. For Ralph Berry (1980, item 104), Joan supplies a necessary corrective; though the audience is conditioned to loathe her (she is Gallic, a witch, and sexually loose), she does challenge the English "inner myopia." Joan's sexuality is not a vice unique to her.

Other women, too, who have been attacked for their conventional wrongdoing, are the subject of feminist reappraisals, including a number of wives. Adriana in *Comedy of Errors* is not to be dismissed as a haranguing shrew. She should be viewed as a rejected wife who does not covet equality with or domination over her husband; she looks for conjugal love and respect, and on that score she deserves our sympathy (Dorothea Kehler, 1987, item 379). Pointing out how stage history has been guilty of misrepresentation, Rebecca Smith (1980, item 137) demonstrates how Gertrude has been falsely labeled as lascivious. There is no stain in the text of any rechy kisses on Gertrude's part. Seeing Gertrude as a figure of "ambiguous morality," Linda Bamber (1982, item 175) concludes she is a neutral character "who takes on the play's moods" (77). Jacqueline Rose defends Gertrude against charges of being responsible for disorder in the text (1985, item 307). While no feminist study surveyed in this volume has exonerated Goneril and Regan, Claudette Hoover (1984, item 256) finds that Lear's wayward daughters do "inspire metaphysical questions." As with Gertrude, Goneril and Regan have been blamed for their lust; yet, as Hoover maintains, they seek union with Edmund for more sophisticated, political reasons.

While not in the same camp of defamed women, many of Shakespeare's female characters in the histories have been the victims of critical neglect, or myopia, which feminist studies have attempted to redress. Marilyn Williamson (1975, item 21) portrays Katherine in *Henry V* as a shrewd and honest critic of Henry's pompous language and manipulative play acting. From a more expansive perspective, George Geckle discusses the links between sex and politics in the second tetralogy (1984, item 252). The women in *King Henry VIII* in particular have received much careful attention from a feminist perspective. Studies by Hugh Richmond (1979, item 94), Linda Micheli (1987, item 385), and A. Robin Bowers (1988, item 406) elucidate the function and thematic significance of the women in this late history play. Henry's wives and incomparable daughter attain a necessary centrality unappreciated by other critical approaches. Katherine, for example, is "the feminine ideal" and Anne "exceeds any other study of romantic sexuality" for Richmond (p. 14).

Dissolving Gender Boundaries

Feminist critics have revolutionized the way we look at Shakespeare's development of his male and female characters. Rather than accepting the binary oppositions of male/female, feminists transcend static and exclusive categories fixed by a phallocentric social and critical discourse (see, for example, Catherine Belsey, 1985, item 275; or Jacqueline Rose, 1985, item 307). Pushing such exclusive dualities aside, feminists have opened Shakespeare's characters up to radically fresh and inventive interpretations. They have shown that Shakespeare's men can possess feminine characteristics while his women can incorporate masculine ones. Extremely significant is feminism's insistence that one gender must not be valorized at the expense of another. At the same time feminist critics warn that an unnatural imbalance in, or warring union of, genders can lead to tragedy. As Peter Erickson (1985, item 284) wisely affirms, we must view gender as both "reversal" and "exchange."

A number of critics see Shakespeare endorsing cross-gendering. Shakespeare is, what might be called, a skillful exponent of *metagender beliefs*. Juliet Dusinberre, for example, argues that he believed that for true manhood, "masculine and feminine must marry in spirit" (1975, item 6, p. 291). Further confirming Shakespeare's endorsement of the feminine side of masculinity, Linda Woodbridge (1984, item 272) maintains that Shakespeare "attacks effeminacy only on the battlefield; he valued tenderheartedness regardless of gender." Turning to Sonnet 20, Donald Furber and Anne Callahan (1982, item 184) conclude that for Shakespeare, procreation is not male dominated; the "father can be the mother." Other feminist critics have found ample historical justification for Shakespeare's blending or combining two genders in one individual. The historical paragon of such a union was, of course, Queen Elizabeth. Dressed like an Amazon to visit her troops at Tilbury in 1584, she said: "I know that I have the body of a weak and feeble woman, but I have the heart and stomach of a king" (qtd. in Louis Montrose, 1986, item 344, p. 80). Interpreting Elizabeth's actions, Montrose points out that she "incarnated a contradiction at the very heart of the Elizabethan sex/gender system" (p. 81). Several studies explore how those contradictions served Elizabeth well and how her political Petrarchianism and male heart/female sexuality actually helped to problematize some of Shakespeare's work, especially *Merry Wives of Windsor* (see, for example, Peter Erickson, 1987, item 365).

Among the most fruitful analyses of gender are those that explore the feminine sources of masculinity. Many of Shakespeare's men fight feminization. Madelon Gohlke (1980, item 115) has correctly cautioned that men feared becoming "feminized mates." Romeo, Hamlet, and Macduff are three Shakespearean men who dread "woman-like" fears and tears. Coppelia Kahn's assessment of a masculine Verona (1975, item 9) and Juliet Dusinberre's commentary on the tragic hero's "incapacitating effeminacy" (1975, item 6) provide helpful background information. Linda Woodbridge (1984, item 272), among others, explores Enobarbus's charge that Antony is feminized by Cleopatra. Hamlet's use of amplification–profusive language–leads Patricia Parker to conclude that a "feminized Hamlet" believes that he can only talk and not act (1987, item 390). Lusting after his mother, Hamlet has been seen as guilty of desire associated with the feminine side of his nature, as Jacqueline Rose emphasizes (1985, item 307).

A number of Shakespeare's men suffer an enforced feminization according to some critics. For Dennis Biggins, Macbeth loses his manhood through the witches (1975, item 3). And Janet Adelman (1987, item 353, p. 95) claims that in *Macbeth* the androgynous parent Duncan is not "an emblem of masculine authority, but of female vulnerability," an easy prey to the maternal malevolence controlling Macbeth. It is troubling for Coriolanus to be both male and female, or a man like his mother, as Page Du Bois claims (1985, item 283). Falstaff, like Ford, suffers emasculation at the hands of the women in the *Merry Wives* (Nancy Cotton, 1987, item 362). Gayle Whittier has shown that Falstaff's "submerged androgyny" in *Merry Wives* makes him a deplorable "counterfeit woman" (1979, item 97). And according to Michael Stugrin, Adonis is Venus's "virginal victim" (1980, item 140).

On a more positive side, many Shakespearean men profit from and/or actively display a feminine side of their natures. Men can acquire the gift of sympathy from women, as Janice Hays points out (1980, item 118). Prospero is a "maternal father," combining authority and nurturing for Jerry McGuire (1982, item 195). Pericles's behavior suggests a feminine role for Davies (1986, item 328). Neely's Chapter Four on *Antony and Cleopatra* (1985, item 298) explores Antony's evolving and redeeming identity possible only because he assumes new values–masculine and feminine. For Neely, Antony refashions his male identity by acquiring and displaying "maternal bounty." Duncan is a benevolently androgynous figure in *Macbeth* for Dianne Hunter (1988, item 419). For David Sundelson (1983, item 241), Antonio's nurturing in *Merchant of Venice* is feminine. In contrast to Kahn's reading of *Romeo and Juliet* (1981, item 160), Edward Snow (1985, item 310) asserts that of all Shakespeare's heroes, Romeo is the "least inhibited by male bonding," even if his love is limited by his gender. Margaret Beckman (1975, item 2) believes that *Romeo and Juliet* symbolizes the harmony of male/female relationships. For Richard Abrams (1985, item 273), Palamon and Arcite acquire different genders in *Two Noble Kinsmen*, and Palamon even dreams of being "ravaged by his manly lady." Claiming that it is misleading to "de-eroticize" the sonnets by seeing them as an expression of friendship, Judith Gardiner (1985, item 288) demonstrates that Shakespeare violated gender roles in painting the young man's relationship with the poet in terms of courtship and marriage. Similarly, Eric La Guardia assesses the "dual sexual identities in *Twelfth Night*" (1984, item 257).

Many of the men in the romances also try to come to terms with the woman inside of them. Diane Dreher (1986, item 330) and Chapter Nine in Marianne Novy's book (1984, item 262) isolate such feminine traits among masculine characters in the romances. Leontes must learn many lessons about femininity in *Winter's Tale*. As Patricia Gourlay

(1975, item 8) stresses, women become the "metaphors for necessary qualities denied by Leontes's masculine society." He must come to understand and participate in Paulina's magic–see, for example, studies by D'Orsay Pearson (1979, item 92) and Charles Frey (1978, item 61). Cymbeline envies motherhood so much he refers to himself as a mother. Coppelia Kahn (1982, item 190) and Carolyn Asp (1986, item 321) call attention to Lear's feminine tactics which are a part of his symbolic stripping and nurturing. Kahn (1986, item 341) also elucidates Lear's use of feminine weapons as he subverts the traditional role of parent/child. Yet, as Kathleen McLuskie stresses, we need to keep in mind that Lear, like a woman, can be deprived of power and control (1985, item 295). Ten years earlier, Joan Klein contended that another patriarchal ruler, Claudius, was metaphorized into a woman; he is transformed into a victimized maid in Ophelia's song (1976, item 27).

As in other critical discourses, *Hamlet* has received intense attention from feminists who have explored gender roles in the play. Linda Bamber appropriately asserts that Hamlet "occupies the position of the cultural feminine" (1982, item 175, p. 89). One of the most influential essays on femininity and the heroes of tragedy is by David Leverenz (1980, item 128), who demonstrates that Hamlet is crushed by blindly following patriarchal values. Being a "manly revenger," Hamlet violates himself by rejecting his feminine side, and it is only by restoring his mother's valid feelings that he can be saved. Judith Wilt (1981, item 172) endorses Leverenz's arguments but urges feminists and other critics to extend them to other plays. Unlike Leverenz, though, Jacqueline Rose (1985, item 307) links Hamlet to "bad femininity." And while Peter Erickson (1985, item 284) declares that Horatio is a maternal substitute for Gertrude, the Stoic is still not a suitable alternative to women.

While some male characters profit from acknowledging and acting upon the feminine sources of their own identity, a few of Shakespeare's women do the same by developing their masculine attributes. Portia borrows wisely from the male world of knowledge for Lisa Jardine (1987, item 377); she gains control of her husband by being his "master-mistress" for Richard Wheeler (1985, item 315). For Mary Mathis (1988, item 424), Portia imitates the best of manhood by becoming "a professional man" in the courtroom. Combining masculine liberality with feminine spirituality, Portia, for Norma Greco (1982, item 186), polarizes sex roles within herself. Rosalind displays an energetic and restorative "active masculinity" for Margaret Beckman (1975, item 2). Helena in *All's Well* reverses gender roles by becoming the aggressor, the pursuer rather than the object of desire for Susan Snyder (1988, item 436). Even Desdemona, once marginalized for her passivity, is praised for her masculine courage and directness (W.D. Adamson, 1980, item 100). As Peter Erickson shows in his Chapter Three on *Othello* (1985, item 284), Desdemona undergoes a gender reversal by becoming the "fair warrior" who achieves power through Othello's stories. Carol Cook argues that the women in *Much Ado* mirror masculine language as a defense against feminine weakness, and consequently the play presents an "unresolved conflict" (1986, item 326). Lady Macbeth does not want to be made masculine by being unsexed, argues Lynn Veach Sadler (1975, item 15), because she wants her husband to be unsexed, too.

Many Shakespearean women are stigmatized for their destructive male qualities. For Linda Bamber (1982, item 175), Joan of Arc is similar to the masculine self, but Bamber offers this comparison not as a compliment. Joan is a "second-class man" (p. 140). Lady Macbeth and Volumnia are the opposites of the Jungian ideal of the fertile for Bamber. David Kastan (1982, item 191) provocatively suggests that Lady Macbeth wants to throw off her femininity permanently, unlike the disguises temporarily adopted by comic heroines. Margaret Loftus Ranald (1982, item 201) characterizes Margaret as a "masculine wife." Patricia Silber warns that as Margaret's behavior in the first tetralogy becomes more masculine, the "kingdom decays" (1979, item 95). Patrick Hogan terms Lady Macbeth and the witches "phallic women" (1983, item 219). According to Judith Gardiner (1985, item 288), the Dark Lady of the sonnets is the young man's ravager. Lisa Jardine perceptively comments on the misogynistic tradition responsible for the presentation of Tamora in *Titus Andronicus* and Lady Macbeth (1983, item 224). For Donald Furber and Anne Callahan, Venus is an ambiguous figure playing male and female roles; she is "the most sexually aggressive woman in modern literature" (1982, item 184, p. 61). Goneril and Regan, the masculine women in *King Lear*, have received much negative criticism because of their masculine traits; for Harry Berger (1979, item 80), Goneril has inherited her father's destructive patriarchal assumptions. After Lady Macbeth, Volumnia, the masculine mother, has received a great deal of attention for her male vices. Janet Adelman (1980, item 101) comments on why and how Coriolanus's mother loves blood more than milk. Frances Helphinstine (1979, item 87) faults the masculine values Volumnia teaches Coriolanus; she is "unfeminine" for extolling violence and "abusing maternal kindness." Phyllis Rackin also discusses Volumnia as a "manly woman" (1983, item 237).

Gender and Theatrical Representation

The critics whose work is the subject of this bibliography have insightfully feminized Shakespeare's theatre in two significant, complementary ways: (1) they have used the language of a theatre company's organization and role playing to describe women's functions, both in the plays and society at large and (2) they have successfully argued that gender itself is related to theatrical representation. Though Elizabethan and Jacobean women were prohibited from appearing as actresses on stage, the feminine presence infuses Renaissance plays and talk of plays. Condemning theatrical fictions, sixteenth-century moralists characterized the playhouses and the plays as loose women who entrap spectators through their illusions, the way a lascivious whore ensnares a man. Timothy Murray, for example, explores the negative implications of associating mimesis with female weakness (1985, item 297).

Of course, much more positive implications of feminine analogues to theatrical practice are found in feminist criticism. Lynn Veach Sadler (1975, item 15) briefly touches upon theatrical roles to characterize Lady Macbeth as playing the audience for and to her husband. Peter Hyland (1978, item 65) maintains that because Shakespeare's heroines share secrets with the audience, they bond with the audience and even become part of it. In greater detail and complexity, Marianne Novy's Chapter Five (1984, item 262) develops comparisons between women as actors in their respective plays as well as their role as audiences in those plays. Novy finds that both actors and women were the dispossessed, outsiders and foreigners, and considered "the Other" by an Elizabethan patriarchy. She maintains that *Antony and Cleopatra* is the only tragedy that "glorifies woman as actor" (p. 91). Matthew Wikander (1986, item 351) similarly explores women's relationship to the actors but from a different angle. He maintains that the sexual rivalry between men and women is best seen in terms of the theatrical rivalry between the boy actors (who played women) and the adults (who took the male roles) and concludes that the boy actors were subservient to the men and had to undergo a mandatory rite of passage, if they expected full rights. Sue-Ellen Case also links women to the boy actors as groups regarded as inferior and subordinate to men (1988, item 410). More positively, Peter Erickson insists that men in Shakespeare must acknowledge their "feminine self," a lesson the boy actor had to learn in order to transcend a narrow masculinity (1985, item 284). A few critics investigate women's roles as playwrights within their own plays. For several critics, Rosalind is the playwright who brings the confusions of *As You Like It* to a happy ending. Marcia Reifer (1984, item 269) interprets Isabella in *Measure for Measure* as one who loses the right of being a playwright to the bungling yet dangerous Duke who is at best "a model third-rate playwright" (p. 68).

If women can be characterized and understood in terms of theatrical management and metaphor, then theatrical representation itself can be related to gender divisions. Two major studies–by Katherine Maus (1987, item 384) and Phyllis Rackin (1987, item 393)–explore the crosscurrents between theatre and gender. Maus calls attention to the productive analogy between male spectators (as jealous husbands) and the feminine spectacle (or play). Eavesdropping scenes, argues Maus, can thereby shed light on the relationship of men to women, and of plays to audiences. Like jealous husbands/spectators, audiences lack control and power. For Rackin, the Shakespearean play is like a "sexual transaction or marriage" with the audience; the boy actor, who is powerless as a woman, can nonetheless exercise power on the stage. Rackin concludes that "stage illusion subverted gender divisions of the Elizabethan world" (p. 38).

Shakespeare's Androgynous Heroines and the Politics of Gender

Shakespeare's androgynous heroines played by the boy actors have received a great deal of lively attention from feminist criticism. These seven heroines appear in five Shakespearean plays–four comedies (*Two Gentlemen of Verona, Merchant of Venice, As You Like It,* and *Twelfth Night*) and one romance (*Cymbeline*). No such heroines appear in the tragedies, a fact that has received some comment in feminist studies. It is worth noting, though, that Cleopatra derogatorily refers to the theatrical practice: "and I shall see/Some squeaking Cleopatra boy my greatness/I' th' posture of a whore" (Act 5.2.

219-221). There is divided opinion among feminist critics as to how well the boys actually portrayed women. Opinion ranges from Marianne Novy's view (1984, item 262) that the boys were psychically associated with the female characters to Judith Cook's caveat (1980, item 108) that the boys could not capture Shakespeare's mature women. See also studies by James Hill (1986, item 338), Douglas Green (1988, item 415), and Sue-Ellen Case (1988, item 410) that are skeptical about the boy actors and their representation of femininity.

Having boy actors portray young, energetic women who then, for a variety of reasons, dress in male costume allowed Shakespeare to explore and exploit a number of conventions associated with femininity, gender, sexual identity, marriage, and society. Of course, Shakespeare was not the first one to use such stock conventions of cross gender dressing (see Peter Hyland, 1978, item 65, p. 25). More than 70 Renaissance plays employed young actors playing women who then disguised themselves as saucy and energetic young boys. But Shakespeare's attitudes toward crossdressing differed markedly from some of his contemporaries, especially Ben Jonson, as Phyllis Rackin (1987, item 393) has shown. There is no doubt, however, as Gayle Whittier (1979, item 97) claims, that Shakespeare used such disguises for constructive, not destructive, reasons. As an example of destructive androgyny, Whittier cites Falstaff as a "false androgyne." Yet Pat Carroll, a woman in her sixties, portrayed a superb Falstaff in the 1990 production of *Merry Wives* at the Folger Shakespeare Library. Carroll's success and credibility raise questions about traditional casting and contemporary gender expectations. (See Dorothy Chansky's "Who Owns Shakespeare?" *Dramatics* [Oct. 1990]: 44-47.)

A number of useful studies sketch in the social and religious background about such crossdressing on stage. David McPherson (1983, item 229 and 1985, item 296) quotes at length from moralists who, on the basis of the prohibition in Deuteronomy, abhorred such actions. Crossdressing was regarded in some quarters as the work of the devil (Nancy K. Hayles, 1979, item 86). Jonathan Dollimore (1986, item 329), among others, discusses the homoerotic feelings the boys excited among the male audience. Sandra Clark (1985, item 278) explores the pamphlets *Haec Vir* and *Hic Mulier* which attacked mannish women and effeminate men, respectively. Hyland (1978, item 65), too, pays attention to such complaints. Female crossdressing seems to have been as popular on the streets of London as in the playhouses (see

Dusinberre, 1975, item 6; Dreher, 1986, item 330). "A wave of feminism [swept over] England from the 1580s onward during which time a number of women 'provoked an uproar' by wearing men's clothes and carrying swords. This practice continued into the early nineteenth century, although the early feminists were officially reprimanded by both King James and the Bishop of London" (Dreher, p. 32).

Boys dressing as women who dressed as boys inevitably raises political questions about women's role and power in society. For the sake of convenience, we might divide feminist critics into two camps—(1) those who argue that such disguises give women the freedom and power denied them by a male culture and (2) those who claim that the disguises only affirm patriarchal hegemony. Among those who view the disguises as empowering women by subverting patriarchy are, for example, Paula S. Berggren (1980, item 103); Catherine Belsey (1985, item 275); and Karen Newman (1987, item 388). For Berggren, the transvestite heroines confirm women's identities but shatter men's. More aggressively, Belsey contends that dressing a woman like a man shakes the very foundations of patriarchy which exist by marginalizing women: "female transvestism throws patriarchy into relief by upsetting the categories that legitimate it." Discussing *Merchant of Venice,* Newman argues that giving Portia's ring to Balthasar "signals the disruption of male hierarchy by admitting Portia/Balthasar into the transaction"; Portia thus opens marriage to the forces of disorder by subverting the rules of male society. Disguised as boys, women could effectively educate men in the ways of love and marriage. Marjorie Garber (1986, item 336) similarly looks at Rosalind's disguise as a way for her to tutor Orlando; unlike other heroines, she does not need to maintain it for safety but to make Orlando feel more comfortable talking to a member of his own sex. And W. Thomas MacCary (1981, item 161) differentiates the roles the girl/boy pages played either to caricature male aggression or to offer a model of the perfect blend of the male/female. The particular role depended on the type of education the young male lover was in most need of receiving.

Yet for other critics the disguise does not, as Mary Free believes (1986, item 334), give women freedom to voice anti-patriarchal sentiments; the boys remain feminine speakers voicing pro-patriarchal sentiments. Mary Mathis asserts that Portia actually upholds the social order of patriarchy (1988, item 424); and Jean Howard (1988, item 418) even maintains that crossdressing in *Twelfth Night* actually privileges the patriarchy, since the crossdressed Viola/Cesario is really less subversive than the female-dressed Olivia. For Matthew Wikander (1986, item 351), Viola does not have the male clout to accompany the disguise. Yet Donald Furber and Anne Callahan (1982, item 184) point out that because Viola does not change into women's clothing, we never actually see the woman Orsino loves. Clara Claiborne Park (1980, item 133) concedes that Shakespeare dressed women in male clothes to give them power but only "temporarily." Marianne Novy (1984, item 262) similarly concludes that women gain freedom from such convention, yet they are controlled by the disguise. More philosophically, Robert Kimbrough (1982, item 192) regards Shakespeare's transsexual disguises as part of a testing ground in which woman might be seen in all of her roles. Because of her disguise, Rosalind grows into a fuller human being; and Viola, through her disguise, teaches that the differences between men and women are really "dissolvable." Matthew Wikander (1986, item 351) stresses that the boy-actress was neither male nor female. In contrast, Judith Cook (1980, item 108) argues that Rosalind never becomes a boy; she is always feminine.

Of all Shakespeare's transvestite heroines, Portia is often set apart by feminist critics for her intelligence. She may be Shakespeare's most learned woman, a character type to which Helena in *All's Well* belongs (see Lisa Jardine, 1987, item 377). Commenting on how and why Portia is separate from the other heroines, Juliet Dusinberre (1975, item 6) explores the ways she behaves differently from Rosalind when both of them appear in male attire. Vera Jiji (1976, item 24) contends that Portia can control her sex at will, and that she is not pressured into a male disguise as Julia in *Two Gentlemen* or Rosalind is. Catherine Wildermuth (1982, item 209) emphasizes that Portia is in complete control in Act 5. By giving Bassanio his ring, she removes the threat of cuckoldry and returns to an "unthreatening femininity" for Anne Parten (1982, item 199). Portia's double self (the Fair Maid of Belmont/Balthasar) is kept quite separate according to most feminist readers, though for Anne Parten again she is a "two-sexed figure" (1982, item 199).

Diane Dreher (1986, item 330) insists, too, that Portia is "the most androgynous of Shakespeare's women" (p. 129). Yet for most readers, Portia as Balthasar shows no signs of the Portia who loves Bassanio as Rosalind's Ganymede does when she swoons under her own shadow. As Keith Geary puts it, Portia's disguise differs from Rosalind's and Julia's;

Portia's "resilient femininity" shows that she is ready to be the lawyer (1984, item 251). For many readers the lawyer and the lady do not struggle for an equal hearing in Portia. Leonard Tennenhouse (1980, item 142) contends that Portia succeeds most when she is dressed in male garb acting like her father; it is a fantasy to assume she is both male and female. As Geary again points out, Portia allows herself to fasten both sexes on herself. For other readers, Portia is a more subversive figure. We have already seen Karen Newman's response above about Portia's undercutting male rule through her hybrid character of Balthasar/Portia (1987, item 388). In her chapter on "Androgynous Daughters," Diane Dreher (1986, item 330) finds that Portia's brilliant courtroom performance threatens gender stereotypes. Dusinberre claims that Portia even mocks the boy who plays her (1975, item 6). Interestingly, according to new historicist Jonathan Goldberg (1985, item 290), Portia is neither female nor male but passes through the text "affirming ... experience."

If Portia has won the reputation for being Shakespeare's most learned woman, Rosalind may well claim the title of Shakespeare's most versatile because of her multiple disguises/sexual roles. She is the only Shakespearean heroine to have the last word in her play, and the Epilogue she speaks has itself been the subject of much feminist criticism. A conventional view of Rosalind's role-playing is expressed by Andrew Crichton (1975, item 5): Rosalind harmoniously reconciles male and female. Discussions by Judith Cook (1980, item 108) and Angela Pitt (1981, item 165) also emphasize the comedic functions of Rosalind's disguise and acclaim her as one of Shakespeare's greatest female creations. Janet Adelman (1985, item 274) sees Rosalind as fulfilling two necessary roles through her disguise–she is simultaneously a male friend and a female lover. W. Thomas MacCary claimed the same accomplishment for Julia in *Two Gentlemen of Verona* (1981, item 161). Rejecting the idea that Rosalind can be "stabilized into male or female," Donald Furber and Anne Callahan (1982, item 184, p. 71) conclude that *As You Like It* exemplifies the "fundamental ambiguity of sexuality itself." From her cultural materialist perspective, Catherine Belsey (1985, item 275) similarly concludes that Rosalind/Ganymede is sometimes feminine/sometimes masculine, a character who asks us to "celebrate the plurality" of roles. For Barbara Bono (1986, item 323), Rosalind's disguise softens the masculine views found in Petrarchianism and allows her to be a good companion to Orlando. Because of the disguise, she is able to test his love and help him revise his wrongheaded and idealistic views of love and women. For Peter Erickson (1985, item 284), Rosalind is not androgynous at all (she has no access to male strength); and she validates patriarchy by submitting to the benevolent control of the men who, rather than Rosalind, "reap the benefits of androgyny." Some dissenting voices have been raised about the positive functions of Rosalind's disguise. For Nancy Hayles (1979, item 86), her disguises mirror and add to the complexities of the play while their removal restores order. In fact, unmasking her makes peace possible. Douglas Green (1988, item 415) refuses to accept Rosalind as an independent woman; she is a creature of the male imagination. And rejecting Rosalind/Ganymede's femininity, Peter Reynolds (1988, item 430) insists that "the Rosalind/Ganymede spoken text is almost entirely masculine" (p. 85); the audience never loses sight of the "actual male self" of the boy actor.

Though she has received less attention than Portia and Rosalind, Viola is the subject of a number of discussions of gender and sexuality and how they are represented through transvestite disguises. Hayles (1979, item 86) believes that while Viola's disguise leads to a loss of control, it nonetheless releases Olivia and Orsino to love and thus has a restorative function. According to Matthew Wikander (1986, item 351), Viola is trapped in boy's clothing, hardly a liberating experience for her. Joel Fineman (1985, item 287) traces the fratricidal implications of Viola's role-playing, comparing her state with her brother's.

Genre and Gender

Feminist readings of Shakespeare stress that a male ideology of gender shapes and restricts genre at the expense of women who are thereby stereotyped, marginalized, or victimized. The unquestioned assumptions that a genre makes about women can lead to a distorted view of female roles and achievements in Shakespeare's plays (e.g., Gayle Greene, 1982, item 187). Genre considerations are part of the cultural repression of women. Bernard Paris (1984, item 263), for example, discusses the negative view of women because they were forced into conventional roles frequently dictated by genre.

A starting point for a discussion of genre and gender in Shakespeare is Marilyn French's *Shakespeare's Division of Experience* (1981, item 155). She divides the plays into two camps–the comedies reflect a feminine world while the tragedies and histories show masculine control. Kathleen McLuskie (1985, item 295) also argues that tragedy implies maleness with its emphasis on heroic deeds and condemnation of women's lust. Perhaps because of tragedy's male bias, Ann Thompson (1988, item 437) believes that feminists should not privilege the tragedies over the comedies or histories. Along similar lines, Marianne Novy (1984, item 262) points out that women as actors are more easily accepted in the comedies than the tragedies. Some feminist criticism of Shakespeare has called for more attention to women's participation in the tragedies and histories in particular and to more feminist readings of the tragedies and histories in general. Jeanne Addison Roberts (1986, item 346) exhorts teachers to include in their courses more comedies where women do dominate. Marilyn Williamson (1982, item 210) explores the relationship of doubling practices, women's anger, and genre. Applauding Williamson's insights into the nature of genre, Greene (1982, item 187) further develops this critic's ideas on conventions: "Williamson's suggestion is fascinating with its implications that the more firmly established the conventions of a genre, the more conventional the conceptions of woman, whereas the more flexible such conventions are, the greater the latitude possible in the conceptions of what women are and what they can do" (p. 10). Novy's Chapter Ten (1984, item 262) shows how when the hold of genre is loosened in the romances, for example, men are eager to be portrayed in feminine terms (as mothers) and women control the ultimate power for reconciliation. Expanding the considerations of genre even further, Carol Thomas Neely (1985, item 298) reminds us that *Othello* is the "terrifying completion of the comedies"; however, unlike the comic heroes, Othello cannot accept cuckoldry. In her Chapter Four, "Gender and Genre in *Antony and Cleopatra*," Neely (1985, item 298) makes this valuable observation:

> In *Antony and Cleopatra* genre boundaries are not dissolved but enlarged. Motifs, themes, and characterization from comedy, tragedy, and history are included. Gender distinctions, too, are not dissolved but are explored, magnified, and ratified. And male and female roles are not equal—not even here. Cleopatra, like the heroines of comedy, engenders Antony's growth and her own, controlling the ending to glorify her submission to him. Like the heroines of

the problem comedies, she endures sexual degradation and uses sexuality fruitfully. Like the heroines of tragedy, she dies, though her death is more self-willed and self-fulfilling than theirs (165).

Several critics have deconstructed the idea of genre itself to arrive at a more equitable view of women's roles in the plays. Brian Shaffer (1988, item 433) breaks down the sexual stereotypes of domestic tragedy. Jean Howard (1986, item 340) shows how and why comic formulas do not work in Shakespeare; what was once assumed to be comedic, including women's role in the larger patriarchal pattern, must be challenged. Richard Wheeler (1985, item 315) explores the stress on genre boundaries in the sonnets, *Merchant of Venice,* and *Othello* because of the tensions between female sexuality and male autonomy. Along these lines, it is wise to heed Peter Erickson's warning (1987, item 365) that "patriarchal control has to be negotiated each time, and the outcome is variable and uncertain–patriarchy is not monolithic but multivalent ... in some plays male control cannot be achieved at all" (pp. 116, 117). Finally, one of the most provocative and productive studies of gender and genre is by Timothy Murray (1985, item 297). Arguing that genre neglects women, Murray coins the phrase *"genderic"* (genre and gender) to describe the types of inquiries feminists must pursue in looking at the relationship of genre and women's roles in Shakespeare's plays.

The Taming of the Shrew–
Marital Battlefield or A Field of Games ?

Of all Shakespeare's plays, perhaps none is as controversial for feminists as *The Taming of the Shrew.* It is a test case for a wealth of different viewpoints about Shakespeare's women and their place in the Elizabethan power structure. Depending on the feminist critic, the problem or solution in *Shrew* resides in Kate's last speech. David Garrick's adaptation of Shrew side-stepped any problem raised by Kate's last speech by giving it to Petruchio (Dash, 1981, item 152). Because of this speech, *Shrew* has been variously interpreted as a canonical statement of traditional beliefs about husband and wife, a romantic comedy, an ironic comedy, a subversive philippic to patriarchy, and even a problem comedy.

Some readings of *Shrew* by feminists see the play as a mirror of the status quo. *Shrew* is an expression of male dominance over women through the institutionalization of matrimony. Arguing that *Shrew* upholds the patriarchy, Eugenia Zimmerman (1976, item 31) characterizes Kate as a shrew who changes her masculine, aggressive behavior to become a submissive wife who can thereby bring reconciliation to her husband. Winfried Schleiner (1977, item 52) judges Kate to be an obnoxious shrew and refuses to see the ending of *Shrew* as either romantic or ironic. Mary Free insists that Kate speaks from the accepted patriarchal point of view (1986, item 334). Peter Berek maintains that Shakespeare's *Shrew* is far less an antifeminist tract than the bad quarto of the play and concludes that *Shrew* accepts patriarchy for social reasons (1988, item 405). Although they voice incredulity at Kate's transformation, Juliet Dusinberre (1975, item 6) and B.J. Pendlebury (1975, item 14) also endorse a relatively traditional reading of the play. Kate's transformation for Dusinberre is a miracle that just would not occur in the real world of Elizabethan patriarchs; and Pendlebury labels *Shrew* a "fantasy to appeal to hen-pecked husbands."

Conceding that Kate's speech is serious and sincere, many more feminists have expressed disgust at *Shrew*. Regarding it as a thorn in the flesh, a sizable group of feminists has denounced the play. Considering himself an ardent supporter of women's rights, George Bernard Shaw exhorted audiences to boycott the play because Shakespeare treated women like property (Lise Pedersen, 1977, item 50). His sentiments are echoed in part by such contemporary feminists as Coppelia Kahn who characterizes *Shrew* as sexist and Petruchio's behavior on his wedding day as "the most shamelessly blunt statement of the relationship between men, women, and property to be found in the literature of the period" (1975, item 9). For S.N. Garner (1988, item 414), *Shrew* is a "bad play based on a bad joke." Petruchio is Kate's veterinarian, not husband, for Dorothea Kehler (1987, item 380); and even Bianca is the victim of stereotyping for Diane Dreher (1986, item 330). According to Carol Heffernan, *Shrew* attacks middle class bourgeois financial values (1985, item 291) typified by Baptista's commercialism at the expense of Kate's rights. Kathleen McLuskie (1982, item 196) decries the capitalistic interpretation of love as a cash transaction, and urges readers to see the ideology through the comedy. Terence Hawkes also points out that *Shrew* "reinforces phallocentric views" (1986, item 337).

For other critics, the fact that *Shrew* upholds patriarchy is a good, not bad, thing. Marianne Novy's Chapter Three on *Shrew* applauds the ways Kate and Petruchio reconcile their love with patriarchy to create a new and better world (1984, item 262). Similarly, Richard Burt argues that patriarchy is reinforced by relocating it in the wife's love of her husband (1984, item 245). Harvey Rovine, too, finds harmony in *Shrew* as Kate is transformed from a shrew into a sober and believable spokeswoman for mutual dependence (1987, item 394). John C. Bean (1980, item 102, p. 70) likewise sees Kate's final speech in a positive light:

> Kate's final speech in *The Shrew,* then, in its use of political analogies and its emphasis on woman's warmth and beauty rather than on her abject sinfulness, is not a rehearsal of old, medieval ideas about wives but of relatively contemporary ideas growing out of humanist reforms. Male tyranny, which characterizes earlier shrew-taming stories, gives way here to a nontyrannical hierarchy informed by mutual affection.

In a highly sophisticated argument, Joel Fineman affirms that while the play is "neither for women nor against men" it nonetheless upholds the rights of patriarchy through the very forces of female subversion (1985, item 287).

Still other feminists believe that *Shrew* is therapeutically comedic. For Lisa Jardine, it is a "good natured comedy" demonstrating that Kate has social freedom and financial power (1983, item 224). Valerie Wayne (1985, item 314) argues that Kate shatters traditional notions of female hypocrisy and feigns obedience because she is in on Petruchio's joke. A more humane way to tame a shrew can be learned from Petruchio's role-playing, Wayne insists. From Marion Perret comes praise for Petruchio's "moral awareness and sensitivity"; he is hardly his wife's veterinarian but rather a good wife himself, and in acquiescing through an act of love, Kate becomes a model wife herself (1982, item 200). Irene Dash (1981, item 152) also characterizes Petruchio as a "sensitive" man of wit, Kate's friend. Joan Hartwig (1982, item 188) even commends Petruchio for his "mild" methods which help Kate to realize herself fully. Similarly, Martha Andresen-Thom (1982, item 173) warns that Petruchio is not a "sinister tyrant"; the real enemy is not Kate but those who would oppose Petruchio's instructive playfulness. Studying

Shrew from a legal context, Margaret Loftus Ranald (1982, item 201) singles out Petruchio for his salutary iconoclasm. It seems that in some feminist quarters Petruchio has been praised for his gamesmanship. Many other feminists debunk a straight, literal reading of *Shrew*. Instead of taking comfort in matrimonial harmony or using the play as a whipping post for its antifeminism, they spy a corrective and subversive irony in Kate's last speech. According to some arguments, Kate mockingly mouths the patriarchal platitudes her husband and his cronies want her to (see Martha Andresen-Thom, 1982, item 173), and in some productions she even winks to signal her mockery. Thus because of Kate's verbal tricks, the promise of even stormier days are ahead for the gulled and gullible Petruchio. Coppelia Kahn, for example, believes that Kate's ironic reversal proves that male dominance is a fantasy (1981, item 160). Other feminist interpretations deny the use of irony at all. Winifred Schleiner attests that the play is neither ironic nor romantic but exhibits a simple set of social conventions (1977, item 52). David Daniell urges readers to move beyond irony in Kate's final speech to see the larger use of "acting" necessary to learning about marriage in the real world (1984, item 248). Yet Dorothea Kehler protests that whether Kate is brainwashed or surrenders is not the point; Kate offers a subversive subtext for women who are treated like property (1987, item 380). The message of *Shrew* for the women in the audience is listen and change, claims Kehler.

Finally, Jean Howard's response to *Shrew* (1986, item 340) attempts to resolve the contradictions others find in the play by accepting these inconsistencies. For Howard, Kate's speech is deliberately problematic and contradictory to frustrate closure, thus reflecting the contradictions found in Elizabethan culture itself. Howard's deconstructionism both detonates and leaves in place the commonplaces out of which Kate's speech is shaped.

Women's Friendships, Language, and Mother-Daughter Relationships

The ways in which Shakespeare's women form friendships with each other reveals much about feminine identity and bonding. Judith Cook's Chapter Five (1980, item 108) is devoted to female friendships; and Angela Pitt (1981, item 165) discusses the bonds of sisterhood in Shakespeare. Female bonding often contrasts with the male variety (see

Richard Wheeler, 1985, item 315) and proves that women's friendships can escape the jealousy and dangers associated with male relationships in the plays. The female bonds in *Richard III* are unholy alliances, to be sure, because some of them are created by force, but they do contrast starkly with Richard's feigned friendships. Accused of destroying male bonds, women have an "emotional stability" (Madonne Miner, 1980, item 131). The confederation of Queens offers a moral consciousness, a female camaraderie for Miner. These women are the intelligencers of the play (Ralph Berry, 1980, item 104), conveying its real sense of history (Marguerite Waller, 1986, item 349). Cleopatra's relationships with her women, Portia's friendship with Nerissa, and the dynamics of the ladies in *Love's Labor's Lost* are just a few female relationships in Shakespeare that illustrate the strengths of female community and the threats to it.

Women's bonds in three plays in particular—*Othello*, *As You Like It*, and *A Midsummer Night's Dream*—have received the most detailed attention from feminist critics. Looking at the women in *Othello*, June Sturrock (1984, item 271), Carol Thomas Neely (1985, item 298), and Eamon Grennan (1987, item 370) contrast feminine loyalty with male treachery. Act 4.3 of *Othello* is an excellent example of a protected female enclave, according to Grennan. Gayle Greene (1979, item 82) had earlier maintained that the defenseless Desdemona needed to be more like Emilia—sturdier, outspoken, realistic. Janet Adelman (1985, item 274) and Susan Carlson (1987, item 357) investigate female bonds and bonding in *As You Like It*; Carlson laments the male restrictions placed on female community in the forest and argues that Celia and Rosalind are drawn apart instead of closer in Arden. Offering a radically different interpretation, Peter Erickson (1985, item 284) concentrates on the forest as a male enclave, a model of male nurturing where female friendships are secondary to Shakespeare's purpose. Hermia and Helena's friendship is explored by S.N. Garner (1981, item 157), Susan Snyder (1988, item 436), and William Slights (1988, item 435). As a number of feminist critics point out, the quarrel between these two comic heroines is the most violent involving women in Shakespeare, and the result of male dominance and male mischief. Garner maintains their friendship is disrupted to make them ready for marriage and male dominance. In a later article, Garner (1988, item 414) finds that patriarchy sets the women of *Shrew* against each other, too. Slights emphasizes Titania's friendship with her votarist as a major example of "indeterminacy" in *Dream*, thus disputing a traditional, comedic reading of the play. Finally, Snyder (1988, item 436) contrasts the female friendships that last in *All's Well That Ends Well* with those that are lost in *A Midsummer Night's Dream*.

Paradoxically enough, studies of women's distinctive language have focused on women's silence. Some critics see women's quietude as a plus; others as a liability. Chapter Four in Juliet Dusinberre's book (1975, item 6) discusses women's silence and speech. In her Derridean reading of *Winter's Tale*, Joyce Wexler (1988, item 439) stresses the power of women's silence. Also exploring women's language in *The Winter's Tale*, Eve Horwitz (1988, item 417) claims that women achieve redemptive power through silence. Similarly, Jonathan Goldberg (1985, item 290) argues that silence is not a sign of subjection or powerlessness and cites the Duke asking a silent Isabella to "ratify his plan." For Jean Howard (1986, item 340), Isabella's silence subversively undermines the comedy of *Measure for Measure*. R.S. White (1986, item 350) praises the eloquent silence of female victims in Shakespeare; silence allows Lucrece to be seen from the inside. David Willbern (1980, item 143) argues that Cordelia's silence is really the grounding for speech. On the other hand, S.N. Garner (1988, item 414) worries that a "silenced" Kate in *Shrew* is forced to speak someone else's (patriarchal) words. Alberto Cacicedo (1988, item 407) maintains that the women's silence at the end of *Much Ado* is a sign of their protest against male oppression. Harvey Rovine (1987, item 394) explores the oppression at the root of Ophelia's silence in *Hamlet*. According to Phyllis Rackin (1987, item 393), "the subversive female voice is never allowed to prevail" in Shakespeare's early histories.

Women's language can be a powerful source for correction and healing. Chapter Five in Neely's book (1985, item 298) provides a useful analysis of women's language. Marion Perret (1982, item 200) emphasizes the power of Constance's and Katherine's words in *Henry VIII*. Inga-Stina Ewbank (1978, item 58) locates women's language at the center of *Much Ado*. Deborah Aquino (1986, item 320) claims that women's speech is more discreet and honest and less cunning than men's. And Joan Klein (1976, item 27) argues that Ophelia in and because of her madness is enabled to tell Claudius what words mean. Exploring the language of madwomen on the Renaissance stage in general, Maurice Charney and Hanna Charney (1977, item 34) argue that in madness women could at the least assert themselves in a male-controlled world. Carole McKewin (1980, item 130) studies women's intimate conversations contrasting them with the bravado in male discourse. Contrasting male and female speech in *Richard III*, Marguerite Waller (1986, item 349) lays bare the weaknesses of Richard III's rhetoric and the power of Anne's discourse. Christy Desmet (1987, item 363) also focuses on the advantages of feminine rhetoric. Clearly, Rosalind in *As You Like It* is one of Shakespeare's most forceful speakers; Charles Frey (1978, item 60) contends that she is "Shakespeare's most talkative woman."

Joel Fineman (1985, item 287) studies the relationship among gender, rhetoric, and feminine language/lunacy in *Shrew*. For Eve Horwitz (1988, item 417), feminine language is associated with flux, change. A number of Shakespearean women have been singled out for praise for their linguistic talents. Betty Norvell commends Margaret's speaking ability in *1 Henry VI* (1983, item 233). Katherine in *Henry V* develops a "growing language of sexuality" (Lance Wilcox, 1985, item 317). Desdemona is a "female worker of words" for Timothy Murray (1985, item 297), and she is praised by Kezia Sproat (1985, item 311) for her witty retorts to Iago. Valerie Wayne (1985, item 314) honors Emilia for killing her marriage with words. Dorothy Wickenden (1985, item 316) laments any attempts to bowdlerize "Juliet's impassioned words"; and Edward Snow (1985, item 310) unites the Veronese lovers by claiming that Romeo and Juliet speak the same idiom. Women's language can be prey to male control and contradiction. Nancy Vickers (1985, item 313), for example, maintains that the descriptive language of the men in *Othello* and *Rape of Lucrece* destroys the women. Madelon Gohlke (1982, item 185) likewise explores the "rhetorical fate of women" in *Othello* and the other tragedies and finds that heroes like Othello fear being feminized by language. Patricia Parker (1987, item 390) links rhetoric to gender to account for ways in which male characters are feminized through their language. Gail Kern Paster (1987, item 391) reveals how patriarchy associates women's bodily functions and language to make women more vulnerable. And Carol Cook (1986, item 326) posits the controlling language of *Much Ado About Nothing* to be male.

Feminist critics have paid considerable attention to mothers in Shakespeare. According to Velma Richmond (1978, item 72), mother figures are more important to Shakespeare than father ones. Similarly, Susan Shapiro (1978, item 75) contends that Shakespeare upholds the traditional views of maternal love. The plays are filled with mother and son relationships–Hamlet and Gertrude; Coriolanus and Volumnia–a terrain feminists have explored carefully and provocatively. See, for example, Janet Adelman's essay (1980, item 101) on Coriolanus and his mother. Betty Norvell's dissertation (1982, item 198) is also instructive. Naomi Scheman (1987, item 396) discusses Othello and his mother. The metaphoric roles of mothers have also been widely discussed. Patrick Hogan (1983, item 219) characterizes Scotland and Malcolm as mothers in *Macbeth*. For Harry Berger (1981, item 148), Portia functions like a Jewish mother because of her "mercifixion," a blend of the mercy and crucifixion she dispenses. And in an article with intriguing biographical speculations, Donald Silver (1983, item 239) provocatively studies Shakespeare's relationship with his own mother.

But while there are many son and mother pairs, the "mother-daughter cathexis" (Myra Schotz, 1980, item 134) is absent, or nearly so, in Shakespeare. Stephen Orgel (1986, item 345) finds that Shakespeare is more interested in "chiastic relationships"–father and daughter; son and mother–than same sex ones. Moreover, Clarice Kestenbaum (1983, item 225) claims that the father/mother/daughter triangle is "disastrous." The reasons are structural and psychological. In the comedies, an intrusive and competing mother would surely dampen the luster of the pert and independent romantic heroines. D.W. Harding contends that in the romances a punishing and severe mother is antithetical to the regenerative femininity Shakespeare presented in his young heroine daughters (1979, item 84).

Of all the plays, *King Lear* has attracted the most attention for its missing (and repressive) mothers. Lynda Boose (1986, item 324) explains that the maternal could not survive in the brutal *Lear* world. Novelist and poet Joyce Carol Oates (1981, item 164) believes that in Lear's queenless land the dangers of male authority become more prevalent. In two articles (1982, item 190; 1986, item 341), Coppelia Kahn looks at the "maternal subtext" of *Lear*. Lear himself acts like a mother with his female attributes (1982); and no actual mother can appear in Lear because his patriarchal society has subverted women (1986). Kahn (1982, item 190) and Carolyn Asp (1986, item 321) recognize that Goneril and Regan act like rejecting mothers to Lear. Steven Cahn (1988, item 408) argues that Cordelia is not at all like her mother while Goneril and Regan do resemble this absent woman. On the other hand, Coppelia Kahn (1986, item 341) believes that Goneril and Regan act as if they had a different father than Lear. Finally, Oates rejects any view of Cordelia as the Terrible Mother.

The romances present a different view of motherhood for daughters, and fathers, too. Marilyn Williamson (1986, item 352) affirms that motherhood is vital to succession in the romances and, conversely, Marilyn French (1981, item 155) emphasizes that men suffer from absence of females in the romances. For Myra Schotz (1980, item 134), *Winter's Tale* is Shakespeare's "most maternal play"; similarly for Stevie Davies (1986, item 328), *Winter's Tale* presents a "mother culture." While still keeping sight of the maternal power of *Winter's Tale*, Coppelia Kahn (1981, item 160, p. 225) claims that the play represents the "richest version of male identity defined within the family." Joyce Wexler (1988, item 439) emphasizes the power and reconciliation inherent in the mother-daughter bond in *Winter's Tale*. Even though *Pericles* is a "womanless play," the absence of women/mothers argues for their central importance for D.W. Harding (1979, item 84). Political life for Davies (1986, item 328) is reflected in the mother/daughter relationship in *Pericles*. Discussing Prospero's missing/absent wife, Stephen Orgel (1986, item 345) portrays Sycorax as a bad mother.

Scope and Organization of the Bibliography

Shakespeare and Feminist Criticism: An Annotated Bibliography is the first annotated bibliography on this subject. Previous bibliographies dating from the early 1980s (see, for example Lenz, Greene, and Neely, 1980, item 127; or Georgianna Ziegler, 1982, item 212) are unannotated, out of date, and now incomplete. The impressive contributions of feminist criticism to Shakespeare studies demand more recent bibliographic coverage. My work surveys feminist criticism, written in English, of Shakespeare's plays and poems from 1975–the date of publication of Juliet Dusinberre's *Shakespeare and the Nature of Women*–through 1988. I chose the publication of Dusinberre's book as my starting point because, in the words of Carole McKewin (1977, item 45), it is "the first full-length study of Renaissance drama in the mode of the new feminist criticism." The year 1988 was the latest, most realistic *terminus ad quem* I could choose to gather my information. These fourteen years–1975 through 1988–have witnessed a remarkable amount of significant, groundbreaking work by feminist critics exploring Shakespeare's work. Lynda Boose has aptly referred to these years as the crucial first phase of feminism's response to Shakespeare (1987, item 355).

While the following bibliography is devoted to feminist studies of Shakespeare, it also includes wide-ranging works on language, desire, role-playing, theatre conventions, marriage, and the complex ideologies of Elizabethan and Jacobean culture as they shed light on Shakespeare's views on and representation of women, sex, and gender. I have also incorporated relevant psychoanalytical studies that address feminist concerns with women, sex, and gender in Shakespeare's life and works. Included here, too, are responses that challenge feminist criticism of Shakespeare (see, for example, Carol Iannone, 1983, item 222; Richard Levin, 1988, item 421; Jonathan Goldberg, 1985, item 290; and Peter Reynolds, 1988, item 430) in order to document some of the ways in which feminist methods and interpretations have influenced the course of Shakespeare studies. While I have attempted to include all relevant scholarship on feminist views of Shakespeare, I dare not claim that my bibliography is comprehensively complete. But it is, I hope, a useful reference source nonetheless.

This annotated bibliography contains 439 entries, including books, collections of essays, articles, notes, and dissertations (though I have not annotated the latter but have given a reference to summaries included in *Dissertation Abstracts International,* abbreviated *DAI*). Each title in this bibliography is classified by year of publication and then alphabetized by the author's name within that given year. Journal titles are spelled out in full to make identifying them easier for users. For each book, monograph, or collection of essays, I have supplied, after its annotation, reviews it has received to assist readers who want to find out how that work was assessed. I have tried to make my bibliography a record of individual scholars' contributions within the larger framework of feminist interpretations of Shakespeare. For example, many articles by feminists have been reprinted (and sometimes revised in the process) for a subsequent collection or as a chapter of the author's own book. My policy is to list an item under the year it was originally published and then record any subsequent reprintings and/or revisions. I do not annotate the original item but wait until it appears in its latest published source, whether that be in an edited collection of essays or in a single-author book. Within my annotations, I also supply cross-references directing readers to works the author of a given article or book found especially useful or took issue with.

I have strived to make my annotations lavishly informative but non-evaluative. My goal is to maintain the author's perspective, supplying a careful and thorough account of the main points of an article, edited collection, or book without simplifying or distorting an argument. That has not always been an easy task, since many feminist readings require attention to complex theoretical principles. To help readers grasp an author's main points, I have provided extensive rather than one- or two-sentence skimpy annotations. Toward that end, in my annotations I have used summaries, paraphrases, and, in many instances, illustrative key quotations (with the page numbers on which they are found). My annotations of books may seem like miniature essays, but I believe these book-length works merit such attention. I annotate each chapter of a book, or essay in a collection, as if it were an article, since many times it originated that way. Except when they appear in titles of articles or books, or within direct quotations from these sources, all titles of Shakespeare's works have been abbreviated according to the symbols found on pages 49-50.

Acknowledgments

In preparing this bibliography over the last two years, I have profited from the kind assistance of many people. At the University of Southern Mississippi, I am happily indebted to Karen Yarbrough, Vice President for Research and Planning, and Glenn T. Harper, Dean of the College of Liberal Arts, for a generous grant to start this project and for their continuing support of my research; to David Wheeler, Chair of the English Department, for all manner of help and encouragement; to Karolyn Thompson, Interlibrary Loan Librarian, for extraordinary patience in processing endless requests for materials and for remarkable diligence in locating them; and to my graduate assistants Anne Stascavage, LaNelle Daniel, Helen Thompson, Joao Froes, and Dawn Herring for their help. To Anne I am especially grateful for all her good work, faithfully done and professionally executed; she has given me invaluable help by checking facts, proofing, and assisting me in preparing the index. I thank my former colleague Linda Elkins McDaniel for her help, too. I am also grateful to Dorothea Kehler of San Diego State University for sharing with me her forthcoming (unannotated) bibliography on Shakespeare and feminism, to appear in her and Susan Baker's collection *In Another Country: Feminist Perspectives on Renaissance Drama* (Metuchen, NJ: Scarecrow, 1991). To Harrison Meserole goes my thanks for his counsel, his assistance in helping me locate some hard-to-find materials, and most of all for his encouragement. My gratitude also goes to Jurgen Wolter, Universitat Wuppertal, for his unfailing friendship in sending me materials that were not readily available in the United States, and to my dear friend Colby Kullman for his help closer to home.

A special debt goes to Jesse Stevens, computer keyboarder extraordinaire, who transformed many drafts of this book into the bright camera-ready copy you are now reading. I applaud Jesse's talents and ask God to bless her for the many words of encouragement she sent my way.

Finally, I thank Janeen L. Kolin for proofreading this book and, as always, for saving me from walking in falsehood's steps.

ABBREVIATIONS USED FOR
SHAKESPEARE'S PLAYS AND POEMS

AC	*Antony and Cleopatra*
Ado	*Much Ado About Nothing*
AWW	*All's Well That Ends Well*
AYL	*As You Like It*
CE	*The Comedy of Errors*
Cor	*Coriolanus*
Cym	*Cymbeline*
Ham	*Hamlet*
1H4	*Henry the Fourth, Part I*
2H4	*Henry the Fourth, Part II*
H5	*Henry the Fifth*
1H6	*Henry the Sixth, Part I*
2H6	*Henry the Sixth, Part II*
3H6	*Henry the Sixth, Part III*
H8	*Henry the Eighth*
JC	*Julius Caesar*
KJ	*King John*
Lear	*King Lear*
LLL	*Love's Labor's Lost*
Mac	*Macbeth*
MM	*Measure for Measure*
MND	*A Midsummer Night's Dream*
MV	*The Merchant of Venice*
MWW	*The Merry Wives of Windsor*
Oth	*Othello*

Per	*Pericles*
R2	*King Richard the Second*
R3	*King Richard the Third*
RJ	*Romeo and Juliet*
RL	*Rape of Lucrece*
TA	*Titus Andronicus*
Tem	*The Tempest*
TGV	*The Two Gentlemen of Verona*
Tim	*Timon of Athens*
TN	*Twelfth Night*
TNK	*Two Noble Kinsmen*
TrC	*Troilus and Cressida*
TSh	*The Taming of the Shrew*
VA	*Venus and Adonis*
WT	*The Winter's Tale*

1975

1. Bamber, Linda Vigderman. "Comic Women, Tragic Men: Genre and Sexuality in Shakespeare's Plays." *DAI* 36 (1975): 2212A. Tufts U.

   See item 175.

2. Beckman, Margaret Boerner. "The Figure of Rosalind in *As You Like It*." *Shakespeare Quarterly* 29 (1975): 44-51.

   Rosalind paradoxically reconciles the opposites of male and female by combining them—emotionally and physically—in the plot, language, and disguises of *AYL*. Rosalind's union of the sexes creates the harmony of marriage which is a *concordia discors* of realism and idealism. Rosalind thus symbolizes the "natural harmony of opposed forces that constitutes man's 'possible perfection'" (49). She and Orlando "often switch traditional sexual characteristics" (41); Rosalind speaks from the head while Orlando does from the heart. It is only when feminine pity overcomes Orlando's "'masculine' anger at his brother" that he can fight the lioness (48). Serving a complex function by joining male and female, Rosalind symbolizes the union of Mars and Venus, the "Renaissance prototype of all combinations" of man and woman (47). She is the "protecting male figure" and the "aggressive lover" as well as a chaste woman with a faint heart with Orlando. Yet while Rosalind displays outside a "man's readiness to fight," she has a woman's fears inside. In "both instances, the inner 'reality' ... [is] ... less real than the disguising outside" (48). Rosalind's wit and puns, which also "bring together contrary meanings" (49), are a sign of an active masculinity, another *concordia discors*. As both shepherd and courtier, Rosalind's estate further "comprises both extremes of the play" (51).

3. Biggins, Dennis. "Sexuality, Witchcraft, and Violence in *Macbeth*." *Shakespeare Studies* 8 (1975): 255-77.

Sexuality has never been considered a major concern of *Mac*; however, there are important links between sexuality and violence in the play. Although they are not full-fledged devils, the Weird Sisters have demonic tendencies, along with witch-like characteristics. "The witchcraft theme coalesces with the themes of fruitfulness and offspring, which are associated particularly with Duncan and Banquo, and of unfulfillment, sterility, and the destruction of progeny, associated with Macbeth and Lady Macbeth" (260). Sexuality that is perverted by the will to do harm, either by violence or witchcraft, results in a "life-denying barrenness." In other Shakespearean plays, witchcraft is associated with "unnatural sexual desires and sexual domination." Macbeth is deprived of his masculinity because he is "spiritually seduced" by the witches. "The exchanges between Macbeth and his wife that lead up to Duncan's murder, tensioned as they are by an eroticism that is sometimes submerged, sometimes overt, but continuously present, culminate in the decisive act of violence, which is envisaged as a kind of rape" (266). Macbeth's tragedy is that his crimes bring him no peace or satisfaction. Ironically, he realizes this before, while, and after committing them.

4. Boose, Lynda E. "Othello's Handkerchief: 'The Recognizance and Pledge of Love.'" *English Literary Renaissance* 5 (1975): 360-74.

The handkerchief ritualistically expresses the themes of marriage and justice that are central to *Oth*. Mentioned 31 times, the handkerchief is vital to the dramatic structure of the play and reflects an audience's awareness of marriage customs. An "emblem of consummation" (368), the strawberry-embroidered handkerchief visually represents the blood-stained wedding sheets that were publicly displayed to prove the bride's virginity. Shakespeare changes Cinthio's description of the "napkin" to elevate its mythic significance and to stress the connection between the love token and the act of consummation. The handkerchief receives dramatic life through the "tragic potential" it possesses. With "terrible irony," Othello destroys this emblem which just a few hours earlier signified Desdemona's fidelity as a bride (368). Echoes of *work, bed, blood* "strengthen the handkerchief/sheets analogy" (371) and deepen the connection between the two most important props in *Oth*. The "ocular proof of the spotted handkerchief and our final indelible vision of the blood-soaked bed towards which the play relentlessly leads come together in the powerful verbal/visual echo 'Thy bed, lust stained, shall with lust's blood be spotted' (Act 5.1.36)" (370). In Othello's thinking, Cassio possessed the virginal Desdemona when he possessed her handkerchief. Shakespeare departs from Deuteronomy which prescribed stoning an unfaithful wife and from Cinthio's inartistic ending by having Othello murder Desdemona in bed. With the tragic loading of the bed Shakespeare offers a "dynamic fusion of handkerchief and wedding sheets, the sanctified union promising life and the tragic union culminating in death" (373). Yet *Oth* tragically fulfills the "holy writ" of Deuteronomy that legally sanctioned executing an adulterous wife and her lover.

5. Crichton, Andrew B. "Hercules Shaven: A Centering Mythic Metaphor in *Much Ado About Nothing*." *Texas Studies in Language and Literature* 16 (1975): 619-26.

The centering metaphor of Hercules shaving his beard is part of a "submimetic system" that "parallels a mimetic heightening of beards with foppish fashion that Benedick must transcend if he is to realize his humanity" (626). Understanding references to *beards/bear'ds* helps to universalize the "struggle between equally strong male and female types at the center of the play" (621). Beatrice, who is stronger than Rosaline of *LLL* or Rosalind of *AYL*, wants to be taken seriously and depends upon her wit "to survive in a male world" (625). In that world, beards are a sign of male disguise, a symbol of "false heroism and male egotism" blocking the "potential marriage of true minds" (625). Shaving his beard in Act 3.2, Benedick realizes he can become a real (not conventional) man and still profit from Beatrice's refining touch. Beatrice learns "the shorter lesson that Benedick's masculine strength exceeds the hormonal powers she has granted him all along" (621). Shakespeare wisely did not develop parallels with the story of Samson and Delilah because of its unflattering lady barber.

6. Dusinberre, Juliet. *Shakespeare and the Nature of Women.* New York: Barnes and Noble; London: Macmillan, 1975.

Chapter One, "The Idea of Chastity," is divided into five sections: "The Puritans and the Playwrights"; "Chastity as Mystique"; "Virginity and Virtue"; "The Double Standard"; and "Chastity and Art."

The Puritans have wrongly been portrayed as kill-joys. During 1580-1625, encompassing the period of Shakespeare's achievements, Puritanism saw its most "creative and fertile years." Many Puritan ideas about love, women, and marriage "were lifted wholesale into the drama" (24), and in fact the Puritans "pushed dramatists into thinking about women" (30). The Puritans vitalized married life by attributing to it a "spiritual prestige" formerly reserved for single life. This Puritan influence is most notably affirmed in the "exuberant celebration in the comedies of married life against celibacy" (27), many of them set in London, the Puritans' stronghold. Shakespeare adapted Puritan ideas, but unlike other playwrights of the period, he wrote "with no explicit reforming purpose" (26).

Challenging the mystique of chastity, the Puritans divorced "chastity from physical virginity" (32) and extended this virtue to married life. Such thinking in life and in drama had significant implications for "attitudes about women" (32). Like the Puritans, Shakespeare and his contemporaries wanted "to define and explain" the nature of chastity.

Chastity took on "new possibilities" for men and women (41). Following Erasmus, the Puritans saw the celibate, single life, as opposed to the fertility of marriage, as unnatural, perverse, and reflecting self-love (as Olivia's in *TN*). Parolles emphasizes such unnaturalness to Helena in *AWW*; and Isabella finds a greater test of her virtue outside the convent. "Playing down virginity benefitted women" (49), since fertility was a blessing to marriage and in no way did married life threaten a "man's spiritual life." As Hermione proves, a good wife "protects a man's virtue" (51).

The Puritans, like the dramatists who inherited their ideas, attacked a double standard which irrevocably held women to virginity while allowing men the opportunity to reform. Virginity assumed an economic value. Elevating chastity made it "a class system and class-based morality" (51). Calling a woman a whore (Desdemona, Hermione) took away "her position in society" (52). Moreover, a woman's loss of chastity (one virtue) symbolized the loss of all others making her "worthless in every other sphere" (53). Unchaste women were thought to "betray their own sex." Against Angelo, the Puritans believed that if a man pursued his wife like a "whoremonger" he "deserved a whore" (58).

For sixteenth-century thinkers, art was the enemy of chastity, and women who practiced artfulness were guilty of seductiveness and sexual misconduct. Unlike Juliet's artlessness (a virtue), Cressida feigns art; the lark speech in *TrC* "reads like a sad parody" of *RJ* (65). Allowed to be artful, men were not held to the same standards. Cleopatra, however, follows "her own moral law" (69). An artist, Cleopatra is "true to her own nature" like Sidney's poet. Unlike Cressida, Cleopatra does not manufacture emotions through art.

Chapter Two on "The Problems of Equality" is divided into sections on: "Women and Authority" and "Women as Property." The Elizabethan and Jacobean age "bred the condition of a feminist movement" (80) through social unrest. Asserting its belief in "mutual consent," Puritan ideology fostered feminism. Shakespeare and other Renaissance dramatists reflected Puritan beliefs about the role of women. Emphasizing a woman's freedom of conscience, her individual identity, and her willing submission in the "mystical union" of marriage, Puritan thinkers deplored authoritarianism and saw "no monopoly of authority" by men in marriage (84). Hence, Portia is true to "the spirit of Puritanism" in retaining her separate identity. A "husband's villainy annulled" his wife's duty to him (Emilia and Desdemona, for example).

Breaking the union between man and wife, as Claudius does with Hamlet and Gertrude, is a mockery of marriage. The Puritans' "gift to their world lay in replacing the legal union of the arranged marriage with a union born of spirit" (104). Thus, woman's freedom–her desire to be wed–is represented in the drama. Beatrice's selecting her own husband and Desdemona's confronting Brabantio accord with Puritan ideology. Adriana in *CE* berates her husband for violating "an equal division of labor" (a Puritan belief) and, like Portia, rightly attacks the sexual "double standard." The Puritan "spirit of ideal union" was also satirized in the drama. How could Shakespeare, who was "more liberal" (105) than any other dramatist, adopt the "most hyperbolic" and absolute view of women in Kate's final speech? That speech, though, occurs in an ambiguous and theatrical setting where "Kate's transformation is a miracle" (108); it would have never happened in the real world. "Petruchio could only play the part of lord if Kate agreed to the game" (110).

Puritans maintained that treating a wife like a piece of property or using her only to gratify a man's senses was equivalent to seeing her as a whore because such actions diminished a wife's role as man's partner, counselor, and spiritual instructor. The Puritans rigorously confronted the problem of sex in marriage. Unlike other Renaissance dramatists, Shakespeare had no trouble with married sex; for him it was not "an act of power and persuasion" but, as Juliet, Imogen, and Hermione exemplify, mutual bounty and Edenic "completion" (121). Shakespeare's contemporaries concentrated instead on the "similarities between whores and respectable women" and the high price of satisfying a man's lust. Parents who forced daughters–like Kate in *TSh*–into marriage behaved like bawds. Women were thereby reduced to property. "Lear, like Richard II, is one of the few men to enter the experience of woman and discover his own nullity ... once he is separated from his property" (125). Adultery and whoredom ravaged and so divided marriages. Claudius characterizes his guilt, for example, as whorish.

Chapter Three, "Gods and Devils," concentrates on idolatry and satire which humanists regarded as "complementary" and equally damnable since they denied women's individuality and their status as "rational creatures." The "male cult of idolatry" was associated with court artifice and often concealed "contempt for women" (149). Such idolatry sprung from pagan rights and, as Navarre in *LLL* proves, Catholic ritual. Through Bertram Shakespeare condemns the courtly pursuit of lust under the guise of the religion of love, an attack sanctioned by middle-class Puritans. Bred at court, Rosalind can see through court folly. Shakespeare, "more than any of his fellow playwrights," wanted to "dissolve the artificial distinction between the sexes" (153) which idolatry established. More objective than men, women in the comedies are detached observers of men's idolatrous folly; "women reach out to the world of the audience while men are contained in the play" (156). Shakespeare does encourage "mutual idolatry" to promote harmony in nature and love whereas male idolatry is based on preconceptions of women. The Ladies in *LLL* shatter the play world set in motion by their suitors' idolatry. Shakespeare puts such idolatry clearly in the larger physical world, away from its "male sanctuary" (169), to show how unreasonable it is. Associated with the "physical world of birth and death" (170), women offer a life-long perspective.

The age-old tradition of satirizing women was popular in the Renaissance theatre, yet Shakespeare and his fellow dramatists "contrived to have it both ways–to reap the audience's laughter at the satirist's sallies against women without compromising their own position as defenders of women" (176). Though the satirist enjoyed "impunity" in poetry, dramatists exposed his lies by pointing out women's virtues. Puritanism and the audience's "alertness" helped Shakespeare to exploit the satirist himself. Associated with the court and viewed as debased by the middle-class Puritans, satire against women "perhaps more than anything else [was] a class symbol" (195). In the drama, "satire tells us more about the nature of the masculine serpent than about the nature of women" (183). Iago, Othello, Posthumus, and Iachimo create their own theatre "peopled" with illusions of "monstrous women" (184). In their fictions these characters see other men in themselves. Because Hamlet obliterates the real Ophelia his "satire initiates tragedy" (190). In *Ado*, Claudio "cures both Beatrice and Benedick of their taste for acting" by satirizing Hero. Women like Isabella in *MM* "disarmed their detractors" by agreeing to their sex's faults and in the process found new freedoms.

Chapter Four on "Femininity and Masculinity" contains sections on "Women and Education"; "Disguise and the Boy Actor"; and "Politics and Violence."

St. Thomas More and other Humanists argued that since women had the same capacity and spiritual equality as men, they should be educated with no fear that they would become masculine through such education. "The prominence of educated women in Elizabethan and Jacobean society made the Elizabethans sensitive to the whole area of masculinity and femininity ... " (212). Forced to be silent, women could not historically engage in disputation, the "medium of instruction" (214). But Shakespeare did not believe that "silence is natural to women" or that "femininity requires silence" (245). Only Virgilia in *Cor* "conforms to the masculine ideal of feminine silence" (214). Cordelia's silence links her to Kent and contrasts with the masculine "ferocity" of her speaking sisters. To see how they are reflected in men's eyes, women "momentarily become men" when they see other women (218), as Gertrude does assessing the Player Queen. Yet Hermione's "orator's subtlety" joined with her femininity shows that in *WT* Shakespeare believes that "conventions of femininity have no relevance in the tribunal of right and wrong" (220). In *H8*, Katherine through her silence "defies" the male world and "outwits her accusers." Eloquence in women always breeds male animosity, and eloquent women such as Portia or Isabella must plead in a "hostile" environment. Their speech is always "coloured by their sex" (224). The eloquent and educated Elizabeth had a tremendous influence on the views of women. Wit and intelligence level gender distinctions, "making Beatrice more akin to Mercutio than to Ophelia" (229).

A moralist like Philip Stubbes inveighed against actors playing women and women wearing breeches since a woman in man's clothes threatened "to usurp his authority" and "to annex his nature" (239). The Elizabethan controversy over masculine women extended to the drama. There were numerous defenses of the theatrical illusions perpetuated by the boy actors who revealed a "more durable femininity" than society allowed. Similarities and differences between the sexes ran deeper than just changes in costume. The disguise effected through costume revealed a deeper truth about gender. Disguises and reactions to them proved that "masculinity is as much a mask as femininity" (244) and that a woman in such a disguise "smokes out the male world, perceiving masculinity as a form of acting" (245).

Portia, like other women dressed as men, "mocks the boy who creates her" as she affirms her own independence and identity. Julia in *TGV* and Cleopatra become the audience to the boy actor who plays them. In playing Ganymede, Rosalind "acquires a Puckish insight into the theatrical nature of masculinity and femininity" (250). Actresses today wrongly put too much femininity into Shakespeare's women's roles, burdening the plays with what they do not have (253). Charges against the boy actors arousing homosexual feelings are unfounded; the boys did play the man with other women (Rosalind with Phebe; Viola with Olivia). Yet like women, the boy actors emphasized elemental femininity through their intimate conversations with other women about such "primal" matters as childbirth and motherhood, their "confederacy" when discussing lovers with other women, and their womanly rivalry over other men. "If the four lovers in the Athenian wood of *MND* all wore breeches, there would be no mistaking the women" (260). Unlike Imogen who found her male disguise deathly, Portia and Rosalind "thrive on masculinity" (260) as they "extend rather than endanger" their sense of self (264). Shakespeare's "heroines integrate their experiences as men with their feelings as women" so well that audiences cannot accept Rosalind returning to her father or Viola in women's weeds. For those reasons Shakespeare brings Rosalind out for the Epilogue. Portia, however, does not arouse such feelings in an audience which "is never private with the young Daniel" and sees no "sense of loss" when Portia returns to Belmont as a woman. Following his own feminism, Shakespeare creates a "mistress of misrule" (266) through the boy actors to give women a new identity. Disguise helped Shakespeare to "explore ... the nature of woman untrammelled by the custom of femininity" (271).

The sixteenth century was "fascinated by the question of women's political capacity" (273). But since manhood was defined by action and power, both denied to women, women were excluded from politics, though there was a "plethora of female sovereigns" whose actions questioned such an exclusive definition of manhood. Discrediting the belief that women were weak, Shakespeare emphasized that politics was "never confined to the male world" (294). When man "lacks physical power he becomes a woman" as Romeo, Macduff, and Hamlet fear in their attacks against their own effeminacy. Shakespeare cherishes men as well as women "whose sphere of action is words rather than deeds" (280). Excluded from politics, women become cunning plotters like Lady Macbeth whose view of masculinity is "devastatingly conventional" (284). Shakespeare believed that in true manhood "the masculine and feminine must marry in spirit" (291), which is why Coriolanus is stigmatized as less than a man. Women like Octavia in *AC* and Blanche in *KJ* who survive men's wars "stand ... for permanence and fidelity against shifting political sands" (294). When Shakespeare's women (Margaret, Goneril, Regan) engage in war, they are as ferocious as the men. Violent women in Shakespeare are "nearly always" adulteresses, and in "some ways the tragedy of adultery is the woman's version of the revenge tragedy" (303).

In sum, "To talk about Shakespeare's women is to talk about his men, because he refused to separate their worlds physically, intellectually, or spiritually" (308).

Reviews: *British Book News* (1975): 688; *Choice* 13 (1976): 364; *Economist* 256 (1975): 109; *Times Literary Supplement* 28 Oct. 1975: 1420; *Yale Review* 65 (1976): 443; Ashley, Leonard, R.N., *Bibliotheque d'Humanisme et Renaissance* 38 (1976): 171-75; Barton, Anne, *Times Literary Supplement* 24 Oct. 1975: 1259; Beauchamp, Virginia, *Clio* 6 (1976): 224; Cary, Cecile Williamson, *Antioch Review* 34 (1976): 379; Gent, Lucy, *English* 25 (1976): 194-96; Greer, Germaine, *Yearbook of English Studies* 8 (1978): 335-37; Hawkins, Harriett, *Review of English Studies* 28 (1977): 209-11; Holm, Janis Butler, *Shakespeare Quarterly* 29 (1978): 110-12; Palmer, D.J., *Shakespeare Survey* 29 (1976): 259; Ranald, Margaret Loftus, *Renaissance Quarterly* 32 (1979): 137-41; Von Schiak, P., *Unisa English Studies* 14 (1978): 69. See also item 45.

7. Flower, Annette C. "Disguise and Identity in *Pericles, Prince of Tyre*." *Shakespeare Quarterly* 26 (1975): 30-41.

Per depends upon conscious illusion, particularly the use of disguise, to interpret reality and discover true identity. The disguises of Antiochus, his daughter, Cleon, Dionyza, and the Bawd "are a denial of truth, whereas the disguises of Pericles, Marina, and Thaisa are affirmations of truth" (39). Pericles establishes his identity as a true prince while disguised as a mere man. His identity becomes complete in his recognition of his restored family. Thaisa and Marina also assume disguises to prove their true worth. For the Renaissance, chastity was an essential ingredient for the true princess: "truth, troth, and chastity are, in the woman, inseparable attributes" (37). Thaisa assumes a disguise which bears out "the congruity of personality and role" (37). As a nun, she emphasizes the chastity which marks her royal blood. Marina's testing under disguise closely parallels her father's testing. She is betrayed by false friends, forced "to rely on inherent princely attributes without the princely symbols, and elevated to the position of respect (even in a brothel) by holding fast to these attributes." Like her mother, the most distinguishing mark of her true identity is her chastity. Although sold into a brothel, Marina remains virtuous.

8. Gourlay, Patricia Southard. "'O My Most Sacred Lady': Female Metaphor in *The Winter's Tale.*" *English Literary Renaissance* 5 (1975): 375-95.

In *WT*, females become metaphors for the necessary qualities denied by Leontes's masculine society. "Because men rule, the 'masculine' values are power, law, and reason; a man is hardheaded, disciplined, practical, as well as honorable" (375-76). Speaking for these values, Leontes rejects the "womanly" qualities of love, art, and nature when he spurns their dramatic representatives in Hermione, Paulina, and Perdita. The Renaissance perception of Venus reflects the dual attitudes toward woman in general—as a symbol for lust as well as the Neoplatonic ideal love. Rejected by Leontes for her alleged sexual misconduct, Hermione actually symbolizes grace through her gentleness and mercy. Paulina typifies art as she combines truth (in her unceasing defense of Hermione) and artifice (in the magic she uses to bring the statue to life). Surrounded by rich, fertile imagery, Perdita stands for a benevolent nature. "Her innocent sexuality is life-creating ... an antidote to her father's barrenness" (388). By finally accepting these three women, Leontes recognizes "those ambiguities of [his] own nature which he has feared and despised, but without which his masculine world is a wasteland" (395).

9. Kahn, Coppelia. *"The Taming of the Shrew*: Shakespeare's Mirror of Marriage." *Modern Language Studies* 5 (1975): 88-102.

    Rpt. in item 42 and rev. for item 160.

10. Kline, Jean, C.S.C. "Othello: 'A Fixed Figure of the Time of Scorn.'" *Shakespeare Quarterly* 26 (1975): 139-50.

    In *Oth*, Shakespeare explores the illusions and conflicts inherent in a naive and dangerous male code of honor emphasizing that a man must maintain his "reputation for valor, for justice, and for possession of a faithful wife" (140). A woman's honor was controlled by male rules. In each act of *Oth* a person's honor is destroyed–Brabantio's in Act 1; Cassio's in 2; Desdemona's as a wife in 3; Othello's as a husband in 4; and Iago's as an honest man in 5. Unlike Othello, who proclaims the honor of his ancestry, Brabantio is dishonored with public scorn because of his daughter's conduct. Though Othello agonizes over the code, he "is concerned about things other than Desdemona's virtue" (144)–his wife as his property, his own reputation, and the loss of his peace of mind and occupation. Iago's "deflation of women's honor is ... somewhat similar to Falstaff's comment about military honor in *1 Henry IV*" (145). Ironically, up until Act 4 Othello "has lost his honor in the eyes of no one but himself" (146). In the end, he has neither killed his wife justly nor taken revenge against Iago, actions forbidden by law but approved by a male code of honor. Desdemona is one of Shakespeare's "rashly judged women" with no comic solution to save her.

11. Neely, Carol Thomas. *"The Winter's Tale*: The Triumph of Speech." *Studies in English Literature* 15 (1975): 321-38.

See item 298.

12. Nelson, Timothy G.A. "The Rotten Orange: Fears of Marriage in Comedy from Shakespeare to Congreve." *Southern Review* [Adelaide] 8 (1975): 205-26.

Not all Renaissance comedies end with happy marriages. Many dramatists, including Shakespeare, "discouraged the audience from idealizing the married state" (206). In *Ado* the couple's "distrust of marriage is very real." *LLL* ends unconventionally with no marriage; disastrous marriages almost always occur when a couple does not scrutinize each other, as Olivia fails to do in *TN*. *LLL* comes closest to the Restoration stock convention of a gallant marrying off his spoiled mistress (the "rotten orange") to a "gull who thinks she is rich and virtuous" (220). Yet Shakespeare modifies the pattern by making the seducer a country bumpkin, not a lord. In fact, Shakespeare "does not allow the leading characters in his comedies to seduce women and then abandon them with impunity" (221). Though forced or tricked marriages take place in the dark comedies, they are not treated lightly as jokes. The only "golden" comedy where a man fears "being overreached in marriage" is *Ado* where Claudio believes he has been deceived by Leonato who wants to get his unchaste daughter "off his hands before it is too late" (223).

13. Newlin, Jeanne T. "The Darkened Stage: J.P. Kemble and *Troilus and Cressida.*" In *The Triple Bond: Plays, Mainly Shakespearean, in Performance.* Ed. Joseph G. Price. State College, PA: U of Pennsylvania P, 1975. 190-202.

TrC went unstaged between 1603 and 1907. John Philip Kemble's unacted promptbook of 1791 sheds light on the morals of his age, the nature of the play and Shakespeare's women, and the distance between our cynical view of "romantic sensualism" and Kemble's. Catering to the "sensibilities of an audience prone to take offense at the bawdy and sexual coarseness" of Shakespeare's play (192), Kemble deleted both "excessive emotion and insistent sexuality" (194) in his much expurgated version of *TrC*. Troilus and Cressida were romantic, not cynical, lovers for

Kemble. Cressida was transformed into a heroine from
sentimental drama; and Troilus became a tragic lover instead of
Shakespeare's "lovesick adolescent." Kemble considerably "refines
Cressida's character" (195) and limits Troilus's sexual desires. The
role of Helen he deleted because it would undermine the tone
Kemble wanted to establish. Cressida first appears as a "blushing
maiden" (197). Kemble also omitted Troilus's emotional cries, the
mocking allusions to cuckoldry, and Thersites's bitter taunts. In
the last act, the "least satisfying in the adaptation" (200), Kemble
gave Troilus's "personal tragedy ... a romantic interpretation" and
supplied extenuating circumstances for Cressida's betrayal. The
effect was a much more "disciplined" ending than Shakespeare's.

14. Pendlebury, B.J. "Happy Ever After: Some Aspects of Marriage
    in Shakespeare's Plays." *Contemporary Review* [London] 227
    (1975): 324-38.

Though it is not possible to assume that Shakespeare "endorsed
the judgements of his characters," particular assumptions do
inform his presentation of marriage. In the early comedies,
marriage was so much the "ultimate good" that Shakespeare "will
often strain probability to bring it about" (325). Seeing marriage
as a sacrament, Shakespeare's audience applauded "a high moral
tone on the subject of female chastity." The social relationship
between partners receives little attention, however. *TSh* is best
seen as "an example of wish-fulfillment, a fantasy designed to
appeal to hen-pecked husbands" (326). The later plays dwell on
female deceptions and masculine obsessions with infidelity.
Viewing man's behavior more leniently and even "implicitly"
condoning "murderous conclusions" (327), Shakespeare "evidently
accepts different standards of conduct for men and women" (327).
Ironically, *Mac*, which shows affection and esteem between
husband and wife, is "the best picture of genuine partnership in
marriage that Shakespeare has given us" (328). Late in his life
Shakespeare became "embittered" about matrimony.

15. Sadler, Lynn Veach, "The Three Guises of Lady Macbeth."
    C[ollege] L[anguage] A[ssociation] Journal 19 (1975): 10-19.

Lady Macbeth, who should be seen as optimistic, is more imaginative than her husband in her "three-faceted portrayal" (10). As the "public Lady Macbeth," she is a figure of disorder who offers a "parody of the ceremoniousness and bounty of Duncan" (11). She is also the woman "who plays to the audience of her husband only." In this respect, she becomes a practical wife allowing her practicality to hide her "own trafficking with the supernatural" (14). Goading Macbeth, she tries to "make the unnatural natural." The "private Lady Macbeth" struggles because of her imagination; she forgets that she can be victimized by time as she ignores "man's fallen condition" (13). Though she privately asks to be unsexed, she is not asking to "be sealed in the virtues of masculinity" (16), for she wishes Macbeth to become unsexed, too, since he is too full of the milk of human kindness. Her powerful imagination leads to her downfall; she suffers because of the "cleavage between her imaginings and the physical power to translate them into action." Ironically, her bold imagination prevents her from sharing "the full extent of her fancy" with her husband.

16. Salter, Nancy Kay Clark. "Masks and Roles: A Study of Women in Shakespeare's Drama." *DAI* 36 (1975): 1535A. U of Connecticut.

17. Schwartz, Murray M. *"The Winter's Tale*: Loss and Transformation." *American Imago* 32 (1975): 145-99.

Leontes's irrational jealousy results from the simultaneous desire and fear of maternal presence. He "follows a regressive path toward the object of his ambivalent desires, Hermione, and he attempts to destroy her in order to reunite himself with a fantasized ideal maternal figure" (145). As the self-appointed advocate for Hermione, Paulina argues for feminine nurturance, but paradoxically, in the early scenes, she embodies and intensifies Leontes's anxieties. During the trial scene, these anxieties, reflected in the accusations directed at Hermione, surface in Leontes as he becomes the thing he most fears–a destructive parental figure denying his wife and child. The penalty inflicted on him for rejecting the oracle is the death of his son, another symbol of his "failed patriarchy." In Bohemia, Shakespeare "re-creates and reverses the psychological sources of Leontes's madness" (199) through Perdita and Florizel. Florizel negates possible disillusionment of an idealized Perdita by engaging in an "idealized symbiosis" with her. The last act, set in Sicily, is consciously theatrical, and thus through art, Shakespeare is able to join and renounce simultaneously, both for himself and his character, "the creative and destructive mother in infancy" (198).

18. Sproat, Kezia Bradford Vanmeter. "A Reappraisal of Shakespeare's View of Women." *DAI* 36 (1975): 3664A. Ohio State U.

19. Voth, Grant L., and Oliver H. Evans. "Cressida and the World of the Play." *Shakespeare Studies* 8 (1975): 231-39.

Cressida is not as simple or corrupt as critics have made her. More interested in discussing Troilus, Cressida's detractors have not recognized her complexity. Not vicious or static, she does change in the course of the play. It is unfair to hold her responsible for the corrupt world she lives in. She is responsible, however, for the folly of "ignoring her knowledge of the world of the play and of giving herself to Troilus's 'ideal' vision" (237). She begins by fully understanding the cynicism of a world that is "stripped of metaphysical and temporal dimensions" (231) and dimensionality. In contrast to Troilus, Cressida has a "more legitimate approach to love" and unlike Troilus, she uses language to "keep herself from remembering how much she loves" him and from revealing too much about her love (234). Yielding to Troilus's corrupt idealism that tries to cover the putrefied core with embellished language, Cressida "loses touch with her earlier, more accurate vision" (235). In the Greek camp, she reluctantly resubmits to the sordid world of the play represented by Diomedes. In fact, she has never really left that world despite Troilus's attempt to seduce her. Her only defense against that corrupt world is her language.

20. Wheeler, Richard P. "The King and the Physician's Daughter: *All's Well That Ends Well* and the Late Romances." *Comparative Drama* 8 (1975): 311-27.

Themes and patterns "central to the design of the later romances are present in *AWW* as intrusions not fully integrated into the comic action" (325). Chief of these anticipations is the relationship of the king to Bertram and Helena. Unlike the festive comedies, *AWW* does not show younger lovers triumphing over an older generation; the king's presence intensifies the frustrations between Bertram and Helena. Nor does *AWW* offer a benevolent atonement as in the romances. Family relations are in disarray in *AWW* as Bertram, devalued, loses his place in the family to an idealized Helena who looks forward to the daughters of romance. Like Marina, Perdita, and Miranda, Helena establishes a strong bond as daughter to the king. She restores her father/king to a "full sense of life," yet by choosing her husband, the king sets Helena up "to be abandoned and disgraced" (316). As in the late romances, *AWW* turns on a crisis of trust which is tied to "the insistence that a man's power to bestow position and wealth within the social structure of life balances a woman's power to create or regenerate the vitality of life itself ... " (318).

The king experiences this crisis in Bertram's rejection of Helena, which threatens the king's own "masculine autonomy," for he regards Bertram as "a symbolic equivalent of his own ... restored potency" (320). Moreover, the king's bond to Helena is expressed in terms of her "sexual legitimacy" (322). Depending on the success of Helena's cure, she will be an honest wife or a strumpet. The king thus displays the incestuous love for a daughter manifested by the fathers in the romances. Bertram and Helena are not joined through magic or miracle, as romance couples are, but through the "manipulations of industrious Helena" (325). Ultimately, the father-king in *AWW* subverts the youthful love of the comedies but does not offer the protection from incest promised by the romances (326). The king's healing neither repairs Helena and Bertram's relationship nor does it "balance his debt" to her.

21. Williamson, Marilyn L. "The Courtship of Katherine and the Second Tetralogy." *Criticism* 17 (1975): 326-34.

The courtship scene in *H5* is far more than a "crowd-pleaser," since it "repeats a basic pattern in Henry's behavior that reaches back to his madcap days" (327). This scene is "entirely gratuitous" (328) because it is, politically speaking, a *fait accompli*. But it reflects Henry's strategy of imitating the common man and adopting "good fellowship." Henry's play-acting, manipulation, and need to get support are repeated "in the courtship of Katherine, where Henry pretends it really matters whether Katherine loves him, while all the time they both know that her father's wishes will settle the issue" (329). Henry's wooing calls to mind his "Hal-like wit" and "realistic, cynical, Falstaffian truth telling," yet his pretense only stresses that he and Katherine are not common individuals with a free choice but royal personages. Even though she must obey her father, Katherine "will not pretend that she is doing anything else or that she loves Henry or that she can speak his language ... she greets his play-acting with a healthy skepticism" (331). As Williams did earlier, Katherine resists Henry's game of "king-and-man" (332). With his "kingly pomposity" (333) and his need for self-justification, Henry has become "a pompous Hotspur, without the saving bluntness and sincerity" (332). The fact that Katherine and he cannot speak each other's language is a "paradigm" of Henry's being "so separated from the rest of humanity that he cannot even talk to his intended wife" (334).

1976

22. Blades, Sophia B. "Cordelia: Loss of Insolence." *Studies in the Humanities* 5.2 (1976): 15-21.

Cordelia does not have to be seen in allegorical or theological terms as a divine figure. She undergoes a change in behavior from being a wilful, insolent girl who does not respect Lear's authority in Act 1 to a "woman, a queen who is driven by love to help her father" (15). Though she wants to "contrast the excess of her sisters' replies," Cordelia nonetheless "commits their error, for she is as guilty of understating her love as they were in overstating theirs" (16). In rejecting her sisters, Cordelia also rejects Lear. Like Lear, she is proud. But when Cordelia returns in Act 4 as the Queen of France and Lear's nurse, she restores Lear's reason and "his position as father." Now possessing an infinite love that resists quantification, Cordelia can "act for Lear without subtracting any of her affection from France" (18). In Act 4, Lear and Cordelia reverse their "motives and statements of love" from Act 1. Daughter and father change because each gains in love; in fact, Cordelia "acquires pure love and loses her insolence through a process parallel to Lear's regenerative situation," though she acquires such love not in England but in France married to a "kind and loving" husband (21).

23. Garner, S.N. "Shakespeare's Desdemona." *Shakespeare Studies* 9 (1976): 233-52.

Many critics view Desdemona as pure and virtuous, completely faithful and loyal to Othello. Hence, she is easily dismissed. Shakespeare presents her as neither standing on a pedestal nor fallen in the gutter, and makes this clear by undermining the two extremes. When questioned about her marriage, she answers her father forcefully without any traces of shyness. Neither does she want to be treated delicately; rather, she prefers to join Othello in Cyprus in order to assume the role of a wife of a military hero. Cassio, who idealizes Desdemona as much as her father did, seems to be the only acceptable white suitor for Desdemona, but his liaisons with Bianca bring his masculine acceptability into question. "The embodiment of style, Cassio is hollow at the core" (243). Iago and Roderigo know they can play on Brabantio's fears of black sexuality and miscegenation. Othello himself sees his blackness as a flaw in his character, associating it with a lack of grace and manners. Desdemona's tragedy is that she idealizes her husband, and does not believe that he can fall victim to jealousy and anger. "Unlike Hermione, Desdemona merely asserts her innocence rather than reproaches her husband, with whom the final blame must lie" (249).

24. Jiji, Vera M. "Portia Revisited: The Influence of Unconscious Factors Upon Theme and Characterization in *The Merchant of Venice.*" *Literature and Psychology* 26 (1976): 5-15.

Portia has a darker side as a threatening castration figure. Although this is one of the submerged themes, it controls much of the action. An ambiguous character, Portia is both the "Goddess of Death" and the "Goddess of Love and Fertility," the cornucopia and the devourer. Hardly heavenly, Portia torments Antonio in the trial scene and as master-mistress controls Bassanio in the mock trial of the rings. Only submissive on the surface, Portia "controls her sex at will" and "moves from female to male and back to female not under the pressure of events from the outside (as Julia, Viola, Rosalind, and Imogen do), but by her own choice of time and circumstance" (8). In venturing for Portia by choosing the right casket (which suggests death and female genitals), Bassanio risks losing his "genital power" and a "normal sex life" (11). The fear of castration, an "unconsciously determined theme" (12), is present in Shylock's bond with Antonio and Bassanio's with Portia; in fact, Antonio and Bassanio are "split halves of one identity" (12). Portia may be a witty and intelligent woman, but her role as a frighteningly powerful "phallic mother" (12) helps us to see unity among the three plots of *MV*.

25. Kahn, Coppelia. "The Rape of Shakespeare's *Lucrece*." *Shakespeare Studies* 9 (1976): 45-72.

In *RL*, Shakespeare uses the rape to examine women's role in marriage within a patriarchal society. A wife's chastity is a material fact, dependent not upon her intent but upon her body. "There is simply no excuse for a raped wife, because the social order depends upon pure descent as a mark of status, legitimate heirs as a means of insuring property rights, and the control of male sexual rivalry through the ownership of sexual rights to women in marriage" (67). As a chaste wife, Lucrece encompasses the paradox of a woman who is almost asexually pure and yet is necessarily intimate with her husband whose possession she is. Her purity and Collatine's ownership of her account for Tarquin's desire more than does his lust for Lucrece. As in *Cym*, "the husband's boasts initiate the temptation, in effect challenging his peers to take that jewel" (53). Tarquin's crime, therefore, is one against husband and state. Lucrece's suicide reinforces the patriarchal view of women. Although others are willing to forgive her, she refuses to set a potentially dangerous pattern for other wives. In her society, she has the role of "chaste wife," and since chastity is a material thing for her, she has no life once she is "stained." By her death she is able to reinstate her physical purity by spilling out her corrupt blood. Although Lucrece accepts the material view of chastity, Shakespeare frequently advocates the more Christian view of spiritual chastity. "The evil that concerns him is that men not only abuse women but also hold women guilty of those very abuses" (68).

26. ---. "Self and Eros in *Venus and Adonis*." *The Centennial Review* 20 (1976): 351-71.

See item 160.

27. Klein, Joan Larsen. "'Angels and Ministers of Grace': *Hamlet*, IV,
    v-vii." *Allegorica* 1.2 (1976): 156-76.

    Not a "pathetic victim," Ophelia is an "active force" who
    becomes a surrogate for Hamlet by ministering to Gertrude in
    rituals similar to those in the order for the "Visitation of the Sick."
    The "mad piety" in her speech and song contains "patterned
    references to sixteenth-century moral, theological, sexual, and
    medical lore" (156). Ophelia's madness shows her to be patient
    and faithful, someone in a state of grace set apart from the
    corrupt court because of her strong senses. Only when she is mad
    can she tell Claudius what words mean (160). Like Hamlet, she
    evokes "the better, holier past" epitomized for her and the prince
    by King Hamlet. A "minister, docent, and physician," Ophelia does
    not use reason but relies on herbs and caring. Her Valentine
    song, "another male version of the debauching of Ophelia" (163),
    is applied to Claudius, who through inversion is cast as the maid
    victimized by seduction. Though a counselor in her first mad
    scene, Ophelia is isolated in her second mad appearance. She
    attempts to bring Laertes and Gertrude to their senses through
    appropriate herbs, but she holds out no hope of grace for the
    "deceiving Claudius." But Laertes, who has become an extension
    of Claudius, does not move away from his sullied self; and
    Gertrude is not protected from Claudius's poisoned cup/chalice.
    Ophelia's nettles suggest Christ's passion and crown of thorns. By
    being taken into nature, which draws her to itself in the pastoral
    tradition, Ophelia is "both like and unlike Hamlet, who allows
    himself to be drawn by providence into a duel which finally brings
    him rest" (170).

28. Novy, Marianne L. "'An   You Smile Not, He's Gagged':
    Mutuality in Shakespearean Comedy." *Philological Quarterly* 55
    (1976): 178-94.

    See item 262.

29. Peter, Lilian Augustine. "Women as Educative Guardians in
    Shakespeare's Comedies." *DAI* 36 (1976): 7443A. Indiana U.

30. Sklar, Elizabeth S. "Bassanio's Golden Fleece." *Texas Studies in Literature and Language* 18 (1976): 500-9.

Bassanio is a morally ambiguous character. He is typical of Venetian society "in a way that Portia, a woman, and Shylock, a Jew, cannot be" (501). He displays a "purely Shylockian ethic" in being preoccupied with money. Confusing love and money, he woos Portia for her wealth and is thus guilty of "covetousness in love" (503). Jason is a "singularly apt prototype" (501) for Bassanio, who shares the vices of covetousness and perjury with this classical figure. *MV* is about breaking oaths, and Bassanio is unable to fulfill his oath to Portia. The last act, in fact, has "adulterous overtones" in describing Bassanio's sexual infidelity to Portia. Jessica and Lorenzo also reflect the sins of the Jason/Medea legend. Like Medea, Jessica abandons her father, steals his wealth, and leaves "emotional devastation in her wake" (506). In the world of Bassanio's Venice, "ideals such as unselfish love and fidelity to truth cannot exist in unadulterated form ... " (507).

31. Zimmerman, Eugenia Noik. "The Proud Princess Gets Her Comeuppance: Structures of Patriarchal Order." *Canadian Review of Comparative Literature* 3 (1976): 253-68.

TSh illustrates patriarchal attitudes toward marriage and the transfer of authority over the proud princess from her father to her suitor-husband. Kate, the proud princess, asserts her shrewishness verbally; and by controlling when Bianca can wed, Kate ensures that the "patriarchal order is twice troubled" (258). Reversal of sex roles in *TSh* is linked to reversal of social roles as well. The page, Bartholomew (a male), is disguised as Sly's wife (a female). Bartholomew thus represents "what Katarina, the shrew, is not, what Bianca first appears to be, and what Katarina, once tame, becomes" (259). Through taming Kate, who initially loses the comforts associated with her rank, Petruchio "changes the nature of her identity and rewrites her definition" (259). She moves from aggressive (masculine) shrewish behavior to "submissiveness, [which promises] restoration of comfort" (260) and finally reconciliation.

1977

32. Asp, Carolyn. "In Defense of Cressida." *Studies in Philology* 74 (1977): 406-17.

    Cressida, who "embodies the play's central metaphysical question" about how value is determined, finds herself manipulated in a hostile masculine world. When Troilus proposes a sincere love for her, a new experience for Cressida, she comes to believe in her intrinsic worth. But she is embroiled in a "conflict of identities" (411). Betraying Troilus for Diomedes, Cressida is forced to surrender her sense of intrinsic worth and enters a relationship "circumscribed by mutability" (414). She must accept Ulysses's philosophy. Her actions in the love plot mirror those in the war plot; Achilles, like Cressida, is tricked into believing that observers confer worth. A "complex woman," Cressida cannot maintain a "consistent identity" because she is the pawn of men's desires (417).

33. Boose, Lynda Elizabeth. "'Lust in Action': *Othello* as Shakespeare's Tragedy of Human Sexuality." *DAI* 37 (1977): 7136A-7137. U of California, Los Angeles.

    See also items 4 and 33.

34. Charney, Maurice, and Hanna Charney. "The Language of Madwomen in Shakespeare and His Fellow Dramatists." *Signs* 3 (1977): 451-60.

Madwomen in Renaissance drama were "more strongly
defined" than madmen. Women's madness was "interpreted as
something specifically feminine, whereas the madness of men
[was] not specifically male" (451). Madwomen allowed dramatists
to explore unconventionally the feminine consciousness and
thereby give women the opportunity to "make a forceful assertion
of their being" (459). Such is the case with Ophelia, the prototype
for many madwomen to follow. Suffering from melancholy, a
classic symptom of love madness, Ophelia exhibits the traits of
female madness with her hair down, her lyrical speeches, broken
syntax, and great powers of imagination. "Her madness opens up
her role, and she is suddenly lyric, poignant, pathetic, tragic"
(456). Thus transformed, she is no longer silent but a threat to
Claudius. Shakespeare was possibly indebted to Marlowe's Zabina
(in *1 Tamburlaine*), "perhaps the first madwoman in Elizabethan
drama" (456). In her madness, Lady Macbeth "comes closest to a
modern feeling of anxiety symptoms" (458) in not being able to
suppress forbidden subjects. The portrayal of women's madness
on stage reveals the "cultural assumptions" of Shakespeare's age
and ours.

35. Cook, Ann Jennalie. "The Mode of Marriage in Shakespeare's
     England." *Southern Humanities Review* 11 (1977): 126-32.

A lack of information about English marriage customs prevents
us from knowing when Shakespeare is following an accepted
practice and when he is departing from it. It was not normal for
girls to marry at 13 or 14; "very early marriages were rare" (127).
Partners married between 20 and 25 years of age. *RJ*, which is
"probably most responsible for perpetuating the myth of early
marriage" (127), goes contrary to Elizabethan custom to minimize
the young lovers' responsibility and to arouse pity rather than
censure for them. Moreover, Romeo and Juliet's young age
emphasized the "premature fruition of sexual desire" associated
with erotic Italy. By contrast, women in the comedies were
married closer to the mature age endorsed by Shakespeare's
culture. Yet, Shakespeare in the romances returns to the child
bride who "is essential to the dream nature" of these plays and the
"theme of endangered innocence" (130). Understanding the rules

that governed matrimony allows us to understand "one of the funniest notions presented in the comedies" (131), that men and women were free to "pair up as they please" in opposition to parental wishes and without concern for adequate property settlements. The daughter of a duke such as Rosalind "did not marry a penniless, undereducated younger brother like Orlando, no matter how virtuous or how much in love he might be" (131).

36. Dash, Irene G. "A Penchant for Perdita on the Eighteenth-Century English State." *Studies in Eighteenth Century Culture* 6 (1977): 331-46.

   See item 109.

37. Fitz, L.T. "Egyptian Queens and Male Reviewers: Sexist Attitudes in *Antony and Cleopatra* Criticism." *Shakespeare Quarterly* 28 (1977): 297-316.

   Sexist readings of *AC* distort the play. Anti-Cleopatra critics reveal their own "difficulties in relationships with women" (298). By comparing Cleopatra only with other women, they stereotype her as Eve, "the quintessential," unpredictable woman. Though Shakespeare may disapprove of her "feminine wiles," he realizes that Cleopatra adopts them to protect herself from "the ravages of age." Major sexist critical faults are believing Antony could have been saved "by the love of a good woman" (i.e., Octavia), being disgusted by Cleopatra's "frank sexuality" (303), and applying a "clear double standard" (304) in interpreting Antony and Cleopatra. While Antony is praised for his political concerns, Cleopatra is condemned for hers; war and politics were not the feminine province. The "most flagrant manifestation of sexism in criticism of the play" (307) is making Antony the sole protagonist, even though Cleopatra survives the last act and speaks some of Shakespeare's greatest poetry. Shakespeare displays a greater interest in Cleopatra than Plutarch did, and his changes from the Roman historian "almost always" mitigate "Cleopatra's culpability" and Plutarch's "harshness" (313). Cleopatra rather than Antony should be regarded as the protagonist based on her death scene, the number of lines she speaks, and the fact that she "learns and grows as Antony does not" (314). Saying she "cannot be understood" is sexist; her acting contrary to what Antony expects is a mark of her infinite variety.

38. Garber, Marjorie. "Coming of Age in Shakespeare." *Yale Review* 66 (1977): 517-33.

    See item 156.

39. Gardner, C.O. "Beatrice and Benedick." *Theoria: A Journal of Studies in the Arts, Humanities, and Social Studies* [Pietermaritzburg] 49 (1977): 1-17.

    Beatrice and Benedick play an "aggressive, paradoxical game" that critics have failed to understand. There is a strong, magical Dionysian element of self-delight in their games. Though Beatrice has been portrayed wrongly as a cantankerous spinster, she is more than just a witty young woman. She seeks union with Benedick while at the same time "feels her self-sufficiency threatened" (7). Beatrice welcomes Benedick "in a spirit of joyous but serious contradiction and denial." Comic heroes and intensive individualists, Beatrice and Benedick are a great deal alike in their protesting society's laws. Yet it is "perhaps slightly less astonishing [for Shakespeare] since we are rather more accustomed to the rebellious and the surprising in the behavior of men" (7). Beatrice and Benedick are close to Falstaff; just as he "stands opposed to all the conventions of virtue and sober respectability and military honor," they "reject the norms of love and marriage" (9) which impose upon each partner's self-respect and freedom. Yet, as Shakespeare emphasizes, "even falling in love is not incompatible with self assertion," since Beatrice and Benedick do gain "another complementary self" (14). Beatrice teaches Benedick a valuable lesson about love in demanding that he kill Claudio. To prove itself, love must fight, and be willing to "risk all and to commit self entirely" (15).

40. Greenfield, Thomas A. "Excellent Things in Women: The Emergence of Cordelia." *South Atlantic Bulletin* 42 (1977): 44-52.

Critics have honored Cordelia allegorically as the perfection of virtue/love; yet paradoxically she is a character who errs, grows, and changes between Act 1 and Act 4 of *Lear.* In her *Shakespeare's Heroines* (1908), Anna Jameson was the first to recognize Cordelia's change, yet her views are dated "because [they] rely so heavily on a stilted perception of womanly virtue that would offend even the most die-hard antifeminist" (45). Cordelia is flawed in Act 1. Her "mindless adherence to the artificial values of conventional femininity" (50) leads to her subjugating herself to family duty (which is neither constructive nor natural in *Lear*), to her speaking a stilted and formal language, and to her holding an "absurd and sterile perception of love as a finite quantity" (48). Seeing Cordelia as blameless and beyond reproach in Act 1 compromises Lear's tragedy. His perfection would be standing in front of him; instead, he has to choose between Goneril and Regan's treachery and Cordelia's weakness, which is perceived as treachery. By the time she appears in Act 4, Cordelia has moved away from the conventional patterns of womanly perfection. She abandons the "oblique language of female convention" (50), speaks directly, openly, and sincerely to and about her father, and is compassionate toward him instead of being self-righteous as she was in Act 1. Now she puts no quantitative limits on love.

41. Hodgson, John A. "Desdemona's Handkerchief as an Emblem of Her Reputation." *Texas Studies in Language and Literature* 19 (1977): 313-22.

To see the handkerchief as a symbol of Desdemona's love is to let Othello's misleading evaluation of it determine our view. Rather, the handkerchief is an "emblem of Desdemona's reputation; and as such it closely parallels in its progress through the play the career of her good name" (314). As Othello describes it in Act 3.4.53-73, the handkerchief is a talisman of man's, not woman's, love. With the help of Iago's "slanderous insinuations" (315), Othello tries to make the handkerchief a proof of Desdemona's love. As soon as she moves from a divine woman to a fallen wife in his eyes, the handkerchief passes to Emilia, who is the kind of Venetian wife who would commit adultery. By the

time the handkerchief passes into Bianca's hands, Desdemona for
Othello becomes the "cunning whore of Venice." While all the
women "seem to regard the handkerchief as an emblem of
reputation" (317), Bianca and Emilia cannot copy the work. Yet
while Desdemona's honest reputation could be copied, the
"inimitable pattern in the play is not that of Desdemona's
handkerchief at all, but that of her love" (318). The handkerchief
"finally disappears" into the wedding sheets, the true and proper
"unsullied emblem of her fidelity" (319). Desdemona sleeps on
spotless sheets; it is Othello who stains them with his blood.

42. Kahn, Coppelia. "*The Taming of the Shrew*: Shakespeare's Mirror
     of Marriage." In *The Authority of Experience: Essays in Feminist
     Criticism*. Ed. Arlyn Diamond and Lee R. Edwards. Amherst:
     U of Massachusetts P, 1977. 84-100.

     Rpt. from item 9 and rev. for item 160.

43. Kiessling, Nicolas K. "*The Winter's Tale*, II, iii, 103-7: An Allusion
     to the Hag-Incubus." *Shakespeare Quarterly* 28 (1977): 93-95.

     Paulina's speech in Act 2.3.103-107 expressing her fears about
     Perdita adopting a "yellow" (jealous) frame of mind is an indirect
     attack on Leontes's vice. The crux of Paulina's words about
     Perdita suspecting that her children are not her husband's is best
     explained in light of the hag-incubus tradition. Falling victim to an
     incubus, or "impregnating male demon," Perdita might find that
     her children were not fathered by her husband or realize that they
     were changelings substituted for her legitimate offspring.

44. Lyons, Bridget Gellert. "The Iconography of Ophelia." *English
     Literary History* 44 (1977): 60-74.

     In the world of *Ham* agreement about iconographic meaning
     is impossible. Ophelia's contradictory representation as the two
     sides of the goddess Flora reflects and reinforces the sexual and
     political confusion of *Ham*. Ophelia ambiguously evokes images
     of Flora the goddess of fertility and Flora the city prostitute
     associated with courtly deception and wealth, and so emphasizes

the gap between the harmonies of pastoralism and the contamination of Denmark. In her role as Flora the fertility goddess, Perdita sharply contrasts with Ophelia. Perdita as Flora is sane, spells out the meaning behind her flowers, and portrays love as rejuvenation and sexually pleasurable. Perdita's "fruitfulness ... is in harmony with social refinement" (68). Ophelia as Flora, on the other hand, is vague about the meaning of her flowers, sings bawdy songs reflecting the "discordant nature of her sexuality" (69), and is victimized by Polonius and Laertes's commercialism. The "iconography of Ophelia as Flora reinforces some of the verbal and dramatic complexities of the play as a whole" (70), most notably the contradictions between Gertrude's pastoral description/explanation of Ophelia's death and the jarring sordid details of its reality. Like Ophelia as the incongruous Flora, Hamlet as Hercules lamentably shows us a figure in a "world that is hostile to ennobling comparisons" (73).

45. McKewin, Carole. "Shakespeare Liberata: *Shakespeare and the Nature of Women*, and the New Feminist Criticism." *Mosaic* 10.3 (1977): 157-64.

Juliet Dusinberre's *Shakespeare and the Nature of Women* (item 6) is "radical and exhilarating" by proposing that Puritanism had a positive influence on the bourgeois audience's views of women and "Shakespeare's insistence on the mutuality of men and women" (158). The result was that Shakespeare's women played by boys were "vital, significant, and searching." Yet Dusinberre's "interpretation of social history totters on overly optimistic assumptions" (159). Despite the importance that marriage and education had in the Puritan view of woman, the "Golden Age of drama was not necessarily the Golden Age for women." Not all dramatists provided a sensitive view of women, and "Even Shakespeare has darker visions of women than Dusinberre will admit, particularly in the early tragedies and history plays" (160). In the comedies, women's power is limited, diminished; a married Portia bows to the mores of her day, and Rosalind in "male dress seems more intelligent and vital than Rosalind of female attire" (160). The "problems and pleasures" of Dusinberre's book reflect "larger issues" in feminist criticism of Shakespeare. Though

feminism has not been widely accepted, and often seen as a
political movement, it "can broaden our understanding" of
Shakespeare rather than "narrowing it" (161). Dusinberre
establishes an important trend in feminist scholarship by
questioning male assumptions/illusions of women, "the images of
woman in the man's mind" (162). Using eclectic methods,
feminism can distinguish between "Shakespeare's use of male
fantasy and his *sanction* of it." Too often anti-feminism resides in
the critic rather than the author.

46. Montrose, Louis A. "'Sport by sport o'erthrown': *Love's Labour's*
     Lost and the Politics of Play." *Texas Studies in Language and*
     Literature 18 (1977): 528-52.

     The message of Shakespeare's art exists in its "affirmation of
     the power and obligation of men and women to exercise their
     minds in a multivalent exploration of the ambiguous reality in
     which they live their lives" (528). *Ham* implies that play can be
     serious and jest earnest. The world of Navarre in *LLL* is a
     playground for the male characters. They celebrate the discovery
     and exercise of creative energies, even though they are misguided.
     For example, much of the action of the first scene of the play is
     a parody of kingship. "Their energies go awry when the ladies
     refuse to cooperate in the roles of passive objects or equal players
     in the fiction" (530). While the ladies are capable of social grace,
     the men are not. Only Berowne has the self-consciousness to
     recognize his role playing. "The frustration of the ritualistic
     masque structure by the ladies' deception and refusal to dance
     makes it a game of discord and irony, a miniature of the larger
     dramatic form" (540). The Princess and her ladies bring with them
     to Navarre worldly concerns that disrupt the male peace.

47. Mowat, Barbara A. "Images of Woman in Shakespeare's Plays."
     Southern Humanities Review 11 (1977): 145-57.

     There is a glaring discrepancy between Shakespeare's women
     and the way they are perceived by male characters. Because of
     male fantasies and fears, women are often wrongly portrayed as
     Circe (Luciana), a witch (Sylvia in *TGV*), or a "lascivious

temptress" (Rosaline by Berowne). Such unfair characterizations "recur throughout Shakespeare's plays" (150) as a result of male anxieties about female power and sexuality. Fearing that a woman is beautiful outside yet a "devilish harlot" inside, Othello, Posthumus, and Leontes stigmatize the women that love them. It is wrong to say Hamlet is jealous over Gertrude, who is "ambiguously related" to the pattern (156); he is distraught that she confirms moralistic views of women's sexual nature. Of the 17 plays involving fathers and daughters, eleven deal with the father "giving–or losing–the daughter in marriage" (152); Brabantio and Capulet erringly attack their daughters for hypocrisy. In *Lear*, however, the "male dreams and fears about the daughter are given fullest expression." Lear suffers from "two of the more terrible" male nightmares–(1) mistaking the virtuous woman for an evil one and (2) failing to "recognize evil in a wicked female" (153). The early comedies are linked to *Lear* in terms of the male-created mystique of a woman as half god, half fiend. With the romances the "pattern suddenly breaks" (153) where the daughter is "female as the male would have her"–pure and beautiful (154). Palpably evil women are "wonderfully destroyed" (154). The male image of woman is comic, grotesque, ambiguous, and only sometimes coincides with truth. The image of woman in Shakespeare, though, is "more complex" than that found in male dreams and nightmares.

48. Nardo, A.K. "Romeo and Juliet Up Against the Wall." *Paunch* 48-49 (1977): 126-32.

The psychological situation in *RJ* is more complex than M.D. Faber's reading of the play as an aborted attempt at adolescent separation from parents ("Adolescent Suicides of Romeo and Juliet," *Psychoanalytic Review* 59 [1972]: 169-82). Though the "elders feed the flames," the sparks of the feud are kindled by the hot-blooded young men with their phallic swords. Reflecting both the violence and the bawdiness of Verona, "sex and aggression are routinely linked" (128) threatening the lovers' "mutual adoration." Romeo is not torn between family and Juliet but "between loyalty to 'the boys' and their code of honor and love for his lady" (129). In killing Tybalt, Romeo fails to break away from his masculine friends. While Romeo cannot separate himself from his masculine milieu, Juliet can be faithful to her marriage vows; yet because of her gender, she is imprisoned, confined to Capulet's house, Laurence's cell, and the tomb. Her "love and spirit are, however, not imprisoned" (130). Betrayed by sterile Verona, the young lovers cannot give the city new life, for "Juliet has finally been thrust to the wall by the phallic power her society has exalted" (131).

49. Neely, Carol Thomas. "Women and Men in *Othello*: 'What should such a fool/Do with so good a woman?'" *Shakespeare Studies* 10 (1977): 133-58.

     Rpt. in item 132 and rev. for item 298.

50. Pedersen, Lise. "Shakespeare's *The Taming of the Shrew* vs. Shaw's *Pygmalion*: Male Chauvinism vs. Women's Lib." In *Fabian Feminist: Bernard Shaw and Women.* Ed. Rodelle Weintraub. University Park: Pennsylvania State UP, 1977. 14-22.

     Shaw criticized Shakespeare for following the conventional morality of the Elizabethan age. *Pygmalion* "seems deliberately designed to challenge and contradict" (15) Shakespeare's views of women and male attitudes toward them. In his reviews, Shaw warned audiences to boycott Shakespeare's play, which presented women as chattel. Similarities between *TSh* and *Pygmalion* stress that physical abuse is "an admission of defeat" rather than a "means of domination" (20) as it is in Shakespeare. Eliza and Higgins believe that male domination over women is wrong, "a concept which is not only supported but actually exalted by the conclusion" of *TSh* (21). Shaw was an early pioneer for women's liberation.

51. Saxon, Patricia Jean. "The Limits of Assertiveness: Modes of Female Identity in Shakespeare and the Stuart Dramatists." *DAI* 38 (1977): 7349A-50A. U of Texas, Austin.

52. Schleiner, Winfried. "Deromanticizing the Shrew: Notes on Teaching Shakespeare in a 'Women in Literature' Course." In *Teaching Shakespeare*. Ed. Walter Edens et al. Princeton: Princeton UP, 1977. 79-92.

Included in a course exploring the motif of "wives willfully tested," *TSh* can be studied in light of Germaine Greer's idea of romance as expressed in *Female Eunuch* (19). There is no "disparity in rank" among the lovers (a potential "source" of Greer's concept of romance); "how seriously we take Kate's shrewishness" determines our view of her as a romantic figure. Kate is a "singularly obnoxious shrew" whom Petruchio cures of her choler. It is misleading to view Kate's final plea for wifely obedience ironically or romantically; it is "based not on a mythic belief in male dominance but on a social conception of male-female hierarchy" well known to Renaissance audiences (87). By contrast, *AYL* represents the "ne plus ultra of romantic fantasy" where Rosalind and Celia are like romantic heroines deeply involved in "male and female fantasy" in ways Kate and Petruchio are not.

53. Schwartz, Murray. "Shakespeare Through Contemporary Psychoanalysis." *Hebrew University Studies in Literature and the Arts* 5 (1977): 182-98.

See item 135.

54. Stone, Lawrence. *The Family, Sex and Marriage in England 1500-1800*. New York: Harper and Row, 1977. Esp. 87, 95, 100, 102, 106, 180, 218, 283, 376-76, 474, 523, 674.

The purpose of this book is "to chart and document, to analyze and explain, some massive shifts in world views and value systems that occurred in England over a period of some three hundred years, from 1500 to 1800. These vast and elusive cultural changes expressed themselves in changes in the ways members of the family related to each other, in terms of legal arrangements, structure, custom, power, affect and sex" (3). These changes occurred specifically in attitudes toward women, children, conflicts between husbands and wives, female friendships and movements, property rights, wife beatings, marriage and orgasm. Part Three is devoted to "The Restricted Patriarchal Nuclear Family 1500-1770." Chapter Four concerns "The Decline of Kinship, Clientage and Community"; and Chapter Five deals with "The Reinforcement of Patriarchy."

Shakespeare's plays and poems expressed the "antithetical ideal of romantic love" (180). Elizabethan audiences would have found the tragedies of *RJ* and *Oth* less in an "ill starred romance" than in "violating the norms of society" (87). Predating nineteenth-century anxieties, Shakespeare's *WT* worries over adolescent sexuality and the "time-lag between sexual maturity and marriage" (376). Shakespeare would have interpreted King Lear's decision to give up his property as an act of insanity. Ultimately, however, we can say that a "fairly sympathetic attitude toward sex in Elizabethan England is reflected in some of the characters in Shakespeare's plays, such as Juliet's nurse, the merry wives, and the flirtatious couples in *As You Like It, Taming of the Shrew,* and *The Tempest.*" But those characters who voice a "love-hate attitude towards sex" (Angelo, Thersites) "are not depicted as likeable or admirable persons" (523).

1978

55. Adelman, Janet. "'Anger's My Meat': Feeding, Dependency, and Aggression in *Coriolanus*." In *Shakespeare: Pattern of Excelling Nature*. Ed. David Bevington and Jay L. Halio. Newark: U of Delaware P; London: Associated UP, 1978. 88-100.

See item 101.

56. Andresen-Thom, Martha. "Thinking About Women and Their Prosperous Art: A Reply to Juliet Dusinberre's *Shakespeare and the Nature of Women*." *Shakespeare Studies* 11 (1978): 259-76.

According to Dusinberre (item 6), Shakespeare's female characters illustrate the female ego ideal, the woman of wit and charm who had been "recently liberated by Puritanism." Shakespeare broke the stereotypes of women; thus his treatment of women was "unorthodox, even radical." While Dusinberre is to be praised for urging a "surprising compatibility between cultural facts hitherto regarded as competing: women, Puritanism, and the public theaters" (265), she begs the question of when does art mirror social reality and when does it "distort these realities" through fantasies and ideals (273). Dusinberre forgets that women are "paradoxically idealized" and as paradigms they are too complex to fit into a restrictively conceived social theory. Desdemona, the Talkative Woman turned Silent Woman, is "deepened by Shakespeare's deliberate hints of stereotypes, whose persistence ... is not acknowledged by Dusinberre" (264). A woman could be both silent and garrulous, submissive and sturdy. Wit in comedies such as *MND* and *AYL* points to separation of the sexes, yet separation leads to "psychic liberation that insures a safer dropping of defenses and a happier interdependence when trust is established" (271). From their male disguises women learn about male fantasies to survive better in a realistic love affair. However brilliant they are, women alone cannot "set things completely right"; masks must be dropped for marriage, and the outer world must cooperate. Most seriously, Dusinberre "frequently lifts female characters out of context from their imaginative worlds and then she tends to measure them against her own idea (ideal) of feminine nature" (273). Women in Shakespeare's plays are not simply a reflection of a liberal, humanist culture but rather an expression of the masculine desire for such a culture/women. Moreover, talented females may express "masculine fears of women" (274), since men are dependent on such women for nurturing.

57.   Asp, Carolyn. "Shakespeare's Paulina and the *Consolatio* Tradition." *Shakespeare Studies* 11 (1978): 145-58.

In her role as counselor guiding Leontes to a "secular beatitude," Paulina occupies a "unique position and function when viewed against conventional expectations of female behavior" (145). The models for Paulina's actions in *WT* are not found in the realistic portraits of women in educational or social tracts or even in the politics of Renaissance England. As a subject, Paulina has "no theoretical right to dominate the court of Sicilia ... " (146). There are "striking parallels" between Paulina in her "figurative function" and female medieval advisors such as Lady Philosophy in Boethius's *Consolation of Philosophy* and Beatrice in Dante's *Purgatorio*. Like these female counselors, Paulina's chief function is to educate a protagonist (Leontes) in the ways of providential justice and benevolence. Like Lady Philosophy and Beatrice, Paulina dominates the relationship and "seems to possess part of the divine *numen*" (150), giving her the authority and consolation she needs for Leontes's reformation. Like Beatrice and Lady Philosophy, Paulina transcends the "constrictions of accepted female roles" (151). Leontes tries to dismiss Paulina with her "stern pity" as a disobedient wife, but with the death of Antigonus, Paulina is released from that role and "assumes a more concentrated resemblance to the female *consolatio* figure" (153). Recalling those figures, Paulina leads her charge Leontes "through the five steps of purgation" (154) and successfully advises against his remarriage. Paulina is the "guardian of the oracle."

58. Ewbank, Inga-Stina. "Shakespeare's Portrayal of Women: A 1970's View." In *Shakespeare: Pattern of Excelling Nature*. Ed. David Bevington and Jay L. Halio. Newark: U of Delaware P; London: Associated UP, 1978. 222-29.

Shakespeare was neither a feminist nor an antifeminist. Though the plays show an "infinite variety of insights into the nature of women" (223), Shakespeare did not deliberately set out to portray women but to dramatize human relationships. Women like Desdemona and Ophelia seem to be stereotypes of the silent, inarticulate woman, but their "apparent inarticulateness ... is in fact dramatically eloquent" (227), a sign of their tragic vision. In opposition to Dusinberre's view (item 6), women as well as men can command the resources of language; witness the comic heroines whose language is therapeutic in *AYL* or the "center of energy" in *Ado*. Cleopatra is verbally adept at dealing with a variety of challenges. Desdemona's and Ophelia's words cannot purge the hero because women and men speak different languages. While confrontations such as those in the brothel scene in *Oth* and the nunnery scene in *Ham* may be characterized as male/female conflicts, the situations are "based *not* on the fact that one interlocutor is female, and thus by definition inarticulate, but on the other interlocutor's absorption in a world ... that he has himself created ... " (225). The fact that Shakespeare's women are articulate is not simply a matter of education but of their experience and wisdom. Though tragic heroes do not always learn from women's language, the women in Shakespeare's last plays "are listened to and *understood*" (228). Marina, Hermione, and Paulina ("the greatest female talker in the romances" [225]) speak powerful words.

59. Frey, Charles. "'O sacred, shadowy, cold, and constant queen':
    Shakespeare's Imperiled and Chastening Daughters of
    Romance." *South Atlantic Bulletin* 43.4 (1978): 125-40.

    See item 113.

60. ---. "The Sweetest Rose: *As You Like It* as Comedy of
    Reconciliation." *New York Literary Forum* 1 (1978): 167-83.

    Like other comedy, Shakespeare's deals with family troubles.
    AYL "makes us laugh sympathetically at our differences while
    reconciling them toward common ends such as fellowship and
    marriage" (168). Directors must decide whether to portray
    Rosalind as a gentle lady "in the style of Helen Faucit,"
    "maddeningly coy in the style of Elizabeth Bergner," or "winningly
    coy like Vanessa Redgrave" (170). The "distinctive metabolism" of
    AYL leads to its "own constant anatomizing" (173); four pairs of
    lovers may reflect "diversified styles of love," yet ultimately all that
    society cares about is generation. *AYL* is not a static debate on
    sex roles; instead, through Rosalind, the play celebrates "excess"
    (175), the metamorphoses of life and love. Appropriately,
    Rosalind is "Shakespeare's most talkative woman" (177), speaking
    more lines in her play (27 percent) than other heroines, including
    Cleopatra, do in theirs. Her words are full of love's impulse and
    desire. Through her "expansive energies" Rosalind elaborates
    imaginatively on the fecundity of love. "She opens up a space for
    desires to play in, a space in which to metamorphose the close
    wrestling into broad measure of the dance" (177). She is able to
    turn the "polarities of the play in a circle." *AYL* shows the
    "harmonization of disparate impulses" (178).

61. ---. "Tragic Structure in *The Winter's Tale*: The Affective
    Dimension." In *Shakespeare's Romances Reconsidered*. Ed.
    Carol McGinnis Kay and Henry E. Jacobs. Lincoln: U of
    Nebraska P, 1978. 113-34.

    The romances are filled with "familial taboo[s]" in which the
    "potency of each hero" is associated with "a loss of power to
    procreate sons" (114). Siring only females, the ruler must forfeit

his daughter in a patrilineal society. The "antithetical structure of the scenes" in *WT* establishes the contrasts and tragic implications in the generative patterns of life. Leontes pushes people away; those he opposes unite. Disengaging himself from the procreative process, Leontes repels family and thus expresses his "hatred of sex, a hysterical misogyny, and obsessive threats of death" (117). In rejecting women, he tries to be self-sufficient, but as a man, if not as a king, he is still "dependent on women to play his part in creation" (118). Contrasting with Leontes's expulsions, the counselors (Paulina, Archidamus, Camillo) in the four interstitial, non-Leontes scenes of Act 2 move forward through their cooperation and pairing to family identity and "the generative continuum that binds us together" (121). Paulina's "tirade" against Leontes (Act 3.2.175-214) is like an exorcism through which Leontes undergoes a "sacred purgation" (123).

62. Greer, Germaine. "Juliet's Wedding." *The Listener* 7 Dec. 1978: 750-57.

Shakespeare would have regarded our view of marriage as "anti-social" (750). *RJ* does not glorify young love but rather questions the Friar's actions in performing a clandestine marriage. The catastrophe begins with that marriage, not with the feud which is simply a condition of the times. Juliet's refreshing youth saves her from being a typical Veronese.

63. Hamill, Monica J. "Poetry, Law, and the Pursuit of Perfection: Portia's Role in *The Merchant of Venice*." *Studies in English Literature, 1500-1900* 18 (1978): 229-43.

Portia fulfills the Renaissance ideal of "poet-lawmaker" as she leads the other characters toward perfection. Her use of "poetic language and fictions ... [is] inextricable from her upholding and interpreting the law" (229). The love between Bassanio and Antonio is flawed because of selfish possessiveness, a fault reflected in Bassanio's mercantile metaphors connecting love with acquisition. Portia, who also uses monetary metaphors, relates love to giving, thereby replacing possessiveness with generosity. A true lover must be prepared to "give and hazard all he hath." The lottery represents destiny, the dead father's will stands for the law, and the choice of the suitors symbolizes human error. In the trial scene, Portia argues for the ideal of mercy as the perfection of justice, but she recognizes "that law is also necessary to constrain those evil-doers who will not acknowledge the spiritual realm" (240). Because Shylock cannot be swayed by her plea for mercy, she defeats him by using law. However, once he is beaten, she restates her plea to a more amenable audience, the Duke and Antonio, and achieves the ideal when they show mercy to Shylock. In the ring-play, Portia's "posture of stubborn jealousy reflects the possessiveness which mars the men's imperfect love, a quality which is exorcised in the fiction she constructs and plays out." Because of love for his friend, Antonio offers his soul as surety for Bassanio. However, Antonio wants to share love rather than possess it. When Portia hands him the ring to give to her husband, it "becomes a gift that ratifies the ideal of love's inclusiveness" (243).

64. Hulse, S. Clark. "'A Piece of Skilful Painting' in Shakespeare's *Lucrece*." *Shakespeare Survey* 31 (1978): 13-22.

Although Tarquin is clearly the villain in *RL*, Lucrece's heroic standing is not initially apparent. When Shakespeare describes her response to the tapestry of Troy, he establishes "her stature as a woman and as the hero of his poem" (13). The last figure Lucrece views is Sinon, whose duplicity and treachery is paralleled by Tarquin's violation of her. Her recognition of this similarity invokes judgment as well as empathy. But her suicide is a product of Shakespeare's misogyny; she is soiled in body if not in mind and must be disposed of, though "she bears no responsibility for what has happened" (20). Her position as woman prevents her from taking up a sword in heroic revenge, but her suicide allows her to become an artistic emblem. "After her confrontation with the Troy-piece, she is prepared to present herself as the image of woe and suffering, and to demand from Collatine and Lucretius the revenge she offered to Hecuba" (23). Where she may falter heroically, Lucrece succeeds artistically.

65. Hyland, Peter. "Shakespeare's Heroines: Disguise in the Romantic
     Comedies." *Ariel: A Review of International English Literature*
     9.2 (1978): 23-39.

     Though disguises suggested deceit and were attacked for being
     a transvestite fashion, Shakespeare moved beyond his
     predecessors and contemporaries in using disguised heroines to
     enrich the role and to deepen the relationship between the
     character and the audience. A disguised heroine gave Shakespeare
     "two distinct characters ... allowing the secondary, male persona
     to participate in the action, and leaving the primary, female
     persona to comment, to satirize, or to manipulate, and in doing
     so to involve the audience by allowing it to identify itself with her
     consciousness" (37). The disguised heroine becomes the audience's
     representative on stage, sharing secrets with them to become
     closer to them. Having his heroine be aware of the artifice of the
     play, Shakespeare employs the opposite of the "Brechtian
     alienation device" (29). Because of her awareness and her
     separateness, Julia in *TGV* shares in the audience's consciousness.
     In *MV*, which is less successful in its "recognition of the
     possibilities that disguise allows" (33), Shakespeare seems
     uncertain of his treatment of disguise. Jessica does not need it to
     escape; and Portia does not draw the audience into her intimacy.
     In fact, her "mockery ... of the male idea of masculinity" is at odds
     with her disguise in the courtroom (32). Rosalind, the only woman
     to have the last word in a Shakespearean play, has her "primary
     female persona step quite consciously out of the action, leaving
     the secondary persona Ganymede to inhabit the same plane as the
     other characters" (33). Less active than Rosalind, Viola is "much
     more fully an observer and commentator, leaving the issues of her
     disguise to work themselves out ... " (35). Unlike the disguised
     heroines of romantic comedy, Imogen is ignorant of much of the
     action and hence there is "no special attempt to align her with the
     audience" (36); moreover, her femininity is "constantly stressed."

66. Kahn, Coppelia. "Coming of Age in Verona." *Modern Language
     Studies* 8 (1977-1978): 5-22.

     Rpt. in item 120 and rev. for item 160.

67. Leverenz, David. "The Woman in Hamlet: An Interpersonal View." *Signs* 4 (1978): 291-308.

    See item 128.

68. McLeod, Robert Randall. "Thanatos and Eros: An Analysis of the Dialectic of Sex and Death in Shakespeare." *DAI* 39 (1978): 1553-54A. U of Michigan.

69. Neely, Carol Thomas. "The Structure of English Renaissance Sonnet Sequences." *ELH* 45 (1978): 359-89.

    English Renaissance sonnets "retained the essential structure of the genre bequeathed by Dante and Petrarch, but adapted it to their own needs" (382). In both cases the metaphor of breeding connects the triple focus of 1) declaration of love; 2) courtship; and 3) poetry composition as tribute, with the poem being the "surrogate child" (365). In Shakespeare's sonnets to the young man, the poet moves from advising him to beget a real child to offering to reproduce him through poetry. The sonnets begin in a typically Petrarchan fashion. However, while Italian models conclude with "solitary sublimation and transcendence" (360), Shakespeare replaces idealized love with sexual love. "The lover is in pain and the lady a tyrant not because of her immovable chastity but because of her insatiable promiscuity" (375). Abandoning the transcendent ending of the Italians, Shakespeare resolves the lover's unrequited love by either stopping abruptly, thus freezing the lovers, or striving for detachment. The refashioned endings come about because of changing attitudes toward marital sex. "The adulterous love at the heart of the Petrarchan sequences became less necessary–because romantic love could be found in marriage–and–more threatening–because as sexual desire gained new legitimacy, it required more stringent restrictions" (383). Thus Shakespeare resolved the hostility between adultery and marital sex.

70. ---. "Women and Issue in *The Winter's Tale*." *Philological Quarterly* 57 (1978): 181-94.

See item 298.

71. Novy, Marianne. "Sex, Reciprocity and Self-Sacrifice in *The Merchant of Venice.*" In *Human Sexuality in the Middle Ages and Renaissance.* Ed. Douglas Radcliff-Umstead. *U of Pittsburgh Publications on Middle Ages and Renaissance* 4. Pittsburgh: Center for Medieval and Renaissance Studies, U of Pittsburgh, 1978. 153-66.

See item 262.

72. Richmond, Velma Bourgeois. "Shakespeare's Women." *Midwest Quarterly* 19 (1978): 330-42.

Though Virginia Woolf praised Shakespeare for his "androgynous mind," he consistently "recognizes and exalts the values of femininity" (331). The history of Shakespeare's age saw the achievements of many women, most notably Queen Elizabeth who "dominated" the age, exploited her virginity, and "enhanced the situation of women" in general (335). Cleopatra echoes Elizabeth in many ways, sexually and politically. "Women dominate the comedies" by teaching men to "avoid the extremes of idealism and passion" (336), excesses that lead to tragedy as in *RJ.* In almost every one of his plays, Shakespeare includes a role for women; these are varied roles, to be sure. Mother figures seem to be more important in Shakespeare than father ones; Juliet is more "competent and assured" (337) than the motherless Desdemona, Cordelia, or Cressida. Shakespeare discourages women from adopting male roles; Lady Macbeth's masculine ambition destroys her. Shakespeare's recognition of the "fundamental dichotomy" between public and private life and his celebration of the personal are "perhaps his finest embracing of the feminine" (339). The limitations of the male preoccupation with world affairs are emphasized in the romances where personal relationships and marriages provide truer rewards. Though it might challenge Shakespeare's androgyny to say it, he saw that "humanity's future lies in the feminine principle" (341).

73. Schwartz, Jerome. "Aspects of Androgyny in the Renaissance." In *Human Sexuality in the Middle Ages and Renaissance.* Ed. Douglas Radcliff-Umstead. *U of Pittsburgh Publications on Middle Ages and Renaissance* 4. Pittsburgh: Center for Medieval and Renaissance Studies, U of Pittsburgh, 1978. 121-31.

Though Shakespeare does not include the "Platonic androgyne," the "very structure of the [sonnet] sequence is androgynous." The male friend and the Dark Lady are "simultaneously male and female, active and passive, lover and beloved" (128), and the product of Shakespeare's own "bisexual sensibility" (129). Shakespeare was fully aware that androgyny was perceived as a dream, yet for him in the sonnets, androgyny "is no longer an abstract ideal, but the paradigm of ambivalent *eros* and *agape*" (129). Shakespeare's love for the young man could be "erotic without being sexual."

74. Sexton, Joyce H. *The Slandered Woman in Shakespeare.* English Literary Studies Series 12. Victoria, British Columbia: U of Victoria, 1978.

Chapter One focuses on "'Slander's Venom'd Spear': The Traditions." Shakespeare's four plays dealing with slandered women–*Ado, Oth, Cym,* and *WT*–veer away from psychologically realistic examinations of motive in order to focus on the theme of slander itself. "Whatever the aesthetic rationale or the ethical intent of a given predecessor, Shakespeare designed each play so as to emphasize the strong lines inherent in the story and to insist on a particular conception: that good name has absolute value" (11). This conception was rooted in sixteenth-century views on slander as Vice personified, views inherited from earlier classical, scriptural, and patristic sources.

In Chapter Two, "*Much Ado About Nothing* and Garter's Susanna," Shakespeare was more interested in defining slander. "Out of the source material he extracted the ethical issues, bringing to the center of his play the old sense–Gower's and Spenser's–of the absolute, devilish evil in calumny" (39). The deviations from the sources bear out this idea. First, Don John is an unmotivated villain, whereas his predecessors were rejected lovers. Second, by omitting the window-scene, Shakespeare removes the "proof" which substantiates the slander; Claudio is convinced by slander alone. Third, Hero, unlike her predecessors, is publicly denounced and helpless to defend herself, an act which "underline[s] the brutality of detraction and dramatize[s] its power over the innocent" (44). Fourth, because the truth must eventually be publicized, Hero's good name is associated with life itself. Fifth, the discovery of truth is providential and does not emerge from changes of heart or the development of the plot; slander is an absolute which can only be overcome by providential means.

Chapter Three on "Villainy in *Othello*: Shakespeare's Anatomy of Envy" argues that "while he had suppressed the psychological element in fashioning *Ado* from its sources, [in *Oth*] Shakespeare now reversed the process, giving Cinthio's flat characters supreme individuality" (50). Iago undergoes the most alteration, but once again, Shakespeare rejects the rejected suitor idea for more complicated motivations. The traditional characteristics of fundamental vice are to be found in "Iago's grief and his mirth, his hypocrisy, his lying, and his ambition" (52). Iago's vice has become Othello's vice, and "while the falsely accused heroine can be vindicated, the hero's innocence cannot be restored" (60).

In Chapter Four, "*Cymbeline*: Shakespeare's Wager Story," Shakespeare changes emphasis from the slanderer and his motivation to the slandered woman and the effects of slander. Iachimo's slander of Imogen is set in a frame story of the persecuted princess. Although the king and stepmother are cruel, they cannot do Imogen much harm. In the wager scene, the good name and honor of Posthumus, enshrined in his wife's chastity, are challenged. In *Cym*, mere words of slander are potentially destructive. In attempting to win the wager, Iachimo tries to seduce Imogen, using as his primary weapon slander against Posthumus. Although Imogen is initially distressed at his bad report, her love and faith win out, and she sees through Iachimo's falsity. Jupiter's appearance underscores the potency of slander and "the defenselessness of slandered women" (73).

Chapter Five, "'The Injury of Tongues': Slander in *The Winter's Tale*," points out that the opposition of love and slander has no villainous equivalent to Iago or Iachimo. "So we focus on the

ruinous power of the false utterance itself and watch while
another paradise is destroyed, even though there is no serpent"
(77). Leontes's suspicions are generated from his diseased
opinion, not inspired by any villain. With traditional and
psychological motivations removed, emphasis falls on the slander
itself. Hermione's good name is equated with her social identity,
more valued than life. The destructive power of slander is
absolute, vanquishing life and love, striking its intended victim,
Hermione, as well as Leontes himself and Perdita, the next
generation. Leontes's faith is restored at the death of his son, but
faith and repentance alone are not enough. Paulina must invoke
supernatural power to restore Hermione to life.

    Reviews: *Shakespeare Newsletter* 29 (1979): 46; Dash, Irene, G.,
Shakespeare Quarterly 31 (1980): 457-58; Rabkin, Norman,
Sewanee Review 88 (1980): 447.

75.   Shapiro, Susan C. "Shakespeare's View of Motherhood." *C[ollege]
    E[nglish] A[ssociation] Forum* 8.4 (1978): 8-10.

    Though not given to stereotyping women, Shakespeare, "the
noblest feminist of them all" (8), does uphold the traditional view
of maternal love. Goneril, Lady Macbeth, even Cleopatra (until
the last scene) reject maternal roles and embrace masculine
aggression. Volumnia, the "most striking example of perverted
motherhood" (9), causes her son's tragedy. Hermione, Lady
Macduff, and Gertrude exemplify maternal concern for a child.
Yet Shakespeare never shows us a caring mother "producing
happy children who become secure adults" (10). Mothers are
absent in the comedies because they would have restricted the
freedom of the androgynous heroines.

76.   Thorssen, Marilyn J. "Varieties of Amorous Experience:
    Homosexual and Heterosexual Relationships in Marlowe and
    Shakespeare." In *Human Sexuality in the Middle Ages and
    Renaissance*. Ed. Douglas Radcliff-Umstead. U of Pittsburgh
    Publications on Middle Ages and Renaissance 4. Pittsburgh:
    Center for Medieval and Renaissance Studies, U of Pittsburgh,
    1978. 135-52.

Both Marlowe and Shakespeare portray love between men as well as heterosexual love, and while some similarities can be found in their depictions of relationships, their works differ in attitude toward love. Marlowe's view of love is basically pessimistic; love is a beautiful desire, but one which can never be satisfied in a limited world. "When we turn to Shakespeare, we find an altogether different portrait of love, for it is those qualities such as 'reasonableness, fidelity, and temperance,' absent from Marlowe's love relationships, which seem to be most highly valued in Shakespeare's portrayal of love, especially in relationships between men" (144). The scope of love in Shakespeare is more inclusive and varied: the most fulfilling relationships are characterized by generosity toward the loved one rather than concern for self. Unlike Marlowe, Shakespeare portrayed love between men more by implication than by explicit description. In the sonnets, the young man is both physically and spiritually beautiful; the relationship to the poet is initially ennobling. The Dark Lady, however, appeals on a baser, more sensual level. The flaw in the poet's love for her is "that the passion of lustful desire, which Shakespeare refers to as a stain, a blot, a fault, and a sin when it is given free rein in either men or women, is the *only* basis for his relationship with the Dark Lady" (147). *AC* demonstrates that it is impossible for the masculine and the feminine principals to become one in a limited world. Only in death can the lovers be united. The androgynous opportunities in some of the comedies, however, create an ideal world where the masculine and feminine meet. "Only in the complicated doubling and redoubling of sexual roles, such as may be found in *AYL*, in which a boy actor plays the part of Rosalind who plays the part of a boy pretending to be a girl, could division in love, the dichotomy which is magnified in the 'two loves' of the sonnets, be resolved" (148).

77. Welsh, Alexander. "The Loss of Men and Getting of Children: *All's Well That Ends Well* and *Measure for Measure*." *Modern Language Review* 73 (1978): 17-28.

Shakespeare explores the "problematic relationship of biology and society" (27) in *AWW* and *MM*. In these plays, sex is

degrading in the Bakhtian sense of reproduction. For men,
marriage and sex spell death since by creating a new generation
a man replaces his own and acknowledges his mortality. Making
love with a virgin who is not to be a wife is timeless; the betrayed
virgin places a man under no obligation. *AWW* views marriage
and generation "from a male and individual perspective" (27).
Bertram's "martial cowardice" (19) signifies male terror. By having
Helena "die" in Bertram's place, *AWW* fulfills the "heroine's myth
of sacrifice" (20). In *MM*, Angelo repudiates marriage but takes
advantage of a virgin. Though Isabella is not the "perpetuator of
the bedtrick," as Helena is in *AWW*, Vienna society in *MM* forces
women into categories of maid, wife, widow based on "institutions
of generation" (23). Politics cannot be separated from sexuality.
Lucio parodies Shakespeare's "theme of generation and death."
Ultimately, Vienna remains unchanged except for marriage; it
exists in a "dangerous state of stalemate" (24), and the problems
of generation are "unresolvable." In the romances, Shakespeare
"reworked" the theme of generation offering a third generation as
a consolation for man's fears. Shakespeare "dissolves death in
daughters" (26); Marina seems a mother and a daughter to
Pericles. Unlike the troubling view of generation in *MM* and
AWW, the romances, which synchronize birth, death, and
marriage, finally subordinate marriage to the idea of generation;
"daughters are as important as wives" (27).

78. White, R.S. "The Tragedy of Ophelia." *Ariel: A Review of
    International English Literature* 9.2 (1978): 41-53.

Ophelia displays an "incompleteness" in her personality. She
and Hamlet are "ideal candidates for a romantic comedy" (42),
except that in listening to the advice of her brother and father on
the "mercurial nature of sexual desire," Ophelia commits a "sin
against the laws" of comedy (43). Though Ophelia is innocent of
all wrong doing, Hamlet interprets her innocence as fraud and
projects upon her the "guilt and pollution" he spies in Gertrude.
His speech to Ophelia in the nunnery scene is filled with doubts
and paradoxes about women's dishonesty, which he fears he may
have inherited. Preoccupied with "sex and the perversion of
marriage by women's infidelity," Hamlet conflates Gertrude and

Ophelia into the "Untrustworthy Woman" (46). Yet, he simultaneously finds women's sexuality frightening and fascinating. To protect her feelings and to make sense of events, Ophelia escapes into another world and unlike Hamlet keeps herself from bad dreams. In her songs she projects her sexual feelings onto another maid, and thus supplies meaning about love missing in her own life. In her dirge for Ophelia, Gertrude reveals her own "capacity for intuitively reaching into the feelings of another character ... " (51). Ophelia's death symbolizes "the meaninglessness and loneliness pervading" *Ham.*

79. Willbern, David. "Rape and Revenge in *Titus Andronicus.*" *English Literary Renaissance* 8 (1978): 159-82.

TA enacts the fantasy of rescuing a woman (Rome, a city; Lavinia, a daughter; Tamora, a mother) from attack or rape. The men in *TA* heroically come to the rescue of the assaulted woman in an attempt to destroy the devouring, malevolent mother and replace her with the benevolent one. Rape and revenge are reciprocal in the play. Women are pure as well as dangerous and seductive. In such an environment, "sexuality is displaced onto vengeance, which becomes its substitute. Revenge is both a substitute for sexuality and a defense against it: it is both threat and rescue" (66). The orality of the pre-oedipal destructive mother is represented by Tamora and symbolized by the loathsome pit which is a mouth, "violated vagina," womb, tomb, and Hell. Linked to both Desdemona and shrewish hussies, Lavinia as the mutilated bride reminds us of the "unconscious proximities of sexuality, rape, death, and dismemberment on which the play builds" (172); she herself symbolizes the "all-consuming bloody pit" (174). Titus's stabbing Lavinia in Act 5 is another example of a pattern of attack and defense, rape and rescue, and a "further enactment of the murderous hostility toward women which informs the play" (175). Eating her own flesh and blood, Tamora shows the extent to which "oral vengeance" can go and represents the "incestuous intercourse" associated with the malevolent mother. At the end of *TA*, Aaron, whose sexuality is more a "means of maintaining masculine power in the face of feminine peril" than an example of lust, is like a child intent on matricide.

1979

80. Berger, Harry, Jr. "*King Lear*: The Lear Family Romance."
   Centennial Review 23 (1979): 348-76.

Lear's sense of "paternal prerogative" is that his children should
always honor their bond to their creator, that is, pay over-zealous
respect to him in recognition of his sacrifices for them. At the
beginning of *Lear*, "he inflicts his generosity upon them with a
show of power which betrays his sense of the weakness of his
position" (353). If the daughters want his power, they have to risk
humiliation by begging for it. The bargain seems to be
imbalanced–land and power in return for flattery–but there is
more for Lear to gain. He has withheld the dowries of Goneril
and Regan until after their marriages, while Cordelia is to get
hers before the wedding. He does this in order to be taken care
of by his youngest daughter; in essence, "he wants to become his
own grandson." Goneril sees relationships only in terms of power.
Her defensiveness is something she has inherited from her father.
"Goneril reveals Lear's basic approach to his children, to paternity
and filiality, by her reflection of it" (357). Cordelia believes that
to give love to a husband is to take it from a father. In adopting
Lear's views, she believes that the father has a right to compete
with the husband. In the last scene, "the oppressed king becomes
the oppressor" by taking France's place and becoming first in
Cordelia's heart. "In hurting and punishing Cordelia, [Lear] is
trying to hurt and punish himself" (358).

81. Diverres, A.H. "The Pyramus and Thisbe Story and Its
     Contribution to the Romeo and Juliet Legend." In *The
     Classical Tradition in French Literature: Essays Presented to
     R.C. Knight.* Ed. H.T. Barnwell et al. London: Grant and
     Culter, 1977. 9-22.

     The two heroines are "parallel examples of maidens who refuse
     to outlive their lovers and of parents who have exercised excessive
     pressure on their daughters and by so doing have been unwittingly
     responsible for their deaths" (9). In the development of the
     Pyramus and Thisbe story, parental opposition to marriage
     becomes a quarrel between fathers that develops into a lifelong
     feud.

82. Greene, Gayle. "'This That You Call Love': Sexual and Social
     Tragedy in *Othello.*" *Journal of Women's Studies in Literature*
     1 (1979): 16-32.

     The tragedy of *Oth* is rooted in "men's misunderstanding of
     women" (20) and women's inability to protect themselves from
     society's conceptions of them. Othello and Desdemona themselves
     supply the causes of their tragedy. Accepting the male view of
     women as goddesses or whores, Othello fails to see Desdemona
     as a real person. He "embodies the essence and extreme of
     certain qualities which are conventionally 'masculine'"–action,
     violence, revenge, honor, and an excessive concern over his
     "occupation" (19). These manly qualities "ill equip" him for
     marriage; in fact, Othello is never comfortable talking about sex
     and is suspicious of women's "physical being" (22). Iago is able to
     manipulate Othello because of the views of women the Moor had
     already possessed. The three women in the play, who "illuminate
     aspects of one another" (24), are the victims of male fantasies and
     prejudices. Their identity is "precarious" because of male opinions
     of them. Desdemona is not the ideal; her quintessential feminine
     qualities of obedience, love, and softness render her "incapable of
     self-defense" (27). She is helpless against Othello. "Bianca
     provides a reflection of what Desdemona is, Emilia a potential of
     what she might be" (29); Desdemona needs more of Emilia's
     voice and less of Bianca's vulnerability. Shakespeare suggests that

women's virtue must be more active and less controlled by male views of chastity.

83. Grise, Martha S. "Shakespeare's Comic Heroines as Women and as Wives: A Study of the Limits of Shakespeare's Feminism." *DAI* 40 (1979): 5873A. U of Kentucky.

84. Harding, D.W. "Shakespeare's Final View of Women." *Times Literary Supplement* 30 Nov. 1979: 59-61.

From a group of plays, *AC, Cor, Mac*, where women destroy men, Shakespeare moved to the romances which present a benign view of women. An "almost womanless play" (59), *Tim* is a bridge between *Cor* and *Per*, by hinting at how important women are as transmitters and custodians of devotion and loyalty. The later plays use a young girl as the ideal of female tenderness, sympathy, and faithful love. Separated from the more formidable aspects of a femininity that a punishing, severe mother represents, this girl has a minimum dependence on mothers. The father's affection for his daughter is not reduced to sexual appetite but helps him to restore his life. As in *Per*, Leontes in *WT* rediscovers what he lost through his daughter, Perdita, and thus sees how mature his wife Hermione has become. Trust in Imogen is central to *Cym*, which also illustrates the dilemma that, in trusting women, men may be duped. Also at stake in these plays is the question of the father regaining his rule and ensuring his succession through the daughter, a motif with biographical implications for Shakespeare as well as James I. Though seemingly as much a "one-sided masculine play" as *Tim, Tem* through Miranda offers the idealization of woman. In presenting these daughters, Shakespeare may be "seeking to discover what at best" Lear and Cordelia's "relationship could have been" (61).

85. Hargreaves, George Brooks. "Love and Identity in Eight Plays of Shakespeare." *DAI* 39 (1979): 4272A. U of Toronto. [*AC, Ado, AWW, AYL, Cym, MND, Oth*, and *TN*.]

86. Hayles, Nancy K. "Sexual Disguise in *As You Like It* and *Twelfth Night*." *Shakespeare Survey* 32 (1979): 63-72.

AYL starts by contrasting the rivalry of men and the intimacy of women. These contrasts, however, are not so clear-cut in the forest where confrontation is brought into a place of cooperation. "The sexual disguise of Rosalind mirrors the complexities of these tensions" (64). Layers of disguise added to Rosalind create conflict while their removal restores amiability. Disguised as Ganymede, Rosalind can articulate "more of her essence" to Orlando than if she were undisguised; her real self contrasts with Orlando's idealized version of her. She reveals herself as a real woman rather than a "Petrarchan abstraction" (65). As Ganymede, Rosalind causes troubles between Phebe and Silvius, but returning to her self brings peace. Rosalind's self-interest is necessary to recognize her needs, but her self-interest must be relinquished to create a successful marriage. In larger societal terms, the "unmasking makes it possible for peace to reign in the forest and the dukedom."

In *TN*, Malvolio's so-called possession by devils is mirrored in the main plot by images suggesting that Viola's disguise is also diabolic. Unlike *AYL*, disguise in *TN* leads to loss of control. In the subplot, Malvolio is controlled by Sir Toby; however, it is uncertain to whom Viola has relinquished control. In the Renaissance, crossdressing was seen as the work of the devil, but Viola's disguise operates in a much more benevolent way, releasing Olivia and Orsino from their deadlock and allowing them to love each other. The sexual disguise leads to happiness. Exceptions to this harmony are Antonio and Malvolio, who suffer from the confusion that fortune, nature, and time can sometimes evoke.

87. Helphinstine, Frances. "Volumnia: The Life of Rome." *Selected Papers from the West Virginia Shakespeare and Renaissance Association* 4 (1979): 55-63.

Volumnia raised no sissy. An ambitious mother, Volumnia sacrificed maternal affection and attachment to teach Coriolanus a "stern and fanatical conception of duty" (56). Her overriding concern with his reputation leads her to desire the high office for her son more than he wants it himself. She is driven like Lady Macbeth. Coriolanus's successes demonstrate that he has accepted and accomplished the goal of absolute manliness that his mother set for him. But Volumnia "misuses" Roman virtue for her own selfish ends. Her obsession with Coriolanus's reputation causes her to "distort the Roman concept of honor" (58) by counseling him to dissemble and to degrade his military feats. She abuses "maternal kindness" as well as the "Roman virtue of paternal respect" (59). Contrasted with the typically feminine Virgilia, Volumnia has a "much more unnatural feminine characteristic of exalting violence and Coriolanus's ruthlessness." When he loses patriotism and threatens Rome, she "bows to him in a deed that is unnatural for a Roman matron"–appealing to him with a legion of women. But moving from an appeal to personal values to those of honor, Volumnia banishes her son to save Rome and ends with the "greatest achievement a Roman matron could desire" (63).

88. Jackson, Russell. "'Perfect Types of Womanhood': Rosalind, Beatrice and Viola in Victorian Criticism and Performance." *Shakespeare Survey* 32 (1979): 15-26.

   In nineteenth-century productions of *AYL*, *TN*, and *Ado*, "Victorian critics and performers established a subtext in which virtuous, modest, and loving women, endowed with uncommon resources of wit and tact, found happiness through marriage" (25). Many of Shakespeare's heroines–Cordelia, Miranda, Imogen, and Perdita–exemplified the qualities praised in Victorian womanhood. Rosalind, Beatrice, and Viola, however, possessed independent spirits which were inconsistent with Victorian ideals. Viola and Rosalind even went so far as to parade in male disguise. Information from nineteenth-century promptbooks and critical commentaries point to how actresses of the period relied on the polarities of farce and strong emotion, staples of Victorian theatre, to project womanliness of Shakespeare's characters.

89. Kuppens, Patricia Frances. "Patterns of Complementarity: Masculine and Feminine Relations in *Othello*, *King Lear*, and *Macbeth*." *DAI* 40 (1979): 3317A. Yale U.

90. Novy, Marianne. "Patriarchy and Play in *The Taming of the Shrew*." *English Literary Renaissance* 9 (1979): 264-80.

See item 262.

91. ---. "Patriarchy, Mutuality, and Forgiveness in *King Lear*." *Southern Humanities Review* 13 (1979): 281-92.

See item 262.

92. Pearson, D'Orsay W. "Witchcraft in *The Winter's Tale*: Paulina as 'Alcahueta y av Poquito Hechizera.'" *Shakespeare Studies* 12 (1979): 195-213.

Shakespeare superimposes on Paulina the characteristics of an urban witch–"a bawd and a bit of a witch" ("alcahueta y av hechizera")–even though she is holy and innocent. In the popular imagination and in some contemporary plays (e.g., *The Alchemist*) urban witches were associated with the forces of evil in their capacity as necromancers, midwives, and procurers. Leontes projects these attributes on Paulina by calling her "callat," "gross hag," and "Lady Margery." He is no more justified in calling Paulina a witch than he is in denouncing Hermione as unfaithful. Yet Paulina's own seemingly demonic and occult actions and her suggestive dialogue "sustain" her role as an urban witch; in fact, "as the play progresses the accusation becomes increasingly a real possibility" (202). In her dealings with Leontes, Paulina "exhibits three qualities" associated with urban witches and so metaphorically plays the role–she has great power over her client; she practices erotic magic; and she is a procuress by insisting that Leontes allow her to find him a second wife. Like a procurer, she thus controls "the male potential for generation." Yet the royal family joins her in the role in bringing Hermione back to life and thus dissipates Paulina's guise. Not being able to bring back her own husband Antigonus proves that Paulina's witchcraft is "nonexistent" (208). By giving Camillo to her, Leontes himself acts like an intelligencing procurer. An enigma and a "gadfly to Leontes' conscience" (202), Paulina functions in Shakespeare's plan to implicate the audience for their misjudgments in the course of *WT*.

93. Ranald, Margaret Loftus. "As Marriage Binds, and Blood Breaks: English Marriage in Shakespeare." *Shakespeare Quarterly* 30 (1979): 68-81.

"For the purposes of their plays, Shakespeare and his contemporaries merely transferred English legal practice to foreign settings" (69). In *TSh*, the financial arrangements for Kate's wooing and marriage are completed quickly because her father wants his daughter to be married soon. However, Baptista does insist that Petruchio win Kate's love, which most likely can be translated into obtaining her willing consent. Unlike her sister, Kate is married in a public ceremony, but not before Petruchio threatens her with humiliation by standing her up at the altar. Petruchio demonstrates "his iconoclasm by reducing the essentials of the marriage ritual to broad humor" (72). From the beginning of his wooing, Claudio in *Ado* seems to be a young man in search of a wealthy wife, concerned with his own advancement. However, the play's action demonstrates that before Claudio can marry Hero, he must learn the importance of love, and that marriage is not simply a business arrangement. In *MM*, Shakespeare provides his audience with a "defective conception of foreign canon law." Both Angelo and Mariana were "liable to ecclesiastical punishment [for the bed trick] under Roman canon law as well as punishment under the statute which is the basic premise of the play" (78).

94. Richmond, Hugh M. "The Feminism of Shakespeare's *Henry VIII*." *Essays in Literature* [Western Illinois U] 6 (1979): 11-20.

By exhibiting a "distinctively Shakespearean feminism," *H8* "offsets the disconcerting negative view of women" found in the *H6* plays (11). From Prologue to Epilogue, *H8* honors the feminine values and sympathies of the three "magnetic" queens. Unlike the men who are "erratic" and pursue "virile self-confidence" like Buckingham or "romantic delusions" like Henry, the women are resilient and triumph over male "misconduct" (13). Neglected by the critics because she speaks barely 50 lines, Anne "exceeds any other study of romantic sexuality" in Shakespeare (14). Like Eve, she both brings disaster and creates new promise.

Shakespeare purposely does not allow Anne to eclipse Katherine who, like Hermione in *WT*, is "woman as generatrix of passions," the feminine ideal. No passive feminist or "servile victim," Katherine (like Kate in *TSh*) vows a powerful devotion to her husband and, like Cleopatra, experiences her own mystical apotheosis. Yet realizing that she cannot avoid defeat, Katherine courageously accepts Providence, as do Richard II, Cymbeline, and Coriolanus, and even blesses her enemies. In the last act, Shakespeare stresses that Katherine's feminine virtues are the model for both men and women. Elizabeth is the "coda" to Katherine's tragedy (18). Her reign is hailed as truly humane by reversing the destructive male cynicism and egocentricism of *H5*. Her "feminine personality" is "the best model for earthly rule" and also parallels Hermione's role. The women in *H8* "define the values and unify the play ... " (19).

95. Silber, Patricia. "The Unnatural Woman and the Disordered State in Shakespeare's Histories." *Proceedings of the PMR Conference* [Augustinian Historical Institute, Villanova U] 2 (1979): 87-96.

   Joan la Pucelle and Margaret of Anjou are damningly portrayed by Shakespeare as unnatural women and the immediate cause of civil disorder. Women dominate much of the action in the first tetralogy while they appear for the most part timidly on the sidelines in the later tetralogy. Joan la Pucelle is "proud and arrogant, coarse-mouthed and scornful, as well as being sexually promiscuous, clothed in male attire and wielding their weapons." As the epitome of female evil, she has renounced her sex. Her unnaturalness parallels the disorder rampant in France. Margaret's transformation from innocent virgin at eighteen to an embittered woman in her fifties parallels both the troubles in England and overall the action in the plays. As her behavior "becomes more masculine than feminine, the kingdom decays even further." In the second tetralogy, no truly unnatural women appear before us. Even the crude women at the Boar's Head Tavern play natural roles.

96. Skura, Meredith. "New Interpretations for Interpretation in *Measure for Measure*." *Boundary* 7.2 (1979): 39-59.

The "problem" which makes *MM* a problem play is that critics explore the issues of law and appetite, justice and mercy, but fail to see that the chief conflict is between the law and the context in which laws exist. "Part of the play's meaning is the way in which we have to change the terms in which we understand the action–and the way we have to question the validity of all terms" (42). All of the characters see law and obedience as absolutes, neglecting the human, sexual, and social context which calls them into existence. The sex act, traditionally a constant, is ambiguous. It is associated with loss of identity and death, in this case death for the male. "It puts Claudio in prison and threatens his head, and Angelo seals his fate even as he embraces Isabel and gives Mariana the means to marry–and behead him" (51). The Duke's failure as ruler is linked to this sexual ambiguity. He can "displace sex (Mariana for Isabel), but he cannot displace death (Bernadine for Claudio)." In Lacan's phallocentric order, all meaning and value are absolute except for the word and symbol *phallus*, "the symbol of meaning and authority itself" (53-54). For the Duke this symbol is his seal, but even his seal fails in light of Bernadine's refusal. Shakespeare removes the authority of all absolutes, substituting "a human context of mutuality in which the process of working together to find or invent absolutes is as important as the lost absolutes themselves" (54). In the last scene, the symbol of threatening woman is transformed as Mariana's forgiveness saves Angelo from death.

97. Whittier, Gayle. "Falstaff as a Welshwoman: Uncomic Androgyny." *Ball State University Forum* 20.3 (1979): 23-35.

Falstaff plays a number of symbolic roles in *1H4*, including a false father, a boy, and a counterfeit woman. Yet it is only his "status as a submerged androgyne–a false woman–[that] fully makes symbolic sense of both the comic and tragic" elements in his character (23). A sexually ambiguous figure, Falstaff abdicates his manhood and imitates women by avoiding battle, by trying to unman the Prince, and by his own appearance suggesting a pregnant woman "whose false pregnancy monstrously demonstrates gestation without release" (29). Falstaff is linked with the rebels' marriages (both to the wives and the husbands) through his distorting sexual harmony. In attempting to unman Hal, Falstaff tries to confine him within the womb of the tavern, the "(feminizing) compass of the tavern world" (29). Hal, however, burlesques Hotspur on two levels, sexual and political, while associating Falstaff with both. As a "static unmanning force," Falstaff regresses unlike Hal who "moves harmoniously in time with nature" (31). By wounding the defeated Hotspur in the thigh, Falstaff symbolically castrates Hal's victim and becomes associated with the Welsh women who did the real thing to the dead English soldiers (Act 1.1.41-46).

A comparison with Shakespeare's other androgynes reveals Falstaff's sexual aberrations. While Falstaff is a trickster like Shakespeare's comic androgynes, he is ultimately a "counter-artistic force" and "never fully acknowledges" his own androgyny. He is closer to the tragic androgynes because of his monstrous state (e.g., Lady Macbeth). But Falstaff violates Shakespeare's custom of having a woman disguised as a man; his androgyny is "destructive." Trying to be both sexes, he is neither, only a sterile mockery. His "generic confusions–no less than his sexual complexities–are never fully resolved in a wholly comic or tragic direction" (35).

98.   Wood, Charles T. "Whatever Happened to Margaret of Anjou? On Olivier's Shakespeare and Richard III." *Iowa State Journal of Research* 53 (1979): 213-17.

Sir Laurence Olivier's film of *R3* had much to do with changing the popular attitude toward Richard III. In rehabilitating Richard, Olivier eliminated his more sinister traits and omitted Margaret of Anjou. Though "far from capricious" since historically Margaret was not present, Olivier's decision may have been based on his desire to achieve greater historical accuracy or his attempt, echoing Colley Cibber's practice, to use a shorter script. An abbreviated text would be more adaptable to "the cinematic form" than Shakespeare's. From the perspective of the modern historian, Margaret does not belong, yet from Shakespeare's view of history as moral example she does. In Shakespeare's quest for the truth, reality could be distorted and so Margaret has a crucial role to play.

1980

99. Adamson, Jane. *"Othello" as Tragedy: Some Problems of Judgment and Feeling.* Cambridge: Cambridge UP, 1980. Esp. 1-9; and Chapter 7, "Self-charity and Self-abnegation: The Play's Women in Love," 214-63.

Oth is unique in the way that it portrays how people make sense of their experience. "Throughout *Oth* we watch how every one of the characters construes and misconstrues things, how they all 'fashion' their view of others to fit with their sense of themselves (or vice versa); and increasingly we become aware–as they themselves never do–of how their fears and desires and needs lead to various kinds of emotional confusion and inflexibility, and how this in turn blacks or deforms their sense of what is and what is not" (4). The women are not merely functional characters, but developed dramatic figures essential to the network of relationships in the play. Desdemona's fate is due in part to outside circumstance and in part to her own disposition. Othello kills Desdemona "because he loves her in the ways he does; but the play also makes us realize that Desdemona is murderable because she has staked her life upon *his* faith and love" (216). Their marriage is based on ideal views of one another. But as Othello begins to pervert his ideal picture of Desdemona into its opposite, Desdemona tenaciously holds on to her ideal picture of Othello. Her definition of her self and her marriage depends upon this ideal, so necessity, more than charity, blinds her to his faults. The two characters thus balance each other. Each is convinced that the other cannot be as he/she seems. The more fair Desdemona appears, the more Othello suspects her foul; the more foul Othello becomes, the more Desdemona maintains his fairness. Othello becomes aggressive in his jealousy: Desdemona becomes passive when she realizes she is suspected. When Emilia advocates that wives return injury for injury, Desdemona abnegates her right to revenge. This abnegation does not generate from charity and forgiveness so much as it does from self-charity, a need to preserve her self-image. Even on her death bed when she denies his guilt, Desdemona's defense of Othello is a "self-charitable act because her love will not allow her to blame or take revenge on him." Throughout the play, Othello cannot adequately articulate his suspicion to Desdemona, and she cannot defend her innocence. The tragic potential of this circumstance is emphasized in exchanges between Cassio and Bianca over the handkerchief and between Iago and Emilia at the end. In each case, the couples freely express charges and countercharges. If these relationships, where communications are open, are doomed, Othello and Desdemona's, with its oblique communication, is much more so.

100. Adamson, W.D. "Unpinned or Undone?: Desdemona's Critics and the Problem of Sexual Innocence." *Shakespeare Studies* 13 (1980): 169-86.

Critics have been divided in their views of Desdemona, idolizing her as a saint whose sexuality is suppressed or renouncing her as a strumpet who, in W.H. Auden's opinion, would eventually take a lover. The anti-idolatrous position of Julian C. Rice ("Desdemona Unpinned: Universal Guilt in *Othello*," *Shakespeare Studies* 7 [1974]: 209-226)–that Desdemona's ambiguous remark about Lodovico being a proper man really undermines her innocence–represents critics who tarnish Desdemona's innocence with pitch. Yet not all negative views of Desdemona can be traced to a "male critical bias": some of her "most dangerous enemies are some of her feminist defenders" (173). S.N. Garner (see item 23), for example, admirably acknowledges Desdemona's normal sex drives but in "overinterpreting the boudoir scene" paints Desdemona as a potentially unfaithful wife, a Madame Bovary. Such a reading counters the "real issue" of Desdemona's innocence. *Oth* reflects Shakespeare's unwavering belief in her "sexual fidelity" (174). Though there is a certain ambiguity in Desdemona's remark about Lodovico, it exists for dramatic reasons to help explain Othello's dilemma. It is "precisely the sort of fatal ambiguity that Shakespeare has made Desdemona exhibit to us and Othello all along and that the prejudiced Moor has misconstrued against her loyalty, just as the critics would" (176). Sentimentalizing idolators as well as cynical "humanizers" forget that for Shakespeare "Desdemona's innocence co-exists with a rich sexuality" (179), providing an alternative to the saint/strumpet dichotomy tragically forced upon her by Brabantio, Othello, Iago (with his "sexual nihilism"), and the critics. Cassio's response to Desdemona highlights this "unperceived alternative" (180). Desdemona's sexuality is neither "ignorant" nor "repressed." And "from an objectively feminist perspective, *Othello* is Desdemona's tragedy, too" (182).

101. Adelman, Janet. "Anger's My Meat: Feeding, Dependency, and Aggression in *Coriolanus*." In Schwartz and Kahn, item 136. 129-49.

The uprising of the plebeians in *Cor* poses a sexual threat. "The fear of leveling becomes ultimately a fear of losing one's potency in all spheres" (130). Hunger is transferred to phallic aggression. The image of the mother who has not fed her children is at the center of the play. Volumnia, who is not a nourishing mother, finds blood more beautiful than milk. She suggests that feeding exposes vulnerability, and for this reason food is poisonous. Coriolanus's "whole life becomes a kind of phallic exhibitionism, devoted to disproving the possibility that he is vulnerable" (132). In this society, the mouth becomes the wound and the breast the sword. Fighting is a poorly concealed substitute for feeding. Coriolanus spits out words, using them as weapons. Using the crowd to bolster his own identity, Coriolanus through his wounds reveals his kinship with the common people in several ways, including that he too has a mouth and is a dependent creature.

102. Bean, John. C. "Comic Structure and the Humanizing of Kate in
The Taming of the Shrew." In Lenz, Greene, and Neely, item
126. 65-78.

Neither the revisionists who see Kate duping Petruchio with
her irony nor the anti-revisionists who see Kate tamed like an
animal are right. Shakespeare's play does not "preach the
subjection of women" or their moral inferiority to men but reflects
through Kate's final speech "a number of humanist assumptions
about an ideal marriage popularized by Tudor matrimonial
reformers" (67). Kate's final speech emphasizes the "notion of
matrimonial friendship" where love for a husband is analogous to
love for a king, ideas which have their roots in Renaissance
humanism. Kate emerges as a "humanized heroine against the
background of depersonalized farce" (66). Kate and Petruchio can
be humanized because of the romantic elements in *TSh* which
oppose the mechanical view of woman found in a farce such as
the misogynistic *Taming of a Shrew.* Kate is transformed on the
road to Padua. Thanks to Petruchio's game-playing, she discovers
her own imagination and "inward self" (66) and the "liberating
power of laughter and play." In this respect, *TSh* looks forward to
the festive comedies. Petruchio's "method of shrew-taming
celebrates life, for Petruchio is playing, and when Kate suddenly
joins him, Shakespeare presents her as cured" (73). Yet *TSh*
"never breaks completely from farce" (74), and what is disturbing
is not Kate's final speech but the "way she is forced by Petruchio
to say it" (74). The bed trick in *AWW* is also a problem in
creating a "humanized woman." Shakespeare's "most erotic
heroine," Helena is involved in an old trick from farce that
encrusts the mechanical–and unflattering–view of woman on the
human.

103. Berggren, Paula S. "The Woman's Part: Female Sexuality as
Power in Shakespeare's Plays." In Lenz, Greene, and Neely,
item 126. 17-34.

The "central element in Shakespeare's treatment of women is
always sex ... a mythic source of power ... that arouses both love
and loathing in the male" (18). An examination of the "resourceful

virgins" in the comedies, the "ingenue tragic heroines," and the "beatified mothers" in the late plays isolates the "differences between masculine and feminine in Shakespeare" (29). The sexes differ greatly in their use and interpretation of disguise. A heroine emerges enlarged from a disguise; it only "confirms her identity instead of shattering it" as it does to the men (20). The disguise celebrates "a flexibility and responsiveness that few men ... can match" (19). Significantly in the "rigid masculine world of Shakespearean tragedy," women are denied this "purgative transvestism" (24). In that world "masculine prudery" contributes greatly to "the powerlessness of the female," e.g., Ophelia, Desdemona, though Cleopatra is able "to renew her femininity" (25). By refusing to dress as a woman, men "cut themselves off from an understanding of the fullest range of human experience" (21). The disguises adopted by Julia in *TGV*, Rosalind, Helena, and Imogen have different functions and significances. Shakespeare "rarely writes a scene that explicitly delineates female sexual longing" (21). While men harbor thoughts of incest, Shakespeare's women do not; "even the troubled women in Shakespeare accept their bodies' limits and claims more easily than do men" (26). In the late plays, the mature heroines are far more resilient than the men and offer "an ideal, curative maternity" (26) fulfilling their role as "savior of the race through childbirth" (28). *Tem* is separate from the other late plays because it is a "masculine stronghold" where female sexuality and natural impulses are restrained and rebuked.

104. Berry, Ralph. "Woman as Fool: Dramatic Mechanism in Shakespeare." *Dalhousie Review* 59 (1979-1980): 621-32.

To understand the "dramatic existence of woman" does not mean exclusively associating a fictional character with "woman." This ontological trap can be avoided by paying close attention to "woman's dramatic mechanism," or function, which varies from shedding light "on the domestic side of their menfolk" as Lady Percy, Portia, Calpurnia do to Lady Macbeth's complex relationship with Macbeth. The "strategic utility of women" is most apparent in the early plays where women are the source of a "critical challenge" by becoming intelligencers. Like the fools, with whom they have a "natural alliance," women "mock authority. And in mocking it, they reveal its limitations" (623). The "clearest instances of woman-as-intelligence" can be found in *LLL* where the women function as "philosophy dons" (627). Through the Countess of Auvergne (a "Gallic Judith") but especially La Pucelle–characters whom the audience is "conditioned to detest" (626)–the English "inner myopia" is challenged. In their role as intelligencers in *R3* the women "are memory and perception" surviving the men. Shakespeare revives this earlier method in *Lear* making Cordelia with the Fool challenge the absurdity of Lear's decisions and divisions. Since he has already fixed the shares of his inheritance, Cordelia's "nothing" is the "most truthful" statement in the play. Saying nothing will not change Lear's choices, thus Cordelia's words are the "impulse of severest logic" (630). Lear's "And my poor fool is hanged" refers to Cordelia who has acted like the truth-speaking Fool.

105. Brooks, Harold F. "*Richard III*, Unhistorical Amplifications: The Women's Scenes and Seneca." *Modern Language Review* 75 (1980): 721-37.

Shakespeare "without historical warrant" moves beyond the chronicles to construct the women's scenes in *R3*. Each of the four women in *R3* "corresponds to one of the four [women] in [Seneca's] *Troads*" (721). Elizabeth is like Andromache; Anne "corresponds" to Polyzena; the Duchess of York is Hecuba; and Margaret, "like Hecuba, is the odd woman out, the alien, the Lancastrian among Yorkists as Helen is the Greek among Trojans" (725). In her Senecan capacity as the voice of vengeance, Margaret continues Joan of Arc's role "with a difference, for she is potentially a new French scourge of the English"; her role is passed on to Richmond who becomes the "minister of chastisement" (722). The women in *R3* are also indebted to Seneca's *Hercules Furens* and *Hippolytus*. In the wooing scene, Anne is like Hippolytus and Richard like Phaedra, "a self-confessed criminal lover" at Anne's feet. In its representation of women, as in other matters, *R3* combines the neo-classical and native traditions.

106. Carlisle, Carol. "The Critics Discover Shakespeare's Women."
     Renaissance Papers 1979 (1980): 59-73.

During the Restoration and through the 1770s, Shakespeare's
heroines were considered slight, were ignored, and were
overshadowed by the competing heroines of other dramatists. In
the Fletcherian mode, heroines suffer "all for love"; creatures of
passion and pathos, they were greatly admired by Restoration and
eighteenth-century critics. By comparison, Shakespeare's tragic
heroines "must have seemed ... not only reticent but emotionally
tame and even a little dull" (64). Because of adaptations, Juliet
and Cleopatra lost their identities as Shakespeare conceived them.
Shakespeare's heroes were the subject of psychological studies
before such attention was paid to the women. William
Richardson's "Shakespeare's Imitation of Female Character"
(1789) "marks a turning point in critical attitudes toward
Shakespeare's women" (59). But "just as the stage had much to do
with the negative attitude toward Shakespeare's women, so it had
much to do with the critical change in their favor" (66). Increased
respect for Shakespeare's heroines can be attributed to the
"newly-intensified" interest in the ideal woman of charm whose
gifts of mind and heart inspired men and balanced their sterner
qualities. These qualities found in Shakespeare's "womanly
women" were praised by such critics as Coleridge, Hazlitt, and
Anna Jameson. The evolution of Shakespeare's heroines as real
human beings together with their idealization was "the most
significant development in the theatre of the period" (71). In
reconciling Shakespeare's heroines with the "womanly ideal of the
romantic and Victorian periods," Helen Facuit helped to make
them "more complex than they had previously seemed ... " (72).

107. Clemon-Karp, Sheila. "The Female Androgyne in Tragic Drama."
     DAI 41 (1980): 2906A-97A. Brandesis U.

108. Cook, Judith. *Women in Shakespeare*. London: Harrap, 1980.

Actresses' comments on Shakespeare's women shed much light
on the great variety of roles they have in the plays. As Chapter
One, "Her Infinite Variety," points out, Shakespeare "reflected the

women of his age, the witty, learned ladies, the independent wives, even the rural simpletons" (6). Though adept at portraying young girls, boy actors perhaps could not realistically capture mature women.

Chapter Two on Rosalind and Viola concludes that "of all Shakespeare's romantic heroines," Rosalind is "the most realistic" (17). The most crucial fact about Rosalind is that she "never becomes a boy at all, her psychology is totally feminine" (20). While Viola takes her boyhood seriously, she is never just a boy and grows into a mature woman by the end of *TN*. Devoted to *TSh*, Chapter Three holds that it is not an unpleasant, anti-feminine play about the subjugation of women. Many actresses portraying Kate stress that she is not tamed. Kate plays in public "the exact game she has been taught in private" by Petruchio (29). *TSh* is a "paean to the secretiveness of real passion" (29). Chapter Four on Portia and Isabella finds them the two least popular heroines. Fond of Portia, actresses emphasize her rebellion against male codes. In the "black comedy" of *MM*, Isabella may be a model of chastity yet she is the victim of "immature enthusiasm." J.W. Lever, in his introduction to the Arden edition (1965), is right: "A real-life Isabella, even in Shakespeare's day, would have received scant sympathy." For actresses, Isabella is drawn between love for the Duke and desire for the convent.

Chapter Five concentrates on women confidants, foils, and friends. *MND* is about marriage and female friendships. A friend and a foil to Beatrice, Hero helps to carry out the plot. Celia is witty and intelligent in her own right; the "staunchest of friends" (49), she is linked with Adam in professing loyalty. Like girls at Elizabeth's court, Jessica and Nerissa are lively, though Jessica has been interpreted as an unfilial daughter as well as "a princess held captive by an ogre" (51). Marina, Perdita, and Miranda in Chapter Six possess a striking innocence, go through a second birth, and are united with families. Of Marina it can be said: "Seldom can a heroine have hung on to her virginity with such tenacity" (56). Unlike Marina and Perdita, Miranda lives in isolation, "enwrapped and protected" by her father (66). Hardly a happy role, Miranda is often played by ingenues.

Chapter Seven looks at historical women, subordinate roles because these women cannot influence events. The only exception

is Volumnia in *Cor.* Calpurnia is far more realistic than Portia in
JC. In the English history plays, only Queen Margaret in the first
tetralogy and Queen Katherine in *H8* have "large parts."
Shakespeare experiences a "tug of war" (68) over Joan who is "the
strangest woman to appear in the histories" (68); she uses evil
witchcraft yet we look forward to seeing her. Chapter Eight
studies Hermione, Imogen, Helena, and Gertrude. The first two
are falsely accused women who personify grace and faith. Helena
is a rebel in *AWW*, a play "about the disparities of rank and how
a virgin can actively pursue a matter of love without incurring
dishonour" (82). Except for the closet scene, Gertrude apparently
has little to say or do. She certainly is not drunk, or neurotic; she
is a sexy woman who can also fall out of love with Claudius.
Whether Gertrude knew of her husband's murder, actress Barbara
Jefford remarked: "I think she knows, but doesn't want to know,
won't talk about it, won't recognize it, won't admit it even to
herself" (86).

Juliet, Ophelia, Desdemona, and Cordelia are the subjects of
Chapter Nine. Conveying Juliet's extreme youth while having her
speak sophisticated verse is an "overriding problem" for actresses.
Ophelia, unlike Shakespeare's other women, has no will of her
own. Variously interpreted, Ophelia has been seen as too soft as
well as independent through madness. Desdemona is not simply
passive; her goodness is not weak. Cordelia is "a difficult role in
that she says very little. What she feels is implied" (99). Her love
is richer than what she speaks.

Chapter Ten on "practical women" discusses Mistress Quickly,
Jacquennetta in *LLL*, Audrey, the Nurse in *RJ*, and Maria. These
earthy women find no great happiness, succumbing to disease, bad
marriages, or lost children. The "villainesses" in Chapter Eleven
include Tamora, Goneril and Regan, and Cymbeline's queen (the
traditional wicked stepmother). Though "Shakespeare wrote very
little about truly evil women" (113), these characters have no
redeeming features. Even though Cressida is included in this
chapter, she is not evil; "she is amoral, and Shakespeare wrote
about her at a time when he seems to have been feeling deeply
disgusted with women" (111). Like Emilia, Cressida is a realist;
and though Cressida can be compared with Gertrude, she is more
subtle.

Chapter Twelve, devoted to Lady Macbeth, examines how three actresses interpreted the role. Sarah Siddons saw in Lady Macbeth "a captivating feminine loveliness" that would charm Macbeth; Ellen Terry conceived of Macbeth's queen as a "small, slight woman of acute nervous sensibility" (127); and though there is a tremendous animal passion between the Macbeths, Judi Dench believed it was Lady Macbeth's ambition rather than her sexuality which drove Macbeth on. Cleopatra, in Chapter Thirteen, is one of the most difficult parts to play because of her changeability. Terry enacted her as an "all-out courtesan" (135) while modern actresses such as Janet Suzman and Glenda Jackson find it hard to get Shakespeare right. The concluding Chapter Fourteen, "Rough Magic," asserts that Shakespeare never underestimated his women characters' weakness nor was he patronizing toward them.

Reviews: Economist 20 Dec. 1980: 83; *Encounter* 57 (July 1981): 60; Masters, Anthony, *Times Educational Supplement* 13 Feb. 1981: 20; Roxman, Susanna, *Dagens Nyheter* 9 June 1981.

109. Dash, Irene. "A Penchant for Perdita on the Eighteenth-Century Stage." In Lenz, Greene, and Neely, item 126. 271-84.

Adaptations of the *WT* during the last half of the eighteenth century by Morgan and Garrick cut the first three acts to emphasize the pastoral and the sentimental at the expense of Shakespeare's women. These adapters "substituted weak women for strong, and strong men for weak" (274). Shakespeare's fearless Pauline, the "scourge of Leontes," is turned into a "displaced, dependent person" (276); her great speech ("I can't repent these things") is given to Leontes by Garrick. Hermione likewise "disappears" in Garrick's adaptation. Though Perdita is not changed much in the adaptations, since she conformed to "the idealized stereotypical woman" (200), the adapters did alter her lines when they thought she was too "outspoken." Even the full-length version of the play done by Hull stresses Perdita, Florizel, and Autolycus rather than the strong-willed Hermione, Paulina, and Leontes to bring out the pleasing pastoral instead of the thornier issues of "children and infidelity" (280). These

adaptations, which conformed to "acceptable female patterns,"
influenced later interpretations of these Shakespearean women.

110. Davidson, Clifford. "Antony and Cleopatra: Circe, Venus, and the
      Whore of Babylon." In *Shakespeare: Contemporary Critical
      Approaches*. Ed. Harry R. Garvin. *Bucknell Review* 25.1.
      Lewisburg, PA: Bucknell UP; London: Associated UP, 1980.
      31-55.

Cleopatra is associated with classical and Biblical models,
iconographically represented in the Renaissance, and partakes of
their negative and positive sides. But Shakespeare "insists upon
transforming the destructive passion that Cleopatra represents
into its seeming opposites" (51). She is the aggressive, fatal
woman whose desire "usurps the phallic role" (37); she is like
Sloth holding a fish that, like Antony, cannot escape. Like her
classical model, the temptress Circe, Cleopatra paradoxically tries
to destroy Antony while symbolizing the generative, fertile source
of power. She plays the role of Eve, as the abundant food and asp
imagery show, and ironically foreshadows the Blessed Virgin (38).
Apocalyptic imagery characterizes her as the Whore of Babylon
with all her negative feminine qualities. Further illustrating her
contrary characteristics, the Egyptian Queen is the earthly Venus,
symbolizing lust and the infidelity of the Dark Lady of the
sonnets. She is also the heavenly Venus associated with harmony
and universal peace. Giving himself to Cleopatra, Antony as Mars
endangers his masculinity and power. But the last two acts do not
offer a "rigidly orthodox moral conclusion" (49). Audience
sympathy for Antony and Cleopatra may rest upon "the sensuous
Cleopatra, but the earthly Venus is purged of her baser elements
and transformed by the immortality of art." Antony's relationship
with Cleopatra is destructive as well as "aesthetically redemptive"
(53).

111. Fineman, Joel. "Fratricide and Cuckoldry: Shakespeare's Doubles."
      In Schwartz and Kahn, item 136. 70-109.

The idea of doubling is built into Elizabethan theatre. Each
actor was required to play several roles, and certain roles were

condensed into one. *AYL* and *Ham* rely on "explicit fratricidal rivalry" (74). In *Ham* "fratricide is not merely a cause, but it is elevated into a fundamental paradigm of all the ensuing dramatic action, functioning as the play's myth ... " (75). Claudius is another Cain who also acts out Hamlet's oedipal desire. Hamlet becomes Claudius's brother when Claudius becomes Hamlet's father. All the women in *Ham* are considered prostitutes, so by nature they appear in disguise. Parricide becomes fratricide, but fratricide becomes incest. To Shakespeare, fratricide is always linked to envy and revenge. *TN* begins with a lost brother who needs a substitute. He is replaced by Sebastian, a found brother, who is miraculously brought to life. Viola's male disguise means that she becomes brother to herself. The violence between brothers is for Shakespeare "the projection into dramatic terms of the infantile experience of cleavage" (104). To be cuckolded is to be castrated by the "whoring phallic mother," who effeminizes men because of her so-called lust for maleness.

112. Fitz, Linda T. "What Says the Married Woman? Marriage Theory and Feminism in the English Renaissance." *Mosaic* 13 (1980) 1-22.

The Renaissance view of women was marriage-oriented. Marriage was viewed as a domestic partnership, a contract rather than a sacrament, where sex was respectable and motherhood honored. This Protestant view of marriage annihilated the alternative to wifehood that was provided for women under Catholicism–the monastic life. Shakespeare favored free choice in marriage rather than the more usual parental arrangement. Pleas for making women subservient point to the fact that they were not. "The number of contemporary ballads about shrews, scolds and domineering wives suggests that the custom of wifely obedience was more honored in the breach than in the observance" (13). Attacking the court of King James and transvestism among women *Haec Vir* claimed that because it was a law of nature differences between the sexes must be preserved. Consequently, women have to adopt masculine attire when foppish men adopt feminine attire. As in Shakespeare's romantic comedies, women felt that they had to adopt the clothing and external attributes of men to be free.

113. Frey, Charles. "'O sacred, shadowy, cold, and constant queen': Shakespeare's Imperiled and Chastening Daughters of Romance." In Lenz, Greene, and Neely, item 126. 295-313.

The "plights and flights of daughters" in Shakespeare's romances show how these women break patriarchal control over their loves and marriages. The matrimonial problems involving unacceptable sons-in-law in romances contrast with the duties of sons in the tragedies. In the son-less late plays (*Cym*, *WT*, *Per*, *Tem*), daughters assume special importance. Their oppressive ruler-fathers are worried about successors when the daughter leaves home. Yet the daughter serves a redemptive function by bringing a husband home and bestowing on the father "a newfound love and forgiveness made possible and believable amid restored patriarchal security" (303). In reinvigorating the family, these daughters substitute virginal renewal in place of the aggression of "patrilineal succession" (304). In the post-romance world of *H8*, women are not valued for their childbearing but instead "the romance pattern is transcended" (305) as Elizabeth and Katherine point us "heavenward." Emilia in *TNK* displays "no sense of familial drive," but even though she does not share the "generational" drive of the romance daughters, her marriage to Palamon is made possible only because of "the warmer eagerness of the Jailer's daughter toward Palamon and love" (309).

114. Garber, Marjorie. "The Healer in Shakespeare." In *Medicine and Literature*. Ed. Enid Rhodes Peschel. New York: Watson Academic Publishers, 1980. 103-109.

A sick ruler in Shakespeare reflects a diseased land. Though surgeons are often called for in the plays, none actually appears, suggesting that their absence is symbolic. In the diseased world of *Ham*, the poisoned cup and rapier symbolize the illness "pervasive in Denmark" as well as "poisoned sexuality: the cup is a traditional symbol for the female, the sword for the male" (105). While actual doctors are limited in their healing, women in the later plays, becoming a type of "Doctor-She," perform "acts of restoration and healing" literal doctors are powerless to offer. Women in healing roles include Helena in *AWW* who works with heaven, her father's talents, and her own energy; Marina who cures Pericles of melancholy; and Cordelia who ministers to Lear. In *Per, Lear,* and *WT,* music is combined with the restoration of the father. Because these women "minister to patients whose suffering is spiritual as well as physical," their powers are truly restorative.

115. Gohlke, Madelon. "'I wooed thee with my sword': Shakespeare's Tragic Paradigms." In Lenz, Greene, and Neely, item 126. 150-70. Rpt. in Schwartz and Kahn, item 136. 170-187.

A "feminist psychoanalytic" sub-reading of the tragedies uncovers the key cultural (metaphoric) "fictions interweaving women with violence" (152). The threat of violence, whether "mutual or self-inflicted," runs throughout the "imagery of heterosexual love" in the plays (161). Men, who have trouble "accepting emotional involvement," use violence as a "denial or defence against femininity" (158). In the tragedies, men regard women as weak and fear becoming "feminized males"; yet paradoxically they are threatened by women's power and the possibility of being victimized by them through betrayal. Hence many women are branded and punished as whores–Desdemona, Helen of Troy, the Player Queen, Gertrude. In *Lear,* woman is seen as untrustworthy in her "maternal functions"; the old man is like "the child being banished by his mother" (i.e. daughters). Macbeth wants to "eradicate femininity itself" (158) by destroying children and the bonds of human society, weaknesses which become strengths for his foes. Antony, like Othello, feels betrayed yet like Romeo "perceives himself as having been feminized for love" (159). In many ways, Cleopatra becomes the "epitome of what is hated, loved, and feared in a woman by Shakespeare's tragic heroes" (160). The values that emerge from the tragedies are "if anything 'feminine' values dissociated from the traditional masculine categories of force and politics ... " (161). A "matriarchal substratum or subtext" exists within "the patriarchal text" and while that subtext is not necessarily feminist, the tragedies do offer a "vast commentary on the absurdity and destructiveness" of male dominance and violence against feminine weakness.

116. Greene, Gayle. "Shakespeare's Cressida: 'A kind of self.'" In Lenz, Greene, and Neely, item 126. 133-49.

Though Cressida is regarded as the "very crown of falsehood," Shakespeare "provides a context that exonerates" her (133), and offers a "more sympathetic" view of woman (145) than the misogynotic assaults in the play indicate. Definitions of Cressida's character are determined by the male society's views of her changing worth. In this mercantile society, market value determines men and women's relationships (136); women are reduced to objects to be consumed. As a merchant in search of Cressida, "predatory" Troilus "impugns his lofty idealism" signaled in his Petrarchan language. Cressida must shape her "selves" for male buyers in this supply and demand economy in order to survive. "Simultaneously victim and critic," Cressida "paradoxically, is in a better position than the men to understand the principles that motivate her world" (139). Though she forfeits any claim to our sympathy in Act 3.1, Cressida experiences anguish at being classed as an object in a price war (142). She and Troilus exploit and stereotype each other–he through his idealization of her and she through her suspicion. Fully aware of her "kind" and "unkind" selves, Cressida understands Troilus better than he does himself. When she meets Diomedes, "in what is perhaps the most loveless encounter between lovers in Shakespeare" (143), Cressida learns that her price has fallen because he refuses to spend words on her, thus depriving her of the "customary means of creating her value" (144). The play "constitutes a critique of stereotyping" in which male games cost Cressida "no less than her self" (145). The tainted male world has so much power over Troilus and Cressida that the "play is thus marked by a fatalism uncustomary to Shakespeare" (146).

117. Guilfoyle, Cherrell. "'Ower Swete Sokor': The Role of Ophelia in *Hamlet*." *Comparative Drama* 14 (1980): 3-17.

A woman can only be considered equal to a man when she is eliminated from sexual considerations. If she is not, she becomes "angel or devil, separately or interchangeably" (3). Ophelia, like Mary Magdalene, is a figure of purity who can atone for the sins of others. She confronts Hamlet in her orisons like a "ministering angel"; however, Hamlet rejects all women as foul and corruptible. While Hamlet pretends to be mad, Ophelia really becomes mad; he meditates on death while she really dies. When Claudius maims Ophelia's funeral rites, his action aligns her funeral with the hasty burial of Christ and Mary Magdalene's visit to the tomb. But Ophelia is not Mary Magdalene's double; she contains the purer half while the other half has been colored by false accusation.

118. Hays, Janice. "Those 'soft and delicate desires': *Much Ado* and the Distrust of Women." In Lenz, Greene, and Neely, item 126. 79-99.

Ado shows how a woman can lead the protagonist away from such limiting male characteristics as aggression and "narrow rationality" toward "empathy" and mutuality so that he can care for others. The Hero-Claudio plot incorporates "the psychological difficulties" of combining a "traditionally arranged marriage" with "romantic and erotic love" (81). Through his silence, male bonds, and idealization of woman (wrongly suggesting incest), Claudio exhibits "the anxieties occasioned by heterosexuality" (85). He is not ready to assume the responsibilities of marriage. "Shakespeare seems to question the limitations of the male instrumental experience ... " (92). Hero is forced to become "a virgin sacrifice," something owned by Leonato. In the patriarchal system, Shakespeare portrays Hero's "infidelity ... as the ultimate betrayal, a fundamental wound to male self-esteem" (87). The resolution of the Hero-Claudio plot depends on Providence, which suggests that a man can act with his heart as well as his head. The "revelation that Claudio's new wife and his 'other wife' are the same woman joins the tender and the sensual in one love object, making it possible for him to entrust himself [to] ... a woman [who] is both sexually desirable and trustworthy" (94).

119. Holland, Norman N. "Hermia's Dream." In Schwartz and Kahn, item 136. 1-20.

Hermia's dream in *MND* can: 1) be used as a clinical study of an adolescent girl; 2) be placed within a system of ego functions; and 3) represent ourselves to ourselves. The sexual symbolism of snake imagery and doubled language establish Hermia's concern with alternatives. She takes the "image of complete truth or candor and dreams it into a snake eating her own heart, an emblem of doubleness, treachery, and hostility" (7). Such transference of one image into another may indicate that the adolescent Hermia is using Lysander to work out a traumatic early relationship with her mother. Marjorie B. Garber *(Dream in Shakespeare: From Metaphor to Metamorphosis*, New Haven, CT: Yale UP, 1974, 72-74) sees the dream in the play as being truer than reality. And Melvin D. Faber ("Hermia's Dream: Royal Road to *A Midsummer Night's Dream*," *Literature and Psychology* 22 [1972], 179-90), using the old one-to-one symbolic equation (snake equals penis), concludes that the dream fulfills Hermia's desire for sex with Lysander. A combination of these two theories sets Hermia's dream in "the whole atmosphere and development of ambivalence in the comedy" (12), including that of overt cruelty, so that the snake represents an aspect of that cruelty, the desertion and indifference of the lovers. As a whole, the play represents "Shakespeare's effort to establish masculine control over unruly impulses associated with the lack of proper boundaries between male and female" (11). Hermia's dream thus takes its life from the relations between men and women.

120. Kahn, Coppelia. "Coming of Age in Verona." In Lenz, Greene, and Neely, item, 126. 171-93.

Rpt. from item 66 and rev. for item 160.

121. ---. "The Providential Tempest and the Shakespearean Family." In Schwartz and Kahn, item 136. 217-43.

See item 160.

122. Kernberg, Otto F., M.D. "Adolescent Sexuality in the Light of Group Processes." *Psychoanalytic Quarterly* 49 (1980): 27-47.

In rebellion against the demands of their respective parents, Romeo and Juliet find an outlet for their adolescent oedipal conflicts by transferring their affections from the parental figure to each other. The consummation of their relationship "unites them and brings them to maturity." Juliet is rebelling against the marital expectations her family has of her. If she responds favorably to their wishes, she is accepting societal regimentation of love and sex. While overcoming the aggression, meaninglessness, and anonymity of the larger group, the couple must be prepared to recognize these things in their own relationship. Love and aggression are emotions closely linked, as exemplified in the suicide at the end of the play. Romeo and Juliet's death is a denial of aggression, even though they turned it on themselves.

123. Klein, Joan Larsen. "Lady Macbeth: 'Infirm of purpose.'" In Lenz, Greene, and Neely, item 126. 240-55.

Despite the critical view of Lady Macbeth as an evil, inhuman force, she is "never able to separate herself completely from womankind unlike her husband who ultimately becomes less and worse than a man" (241). In light of the precepts in contemporary marriage manuals and treatises, Lady Macbeth "epitomizes at the same time she perverts Renaissance views of the woman's role" (243). Though Lady Macbeth fails to put God first and to act out of charity, she "conceives of herself almost exclusively as a wife, a helpmate" (243). In a "grim perversion of married companionship" (244), she tries to assist, counsel, and support her husband; her behind-the-scenes activities are true to the Renaissance belief that "women are passive, men active." In her role as hostess and housekeeper, Lady Macbeth's preparations for and cleaning up after Duncan's murder become a "frightening perversion of Renaissance woman's domestic activity" (245). Yet, after Duncan's murder, she "begins to lose her place in society and her position at home" (246); her husband's "union" with the witches replaces his relationship with her. In the banquet and sleepwalking scenes, Lady Macbeth lives in isolation, no longer needed by her husband. To the end, though, she follows the Renaissance injunction that a woman should confess her sins alone, as opposed to Macbeth who does so publicly. Lady Macbeth is "guilty in ways which are particularly 'feminine'" (241).

124. Kott, Jan. "Head for Maidenhead, Maidenhead for Head (The Structure of Exchange in *Measure for Measure*)." In *En Torno A Shakespeare: Homenaje T.J.B. Spencer.* Ed. Manuel Angel Conerjero. Valencia: Univaersidad de Valencia; Inst. Shakespeare, 1980. 93-113.

Like Shakespeare's source, George Whetsone's *Promos and Cassandra, MM* demonstrates that "corrupted law and corrupted sex are reciprocally destructive" (94). The plots of both works function in terms of "oppositions of deficiency and excess, of below-the-measure and above-the-measure, between the underrated and the overrated" (95). Virginity, sexual abstinence, is below-the-measure; Claudio and Juliet experience an excess of desire with "too few legal bonds" while Angelo and Marianna have "too many legal bonds without sexual desire" (97). The four female roles in *MM* illustrate Shakespeare's system of mirrored doubles. If the bawd is Mistress Overdone, Isabella is Mistress Underdone. Linguistically and structurally, *MM* is based on a system of "trading sex and law [where] everything is paid for in 'heads'" (98). Sex and death are constantly connected; executioner and bawd both cut off heads. Both represent "Law and Sex beyond measure" (102). In fact, sex and law are associated with violence and death (106). Isabella, who regards sex as an execution, has a "sado-masochistic imagination." The forced marriages in *MM* are used for "blackmail and a trap" (107); Isabella pays the price of a maidenhead for her marriage. There are four wedding couples: Juliet/Claudio; Angelo/Marianna; the Duke/Isabella; and Lucio and the Provost; the last pair emphasize the relationship of corrupt sex and law. Whetstone's Cassandra is "split into Isabella and Marianna" (111). The ideology of *MM* depends upon exchanges which do not transform.

125. Leininger, Lorie Jerrell. "The Miranda Trap: Sexism and Racism
      in Shakespeare's *Tempest*." In Lenz, Greene, and Neely, item
      126. 285-94.

      Regarded as her father's "foot" (Act 1.2.472) who must render
      "absolute unthinking obedience" (288), Miranda is forced to
      occupy a subservient place in Prospero's hierarchy. Prospero also
      uses Miranda as "sexual bait" (289) to "counter-balance Caliban's
      lust." Her chastity becomes the political excuse Prospero needs to
      enslave Caliban. In Jacobean England, there was a "tendency of
      allegory to link virtue with privilege and sin with misfortune," thus
      justifying "virulent attacks on social minorities and outcasts" (290).
      Caliban's lust accounts for his lowly station. "Unaccountable
      aristocratic power" thereby becomes equated with "benevolent
      infallibility" (291). A "modern" Miranda would speak a "new
      Epilogue" denouncing the "Miranda trap" which forces her to use
      her body (wrongly located "symbolically in one part of my
      anatomy") to exploit the oppressed. "I need to join forces with
      Caliban," this modern Miranda asserts.

126. Lenz, Carolyn Ruth Swift, Gayle Greene, and Carol Thomas
      Neely, eds. *The Woman's Part: Feminist Criticism of
      Shakespeare*. Urbana: U of Illinois P, 1980.

      Reviews: Bank, Rosemary K., *Theatre Journal* 35 (1983): 129;
      Brown, Keith, *Times Literary Supplement* 22 Aug. 1986: 917-18;
      Callies, Valerie W., *Modern Philology* 79 (1981-1982): 318-20;
      Cary, C.W., *Comparative Drama* 15 (1981): 280-81; Diziwas,
      Doris, *Shakespeare Jahrbuch* (1982): 175-77; Ferguson, Margaret
      W., *Yale Review* 71 (1982): 414-26; ---, *Yearbook of English Studies*
      14 (1982): 313-14; Gottlieb, Sidney, *Sixteenth Century Journal* 13
      (1982): 101-03; Gravlee, Cynthia, *South Atlantic Review* 46 (1981):
      119-22; Heilbrun, Carolyn G., *Signs* 8 (1982): 182-85; Margolies,
      David, *Red Letters* [London] 11 (1982): 46-49; Marsh, C.P., *CLA
      Journal* 25 (1981): 121-24; Priest, Dale G., *South Central Review*
      1 (1984): 82-84; Roberts, Jeanne Addison, *Shakespeare Quarterly*
      33 (1982): 533-36; Schabert, Ino, *Shakespeare Jahrbuch* (1986):
      223-29; Simons, J., *Review of English Studies* 35 (1984): 108;
      Smidt, Kristian, *English Studies* 63 (1982): 74; Taylor, M., *Ariel*

[Calgary] 12.4 (1981): 97-99; Wayne, Valerie, *Modern Philology* 79 (1982): 318-20.

127. ---. "Women and Men in Shakespeare: A Selective Bibliography." In Lenz, Greene, and Neely, item 126. 314-35.

Listing non-sexist criticism published primarily since 1960, this bibliography includes "Shakespearean criticism in English which is feminist or otherwise appropriate to the concerns of those interested in the position of women, in relations between men and women, and in love, sexuality, courtship, marriage, and the family in Shakespeare" (314). The bibliography is divided into five sections: General; Comedies; Histories; Tragedies; and Individual Plays and Other Works.

128. Leverenz, David. "The Woman in Hamlet: An Interpersonal View." *Signs* 4 (1978): 291-308. Rpt. in Schwartz and Kahn, item 136. 110-128.

Freudian explanations based on sexuality (oedipal conflict; divided view of the father) do not hold the answer to Hamlet's problems. Instead, "interpersonal expectations, more than self-contained desires, are what divide Hamlet from himself ... " (111). Hamlet is adrift in a sea of ambiguity because of the false values and roles that a patriarchal system imposes on him. It is a world where what fathers say and do is fraught with "multitudinous double-dealings" (112). The source of Hamlet's tragedy resides in the conflict between "filial duty" and sensitivity (which is the woman's part in Hamlet). Claudius denies such feelings, and through his public speaking emphasizes reason, war in terms of love, and joins obedience to reason in a "unity of opposites." In this male world of ambition and lust, reason is made to exclude feelings, words, and roles that match self. The Ghost demands conformity and filial duty, sending mixed signals to Hamlet, as Claudius does. Both "speak with the arrogant abstractedness of majesty" (117). Ophelia "mirrors in her madness the tensions Hamlet perceives" (117); like him, she is a victim of the father figures and must "continually respond to commands" that ask her to deny her feelings. In demanding "falseness to others" from his daughter, Polonius is uncaring, "preoccupied with only how he looks" (118). Hamlet himself is guilty of sending Ophelia mixed signals when he acts like the manly revenger. Hence, Ophelia is driven mad having to listen to other voices, "contradictory directives" (119), and makes of "herself a play within a play." Her suicide becomes "a little microcosm of the male's world banishment of the female, because 'woman' represents everything denied by reasonable men" (121). Hamlet's tragedy is that he "becomes his own violator" in having to follow the prescribed roles appointed him in the world of the fathers. Tears, feelings, the heart, language are all excluded in this male world of custom and ambition. While Hamlet's final silence suggests the "female dove in him" (123) joining with Ophelia and Gertrude, the play nonetheless ends with the "mindless sequence of ritual male duties, roles without meaning" (124) where Fortinbras, who does not have a "touch of the woman in him" returns us to the "paternal duplicity" of the first act. Hamlet's "real struggle is to restore his mother's validation of his feelings" (125).

129. Mathieson, Barbara Jean Offutt. "Patterns of Misogyny in Jacobean Tragedy." *DAI* 40 (1980): 4055-56A. Stanford U. [*AC, Cym, Ham, Lear, Tim, TrC,* and *WT*].

130. McKewin, Carole. "Counsels of Gall and Grace: Intimate Conversations between Women in Shakespeare's Plays." In Lenz, Greene, and Neely, item 126. 117-32.

Nineteen of the plays contain scenes where women talk intimately with each other allowing them to "express their own perceptions and identities, comment on masculine society, and gather strength and engage in reconnaissance to act in it" (118-19). Unlike corresponding scenes of masculine conversation, women's talk occurs in more private settings and does not move back and forth between "public and private concerns" (119). Women's conversation is sometimes "sheer talk" or "preparation for action"; more commonly, though, these scenes "explore the possibilities and limits of women's action, often leading indirectly to it" (221). However, such feminine conversation is "often shaped by the larger world of the play" (122). Perhaps the best example is in *AYL* where Rosalind and Celia converse "under constraint and freedom" (122), in two different settings–the court and the forest. Their "heady conversations have no equal in Shakespeare's other plays" (124), least of all *Ado* where the talk of Beatrice, Hero, and Margaret has a "curious unease about it" (124). In the patriarchal world of the tragedies, women "talk less to each other"; their self-expression is "imperfectly realized, perverted, or blocked" (127) as with Juliet and the Nurse, Ophelia and Gertrude. Despite Cleopatra's conversations with Iras and Charmian, there is "never ... adequate time ... [for] mutual sharing" (127). In *Oth* the conversation between Emilia and Desdemona "reflects the texture" of male oppression.

131. Miner, Madonne M. "'Neither mother, wife, nor England's queen': The Roles of Women in *Richard III*." In Lenz, Greene, and Neely, item 126. 35-55.

Women in *R3* "take on an emotional stability, a roundness of humanity" (48). Richard sees women as scapegoats, as enemy, as "Other," allocating to them "guilt along sexual lines" so that they "are invariably at fault" for breaking "the bonds between men" (39). Further reducing women from "person" to "things exchanged," Richard views them as "having value only in relation to men"; they lose "title, position identity, as Richard destroys those by whom the women are defined: husbands, children, kings" (41). He ultimately turns women into "ciphers" by making them "abandon traditional titles, to de-identify themselves" (44); Margaret serves as a "model for the women" in *R3* (41). Richard also systematically denies "the human identity of women" (45) altogether, a tactic that is undercut, though, by "women-aiding-women," in which they move from "battling among themselves ... to a condition of camaraderie, sympathizing with each other" (52). Birth metaphors in *R3* illuminate "the paradoxically double presentation of women." A "counterprocess" in *R3* "insists upon the inherently positive value of women" which runs against Richard's views of them as having no value.

132. Neely, Carol Thomas Neely. "Women and Men in *Othello*: 'What should such a fool/Do with so good a woman?'" In Lenz, Greene, and Neely, item 126. 211-39.

     Rpt. from item 49 and rev. for item 298.

133. Park, Clara Claiborne. "As We Like It: How a Girl Can Be Smart and Still Popular." *American Scholar* 42 (1973): 262-78. Rpt., with revisions, in Lenz, Greene, and Neely, item 126. 100-16.

     Unlike his contemporaries, Shakespeare included many women in his plays, even if he never titled a play completely after a woman. Shakespeare respected women, especially those who were assertive without being threatening to men, which is "one of the secrets of his perennial appeal" (103). Shakespeare had to find ways to "mediate" their power, "to temper their behavior to the vulnerability of the male" (l06). He limited their spheres of action by not presenting them as rulers (Cleopatra trades in love, not politics) or scholars. Instead he delighted in glorifying "as never before the image of the bright young girl" (104), plucky and intelligent. Yet to be acceptable to audiences, this young girl's "equality [with men] is kept nominal" (105). Beatrice, for example, tames her own wild heart and thus is nonthreatening to the men in the play and in the audience. Unique among Shakespeare's women, and so unlike Beatrice, Portia and Rosalind control the outcome of events in their plays, which provide "no male rivals." Bassanio is "the most firmly nonmemorable of Shakespeare's characters"; and Rosalind is "twice the person" Orlando is (109). Shakespeare's mitigating factors control female forcefulness. Rosalind's targets are the acceptable "sighing lovers and women"; Portia's are more serious but still "reassuring" for an audience–a "misbelieving Jew" (110). Moreover, both these women submit to their men; Portia does so in Belmont before she leaves for Venice. Shakespeare found mediating advantages in dressing women in male costume which allows them more freedom but only temporarily.

134. Schotz, Myra Glazer. "The Great Unwritten Story: Mothers and Daughters in Shakespeare." In *The Lost Tradition: Mothers and*

Daughters in Literature. Ed. Cathy N. Davidson and E.M. Broner. New York: Ungar, 1980. 44-54.

Shakespeare was truly androgynous. His presentation of daughters is particularly important, since they often symbolize reconciliation. Yet the "mother-daughter cathexis" is missing in Shakespeare. *Mac* and *Lear* show a "motherless world." In *Mac*, where a "beneficent female principle is suppressed" (45), nature is forced to carry the "burden of [the] male fear" of perverse feminine sexuality. Only Macduff, unborn of woman, escapes a distorted masculine heroism. Tragedy results in *Lear* because of a lack of a feminine counterbalance to male rule. The suppressed mother/woman in *Lear* unleashes imagery of woman as lustful, perfidious. Lear tragically consolidates the roles of daughter and mother in Cordelia whom he "sacrifices at the altar of [his] desperately undifferentiated need for the feminine" (49). In the romances the two roles are separated and embody the myth of Demeter and Persephone. *Per*, however, is an "unsatisfying" play, since the daughter and the mother are "contained" by the male; when Marina usurps Thaisa's role, incest and revulsion follow. These two women are "purged of the threatening aspects of the feminine that so obsessed" the tragic heroes (50). Opposed to *Lear*, *WT*, Shakespeare's most maternal and most androgynous play, celebrates the feminine mysteries of birth and new life essential to the psychic health of the male. Leontes separates mother and daughter, but he himself is healed by their reunion effected by Paulina who demonstrates that "true art is feminine" (53). The bond between Hermione and Perdita, marvelously reflected in the Demeter/Persephone myth, is not repeated by Shakespeare who instead turns to the world of Prospero who lives "in the shadow of Cerimon" (51).

135. Schwartz, Murray M. "Shakespeare Through Contemporary Psychoanalysis." *Hebrew University Studies in Literature and the Arts* 5 (1977). Rpt. in Schwartz and Kahn, item 136. 21-32.

A radical shift in psychoanalysis emphasizes how the interpreter shapes the interpretation. D.W. Winnicott's construct of "potential space" (*Playing and Reality* [1971]) helps explain

Shakespeare's development and his plays. In potential space there, is a "dialectic of contraries" where illusion/reality, male/female, work/play are denied and continuities are affirmed. Male and female are integrated. Trust in women is essential for generational succession and potential space. Hamlet degrades "femininity as a projected location for his frustrated desires" (26) because he is a victim of his divided selves. Thwarting "continuities," the playing space in *Ham* is brutalized by a "war of masculine wills" where mutual trust is impossible. Instead of having an interplay based on trust, Lear narcissistically wants to assimilate his daughters into himself, foreclosing potential space. At the end of *Lear*, "as always in Shakespearean tragedy, the feminine sources of masculine identity are dead or powerless ... " (28). A common theme in Shakespeare is that the mistrust of the feminine and the breakdown of potential space lead to the heroes' "denial of separation from others or their violent rejection of dependency on others" (29). Unlike the other tragedies, *AC* provides a potential space where the contraries of female and male are synthesized by Antony accepting the female side of himself. Working through his own struggle with rage, Shakespeare learned the necessity of acknowledging the masculine and feminine sides of self to produce the "double re-creation" of illusion in and of the drama (31).

136. Schwartz, Murray M., and Coppelia Kahn. *Representing Shakespeare: New Psychoanalytic Essays*. Baltimore: Johns Hopkins UP, 1980.

   Reviews: AB Bookman's Weekly 6 Apr. 1981: 2641; *Canto: Review of the Arts* 4 (1981): 148; *Choice* 18 (1980): 532; Charney, Maurice, *Review of Psychoanalytic Books* 1 (1982): 65-69; Danson, W. Laurence, *Studies in English Literature, 1500-1900* 23 (1983): 347-48; Kirsch, Arthur, *Shakespeare Quarterly* 33 (1982): 252; Newman, Karen, *Poetics Today* 3 (1982): 173; Weiland, Steven, *College English* 45 (1983): 705.

137. Smith, Rebecca. "A Heart Cleft in Twain: The Dilemma of Shakespeare's Gertrude." In Lenz, Greene, and Neely, item 126. 194-210.

Traditional interpretations of Gertrude as a "deceitful and highly sexual" woman on stage and in film are unjust. This "accommodating" and loving woman is "both figuratively and literally defined by other characters" (207), especially Hamlet who "encourages one to see all events and people from his perspective" (204). As a result, Gertrude is reduced to a "sexual object" about whom Hamlet, the Ghost, and Claudius have "violent conflicting emotions" (198). In Gertrude's speech and actions there is little that "hints at hypocrisy, suppression, or uncontrolled passion and their implied complexity" (199). Gertrude did not know Claudius murdered Hamlet Senior; her "actions are as solicitous and unlascivious as her language" (200); and she "was not guilty of sexual liaison with Claudius before her husband's murder" (202). She has "married in innocence and good faith" (203). Her response to the Player Queen conveys not a sense of her own guilt but rather her irritation at the Player Queen's "verbosity" (205). As a mother, she is also in great distress for Hamlet. Although Gertrude neither changes nor exhibits the level of complexity of some other characters in *Ham*, her death is "symbolic of the internal disharmony caused by her divided loyalties" (206).

138. Snow, Edward A. "Sexual Anxiety and the Male Order of Things in *Othello*." *English Literary Renaissance* 10 (1980): 384-412.

One of Shakespeare's "most cynical plays," *Oth* offers "neither transcendence nor catharsis" (385). The cause of the tragedy lies in the "pathological male animus toward sexuality" (389). Desdemona's sexuality threatens the "stability of the male world" (393), arousing Othello's guilt and his anxieties. The wedding sheets represent the "lust's blood" of Desdemona's "orgasmic discharge" as well as Othello's own blood and convince him to suppress Desdemona's sexuality. Iago transfers the guilt from a "fantasized Cassio" (394) onto Othello. Appealing to Othello's superego, Iago makes the Moor an adulterer and a cuckold in his marriage that suffers from "sexual confusion and self-contempt" (401). Iago "calls up the father" in Othello (398) when the Moor replaces Brabantio, the wronged father suffering from a "patriarchal conscience" (402). Jealousy is part of the symbolic

male order of fathers and husbands who see in women the
betrayals representing an "eternally recurrent Oedipal triangle"
(403). The handkerchief arouses male fantasies about these
maternal betrayals. The true tragedy of Othello becomes "the
inability of Desdemona to escape or triumph over restrains and
Oedipal prohibitions that domesticate women to the conventional
male order of things" (407). Hardly a castrating female,
Desdemona loses her freedom, confidence, and ability to act in a
guilt-free world and becomes the "thing" that men "fear and
despise" (407). She is forced to nullify herself. *Oth* is not an
example of the bestial (the id) breaking lose but the superego, or
the voice of the father wanting patriarchal order, creating the
tragedy.

139.   Stimpson, Catharine R. "Shakespeare and the Soil of Rape." In
        Lenz, Greene, and Neely, item 126. 56-64.

        Though Shakespeare was "more generous and less foolish than
        many of his contemporaries" (56) in dramatizing rapes, he still
        upholds   patriarchal values. The nightmare setting for rape in
        Shakespeare involves a perversion of nature in which classical
        antecedents are frequently cited. However tragic for the victims,
        rape inescapably is part of a "disastrous element of male rivalry"
        (58) in which the woman's body becomes property in a game men
        play to deprive each other of rights. A victim of a severe, "cureless
        crime," the woman is forced to die as a punishment for "an
        aggression she never sought" (59). No moderate women speak for
        the raped woman; some women even assist the rapists, e.g.,
        Tamora in *TA*. A "more darkly comic study" (61) of rape occurs
        in *Cym*. The raped victim "may be painfully emblematic of the
        plight" of women during 1580-1640 when patriarchy mattered
        "more than the destruction of a woman's body and sense of being"
        (63).

140.   Stugrin, Michael. "'But I must also feel it as a man': Pathos and
        Knowledge in Shakespearean Tragedy." *Iowa State Journal of
        Research* 54 (1980): 469-79.

The expressive power of pathos manipulates an audience's feelings in Shakespearean tragedy. Yet the pathos for suffering victims is distinct in feeling if not in intensity from the suffering experienced by Shakespeare's tragic heroes. Pathos allows us to have an "intimate identification with characters" like Cordelia. *RJ*, with "its sustained pathos" (474), witnesses the destruction of the vulnerable lovers whose love the world will not tolerate. Extinguishing their own flame, the "lovers themselves teach no regrets" (475). The "rhetoric of pathos" is also found in *VA* where Adonis's "neo-Platonic view of love" contrasts with Venus's eroticism. Adonis is a virginal victim–sensuous and moral–while Venus through her rhetorical performances celebrates human passion and animal lust (476). The strongest expression of pathos occurs in the exchange between Lucrece and Tarquin in the *RL*. Tarquin's passion, however, is "far more a product of a perverted imagination than of unbridled animal lust" (477). Through her pathetic speeches, Lucrece has "in a sense distanced herself" from her plight.

141. Sundelson, David. "So Rare a Wonder'd Father: Prospero's *Tempest*." In Schwartz and Kahn, item 136. 33-53.

See item 241.

142. Tennenhouse, Leonard. "The Counterfeit Order of *The Merchant of Venice*." In Schwartz and Kahn, item 136. 54-69.

Elizabethans tended to insist upon those aspects of a cultural self-image that contradicted historical fact; for example, the rivalry and competition between men, dominating economics as well as politics, could be countered by displays of ideal male friendship such as Antonio's and Bassanio's. "The terms by which Shakespeare set up his play, the characters he created, the needs he had them express ... reflect not only the contradictions in his culture, but also the ambivalence of his own desires" (55). Shakespeare's effort to create a stable dramatic world based on a series of oppositions (geographical, moral, and economic) ultimately emphasized disturbance, conflict, and anxiety in himself, his world, and his dramatic creation. Venice and Belmont are opposites, one a masculine world so firmly rooted in mercantilism that women must enter it disguised as men, and the other a romance world that seems maternal, bountiful, and generous, a safe harbor for lovers. *MV*, therefore, must end in Belmont, the softer world, but by that time, the city has become less lyrical, saturated with sexual contests, threatened betrayals, and competitive rivalry. Venice remains a harsh economic reality. Antonio is an excessive exhibitionist. The excesses of his virtue, his oral dependency, his isolation and loneliness characterize his disturbing narcissism.

The network of relationships established in *MV* is "based solely on forms of dependence and trust and hence is constantly subject to the threat of betrayal" (58), a threat first realized in Jessica's betrayal of her father but presented to deny its reality. Jessica's subsequent prodigal spending of the ring psychologically and symbolically dissolves her parents's marriage and cheapens the mother's pledge of love and fidelity. "The violation of the bond between father and daughter becomes the occasion for the testing of other bonds and the enactment of other betrayals" (58). Portia succeeds most when she is wearing male garb, acting like her father or threatening to cuckold her husband hermaphroditically. Behind all the bawdry in *MV* is the anxiety-arousing fantasy that Portia is sexually and simultaneously enclosed as male and female. Although "the theology" of *MV* may be just, the "economics are suspect and, like Portia's sexuality, most effective when counterfeit" (66).

143.   Willbern, David. "Shakespeare's Nothing." In Schwartz and Kahn, item 136. 244-63.

Shakespeare's plays represent "Renaissance No-drama." By banishing Cordelia, Lear "shuts out a symbolic vision he cannot bear to see" (247). Cordelia's refusal to give Lear the flattery he desires is a negative sign of nothing, one of denial. As a result, Cordelia is stripped of her father's love, and she becomes the "queen of silence." Yet, silence is the grounding for speech, and nothing is the grounding for being. Positive nothingness hints at infinite possibilities. In this sense, nothingness provides the potential for creation. Leontes in *WT* creates something out of nothing; he sees hidden meaning in Polixenes's smile. There are many interpretations of nothing, psychoanalytically, sexually, socially. The cipher signifies presence and absence simultaneously. In psychoanalytic terms, the void of nothingness represents the fear of castration. The circle represents the elements–the stars, planets and orbs. "God is a circle (or sphere) whose center is everywhere and whose circumference is nowhere" (254). On the other hand, the magic circle is a parody of God's creative energies. Paradoxically, the Globe Theatre itself is a "wooden O."

144. ---. "A Bibliography of Psychoanalytic and Psychological Writings on Shakespeare: 1964-1978." In Schwartz and Kahn, item 136. 264-88.

This bibliography, which includes 461 entries, is "elastic" and "wide enough" to include "studies of Shakespeare and his art that focus on such issues as identity, family, sexuality, irrationality, creativity, aggression, narcissism, role playing, dreams, play, ambivalence, or anxiety and that employ the terms and techniques of psychological theory or use interpretive strategies that rely on an awareness of such theory" (264).

145. Williams, Mary C. "So Loving-Jealous of His Liberty: Possessiveness and Dependency in Shakespeare's Women." In *A Fair Day in the Affections: Literary Essays in Honor of Robert B. White, Jr.* Ed. Jack D. Durant and M. Thomas Hester. Raleigh, NC: Winston, 1980. 55-66.

The wedding is a symbol of reconciliation in Shakespeare's comedies, yet a complete picture of a married women is never given. One of the problems of marriage in Shakespeare is the possessive wife who wants to control her husband. Ironically, a woman's possessiveness stems from her absolute submission to her spouse. Juliet wishes to adopt the traditional role of woman and be governed by Romeo, but her love transforms him into a prisoner of her love and possessiveness. Unmarried women and newlyweds have more independence than do hardened wives. "However motivated, women are given a dominating role that can continue so long as a marriage has not been consummated or the couple has not really settled down together" (58). Because Shakespeare's women are relatively independent, they do not readily accept the complete obedience required through submission. The benign power they possess makes them more self-sufficient. In marriage, "the assumption of male garb and roles is no longer possible" (60). Possessiveness grows from their passive and dependent lives. Women like Kate Percy need to know their husbands' business in order to have some influence over the male decision-making process. If Hotspur does not tell Kate what is making him uneasy, it means that he does not love her; if Hotspur doesn't love her, then Kate cannot love herself.

146. Wolf, Alexander. "Diegophrenia and Genius." *American Journal of Psychoanalysis* 40 (1980): 213-26. Esp. "Shakespeare," 213-17.

Shakespeare may have suffered from diegophrenia, a split personality producing ambivalence and associated with denied maternal love. Developed between birth and age two, this personality trait is reflected in Shakespeare's family history (with his mother and his wife) and in his plays. Mothers are loving and destructive. Through Romeo, Shakespeare associates "death with his mother's mouth." Shakespeare is ambivalently "crying out to his mother" in need of her and yet expressing "his wish for her death in her unavailability to him" (215). Shakespeare's "heroic selves slay their mothers in his plays" yet seek silence in a peaceful, maternal earth. Acting through Hamlet, the "clearest clinical description of diegophrenia to the present time" (216), Shakespeare poisons "his mother surrogate in Gertrude." Lady Macbeth, the mad Ophelia, and the untamed Kate all point to Shakespeare's ambivalence toward women. Shakespeare "sought ego-reinforcement" in his all-male theatre troupe and like Hamlet asserted his own ego by devising plays. Like other diegophrenic geniuses, Shakespeare was "unwilling to let things be as they are" (224).

1981

147. Asp, Carolyn. "'Be bloody, bold and resolute': Tragic Action and Sexual Stereotyping in *Macbeth*." *Studies in Philology* 78 (1981): 153-69.

Sexual stereotyping is "central to the tragic action" of *Mac* (153). Macbeth adopts a stereotypical model of manliness based on violence and murder to be free from fear and conscience and acquire godlike powers. Yet in overcoming the limitations imposed on him by the stereotype, Macbeth becomes inhuman. In his warrior society, judging from Malcolm and Macduff's actions, women are considered weak victims, not privy to their husbands' plans. Yet Lady Macbeth rejects her own womanliness that she associates with such stereotypical weakness. Unchauvinistically, Macbeth at first confides in her as she couches the entire matter of murder in "sexual terms," chiding him for "arousing her expectations and then failing to follow through ... " (160). Exhorting him to potency, Lady Macbeth negates the very feminine powers which allowed her to manipulate Macbeth. By assuming a masculine role, she does not bring them together but drives them farther apart. The Weird Sisters, whose hermaphroditic appearance removes them from sexual stereotypes, promise Macbeth preternatural knowledge which for him is a "kind of masculine sexual equivalent" (165). The end of the play finds Lady Macbeth isolated from the masculine world and Macbeth surrounded by boys who display a "feminine principle" (167). Ironically, the manly valor Macbeth displayed in

Act 1 is mirrored by Macduff, showing that "society's continued
acceptance of the values and stereotypes ... paradoxically both
threaten it and guarantee its continuation" (168).

148. Berger, Harry, Jr. "Marriage and Mercifixion in *The Merchant of
     Venice*: The Casket Scene Revisited." *Shakespeare Quarterly* 32
     (1981): 155-62.

     The father-child conflict central to *MV* leads to the "consequent
     overlapping of family politics with sexual politics" (157). Fathers
     like Gloucester in *Lear* see sons as an investment while daughters
     are "assigned the role of commodity in the alliance market" (156).
     In bondage to her father's will, Portia is like Hesione (Act 3.2.56),
     a maiden to be sacrificed. Her own words "I stand for sacrifice"
     to Bassanio are fruitfully ambiguous. One meaning, though–"I
     demand sacrifice"–sheds light on whether she gives Bassanio clues
     about choosing the lead casket. While the script is not clear-cut
     about such help, the possibility "hovers tantalizingly in the air of
     their language" (160). Portia is caught between her desire from
     the "law of love" and her apprehension that she is not "the rightful
     owner" of her own person. While she and Bassanio may not be
     fully aware of the "conspiratorial possibilities," the script offers
     "submerged resonances" and "subtextual implications" (160) for
     such betrayals. Of course, Portia would like to help Bassanio, but
     she does not want to be forsworn. Undeniably, she departs
     company from Jessica who blatantly gives Lorenzo a casket.
     Released from her father's will, Portia establishes "control over
     herself and Bassanio" through her generosity. Bassanio's defense
     that he gave Portia's ring to another man indicts male pride and
     superiority over women by revealing his belief that a male pledge
     of sacrifice supersedes any made by a woman. Unlike Antonio
     who welcomes crucifixion, Portia like a Jewish mother uses acts
     of sacrifice and mercy ("mercifixion") to "sink hooks of gratitude
     and obligation deep into the beneficiary's bowels" (161).

149. Blits, Jan H. "Manliness and Friendship in Shakespeare's *Julius
     Caesar*." *Interpretation* 9.2-3 (1981): 155-67.

"No one in *Caesar* has a good word for women" (155). Even Portia denigrates her sex. Manly qualities of strength, honor, and independence are judged superior to womanly softness, sharing, and dependence. The private world and sleep for Brutus and other Romans destroy manliness. Through her "self-inflicted wound," Portia tries to prove her constancy but her "manly endurance quickly" vanishes. Manliness in Brutus's Rome means more than love or friendship as signaled in his quarrel with Cassius whom he chastises for anger, "a womanish spirit" unbecoming a man. Manliness in *JC* is ultimately "a contentious virtue" (159), "self-consuming" and unaffectionate. Cassius becomes the "leading republican example of the tension between manliness and womanliness" (161), pulled between being close to someone else and being pulled away. "As Cassius's suicide points to the limits of closeness among Roman men, so Portia's shows the limits of sharing in a Roman marriage" (162). Unable to dwell in Brutus's heart, she is denied his intimacy and confidence. Ironically, she can get no closer to Brutus than can the men around him. While her suicide is done for conjugal love, his is to master other men's hearts which ultimately separates him from family, friends, and Rome itself.

150. Bowers, Robin A. "Iconography and Rhetoric in Shakespeare's *Lucrece.*" *Shakespeare Studies* 14 (1981): 1-21.

Critics such as Roy Battenhouse (*Shakespearean Tragedy: Its Art and Christian Premises* [1969]) blame Lucrece for being a "guilty accomplice" to her own rape and decry her rhetorical excesses as characteristically feminine. Challenging such views, Shakespeare's poem follows the literary and artistic tradition that bestowed a "stellar reputation" on Lucrece for her chastity, constancy, and suffering. Lucrece was a popular subject in conduct books, exempla, plays, and paintings (by Titian and Veronese, for example), all of which emphasized her virtues "to be more important than the violence of her death" (9). Shakespeare "symbolically individualized" (17) Lucrece to illustrate a key Renaissance theme that personal decisions have "social consequences" (16), that rape leads to destruction. The "forensic

structure" of *RL* vindicates Shakespeare's heroine from
Battenhouse's vengeful Augustinianism. The internal monologues
by Lucrece and Tarquin as well as "the extensive use of narrative
commentary" (11) arouse pity for her. The omniscient narrator
"belies" the critics' claim that Lucrece was guilty by her silence;
instead, her cries for help are "stifled in the silence of narrative
report, just as Tarquin stifled them" (13). Lucrece's extended
expression of grief and despair are justified. Beyond doubt *RL*
"confirms the Renaissance admiration for its heroine" (18).

151. Cook, Ann Jennalie. "Wooing and Wedding: Shakespeare's
     Dramatic Distortions of the Customs of His Time." In
     Shakespeare's Art from A Comparative Perspective. Vol. 12.
     Proceedings of the Comparative Literature Symposium. Ed.
     Wendell M. Aycock. Lubbock: Texas Tech UP, 1981. 83-100.

Accepted Elizabethan marriage practices differed radically
from ours. Social history documents when Shakespeare distorted
or reflected these customs, providing a better sense of his
dramatic purpose. Renaissance marriages were based on financial
considerations (not romantic love); the authority for arranging a
marriage rested with parents, guardians, or the court, which
expressed sharp disapproval of any transgressions. In *TSh*, the
"earliest, longest, and most obvious commentary on the marriage
market" (87), Petruchio conforms to the orthodox image of a man
marrying to enlarge his estate. While Petruchio's wooing is
realistic, the wooing of Bianca is absurd. Gremio could not give
all his wealth as a jointure; nor could Tranio sign away his father's
estate. Lucentio and Bianca violate marriage laws since their
contract was not approved by Baptista. Following conventions,
Petruchio secures a better deal than do Lucentio and Hortensio.
Nonetheless, Shakespeare "may be arching an eyebrow at
marriage-for-money" as well as "marriage-for love" (92). Bassanio
would not be regarded as "mercenary or selfish" but as a wise
man to replace his lost fortune. In *MV* Jessica is entitled to the
judgment for her inheritance, and Antonio would be praised for
serving as a loving father surrogate to her as well as to Bassanio.
Buying and selling wives is at the heart of *MM*, though the men

do get more than they deserve. It is unlikely that Shakespeare "held firm, consistent views on the marriage practices of his day" (97).

152. Dash, Irene G. *Wooing, Wedding, and Power: Women in Shakespeare's Plays.* New York: Columbia UP, 1981.

Chapter One, "The Introduction: Their Infinite Variety," explores the multiple virtues of Shakespeare's women who challenged accepted patterns for women's behavior by displaying independence and self-control–Hermione will not cry, but Leontes cries in self-pity; Desdemona and Juliet defy their fathers and society. Illustrating the inequity between men and women, Shakespeare's portrayal of strong women questions the power structure. Queen Elizabeth's life dramatized a woman's potential for greatness as well as the subordination that a patriarchal society mandated for her if she were to marry. Shakespeare's women develop self-confidence when they discover that they are merely "Other." Through cuts and changes in lines and stage directions, critics and directors have through the centuries often distorted and limited the women's roles. But the plays "show the diversity of the mind of a sixteenth-century man whose understanding of the human condition extended beyond his own sex and beyond his own time" (6).

In Chapter Two, "Oath-Taking: *Love's Labour's Lost*," women constitute the subject of the men's vows that Shakespeare mocks. The male tradition of oath-taking is forcibly linked with honesty as the women reject the timeless oath of marriage. It is the women who are skeptical about oaths. Navarre demands compliance to his oath, and threatens exclusion from the group if his comrades do not comply. Although women are not seen as equals, the Princess of France is more independent because her father has endorsed her as a person. She expresses ideas common to women but seldom articulated and laughs at the Petrarchan tradition that dictates praise of a woman's beauty and insists on honesty and rejects flattery. More than a creature sent to flatter the king's ego, the Princess is a competent administrator showing women's intellectual and moral strengths. *LLL* explores the "meaning of woman as a key to perceiving truth" (30). Ultimately, the play asks us to adopt "new attitudes toward women. It suggests seeing them as full, complex individual characters."

Chapter Three, "Challenging Patterns: *The Taming of the Shrew*," argues that though Kate has no soliloquies, she reveals herself through her actions and speeches. David Garrick wrongly assigned her last act speech on obedience to Petruchio, characterizing Kate misleadingly as "a woman beaten rather than as a person who has learned a new game and who will eventually excel in it" (58). The marriage between Kate and Petruchio is not consummated on the wedding night because it would be rape, and Kate has to learn to behave in a way that will allow the sexual act to take place properly and with dignity. Petruchio's "respect for Kate's right to ownership of her body, while it may take time for her to appreciate, eventually becomes an important key to their relationship." Shakespeare does not release Kate's shrewish behavior until Act 2. He creates surface portraits of a shrew and a beautiful woman in the sisters. Petruchio's wooing of Kate is a contest of wits, demonstrating Kate's intelligence and quick wit. A man of imagination and humor, Petruchio is sensitive to her as an individual. Thus, she is willing to accept him as an equal because of the status and respect she receives within the marriage. She discovers in Petruchio "more than a husband in a hostile world: she has found a friend" (61).

In Chapter Four on "Growing Up: *Romeo and Juliet*," critics and directors find Juliet's young age a problem and in productions references to her age are often removed. Yet the emphasis Shakespeare places on Juliet's age suggests a determination to explore the responses of a teenage girl to the process of growing up and the meaning of marriage. We need to look at Juliet from the perspective of Simone de Beauvoir's theory of adult female development; the fourteen-year-old Juliet reflects Shakespeare's desire to "catch that wonderful struggling age before docility begins" (86). Juliet has both her mother and the Nurse as adult women role models, but they ultimately fail her. There is formality and distance between Juliet and Lady Capulet. Exchanges between Juliet and the Nurse further develop Shakespeare's portrait of the adolescent who seeks an acceptable model for her actions. Juliet regards herself as the "essential" person. Shakespeare shows Romeo's immaturity at the opening of the play in order to reveal his growth as well as Juliet's as the drama progresses. Juliet's tragedy grows out of the "conflict between her humanity and her gender." Because of her youth, she has not yet learned to renounce her self-sovereignty. Juliet can lay claim to courage and directness of action more truly than Romeo can. The "play's uniqueness lies in its portrait of a young girl who remains strong during her swift growth to womanhood" (93). Like Garrick, nineteenth-century critics transformed Juliet into a pawn; Juliet must be seen as a "major tragic protagonist" (98).

Chapter Five on "A Woman Tamed: *Othello*" explores how *Oth* raises questions left unanswered by the swift deaths of the star-crossed lovers. *Oth* asks whether the passion and idealism of two lovers who have courageously crossed color lines and defied conventions can be sustained in marriage. Although *Oth* examines marriage, it is not a domestic tragedy; it is the tragedy of a woman shaped by convention. Desdemona speaks for youth, sexual honesty, and passion. Until Othello and Desdemona marry, they do not experience tragedy since they do not have to conform to any set roles; they function as two individuals. Marriage, however, imposes new constraints. Tragically, man and woman have entered into an unconventional marriage but lack the strength to maintain it. Desdemona submits to a role–a wife–society imposes on her. In numerous productions, she is transformed from the assertive and persuasive woman of Act 1 to someone who loses her individuality. Desdemona's tragedy is "a slow wearing away of the resistance, a slow imposition of patterns–a slow loss of confidence in the strength of self, always with the aim of adjusting to marriage" (104).

In Chapter Six, "Courageous Wives: *The Winter's Tale*," Shakespeare develops two strong women who learn the limits of marriage and the importance of their own personal value. Hermione appears happy in her own sexuality while Paulina is satisfied with her marriage and confident of her husband. But unlike Hermione, Paulina is less a conformist, more an independent person. Both women learn to "defy the dominance of male rule and find their own human worth." Male jealousy forces the women to rethink their priorities, learning that dependency, while it may be comfortable, is also threatening. Hermione and Paulina manage their own lives. Shakespeare first presents his characters in traditional roles before he "chips away at their sex-linked differences." Leontes's irrationality contrasts with Paulina's rationality. His jealousy may spring from the reverse of penis envy; he envies Hermione because she is pregnant. Antigonus is Shakespeare's more subtle counterpart to Paulina. As she assumes more male qualities, he assumes more of the weaknesses supposedly characterizing the female. Rather than being pure fantasy, *WT* presents women at different stages of self-knowledge, who mature and discover their own strengths. Shakespeare questions the validity and assumptions behind gender stereotypes. To present Hermione and Paulina as mystic figures diminishes their power as women, as "fully developed characters ... exciting models ... liberated women" (138).

In Chapter Seven, "The Paradox of Power: The *Henry VI–Richard III* Tetralogy," Shakespeare dramatizes the meaning of power for women–its nearness and its distance. Unlike Hermione and Paulina, the queens and duchesses in *R3* have great difficulty sympathizing with others of their sex. For "a brief moment, a wielder of power" (191), Margaret shows and believes power may erase differences with the men with whom she deals. That women imitate men in seeking success indicates they rely on the frightening political models from men. Unfortunately, she has seen few worth imitating. Like the men, Margaret trains for war and acquires the necessary callousness to engage in war's violence. Even though Margaret goes into battle, she retains a sense of herself as a woman. Still, she is callous, dangerous. For that reason Olivier omitted her from his production of *R3*. While *2H6* dramatized a husband's control of his wife's right to exercise power, *3H6* reveals a woman's new role as parent. Margaret acts the warrior to regain the title of king for her son. By the close of the play, the women's roles have shifted. Margaret, widowed and childless, is a bitter person while Elizabeth, although previously widowed, is wife, queen and mother of new life. Widows in *R3* learn that their husbands were not the only source of their power or their identity.

In Chapter Eight, "Union of Roles: *Antony and Cleopatra*," Shakespeare suggests that a woman of power has the unusual opportunity of combining her sexual and political selves. Cleopatra is a "woman of genius." The male characters express society's views and so challenge Cleopatra's self-sovereignty. The patriarchal men find it difficult to accept such a woman who is sexually alive and politically aware of her role as ruler. It is wrong to "identify" with Enobarbus's "point of view" about Cleopatra (212). Antony only speaks to her as a woman. Yet like Cleopatra, Antony shifts back and forth between presenting himself as a sexual being and as a political person. "Because [Cleopatra] owns herself and is not dependent except when she herself wills a dependency, Antony has great difficulty trusting her" (237). The real stereotypical woman is Octavia who derives her identity from her relationship with husband and brother. Shakespeare "minimizes audience sympathy for Octavia" in part because of a possible "incestuous bond" between her and her brother Caesar (226). In front of Caesar, Cleopatra speaks of her own womanly frailties, which she knows he believes belong exclusively to the weaker sex. Even at the moment of death, Cleopatra links her personal with her public self.

In the last chapter, "Emerging from the Shadows," Shakespeare's women exist within a patriarchal world where they must think of themselves as "Other" and man as primary or "Subject." But they are women of intelligence and intellectual vigor. The boy actors do not seem to have diminished the validity of the portraits of strong women, for the women transcend stereotypes. A woman's right to control her own body is an issue for many of Shakespeare's characters. Concentration on the women illuminates the conflict between the ideals and perspectives that women and men may bring to marriage.

Reviews: Bank, Rosemary K., *Theatre Journal* 35 (1983): 129-32; Carr, Virginia M., *Shakespeare on Film Newsletter* 7.1 (1982): 7; *Choice* 19 (1982): 1066; Free, Mary G., *Shakespeare Studies* 16 (1984): 340-43; Hageman, Elizabeth H., *Shakespeare Quarterly* 35 (1984): 126-28; Halten, Burton, *Review* 8 (1986): 241-64; Hoy, Cyrus, *Sewanee Review* 92 (1984): 256-70; Leimberg, Irene, *Shakespeare Jahrbuch* 118 (1983): 242-48; Lerner, L., *Times*

Literary Supplement 4 June 1982: 619; Pugh, Elaine Upton, *Medieval and Renaissance Drama in England* 2 (1985): 311-13; Rose, Mary Beth, *Modern Philology* 81 (1984): 308-11; Roxman, Susanna, *Dagens Nyheter* 5 (Apr. 1982).

153. Erickson, Peter B. "The Failure of Relationship between Men and Women in *Love's Labor's Lost.*" *Women's Studies* 9 (1981): 65-81.

   See item 284.

154. Ferris, Diane. "Elizabeth I and *Richard II*: Portraits in 'Masculine' and 'Feminine' Princes." *International Journal of Women's Studies* 4 (1981): 10-18.

   Because of her "masculine" triumphs, Queen Elizabeth "had unmistakenly belied the female stereotype" of a weak woman (10). Denying "the sexual hierarchy" (11), Elizabeth remained a virgin so as not to lose control of her own fate. Yet having to depend on a woman for their well-being created tensions for many men. Shakespeare's plays offered a subtle protest to a woman on the throne by "indicating a dissatisfaction with women ... that runs deeper than mere sexual preference can explain" (13). Hence, the plays present evil queens, masculine-acting women in need of taming, and a-political heroines who seek love, not political power. The "culmination" of this critical "impulse" (13) was *R2*, where a womanly King Richard injures his face in "the looking-glass episode" the way a raped woman seeks self-destruction. A queen with Richard's characteristics would allow us to label Shakespeare's play a "feminine tragedy" (14). Shakespeare's audience would agree it was bad to have a woman as king, yet they would have taken pity on her (as with Richard) for her weakness. Elizabeth, who saw herself as Richard, doubtless read Shakespeare's hidden message (17), though she magnanimously did not punish him for it.

155. French, Marilyn. *Shakespeare's Division of Experience.* New York: Summit, 1981.

The "Introduction" maintains that all human traditions define gender principles and their relationship to nature. The "most realized expression, the most complete awareness" of these principles is found in Shakespeare (16). Beginning his career with suspicion of female qualities and respect for masculine ones, Shakespeare by the end of that career "had come to fear and deplore the power and capriciousness of the masculine principle, and to idealize certain aspects of the feminine" (17). He tried throughout his life to synthesize, harmonize these two principles.

Chapter One, "The Gender Principles," defines the masculine as "linear, temporal, transcendent," occupied with the individual's quest for immortality. The feminine principle can be split into inlaw and outlaw aspects. The outlaw, which subverts the masculine, is "associated with darkness, chaos, the flesh, the sinister, magic, and above all, sexuality" (23); it also glorifies pleasure, rebels against masculine permanency, and attempts to castrate the male. Yet this inlaw feminine principle represents the "benevolent manifestations of nature," and nourishes the masculine principle associated with civilization. Women, who are seen as nonhuman and under male control, must not challenge legitimate male power. Shakespeare's women are not changed by their experience but the men are. Women are utterly good or utterly bad. While men are urged to incorporate the inlaw principle, females must not incorporate the masculine (except in disguise) or, like Lady Macbeth, Joan of Arc, and Goneril, risk being branded as unnatural. Men have some sexual freedom in Shakespeare; women, however, must bear the "onus of sexuality." The inlaw principle has been seen as divine, linked to Christian selflessness. Shakespeare's "nightmare visions always involve the destruction of the qualities of the feminine principle by masculine abuse of power" (30). Though Shakespeare experienced a "dis-ease with sexuality supposedly incarnate in women," which turned to a "terrified loathing," he still maintained that rulers must possess the benevolent qualities of the feminine principle.

In Chapter Two, "Formal Equivalents of the Gender Principles," literary forms are seen as masculine or feminine. Feminine works are concerned with interior experiences, emotions, love, and sex rather than with the masculine emphasis on power and justice. Shakespeare's works "may be roughly divided into gender categories by division into comedy and tragedy" (34), though most of the plays demonstrate Shakespeare's attempts to synthesize the two. Shakespearean comedy is feminine, dealing with community and harmony; it is "circular, tied to nature and eternal recurrence" (37). The comedies lack strong plots, move by elaboration, and show multiple characters with multiple goals. Embodying the paradoxes of the masculine principle, the tragedies deal with power, are hierarchal with one character dominating, and end in disintegration as opposed to comedy's expansiveness. Because of their focus on "power-in-the-world," the histories are "primarily" masculine (38). The problem plays are "mixtures."

Chapter Three deals with "Power: The First Tetralogy. *Henry VI, Parts One, Two, and Three; Richard III.*" In *1H6*, the English represent the masculine principle of power, prowess and courage; the French because of their magic are associated with the outlaw feminine principle. Hence, the war is between the two most powerful areas of the gender principles. Gloucester and Winchester accuse each other of being under the domination of a woman or the feminine principle. The influence of women is seen as malign throughout the trilogy. In portraying Joan of Arc as sexually promiscuous and an evil figure, Shakespeare goes far beyond his sources that declared Joan a virgin. In *2H6*, Margaret takes over Joan's role; women, love, and marriage are corrupting. The problem of legitimacy is connected with the relations between man and woman. We are shown the feminine principle in revolt, and women striving for mastery. Richard III's misogyny is a general attitude toward life.

Chapter Four, "Marriage: *The Comedy of Errors* and *The Taming of the Shrew,*" argues that the main focus in these plays is on the male characters, and the major interest is disguise. Ephesus is identified with witchcraft, and sexual freedom–the outlaw feminine principle. However, the surface life is firmly in control of the masculine principle. The two gender principles appear at their worst at the opening of the play. The feminine is outlaw, connected with sorcery and the rebellious; the masculine is oppressive and inhumane. *CE* comes out firmly on the side of bondage as opposed to freedom. *TSh* focuses on marriage as the foundation of a happy and orderly life, but marriage is a purchase agreement made between two men. If the audience condones Petruchio's actions, then his treatment of Kate is judged humane because he does not beat her. Without audience approval, his actions are judged as torture and brainwashing. Kate's transformation is an education in upholding the inlaw feminine principle, and she is taught this by being punished by oppressive masculine power.

Chapter Five, "Constancy: *The Two Gentlemen of Verona, Love's Labour's Lost,* and *A Midsummer Night's Dream,*" finds that in *TGV* magnetic power, or the power to draw others to one, is feminine. Inlaw qualities are located in the female hero, while outlaw qualities are invested in clowns, thus diffusing the feminine principle. The political attitude inherent in the feminine principle is anarchy. Constancy fuses the gender principles. "The core of Shakespeare's vision synthesizes the gender principles, and the beauty of that union ... irradiates the comedies. Where this synthesis is lacking, it is palpably lacking, and edges the play towards or into tragedy" (92). Constancy works as a moral standard and also connects language and sexuality. It is magic in the female characters. As in *TGV*, constancy is abused by men in *LLL*. The ladies stand largely as the ideal in this world that abuses the feminine principle. Finally, in *MND*, constancy is opposed to imagination. Love is a principle of the universe; but like the moon, it is inconstant only within a larger pattern of constancy.

In Chapter Six, "Money: *The Merchant of Venice* and *The Merry Wives of Windsor,*" love in *MND* is "primarily erotic"; in *MWW*, love is treated as possession. In *MV* Venice is dominated by the masculine principle, while Belmont is controlled by the feminine. Venice is absorbed by money matters tied to such masculine values as honor, reputation, and fame. Money is the equivalent of love. Women are usually bought and sold in marriage, but as a wealthy woman, Portia is able to buy herself a husband. Because of its moral flexibility, Belmont tries to balance human needs and desires. Portia adopts her disguise and enters the masculine world to save a fellow human being. The setting of *MWW* is

overwhelmingly masculine, valuing the possession of property and
woman and fearing theft. Ford's fear of cuckoldry is a fear of
theft. "The feminine elements of the play–chaste constancy in the
wives, love in Anne, and Falstaff's outlaw feminine sexual
rebellion–become mere counters in a conflict over property" (107).
In Chapter Seven on "The Realm of Emotion: *As You Like
It* and *Twelfth Night*," *AYL* portrays the underside of society,
which includes women, exiles, the poor, and the low-born. To
these, power looks oppressive, and those who have it are tyrants.
Even though Celia and Rosalind are well-born, they still have
fringe status, which they do not complain about. Like these two
women, Orlando is portrayed as androgynous. Arden is a feminine
world which exists in anarchy. In coming to the strange land of
Illyria, Viola lacks a gender identity. Love of life as well as sexual
love are questioned in *TN*. Sir Toby and his friends, who love life
in a basic child-like way, exemplify the outlaw feminine principle
because they enjoy sensuous pleasure and defy order. The villain
of the play is Malvolio; all of the characters except Malvolio and
Feste are connected through love or love of pleasure with the
feminine principle.

"Chaste Constancy: *Much Ado About Nothing*," the subject of
Chapter Eight, explores the concept as a synthesis of gender
principles that Shakespeare usually associates with women.
Female constancy is linked to chastity which, in turn, is a symbol
of female integrity. Chastity is an active virtue rather than a
passive one, but chastity defers to male ownership of females. In
Ado, chaste constancy is the foundation of civilization. For
Shakespeare, female sexual power was "mainly political because
free sexuality is rebellion." Rebellion in the feminine form arises
out of a sense of powerlessness. Female sexual freedom
constitutes a threat as great as a natural catastrophe. Men who
surrender themselves to sex were seen as unmanly and bewitched
by the power of the outlaw feminine principle. Don John is an
example of the outlaw feminine because of his opposition to the
established order. Beatrice mocks male pretenses and
prerogatives.

Chapter Nine, "The Problem Plays: *Hamlet, Troilus and
Cressida, All's Well That Ends Well*, and *Measure for Measure*,"

finds the romantic attachment in these plays creates an atmosphere of sexual disgust arising from the insistence that human nature transcends animal instinct. Moreover, for the masculine principle to gain complete power over the feminine principle, sex has to be illegitimated and degraded. Thus in *Ham*, Claudius's treachery is damned by the Ghost, not because of the murder, but because of his seduction of Gertrude. The Ghost's real fury is directed against Gertrude. Her remarriage violates Hamlet's sensibilities because it betrays his mother's sexual desire which existed before King Hamlet's death. Loss of faith in the inlaw feminine principle leads to loss of faith in male legitimacy. The love theme of *TrC* rests on an assumption of female infidelity. "Cressida shows herself easy in the world and knowledgeable about sexual matters in a way no other Shakespearean heroine is; not even Cleopatra is shown in such a light" (164). Chaste constancy has value in *AWW* and therefore power. The inlaw feminine principle, which wars with the masculine, insists on its ability to heal society. Unlike *AWW*, *MM* is set in an atmosphere of sin and filth where sexual revulsion surfaces. In Vienna the outlaw characters revel in sexuality which is on trial because it is judged a crime. Claudio and Juliet emphasize the pleasant and loving nature of sex while Isabella escapes from this tainted world of sexuality to a convent.

In Chapter Ten on "The Late Tragedies," the city of Venice in *Oth* is dominated by reason, which suggests control of human nature, but man's nature is seen as depraved. Othello represents ideal control while Iago is too controlled. Othello idealizes love while Iago demeans it, hating the feminine principle. Women and the qualities they possess are trivialized. When Othello thinks he is finally unable to domesticate Desdemona, he has to kill her, illustrating the only two methods of control available to him. "With Cordelia and Hermione, Desdemona represents the inlaw feminine principle at its most superhuman" (216). The witches in *Mac* portray ambiguity of gender; they are female, but have beards. The outer world of the play maintains itself by violence, while the inner world unites the gender principles. Whereas Macbeth violates moral law, Lady Macbeth violates natural law by failing to uphold the feminine principle. In a more positive way,

AC presents the outlaw feminine principle embodied in a powerful female. Roman values are concerned with masculine power while Egypt is rooted in the feminine. *Cor* and *Tim* take place in worlds where the feminine principle is almost completely lacking.

In the final chapter, "The Romances: *Pericles, Cymbeline, The Winter's Tale,* and *The Tempest,*" these plays represent a kind of peacemaking with the world, reconciling masculine and feminine principles. In all four plays the masculine element has worldly power while the feminine does not. Without its erotic component, the feminine principle is divine in Shakespeare. The problem with the romances is that "drama requires conflict, action, and does not lend itself easily to the depiction of the feminine principle" (289). The feminine principle is exiled, just as it is in the tragedies; but in the romances it endures the exile while the males suffer from its absence. Men learn that the responsibility for maintaining chastity is no longer placed exclusively on the female. In *Per,* father-daughter incest combines abuse of power with sexual abuse and is a prime symbol for misuse of both gender principles. Because of the feminine nature of Cymbeline's Britain, it is necessary that it be protected by a masculine power. Masculine power operates in the romances mainly in the domestic sphere. Paulina supports the feminine principle, but does so in an assertive and forceful way. Hermione is a representative of the inlaw feminine principle. In *Tem* Caliban, who is an amoral not an evil character, is a mother's child and so represents the outlaw feminine principle. He cannot be tamed and brought in line with masculine values. Miranda, on the other hand, represents the inlaw feminine principle.

Reviews: Ashley, Leonard R.N., *Bibliotheque d'Humanisme et Renaissance* 47 (1985): 186; Bank, Rosemarie K., *Theatre Journal* 35 (1983): 131; Bayley, John, *London Review of Books* 20 May-2 June 1982: 5-6; Burgess, Anthony, *Observer* 14 Mar. 1982: 30; Burrows, Jill, *Times Educational Supplement* 8 June 1984: 32; Cohen, Eileen E., *College Literature* 9 (1982): 69-70; Desai, Rupin, *Hamlet Studies* 8 (1986): 115-26; Gibbons, Brian, *Shakespeare Survey* 37 (1984): 179-80; Greer, Germaine, *Sunday Times* (London) 4 Apr. 1982: 41; Hartman, Geoffrey, *New York Times*

Book Review 22 Mar. 1981: 11-19; Heilbrun, Carolyn G., *Signs* 8 (1982): 182-86; Hunter, G.K., *Sewanee Review* 90 (1982): 273-79; Kimbrough, Robert, *Shakespeare Studies* 15 (1982): 343-47; Lerner, Laurence, *Times Literary Supplement* 4 June 1982: 619; Schabert, I., *Shakespeare Jahrbuch* 122 (1986): 223-29; Schoenbaum, S., *Book World* 8 Mar. 1981: 1-2; Scragg, Leah, *Critical Quarterly* 24 (1982): 83-84; Widmann, R.L., *Library Journal* 106 (1981): 1223; Williams, David, *Punch* 5 May 1982: 746. See also items 180, 217.

156. Garber, Marjorie. *Coming of Age in Shakespeare.* London and New York: Metheun, 1981. Esp. "Women's Rites: 'As Secret As Maidenhead,'" 116-73.

Elizabethan marriage rites had five steps: 1) financial contract between parents; 2) spousals; 3) proclamations of banns; 4) church ceremony; and 5) sexual consummation. Marriages in Shakespeare's plays are placed in the context of these rites. The relationship of Claudio and Juliet in *MM* is complicated by the betrothal process. *RJ* presupposes some guilt on the part of the young lovers for rejecting parental counsel. However, Shakespeare frequently emancipated his protagonists from rigidly prescribed gender roles in their sexual rites of passage. These rites can be divided into three phases: "sexual self-knowledge as manifested in attitudes towards virginity, chastity, and sexuality; actual rites, like marriage, defloration, child-bearing, and nursing; and symbolic or metaphorical representations of sexual themes" (128). Shakespeare advocates virginity, but only as a stage in the sexual process. Miranda, Diana in *AWW*, and Marina are all praised for their chastity, but all three are on their way to becoming brides. The characters who militantly embrace abstinence as a way of life, however, are not so generously drawn.

In *MM*, Angelo's avowed celibacy thinly covers his lustful nature, and Isabella's ritualized chastity parallels her passionless insensitivity. Shakespeare's characters, in order to mature, must acknowledge and accept their own sexuality. Defloration acts in the plays are represented through aubades and sometimes through symbolic staging, such as Desdemona's spotted handkerchief. In

AYL, the bloodied napkin is clearly a symbol of sexual initiation. "Orlando, the male lover, participates in a symbolic ritual exclusively associated with women, offering a cloth spotted with his own blood as a sign of his purity and fidelity" (146).

Childbirth and pregnancy are ritualistically portrayed and associated with the fecundity in nature while barrenness is linked to spiritual sterility. Infertility in *Lear* symbolizes an "unnaturalness" which is carried to extreme in metaphors describing parents feeding on children and children feeding on parents. In *TA*, cannibalism is literal rather than metaphoric in a pathological inversion of the birthing process.

Sexuality is symbolically represented in the flower imagery of Ophelia and Perdita, maidens who, instead of being "deflowered," give their flowers away. Whereas flowers represent the fragility of virginity, the "treasure" in *Cym* and *MV* demonstrates its value. In *MV*, once the casket is opened, the treasure is replaced by another sexual symbol, the ring. "Of all the symbols Shakespeare uses to denote sexual activity and sexual rites of passage in the plays, the most traditional of all is the walled garden" (163). This image contains the other symbols: it is a circular enclosure which contains flowers. The best example, of course, is in *RJ*. Juliet progresses from "paternal domination to sensual submission and thence to individuation through pain and sacrifice" (170).

157. Garner, Shirley Nelson. "*A Midsummer Night's Dream:* 'Jack Shall Have Jill/Nought Shall Go Ill.'" *Women's Studies* 9 (1981): 47-63.

The resolution of *MND*, which "resembles a fertility rite" (47), depends on the men breaking the bonds the women have established with each other. In doing this, the men also satisfy their own "homoerotic desire" (54). Oberon covets the Indian boy whom he sees as a threat because of Titania's love for the child. In gaining the boy, Oberon further separates Titania from the boy's mother whom she loved. Having a reputation as a "deserter of women" (53), Theseus conquers Hippolita; yet her "androgynous appearance," fitting for an Amazon hunter, suggests that through her Theseus may "fulfill a male fantasy." By insisting that his daughter marry a man she does not love, Egeus wants to have her "exclusive love" as well as "to accommodate his homoerotic feelings by binding Demetrius to him" (56). Hermia and Helena are the only "women characters in Shakespeare's plays [who] come close to fighting physically" (58). Their friendship is permanently disrupted to make them ready for marriage and male domination. They never "reconcile" with each other, and their silence in Act 5 underscores their subjugation to their husbands. The return to order, therefore, signals "the restoration of patriarchal hierarchy" (59) and the end of feminine bonds. In contrast, Portia and Nerissa maintain a strong bond of friendship in *MV*, though there is "reconciliation, but not celebration" (60).

158. Greene, Gayle. "Feminist and Marxist Criticism: An Argument for Alliances." *Women's Studies* 9 (1981): 29-45.

Feminist criticism of Shakespeare exhibits "certain similarities with Marxist criticism" (30), most noticeably in the "critique of the values of patriarchy" which are "inherent in capitalism" (41). In addition to examining patriarchy, feminist critics of Shakespeare "explore such questions as the relation of his characterization of men and women" and the "assumptions of his time and ours" (32). Feminist critics are "nearly as concerned with the biases of Shakespeare's interpreters" as they are with Shakespeare. Feminist criticism is "in fundamental accord with Marxist criticism" (32); the two revolutionary movements are eclectic, interdisciplinary, and dialectical. Concerned with social change, they are "radical and radicalizing" in challenging the myths on which oppressive political structures are based. However, Marxist interpretations of Shakespeare "tend to be stuck in one groove" (36), ignoring the ways in which form promotes ideology. Being "notoriously silent on the subject of women" (39), Marxist criticism does not address the basic questions feminism can raise and consequently is limited. The insights offered about women's identity by feminist critics as well as the misrepresentation of women by male characters and directors would enrich Marxist readings of the plays. Though "Marxist criticism has the most to gain" (41), because feminism opens new subjects for discussion and is "more versatile," Marxist social and economic theory nonetheless can assist feminists from "being co-opted by the society" they want to change (41). The two approaches can correct and complement each other.

159. Greer, Germaine. "Love and the Law." In *Politics, Power, and Shakespeare*. Ed. Frances McNeely Leonard. Arlington, TX: Texas Humanities Resource Center; U of Texas at Arlington Library, 1981. 28-45.

Shakespeare had a "very high ideal of marriage" where love and the law meet. *MND* explores "the great conundrum of how to civilize love which is in itself lawless" and make it support the state (45). Sixteenth-century marriage and divorce laws were "garbled," making it easy to get into and out of marriage. Marriages could be arranged through *per verba* contracts, "handfasting in the greenwood." Queen Elizabeth made but could not easily enforce strict laws about young men seducing country girls (into marriage) with Petrarchan poetry. Elizabethan culture was "madly interested in marriage [yet] ruled over by an unmarried Queen who alternately claimed she was married to the state and a pure and magical virgin" (35). The central problem of *MND* is the conflict between lovemaking and the hard work of marriage expressed through the dialectic between Diana, the guardian of fertility and chastity, and Venus, whose son Cupid wreaks havoc in the Athenian woods. Hermia and Helena, votaries of Diana, do not break their vows as the men do. Diana wins in *MND* but by "foul means" in "harnessing enchantment" (41). In *MND*, Shakespeare warns the "people at whose feast the play was staged" about "erotic delusions" and asks how "human preference for one another" can be made the "lifeline of the family" (40). Too many Elizabethans were caught in "anti-social and destructive matches" (43).

160. Kahn, Coppelia. *Man's Estate: Masculine Identity in Shakespeare*. Berkeley: U of California P, 1981.

Chapter One introduces the psychological and historical foundations for male anxieties about masculine identity. "Problems of sexual identity, family relationships, and gender roles fill Shakespeare's works ... " (1). The awareness of being masculine comes from men separating and differentiating themselves from the mother (the feminine). Not breaking away from engulfment by the mother, a man is dependent on woman and cannot confirm his masculine identity. This separation, however, can lead to the extreme polarization of sex roles, something Shakespeare strongly objects to, as well as the "devaluation of femininity by men" (11). In fact, Shakespeare's "interest in masculine identity centers on this adult struggle to achieve a second birth into manhood" (12). Yet, after a long separation from women, men "must as adults reunite with women in marriage to fulfill their roles in society" (12). Renaissance marriages were built on patriarchy. Tudor-Stuart views of the state as a father as well as Puritan fundamentalism reinforced patriarchal authority. Shakespeare's works "reflect and voice a masculine anxiety about the use of patriarchal power over women, specifically about men's control of women's sexuality" (17). Patriarchy carried a "burden of authority" which produced ambivalence toward mothers and wives. Men could control women yet were dependent on them to "validate" their manhood and ensure their lineage. Shakespeare "explored ... and sometimes attempted to resolve these problems of masculinity" (17). Subsequent chapters examine this dilemma by focusing on the "Ages of Man" from adolescence through fatherhood to death.

In Chapter Two, "Self and Eros in *Venus and Adonis,*" Shakespeare turned the myth of Adonis into "a *rite de passage* in reverse." Instead of leaving his youth behind, Shakespeare's Adonis is caught between intimacy with Venus and the "emotional isolation of narcissism, which constitutes a denial of growth, change, and the natural facts of mortality that underlies them" (21). The conflict between Venus and Adonis is between "eros and death," fought within the narcissistic self where paradoxically "the one who seems to love himself does not really have a self and thus is not capable of loving himself or others" (25). In rejecting Venus, Adonis rejects love. Venus is a mother figure who asks for a kiss in order to achieve physical union like that of a mother suckling her chid. But the kiss is also an intimate act that requires Adonis to recognize himself as a man. The oral contact has aggressive undertones that dehumanizes Venus. Adonis's hunting the boar is a defense against his masculine self. When Venus picks the flower and puts it in her bosom, sexual union is equated with death. Engulfing Adonis completely, she deprives him of his identity.

Chapter Three, "The Shadow of the Male: Masculine Identity in the History Plays," argues that, in the patriarchal world of the history plays, sons identify with their father but remain separate from their mother. Patriarchy follows a linear principle where the son inherits his identity from his father. In the history plays, the "means of masculine self-definition" is aggression. Henry VI cannot attain paternal authority like his father because he never reaches full manhood or assumes rule firmly. Remaining effeminate throughout the play he weeps instead of commands. Talbot is a shining example of masculinity, the model of chivalry. By being fiercely valiant and fiercely loyal to his sovereign, Talbot submits to his father-figure. Similarly, his son, John, will die to keep the name of his father honorable, even though the family line will die out with him. "The son's difficult task is to mold his identity on his father's without threatening his father's superiority" (55). Liaisons with women are fruitless because they endanger male alliances. Joan of Arc, for example, is particularly dangerous to men because she adopts the masculine role of warrior, but uses her feminine sex appeal to dominate. Richard III pursues the crown for himself alone. Though he resembles his father in pursuing ruthless ambition, he neither emulates him nor competes with him. Both Richard II and Richard III are narcissistic in that they are unable to form or sustain bonds with others. In the second tetralogy, Hal is portrayed as rebelling against patriarchy but "by reestablishing hereditary succession, Hal assumes his identity [as Bolingbroke's son] and lifts the cloud of guilt from his father" (18).

Chapter Four, "Coming of Age: Marriage and Manhood in *Romeo and Juliet* and *The Taming of the Shrew*," focuses through these two plays on man's passage into adulthood through marriage. *RJ* cannot be viewed as a tragedy of character but as a response to the consequences of the feud. That feud, which reflects the social values of Verona, illustrates the "death hold" patriarchy has by "promot[ing] masculinity at the expense of life" (84). Youth in Verona must engage in destructive "phallic competitiveness" in which love is seen as a "contest in which men must beat down women or be beaten by them" (97). Romeo's choice is ours (90). Ironically, Mercutio, the witty railer against love, dies of a "real wound occasioned in part by Romeo's love," and his Queen Mab speech paradoxically reveals "his fear of giving in to the seething nighttime world of unconscious desire associated with the feminine" (92). When Romeo slays Tybalt, Romeo's conflict "between manhood as aggression on behalf of the fathers and manhood as loving a woman is at the bottom of the tragedy" (93). Yet the lovers transcend the roles and the names an oppressive patriarchy imposes on them. Romeo's refusal to validate his manhood by phallic violence is aptly symbolized by his dying in the Capulet tomb. He achieves manhood by loving a woman, and Juliet overcomes both "the phallic violence and adolescent motherhood in Verona" through her "rebirth into a higher state of existence" (102), which Romeo also desires.

   TSh is a "test of manhood" (83). Shakespeare does not satirize "woman herself in the person of the shrew, but the male urge to control women" (104), thus challenging Petruchio's male supremacy. The role of a shrew is wrongly forced on Kate by a mercenary male society that treats women like chattel in its "venal" view of marriage. Shakespeare could not possibly endorse Petruchio's view of Kate as his "goods" (Act 3.2), "the most shamelessly blunt statement of the relationship among men, women, and property to be found in the literature of this period" (110). In his violence and loudness Petruchio himself behaves like a shrew. Asking Kate to call the sun the moon reveals the absurdity upon which male dominance is based; Shakespeare "never lets us think that she believes it is right, either morally or logically, to submit her judgment and the evidence of her senses to Petruchio's rule" (112). True to the demands of romantic comedy Kate falls in love with Petruchio and finds "in words a way out of subjection." Through the farce she "completes the fantasy of male dominance, but also mocks it as mere fantasy" (116). Her lengthy ostensible support of Petruchio's rule reveals an ironic reversal. Kate "steals the scene" from him, mocks his platitudes, acts with the authority of a male preacher, and through excessive rhetoric undercuts Petruchio's victory. He may even know she is playing such a game, for her feminine weakness validates "a contrary myth: that only a woman has the power to authenticate a man, by acknowledging him her master" (117).

Chapter Five is on "The Savage Yoke: Cuckoldry and Marriage." Shakespeare's comedies of courtship always end in marriage representing the ideal union of love and society. In this view of marriage, women betray and victimize their husbands. Cuckoldry, which is damaging to men because it weakens the masculine identity, arises out of three beliefs–first, all women are lustful and fickle; second, man's infidelity is tolerated while a woman's is not; and third, a husband's honor depends on his wife's chastity. The horns of cuckoldry represent two premises. The wife has blinded and dominated her husband sexually making him a yoked beast. The horns also make visible the link between jealousy and cuckoldry. Othello is manipulated by means of jealousy into believing he is a cuckold; Leontes follows the same sequence but deludes himself. While Leontes is obsessed with his horns, Ford in *MWW* is more worried about the loss of his good name and public shame than the reality of his wife's actions. Seeing his father as a cuckold, Hamlet finds it more difficult to avenge his murder. In *Oth*, cuckoldry is a lie, but the Moor is easily convinced because it confirms his preconceived notions of women. "Cuckoldry, like rape, is an affair between men, rather than between men and women or husbands and wives, though men blame women for betraying them" (150).

Chapter Six, "The Milking Babe and the Bloody Man in *Coriolanus* and *Macbeth*," maintains that sexual tension is predominant in these two plays. The heroes' manhood is not their own because it is endorsed by women. These women live vicariously through the men they control, making the men believe that "violence will make them manly" (19). In both plays we find the image of the nursing babe, symbolizing the disrupted relationship between men and women. "What the woman wants is to transcend her femininity, to gain another identity through masculine action" (154). These women want to become half men. Feeding changes to aggression, and nurturing to killing, as the man tries to become independent of the mother-figure. Yet he becomes fused with her. As warriors, Coriolanus and Macbeth gain supremacy but lose humanity. As these two characters show, the warrior self is completely distinct from the human self. Volumnia sees no distinction between herself and her son. To her, indoctrinating Coriolanus is the same thing as nourishing him; hence, for Coriolanus, duty to his mother and to Rome become intertwined. Macbeth cannot separate himself from the "feminine source of his identity," which includes the witches and his wife. "As the play proceeds, Macbeth follows a pattern of first imbibing encouragement from female sources, then attacking male antagonists" (174). Macbeth is denied the chance to procreate and have sons; and since fatherhood signifies masculinity, his male identity is thus invalidated.

Chapter Seven, "The Providential Tempest and the Shakespearean Family," explores the stage of the formation of male identity from son to father in five family romances, even though there is an "intense ambivalence" toward the family. The male's goal is to get free from the family while benefitting from its nurturing. These plays show a compromise between the man's autonomy and union which "turns on finding a mate." In *CE* and *TN*, dealing with the loss of self, the double/sibling ties the character to the filial past, yet through this double, the character finds a mate and forges his future (201). Antipholus of Syracuse narcissistically wants to make his brother a "mirroring mother" but after fearing possession by a woman (Luciana) moves into adult selfhood. *TN* shifts to the loss of sexual identity where the twins are first an obstacle to identity and then the means of fulfilling it. Because of the twin/sibling, Orsino and Olivia progress from "sexual experimentation to adult intimacy" (206). Yet the twin/sibling shows that Viola and Olivia are not differentiated from the mother, keeping them from further development. Viola's transsexual disguise forces an audience "to conceive ... ways in which sexual identity might be detached from personal identity" and can free us from "our habitual assumption that the two are inextricable, that the person is defined by his or her sex" (208). *Per*, *WT*, and *Tem* focus more on incest than doubles as a threat to the loss of identity. However father and daughter in *Per* are a different set of doubles. Through Marina, Pericles gains his identity by severing his pre-oedipal ties and breaks into the future as a husband and father. *WT* represents the "richest version of male identity defined within the family" (225). Split between being a "boy of the past and a father of the present," Leontes moves from love for Polixenes (as an escape from the death imminent in loving a woman) toward reunion with his family thanks to Perdita. Acknowledging Perdita as his daughter, Leontes accepts "the sexuality he had wanted to repudiate" (219). Perdita is both the chaste pre-oedipal mother as well as the sexually desirable mother. Leontes's paternity is effectively based on his "separateness from femininity and his union with it" (209). Though Prospero "controls" and "creates," he "never recognizes and accepts his sexuality and his relationship to women as Leontes does" (200). Not uniting with a woman, he does not work through his oedipal past and is not restored to his family. Unlike Marina or Perdita, Miranda's sexuality is defined and guarded by her father. Prospero lives in "sexual and social isolation" (225).

Reviews: Ashley, Leonard R.N., *Bibliotheque d'Humanisme et Renaissance* 44 (1982): 488-89; Barton, A., *New York Review of Books* 11 June 1981: 20; Endel, Peggy Goodman, *Shakespeare Studies* 15 (1982): 252-62; Heilbrun, Carolyn G., *Signs* 8 (1982): 182-86; Kirsch, Arthur, *Shakespeare Quarterly* 33 (1982): 252-54; Leimberg, Irene, *Shakespeare Jahrbuch* 118 (1983): 242-48; Logan, Robert A. III, *Hartford Studies in Literature* 14 (1982): 77-79; Rudnytsky, Peter, *Renaissance Quarterly* 36 (1983): 295-97.

161. MacCary, W. Thomas. "The Comic Significance of Transvestism in Plautus, Shakespeare and Beaumarchais." *Letterature comparate: Probleme e metodo. Studi in onore di Ettore Paratore*. Universita degli Studi di roma: Facolta di Lettere e Filosofia. Bologna: Patron Editore, 1981. 293-308.

Transvestism in Shakespeare's comedies is "an indication of the ambivalence of desire and the ambiguity of sexual objects" (306).

Men can have attributes traditionally assigned to women, and women can have attributes traditionally granted only to men. In *TGV*, the sexual world view equates youth and inexperience to the home and woman; education, self-expression, and self-fulfillment are worldly pursuits accorded only to the male. Julia's pose as a boy gives her access to both worlds. Proteus leaves her to follow his friend Valentine. His narcissistic love for his friend is displaced by Silvia, the object of Valentine's desire. Julia's disguise encompasses both the masculine and the feminine, the hetero- and homosexual choice of object, and thus resolves the love/friendship conflicts in the play. In *MV*, Portia's persona is basically a caricature of male excesses. In *AYL* and *TN*, Viola and Rosalind in disguise achieve a balance between male and female qualities. The conclusions of these three plays show that "the man who makes love to a woman through the intermediary of a boy-girl-boy ... will arrive at one of two conclusions depending upon [who] his intermediary is: ... if he makes love to a woman through a page who is a caricature of masculine aggression, then he will begin to see the absurdity of himself and drop his pretenses; if he makes love to a woman through a page who is the perfect combination of male and female qualities, he himself will assimilate to that pattern and fall in love with the page" (305). *AYL* and *TN* use transvestism to show that men and women have much in common and can develop a love based on this commonality; love does not have to be a "conquest of the passive female by the aggressive male" (305).

162. Neely, Carol Thomas. "Feminist Modes of Shakespearean Criticism: Compensatory, Justificatory, Transformational." *Women's Studies* 9 (1981): 3-15.

See item 298.

163. Novy, Marianne. "Demythologizing Shakespeare." *Women's Studies* 9 (1981): 17-27.

See item 262.

164. Oates, Joyce Carol. "'Is This the Promised End?': The Tragedy of *King Lear*." In *Contraries: Essays*. New York: Oxford UP, 1981. 51-81.

In *Lear* grim history destroys transcendence "expressed by women." Cordelia is "the only savior possible," yet she is an inevitable victim. The incompatibility between the visionary and the tragic in *Lear* is seen in the presentation of women. Denied intelligence and individuality because of her social role, Cordelia rebels and "declares *herself* as a self" (59). Yet *Lear* projects a terrible pessimism because, by the time of Lear's redemption, transcendence and the rejuvenation of nature through Cordelia is impossible. Women are loathed because they are seen as Nature, and so Cordelia as Nature is the enemy who must be murdered. In purging his kingdom of all women, Lear denies the very life force itself. Therefore, the play "as a whole will impress us as the aesthetic equivalent of a suicide" (63). It is a "tragically false dualism" to oppose Edmund's anti-social nature against Cordelia's; both lead to the Apocalypse. *Lear* articulates a deeper disgust of women than that found in *Oth* or *Ham*. Contrary to Freud's assertion, Cordelia "as a form of Death cannot be supported by any evidence within the play" (69). In a kingdom without a queen (like Shakespeare's in 1605), Lear rules one-sidedly over a nightmare world where Cordelia's rebellion is essential for a "synthesis of self and 'Other,' time and eternity, the finite and the infinite, poetically symbolized by a union of male and female elements" (72). But the female is eradicated; the queen-less land emphasizes the danger of masculine authority. Psychologically, the absence of woman stresses her essence. Shakespeare, however, was "too involved in Lear's sexual paranoia to clearly delineate the psychopathology that has gripped the king" (76). Unlike the Terrible Mother, Cordelia as an anima figure is the male's helper, but her virtues "die with her."

165. Pitt, Angela. *Shakespeare's Women*. London: David and Charles; Totowa, NJ: Barnes and Noble, 1981.

Chapter One asserts that English women in the Renaissance had more independence and sense of identity than their European counterparts. However, Elizabethan law specified no particular position for women, except in terms of marriage and inheritance. Unmarried women had virtually all the rights of a man, but remaining single was virtually impossible; a nunnery was the only viable alternative. The socially accepted state for a woman was to wed and become the property of her husband. Widows had more power than most women. In the eyes of the church, "women were the daughters of Eve, temptresses who would lead men down the primrose path to fornication" (15). Queen Elizabeth suffered her female form as a disability. Under James I, many new treatises on the wickedness of women were published, aided by the king's fear of witches. Women were educated, but their choice of reading material was highly restricted.

Chapter Two, "Shakespeare's Tragic Women," argues that he avoided the two-dimensional stereotyping of women that many of his contemporaries fell prey to. However, in the four great tragedies, the focus is on the male character. But women are also important when tragedy arises from a mutual passionate love, such as in *RJ* and *AC*. "The tragic hero must have power and influence so that his fate will affect the condition of more than just his immediate family ... . It is immediately apparent, given the situation in Elizabethan England, that very few women could be imagined in this way ... " (34). Cleopatra and Juliet may be exceptions. Cleopatra is not presented with a fatal flaw; rather, she is a threat to Antony and Rome. She is promiscuous sexually and politically. It is only when Antony is dying that she musters her dignity and courage. The strength of Antony and Cleopatra's passion is equally balanced; hence Cleopatra is not the instrument of her lover's downfall. While Antony's character deteriorates, Cleopatra's is strengthened. In contrast to Cleopatra, Juliet is a young, innocent girl. Neither she nor Romeo has a character flaw; but they are victims of circumstance, sacrificed in order to end the feud. Their sexual yearnings are displayed only within the confines of marriage. A victim of events beyond her control, Desdemona is "a saintly figure." The ideal wife, nonetheless, she marries without parental consent showing she has a mind of her own.

Since she does not develop as a character during the course of the play, she is best seen as a symbol of purity. Ophelia's tragedy results because she is too weak to understand the will of her father. Yet she has entertained Hamlet without a chaperon or paternal consent. "Desdemona, Ophelia and Gertrude all die because of direct association with the fate of the tragic hero" (59). Cordelia acts as a measure for honesty and dishonesty. Lady Macbeth is not a tragic character because her nature is pure evil.

Chapter Three explores "Women in the Comedies and Lost Plays." While men dominate the tragedies, women dominate the comedies in the "game of love." The women may transgress social expectations of behavior, but are always redeemed at the end of the play as "agents of happiness." Adriana in *CE*, who is diseased with jealousy, is envious of men's liberty and angered by women's subservience. Her reaction is unnatural and her reconciliation means returning to the role of wife. Sylvia in *TGV* is first presented as an idealized image of female beauty, but she reveals more sensitivity and integrity as the play progresses. Her virtue and constancy contrast with Proteus's behavior. Julia is her foil and the first of Shakespeare's heroines to be allowed a disguise. The only aspect of Hippolyta's personality in *MND* that is revealed is the acceptance of her husband's superiority. Hermia and Helena are parallel characters yet different physically and temperamentally. Failing to obey her husband Titania is portrayed as deviant. Portia in the court scene of *MV* dons her disguise, but not to win back her lover, as so many of Shakespeare's heroines (like Helena) do. Portia "would never have been allowed to speak had it been known that she was a woman" (92). Exemplifying some of Elizabeth's virtues, Portia has an intellect that surpasses all those in court. Kate in *TSh* is presented as a stereotypical shrewish woman who is never allowed to reveal her inner thoughts. She develops into a stereotypical submissive wife, although it is debatable as to how seriously we can view her final speech.

As Chapter Four, "Women in the Histories," maintains, the histories are predominantly concerned with male authority with women only clarifying the hero's character. The women characters are less complex and more predictable. Mistress Quickly in *1H4* and *2H4* suggests the temptation of a decadent life that Prince Hal could fall prey to; she appears only briefly in *H5* because she no longer poses a threat to the throne of England. The relationship between Troilus and Cressida is founded on sexual indulgence. Portrayed as unfaithful and flirtatious, Cressida is worldly whereas Troilus is naive. Joan of Arc in *H6* is a whore. Symbolizing the "treachery and cowardice in France" (148), she also represents the unnaturalness of anarchy by upsetting the hierarchy. Margaret of Anjou is a prototype of Lady Macbeth; both are terrifying female figures. Margaret represents all that is unnatural because she lacks feminine qualities. Volumnia, the matriarch in *Cor*, contrasts with her son's fearful wife Virgilia.

Chapter Five on "Shakespeare's Women on Stage" concentrates on the implications of the English tradition which "stuck conservatively to the tradition of [using] male actors only" (164). The life of an actress was considered unsuitable for an Elizabethan lady because acting companies always had an army of prostitutes in tow. "The Puritans saw the theatres as dens of theft and whoredom, pride and prodigality, villainy and blasphemy" (169). Boy actors played the female roles until their voices broke and they grew beards. They would then be promoted to playing male characters. Shakespeare wrote for boy actors who played female parts. It can be assumed that the boy actors did not try to offer a realistic representation of a woman because they would be unable to convince the audience.

Reviews: *Choice* 18 (1981): 1587; Bank, Rosemary K., *Theatre Journal* 35 (1983): 129; Jones, K.D., *Times Literary Supplement* 17 Apr. 1981: 433; Leimberg, Irene, *Shakespeare Jahrbuch* 118 (1983): 242-48; Masters, A., *Times Educational Supplement* 13 Feb. 1981: 20; Ollen, Theresa, *Kvallsposten* 29 Dec. 1982; Roberts, Jeanne Addison, *Shakespeare Quarterly* 33 (1982): 533; Roxman, S., *Dagens Nyheter* 9 June 1981.

166. Shepard, Simon. *Amazons and Warrior Women: Varieties of Feminism in Seventeenth-Century Drama*. New York: St. Martin's P, 1981. Esp. 38-39; 107, 122, 100-102; 151-54; 156-61; 163-66; et passim.

The tradition of the warrior woman lies behind many situations and characters in Shakespeare's plays. As other women are, Lady Macbeth is an outsider trapped in a male world; she is "caught between two definitions of maleness, the social and the biological, and she confuses the two" (38). Female martyrdom does not have to be passive, as Cleopatra proves. Violated, abused women, such as Lucrece, Lavinia, and Cassandra, reject male rule and with it "communication with the male world" (187). All of these women are eager to show "their gored bodies" to retaliate. The comedies "draw their feeling from the tradition of the warrior woman, because it is with the issues of that tradition that the comedies are concerned" (165). Those issues include equal partnership and mutual affection. Because of such warrior women, we can "break through the sterilizing cloud of enchantment" and see the struggle that shapes the comedies. Rosalind, for example, must assume the role of a warrior woman to find a test love. Like other Shakespearean heroines, she mocks male affectation and observes male types. She is like Spenser's Britomart, chaste and strong. In her "manly moments," Rosalind is a positive figure in contrast to Touchstone or Jaques. Ultimately, *AYL* says that gender differences based on biology are irrelevant. Portia also attacks male foibles through her wit which helps her to navigate in an area of traditional male decision making beyond her immediate control.

167. Staton, Shirley F. "Female Transvestism in Renaissance Comedy: 'A Natural Perspective, That Is and Is Not.'" *Iowa State Journal of Research* 56 (1981): 79-89.

Disguise, such as female transvestism, is perhaps "the central Renaissance trope" (79). Gender assumptions like space, time, and location can order experience and shape dramatic structure. Shakespeare's six comedies that employ this "complicated double transvestism" can be divided into two groups. In the first (*MV*, *AYL*, and *TN*) such a disguise frees heroines to discover themselves. Rosalind's "masculine-feminine dualism" (82) reconciles opposition in *AYL*; similarly, Viola/Cesario, who subverts the conventions of courtly love, helps us to "rethink supposed sexual opposites" (82). Sapphic scenes, especially in *MV*, emphasize sisterhood through transvestism disguises. Because of transvestism, "we travel beyond gender" for a carnival experience (83). In contrast to the first group of plays, female transvestism in *James IV, TGV, Cym*, and *Philaster* leads a woman to "sacrificial suffering" and upholds patriarchal values. Julia/Sebastian and Imogen endure tragedy in their male attire and so become symbols of "Holy Chastity" to "redeem male evil" (85). However, such chastity is valorized by and thus legitimatizes "paternal rights." While women in the tragicomedies are polarized into good or evil, the men are "free to be human" (86), deformed and reformed. Although disguised heroines (Rosalind and Imogen) are responsible for reconciling men, these women must surrender their new identities and accept "passive silence" (86) at the end of the play.

168. Stiller, Nikki. "Robert Henryson's Cresseid and Sexual Backlash." *Literature and Psychology* 31 (1981): 88-95.

Henryson's *Testament of Cresseid* offers a "northern backlash" against the courtly love tradition found in Italy and in Chaucer that idolized women and gave credence to the appetite. Such code was foreign to Shakespeare, too, and his *TrC* "seems at times an attempt to debunk all the tropes, aims and attitudes of courtly love at once" (94). Shakespeare's play is "perhaps ... one of the most accurate pictures we have" of destructive desire (94). Cressida is a "barometer or weathervane" of the ways in which "attitudes towards love, women, and the sexual self" change from one time and one place to another.

169. Sundelson, David. "The Dynamics of Marriage in *The Merchant of Venice*." *Humanities in Society* 4 (1981): 245-72.

See item 241.

170. ---. "Misogyny and Rule in *Measure for Measure*." *Women's Studies* 9 (1981): 83-91.

See item 241.

171. Traci, Philip. "*As You Like It*: Homosexuality in Shakespeare's
     Play." *C[ollege] L[anguage] A[ssociation] Journal* 25 (1981):
     91-105.

     AYL explores the themes of sexual role playing and diversity
     of love. A homosexual reading of the play can clarify the "multiple
     sexualities of Rosalind/Ganymede/boy actor" (102). The audience
     experiences a double or even triple consciousness in viewing "boys
     playing girls and yet remembering them as both" (104). Phebe and
     Rosalind were boys as well as women. Though he defended the
     boy actors against the charge of homosexuality, Thomas
     Heywood's comments on the audience knowing the boys' names,
     on the deplorable sexual practices of pederasty, and on
     transvestism lend credence to the charge. Shakespeare stresses the
     "similarity between boys and women to encourage our suspended
     belief of the difference between them" (97). Throughout *AYL*
     homosexuality is reinforced through the numerous reminders that
     Rosalind was not a woman, through the mock marriage of the
     boys in Act 4.3, and through the "suppositional mood" signaled by
     Touchstone's *ifs*, which can refer to sexual roles as well as the
     courtly conduct of lying. The jokes in the play depend on and
     exploit homosexuality. The homosexual/heterosexual dualities are
     especially strong and innovative in the boy actor's flirtatious
     Epilogue in which he regards the men in the audience as women.

172. Wilt, Judith. "Comment on David Leverenz's 'The Woman in
     Hamlet.'" *Women's Studies* 9 (1981): 93-97.

     Leverenz (item 128) is correct in claiming that in *Ham* "the
     male world's banishment of the female" results in a "return to a
     military ethos." Leverenz's comments need to be extended to all
     the great tragedies. The healing alternative offered by Ophelia,
     Cordelia, Desdemona, even Lady Macbeth, is rejected by the
     tragic heroes for their sick and stark male plots. Ironically, these
     banished women return (e.g. Lady Macbeth offers the last "spark"
     of fear for her husband) and even "more interesting" Ophelia,

Gertrude, and Hermione "make appearances onstage after their spirits are essentially destroyed" (95) while Cordelia and Desdemona come back from the grave. Although Othello and Lear brand female chastity as cold and absent, they nonetheless "look with renewed spirit to the lips of the healing women at the very end, and receive a great warm message from them" (96).

1982

173. Andresen-Thom, Martha. "Shrew-Taming and Other Rituals of Aggression: Baiting and Bonding on Stage and in the Wild." *Women's Studies* 9 (1982): 121-43.

There are two ways of solving Kate's troublesome obedience speech–seeing it as a triumphant sexual union or a sign of female deviousness signaled by a wink from Kate. Theories of animal behavior found in Konrad Lorenz's *On Aggression* provide illuminating analogies with Kate and Petruchio's behavior. In the animal kingdom, as in *TSh*, mating rituals transform sexual rivalry and aggression into heterosexual bonding and creation. Male bonding among young men directed against old men occurs in the predatory world of Padua as Shakespeare mocks the self-deception of wooers. Since female bonding does not exist, women are pressured to bond with men. Like Lorenz's animals, Petruchio's "first tactic" with Kate uses "dominance through appeasement" (137). To separate himself and his mate from the rest of society, Petruchio then redirects his attack from her "to a larger, less defined target" (132), social customs and rules. A self-ironist, Petruchio acts out his "anti-social behavior" to show Kate how he mirrors her as well as the on-stage audience. The real enemy is not Kate but the "literalists" opposed to Petruchio's play. He is not a sinister tyrant but a teacher; "his taming has been teaching Kate how to play so that they *both* may win" (136). An ironist, too, Kate learns to play and in fact she "overplays female acquiescence in order to undercut it" (136). Her appeasement of

Petruchio is not submission–saying what he wants is not being what he wants. Fredi Olster's Kate, in the Actors Conservatory Theatre production, stood for her last speech, while everyone else sat, making Kate "positionally ... superior." While an audience on stage sees only the taming, we perceive the transformation of aggression through ritual. Kate's behavior is part of a play that helps Petruchio save male "face." He risks everything on her; her "response expresses reciprocally her dependence on him" (139). Kate and Petruchio live in a special world where patriarchy works for them both.

174. Arbery, Glenn Cannon. "Women, Christianity, and the Stage in Four Shakespearean Comedies." *DAI* 43 (1982): 1976A. U of Dallas. [*Cym, MND, MV,* and *TSh.*]

175. Bamber, Linda. *Comic Women, Tragic Men. A Study of Gender and Genre in Shakespeare.* Stanford: Stanford UP, 1982.

Chapter One, "Comic Women, Tragic Men," argues that Shakespeare seems to take the woman's part because women in the comedies are more brilliant than the men. But in the tragedies, the females are nightmare figures; they "are not just women who happen to be evil; their evil is inseparable from their failures as women" (2). However, all of the plays are governed by Shakespeare's masculine perspective so that the Self is male and the Other is female. Nevertheless, the idea of the feminine is central to his work. "Masculine identity and masculine self-achievement in every genre are systematically related to the nature of the feminine in that particular mode" (5). In the tragedies, the heroes' confidence in conventional forms of manliness is shaken as they "project their sexual disorientation onto women." *Mac* and *Cor* are exceptions where misogyny seems to be within the text as a whole, not within the psyche of the heroes. Manliness in Shakespearean tragedy involves detachment from the feminine, an independence from the Other. In the comedies, the feminine either rebels against the restraining social order or, more commonly, "presides in alliance with forces that challenge its hegemony." Non-rebellious women seem to be more successful and have more freedom than their rebellious counterparts. Male dominance is merely a social form irrelevant to the private relationship, as implied in *TSh*.

Chapter Two on *"Antony and Cleopatra"* finds that there are three Cleopatras–Cleopatra-as-Egypt who is "radically ambiguous and who never is fully known" (46); Cleopatra as the Other with whom the hero or Self is "confronted in tragedy"; and Cleopatra as character. Rome and Egypt are not opposites. Egypt is a new world Antony must live in because the old Rome of honor has become soft and died. Rome is opposed to sex because it interferes with business. In the new world, a dialectic is at work between Self and Other; the Self goes through phases from misogyny to connectedness. Departing Egypt for business and marriage to Octavia, Antony shows that his relationship with Cleopatra is only romantic. Unlike Cleopatra, Octavia is unaware of Antony's breach of faith; she poses no threat to the "integrity of Self." Antony's relations with Cleopatra in the second movement of the play (from Act 3.4) are less theatrical and given to strategy. Like other tragic heroes, he is forced to abandon the security of "the patriarchal system and confront the Other dialectically" (53).

Cleopatra controls Antony's destiny; he no longer thinks about his fate but only hers. Though more diffuse and less absolute than in *Lear*, nature in *AC* does bring a resolution. We never see Cleopatra's inner life or feel her suffering, as Linda Fitz (item 37) has argued. A performer, Cleopatra does not reveal a struggle. While Antony quests as the Other to establish a fixed identity and become his own ideal by controlling himself, he becomes divided from himself. Not so Cleopatra who is never at work on herself and never takes instructions from anyone. Unlike Octavia who is defined by Antony and Caesar, Cleopatra defines herself and sees these men as a threat to her identity. Faithful to herself, she is faithful to Antony. As Antony struggles to make absolute judgments, Cleopatra is more eager to elicit "judgments rather than [being] the one who makes them" (64). Cleopatra and Antony confront nature differently. She as the feminine Other "faces the challenge of Nature, of the world outside the Self, with an identity as fixed and unyielding as Nature herself" (69); Antony views nature as "humanistic, synthesizing, responsible" (66). It is the third Cleopatra as character who gives us the sense of resolution.

Chapter Three on *"Hamlet"* finds the play unleashing a pervasive sex nausea greater than in the other tragedies. Hamlet's misogyny is the result of his losing the old, father-centered world. We do not see this first phase of the tragedy. In the second phase, Ophelia, as a "pathetic May Queen" or "inverse Perdita," represents the innocence that might have been. A figure of "ambiguous morality" like Cleopatra, Gertrude talks about sexuality in natural terms at Ophelia's funeral. It is misleading to speak of Gertrude's innocence or guilt. She and Ophelia "are psychologically and morally neutral characters who take on the coloration of the play's moods" (77). Seeing Gertrude's evil through Hamlet's eyes, we lack the evidence about her and so lose the "investment" that would come from our own judgment. The idea of Woman is a "spiritual barometer" in *Ham*, yet the idea "fades into the background toward the end of the play," decreasing any disfunction we may feel. Gertrude's reactions in the last part of the play are meant "to sound the note of poignant femininity" (79). She is not playing a role. Contradictory clues about Ophelia (is she spunky or her father's pawn?) do not matter. Though she has her own personality, Ophelia is "not developed as a woman with a choice to make" (79). As an "icon of positive sexuality," Ophelia as the image of Woman is "a function of a change in Hamlet" himself. There is a contrast in sexual patterns and Hamlet's own view of woman before and after his trip to England. He undergoes a psychosexual transformation. Until this last phase of the play, Hamlet "may be said to occupy the position of the cultural feminine" (89); female aggression was "traditionally domestic or sexual" (89). Hamlet had to experience the aggression of the history hero to confront something beyond the code of manliness. Once he does, he is ready to resolve his metaphysical problems, rid himself of his "negative sexuality," and stand for the Self, Hamlet as the individual.

In Chapter Four, "The Comic Heroine and the Avoidance of Choice," our response to the comic heroine is direct and unmediated by her father, lover or husband. Shylock is the closest thing to a tragic Self in all of the comedies; he has a tendency to deflect his rage toward the feminine. The comedies exhibit "low-grade anxiety" about cuckoldry, fear of which tends to stand for a general discontent. Shakespeare's hatred of women has been seen as being concealed by the conventions of the comic genre, yet good humor toward the feminine in the comedies is part of a more general good humor toward the general conditions of life.

In the tragedies, anxiety develops because the feminine Other, like the masculine Self, is forced to make choices, and these choices may go against the hero. In the comedies, however, the women tend to avoid making choices. If a father opposes a daughter's marriage at the beginning of the play, he is sure to come around by the end. The two exceptions are the sexual tensions that arise between Hero and Leonato in *Ado* and Jessica's betrayal of Shylock. In the world of comedy, "the barriers are lowered between alternatives, making choice unnecessary." But it is the feminine Other who is most at home in the alternative world; the male Self is less brilliant in this setting. The comic heroine is generic as well as individual. She is the marriageable type, young, pretty, and available–the "constant element" in comedy. Her prerogatives are Shakespeare's.

Chapter Five, "*1 Henry VI* to *Henry V*: Toward Tragedy," argues that the masculine Self in the histories is always defined in terms of his place in the world of men. His "central activity is to gain, maintain and exercise power." Joan of Arc is similar to a masculine Self in *1H6*. She fights and kills like a man, desires only victory for her party and power for herself. On the other hand, Isabel in *R2*, as feminine Other, is queen of the realm of the garden. She is the only one defined by something beyond history. In *2H6* and *3H6*, Margaret is as eager for power and vengeful as any of the male characters. Unlike Joan, she always has a male protector or conspirator who does much of the fighting for her; and her ambitions have a "motherly motivation." Margaret's actions are measured against a norm of female behavior; Joan's are not. "Women in the early history plays do not participate in history as women. Joan is a kind of second-class man and Margaret is presented as a woman who has betrayed her own gender" (140). In *R3*, the women are "embittered observers" of the struggle for power. There is no kindness among them to contrast with Richard's cruelty; they are defined by their position in the male world. In the history plays, woman is merely the adjunct of the man. "The histories are in the process of differentiating the Self from the Other, the Other being defined in terms of gender on the one hand and generation on the Other" (153). Shakespeare solves the problem of the generational Other, but not the feminine Other. Only as the Other are women in Shakespeare consistently the equals of men. But because the feminine Other is too explosive a figure for the history plays, Shakespeare saves her for tragedy.

Chapter Six on "*Macbeth* and *Coriolanus*" maintains that *Macbeth* and *Coriolanus* are committed to a code of manliness that emphasizes power, honor, war, and revenge. Volumnia and Lady Macbeth are opposites of the Jungian idea of the feminine representing natural fertility and family love. They are not Others to the heroes because they act as collaborators. Rather than being motivated by self-interest, they do not oppose the male sense of Self. In *Cor* the closest we come to the feminine as Other is Virgilia who speaks for the opposition to Rome. Yet her protest is weak. The process of Coriolanus's separation from the feminine, his mother, comes too late in the play; and under the threat of his mother's suicide, he calls off his revenge. The "dialectic in these plays is confined to the world of men, rather than between masculine Self and feminine Other." There is no revulsion at the treachery and sexual betrayal of women common to the other tragedies. "In *Macbeth*, as in *Coriolanus*, the absence of a significant feminine Other is a sign of a failure to engage in a dialectic with the outside world" (105). Macbeth's attention is constantly on his inner life, where the real terror lies for him.

Chapter Seven turns to "After Tragedy: *The Tempest*." Unlike the other romances, especially *WT*, *Tem* does not offer the "Return of the Feminine." There is no reunion of husband and wife; the family is incomplete. The absence of Prospero's wife is the central, basic structural element of *Tem*, which is "a kind of holocaust literature." The death of Prospero's wife is both "a gift and a deprivation" (174). *Tem* is like a comedy turned inside out; the sexuality of the father dominates, though Prospero lives in sexual isolation. Sexual bestiality associated with other romance heroes is displaced onto Caliban. Excluded from lawful sexuality, Prospero must find the Caliban within himself. Yet Prospero is also liberated by his wife's death, freed from the desire for the lost Other. The "feminine is a principle of death as well as a principle of recurring life" (178). Prospero's freedom from desire is not absolute, for his repression of sex is unnatural. Ariel, who dominates the mood of *Tem*, is Prospero's "unanxious creativity" (179). While the early comedies "move toward sexual liberation," *Tem* conveys a "sense of liberation" that is "spiritual and postsexual" (180). In other romances, it is the woman's will, or no one's will, that makes things happen. Prospero controls the feminine Other. Simultaneously obedient and independent, Miranda is used by Prospero for his own plans, thus diminishing her dramatic significance. Drama is created by the masculine imperative of "Who shall be king."

Reviews: *Choice* 20 (1982): 424; Almasy, Rudolph P., *Sixteenth Century Journal* 14 (1983): 534; Barton, Anne, *London Review of Books* 18-31 Aug. 1983: 19; Bement, Peter, *Review of English Studies* 36 (1985): 82-83; Boose, Lynda E., *Modern Philology* 82 (1984): 91-95; Cotton, Nancy, *Theatre Studies: Journal of Ohio State University Research Institute* 30 (1983-84): 72-74; Danson, Lawrence, *Studies in English Literature, 1500-1900* 23 (1983): 334-36; Erickson, Peter, *Women's Studies* 10 (1983): 342-49; Halio, Jay, *College Literature* 10 (1983): 195-97; Kahn, Coppelia, *Modern Language Studies* 15 (1985): 329-32; Kermode, Frank, *New York Review of Books* 28 Apr. 1983: 30-33; Leimberg, Irene, *Shakespeare Jahrbuch* 118 (1983): 242-48; Rebhorn, Wayne A., *Renaissance Quarterly* 36 (1983): 471-74; Rose, Mary Beth, *Shakespeare Quarterly* 35 (1984): 123-26; Sabol, Cathy, *Library Journal* 107 (1982): 1660; Snyder, Susan, *Shakespeare Studies* 17 (1985): 244-47; Volpina, N.M., *Referativnyi Zhurnal Obscestvennye Nauki v SSSR Ser VII Literaturoverdenye* 6 (1984): 79-81.

176. Berger, Harry, Jr. "Against the Sink-a-Pace: Sexual and Family Politics in *Much Ado About Nothing.*" *Shakespeare Quarterly* 33 (1982): 302-13.

Beatrice's metaphor of dance summarizes the sexual and familial politics of Messina: "wooing, wedding, and repenting is as a Scotch jig, a measure, and a cinquepace" (Act 2.1.63-64). The passionate pace of courtship is tempered by the stately marriage ceremony, a ritual of the older generation to ensure the continuance of the patriarchal system. Life after marriage, however, is spent in unnatural confinement, hence the cinquepace,

or as Sir Toby pronounces it, sink-a-pace. Although Hero plays
the traditional role of woman in this male-dominated social dance,
she is frequently aware of her complicity in the system. She both
envies and disapproves of Beatrice's freedom from men, but her
attempts to emulate this freedom fail. Her ambivalent feelings
toward the patriarchal system are revealed in her epic metaphor
of the bower: "Where honeysuckles, ripened by the sun,/Forbid
the sun to enter" (Act 3.1.7-8). Both images reflect Beatrice's
refusal to subjugate herself to the paternal influence which has
nurtured her although condemning the courtly metaphor is
tempered by the dignity of the honeysuckle. Many males in *Ado*
seem to share Beatrice's views of marriage–women are not to be
trusted. The song in Act 2, however, points to a contradictory
philosophy, also held by men. Men, too, are by nature unfaithful
and devious. "The difference between men and women in this
respect–so goes the regnant ideology of the play–is that women
are responsible for their sins, but men are not. Male deception
and inconstancy are gifts that God gives, and their proper name
is Manhood" (307). The members of The Men's Club of Messina
follow a fashion which they themselves have shaped whose chief
precept is to avoid cost.

  Although the complications in the play are symptomatic of the
patriarchal society, the men are quick to lay the blame on Hero,
a woman, and Don John, a bastard who "is a testimony both to
his father's prowess and to his mother's sin" (311). Pursuit of war
and love further bond the members of the Men's Club, but
marriage itself destroys their fraternal union. "It is an accidental
inconvenience of the system that after a man has amused himself
in hunting his lawful prey, and succeeded in trapping her, he is
then expected to deny his nature and spend his life by her side"
(312). The conclusion is happy only because it ends before trouble
can erupt again. Hero and Claudio "would have to be reborn in
a new heaven and earth, a new Messina, before they could enter
into a relationship free of the assumptions of their community"
(313).

177. Boose, Lynda E. "The Father and the Bride in Shakespeare."
     PMLA 97 (1982): 325-47.

The wedding ceremony provides the "paradigm of all the conflicts that define father-daughter relationships–a ritualistic pattern of the bride's separation from the father, a transition, and a reincorporation with the groom" (326). Ideally, the father must release his daughter from "family bonds that might otherwise become a kind of bondage" (327) so that she can make the transition from daughter to wife. In *RJ*, the ritual is violated by having two husbands (one upstairs–Romeo; and one downstairs–Paris); a father who acts like a "tragic nemesis"; "doomed epithalamia"; and an "inverted marriage ceremony" at the end of the play. Similarly, the nunnery scene in *Ham* inverts the marriage rite by having the bride (Ophelia) wait for the groom (Hamlet), return his gifts, and be redelivered to her father. In *RJ* and *Ham*, "two incompatible rituals" (marriage and funeral) collide, and lead to "violated sacramentality" (330). Unlike Hymen and Duke Senior in *AYL*, Brabantio and Lear frustrate the separation phase of the ritual by refusing to give the daughter away. Rather than going from father to groom, Cordelia must return to Lear in "a sterile circularity of ... violated ritual" (340). The "daughters of tragedy" are "guiltlessly agentive" in destroying the family and "tragically incapable of creating a new one" (335). Daughters Jessica and Portia in *MV* offer distinct solutions to a repressive father. Selling her mother's ring and her father's stones, Jessica is guilty of "delegitimizing" (336) herself; her theft prevents her from moving successfully from paternal to conjugal bonds. Portia, however, reaches "independence within given structures" by ethically giving Bassanio a hint and by properly honoring the symbolism of the ring. A "regenerating daughter" makes family union possible in *WT* and *Per*. Prospero, "undoubtedly the most successful" father in Shakespeare (341), allows his daughter to choose her suitor and, Hymen-like, gives her a "dowry mask," though he suffers pain at losing Miranda.

178. Cohen, Brent Martin. "Sexuality and Tragedy in *Othello* and *Antony and Cleopatra*." *DAI* 42 (1982): 5127A. U of California, Berkeley.

179. Erickson, Peter B. "Patriarchal Structures in *The Winter's Tale*." *PMLA* 97 (1982): 819-29.

See item 284.

180. ---. "Review of Marilyn French, *Shakespeare's Division of Experience*." *Women's Studies* 9 (1982): 189-201.

French's work (item 155) is closely related to Leslie Fiedler's. She concentrates on the twin themes of male "sex nausea" and "denigration of women" (189). She offers a sophisticated view of Shakespeare's authorial presence. The strongest points of the book are her discussion of gender and her portrait of Shakespeare as an artist. Yet her work fails in that no play is treated with sufficient thoroughness or extended analysis. Also, she cites no other feminist critics. The allocation of tragedy to a masculine form and comedy to a feminine form is too arbitrary. She does not take the comic form seriously, oversimplifying the genre. Her gender principles are not at fault, rather, her "haphazard application of them" (196) are.

181. ---. "Sexual Politics and the Social Structure in *As You Like It*." *Massachusetts Review* 23 (1982): 65-83.

See item 284.

182. Estrin, Barbara. "'Behind a Dream': Cleopatra and Sonnet 129." *Women's Studies* 9 (1982): 177-88.

Cleopatra goes beyond the limits lamented by the male narrator of Sonnet 129 who ends helplessly frustrated by the illusions of desire. Cleopatra picks up where this narrator leaves off and pursues "the dream for its own sake" (178) by appreciating "the mutability of her being" (186). The changing tone of her speeches from Act 1 to Act 5 shows how Cleopatra progresses in her triumph in love. In Act 1, she idealizes the past which brought her perfection in love; the present, by contrast, brings "diminished love" (181). Antony's absence symbolizes lost hope, for immersed in him, Cleopatra will be forgotten when he is away. In Act 2.5.10-23, she "recreates a past" and a dream to make it possible and so "playfully overcomes oblivion" (182). Dreaming of Antony in Act 5, she fulfills the fantasy of him she expressed in Act 2, obtaining "perennial pleasure" from an "inexhaustible" Antony who becomes the "regenerative source of mutual fulfillment" (185). Consequently, Cleopatra's dream replaces "both the 'before' and 'behind' of Sonnet 129 with an abiding presence of desire, eternally renewed, and hence, constantly renewable" (184). Entering the world of her own dreams, Cleopatra achieves what the speaker in Sonnet 129 could not–the pleasure of physical love and the courage to anticipate death as eternal regeneration.

183. Fienberg, Nona. "Marina in *Pericles*: Exchange Values and the Art of Moral Discourse." *Iowa State Journal of Research* 57.2 (1982): 153-61.

Marina plays a major role in Acts 4 and 5 of *Per*, for through her moral discourse, she is able to transform the lives of the brothel residents, Lysimachus, and her father. Though she is "initially selfish," Marina acts as "the thematic and structural pivot between two contrasting economies, that which values women as a commodity to exploit and that which values their wholeness and integrity" (154). In place of the debased economy of Pander, Boult, and Bawd, where views of women are reductive, Marina "creates a market for her moral discourse" (155). She thereby teaches Lysimachus to value her not as a prostitute but for her virtuous selfhood and so helps shape him as a new man and governor. She has a "curative" or medicinal function. Through her eloquence, she assumes control over her role in the brothel, functioning like the narrator Gower and retaining her chastity "which serves as a synecdoche for her inner value as well as her value in the marriage market" (158). Her greatest test, however, is in Act 5.1, where she teaches Pericles about the spiritual dimension of relationships involving man and God. She frees the entire play to "celebrate action carried out in a spirit of charity" (153).

184. Furber, Donald, and Anne Callahan. *Erotic Love in Literature: From Medieval Legend to Romantic Illusion.* Troy, NY: Whitston, 1982. See Chapter 2: "Ritual and Role-playing in the World of the Hero," esp. "*Venus and Adonis*," 61-65; "The Boy

Actor and Erotic Illusion," 65-71; and "The Master-Mistress," 71-76.

Venus is an ambiguous figure playing both male and female roles. As the "most sexually aggressive woman in modern literature, she certainly has few rivals" (61). With Adonis she is tender and brutal; she seduces him as if she were a man yet she is the Ovidian symbol of "eternal love." She tries to convince the androgynous youth that the hunt is an "emblem" of male aggression he must avoid.

Though the "real sex lives" of the boy actors were questioned, Shakespeare exploits these actors to explore the psychological and physical ambiguity of sexual identity. In *TN*, Viola/Cesario exhibits the same "melancholic passion characteristic of the perfect Platonic lover" (68); the ambiguity surrounding Sebastian/Viola also pertains to Viola/Cesario. Because Viola does not change into woman's clothing at the end of *TN*, "we never really see the woman whom Orsino now loves. Her existence is as illusory as the image of woman that has been created by the actor himself" (69). Similarly, the hybrid Rosalind/Ganymede is a magical character illustrating a "constant shifting of sexual identity." Because the character's sex cannot be "stabilized into male or female," *AYL* attests to the "fundamental ambiguity of human sexuality itself" (71).

The phrase "master-mistress," referring to the young man in Sonnet 20, beautifully and succinctly expresses "sexual fantasy in its purest form"–this love object places male/female on an equal plane; procreation is not male-dominated since "father can be the mother" (74).

185. Gohlke, Madelon. "'All that is spoke is marred': Language and Consciousness in *Othello*." *Women's Studies* 9 (1982): 157-76.

The language of men and women differs fundamentally from the comedies to the tragedies. In the comedies, the women use "complex speech" involving lies and riddles about the "threat of sexual betrayal" (168) reflecting a "complex consciousness." They can break male bonds for the purpose of heterosexual love. The tragedies reverse this pattern. Women "lapse into silence, madness or radically ambiguous speech" (157) while the tragic hero, "sometimes against his will" (172), finds himself in the "feminine posture of telling the truth through lies" (172), violating the codes of honest male discourse. Vulnerable to female betrayal, the tragic hero acquires "inferiority."

Paradoxically, Iago both hates Othello and wants to bind himself to the Moor to eliminate Othello's intimacy with Desdemona and Cassio. Because he has to be the master with Othello before he can be the servant, Iago vicariously associates with his victims (160) to reveal how he has been robbed of intimacy. Iago teaches Othello, who begins the play in a position of "rhetorical innocence," to look for hidden meanings which results in Othello's adopting a "language of paradox and indirection" (164). Othello misreads Desdemona by believing that men are more "trustworthy" than women. In light of the "rhetorical fate" of female characters in the tragedies, Desdemona, like Ophelia and Lady Macbeth, "retreats into a kind of speech which she herself cannot interpret" (165). Avoiding sexual language, Desdemona unintentionally uses ambiguity which Othello turns against her. Unlike the manipulative Iago or Othello, Desdemona "never gives any indication that she herself is aware of the interpretive possibilities contained in her speech" (166). Having to admit the "'femininity' of his own consciousness," as expressed through his ambiguous language, Othello fears losing his "'honest' masculinity" (172).

186. Greco, Norma A. "Sexual Division and Revision in *The Merchant of Venice.*" *Pennsylvania English* 9 (1982): 39-45.

MV shows a "dichotomy between the traditional 'masculine' and 'feminine' domains"–the public world of government and commerce (Venice) and the inner world of spirit and emotions (Belmont). The play is "about the need both for the individual to 'unite' these 'parts' of the self and for society to integrate the resources of the female into the public realm" (44). A materialist who tries to buy love, Antonio "lacks understanding of a deeper, more unconscious self" (40). Like Antonio, Shylock is wifeless and loveless, symptoms of a drained Venetian society. In Belmont, "the female sphere where males enter only with permission" (41),

Portia is right to attack her suitors, a sign of her rebellion against confinement and proof of her intellectual control. She teaches Bassanio that love is a union between male and female and that marriage is a "metaphor for the psychic union within the individual" (42). She gives her feminine possessions to Bassanio as he must give his male ones to her. Gaining access to the male world, Portia fuses masculine liberality with the "direction of the inner spiritual self" (42). Depolarizing the sexual roles within herself, Portia is "both merciful and scornfully witty, giving and harshly rigid, 'feminine' and 'masculine'" (43). Reinforcing the themes of the main plot, Jessica and Lorenzo fuse "the sex roles between and within themselves" (44). Jessica is the "loving spiritual transformer."

187.   Greene, Gayle. "Women on Trial in Shakespeare and Webster: 'The Mettle of [Their] Sex.'" *Topic* [Washington and Jefferson College] 36 (Fall 1982): 5-19.

Though he portrays women more sympathetically than his contemporaries do, Shakespeare is far more conservative in the conventional roles he gives women as compared with John Webster who portrays tragic, heroic women of "masculine strength" not defined sexually or in relationship to men (17). Roles in Shakespeare are tied to genre considerations. Shakespeare was prevented from "centering a tragedy on a woman" (17). Shakespeare's portrayal of female characters is consistent with Renaissance views that confined women to a separate, inferior domestic sphere and that regulated female sexuality to ensure dependency on men and the legitimacy of heirs. Wifely ideals were obedience and chastity, hardly active or heroic, as suggested in Kate's Act 5 speech. Shakespeare's comic heroines–Portia, Rosalind, Viola–may be strong and independent, but they still reaffirm and are assimilated into the patriarchal hierarchy. Like comic heroines, romance women are judged by their sexuality. Though paired with lively and assertive companions, Desdemona, Hero, and Hermione may reach androgyny, as Williamson argues (item 210), though *Tem* conclusively disproves that interpretation. The problem comedies are problematic because of the less conventional notions of a woman's role. Isabella's cold, diseased fidelity to an abstraction puts her virtue to the test but discredits her as a sexual agent. Tragedy is a masculine genre with its emphasis on warfare and death as opposed to comedy's focus on life forces. Women in the tragedies are "not conceived in particularly sexual terms" (13) in their barren worlds; they are seen as virtuous or evil. Though Cleopatra is associated with the power of women's sex found in the comedies, she goes beyond comedy to embrace tragedy in the last act. Departing from Shakespeare's female characters, Vittoria in Webster's *White Devil* does not derive her strength from her relationships as wife, mother, or mistress. She gains heroism from "the very antithesis of the Renaissance ideal of woman" (15). No one in Shakespeare comes close to her. She operates in a wider sphere than does Cleopatra, and even Portia supports the society of which she is a part. *The Duchess of Malfi* "presents a heroic image of woman unmatched in Renaissance literature" (17).

188. Hartwig, Joan. "Horses and Women in *The Taming of the Shrew*." *Huntington Library Quarterly* 45 (1982): 285-94.

The analogy of women to horses was conventional in the Renaissance. Like horses, women were regarded as commodities to be bought and sold. Kate is likened to a wild horse to be purchased and trained by Petruchio. But in comparison to contemporary methods used to train horses and punish wives, Petruchio's "harsh treatment of Kate is not out of line" (288); in fact, it is "mild" (291). On the journey from Padua to Verona, the horse (Kate) is not in harmony with the rider (Petruchio), thus exemplifying a lack of concord of man with nature. Seen as a metaphorical analogue, Petruchio's "insistence on Kate's submission seems quite reasonable" (291). While the tactics adapted by Bianca's suitors make Kate a shrew, Petruchio helps her "to realize her self fully" and so challenge "the entire social structure." In their complementary relationship, Petruchio and Kate can be like the harmonious horse and rider, "figures of nobility" (292).

189. Hull, Suzanne W. *Chaste, Silent, and Obedient: English Books for Women, 1475-1640*. San Marino, CA: Huntington Library, 1982. Esp. 15, 78, 117, 136, 180, 197.

     Shakespeare's influence can be seen in books directed to female readers. A female name came before a male one "for a change" in *VA*. *TSh* is indebted to the debate on whether women should be beaten or not, and whether they were worthy or not. As the seventeenth-century progressed, more titles contained the words *lady*, *women*, etc. "Perhaps thanks are due to Shakespeare as much as to any author for focusing on heroines" (136). His "lively female characters" had a strong impact on women's books.

190. Kahn, Coppelia. "Excavating 'Those Dim Minoan Regions': Maternal Subtexts in Patriarchal Literature." *Diacritics* 12 (1982): 32-41.

     Dorothy Dinnerstein's *The Mermaid and the Minotaur: Sexual Arrangement and Human Malaise* (1976); Adrienne Rich's *Of Woman Born: Motherhood as Experience and Institution* (1976; 1977); and Nancy Chodorow's *The Reproduction of Mothering: Psychoanalysis and the Sociology of Gender* (1979), all under review here, discover and restore the feminine perspective of motherhood. These studies challenge the patriarchal (and contradictory) notions of motherhood (she is a superhuman, altruistic figure and a weak woman) found in Freud who devalued woman. A feminist reading of the maternal subtext of *Lear* can elucidate male identity by questioning the faulty assumptions on which it is based. The "imprint of mothering on the male psyche" is found in *Lear*. Though mothers are absent in the tragedies, as in *Lear*, they are "present nonetheless in the character structures of its heroes, scripted there in a code derived from the structure of the family" (41). Lear re-enacts "the original crisis of masculine identity" which struggles to break away from the mother. Yet the maternal subtext in *Lear* strongly points to "the hidden presence of the mother in his psyche" and a "repressed identification with her" (37). Lear is like a mother by suffering from hysteria (called "the mother"), a "decisively" feminine disease, and by seeing his connections to his daughters as a recapitulation of "his pre-oedipal relationship with the mother" (38). The "oral rage" in *Lear*, represented through the mouth and eating references, reflects Lear's infantile stage as well as his defense against "his 'feminine' neediness as figured in the daughters he would make into his mother" (39). The daughters also are like unfaithful wives and by shaming Lear, they bring out "the woman in him–the dependency and vulnerability attributed to women ... " (40). Lear pays a price for inflicting heavy patriarchal punishments.

191. Kastan, David Scott. "Shakespeare and 'The way of womenkind.'" *Daedalus* 111 (1982): 115-30.

Unlike the women in the comedies who are not subordinate to their men, the women of the histories are denied participation in the male political world. Though crucial to the dynasty, Richmond's Elizabeth is not even on stage at the end of *R3*. Women occupy an even "less central" position (116) in the second tetralogy than in the first. Their fruitful and nurturing role is "taken over by England herself" (117). Kate in *1H4* and Portia in *JC* are marginalized by their husbands who could have profited from their involvement; "Brutus is Hotspur writ large" (118). In the tragedies women are accused of betrayals, banished, and destroyed. Love fails because male and female cannot be joined into one. Both Hamlet and Ophelia are victims of their family, and, by cutting Ophelia off, Hamlet displays his "discomfort with sexual desire" and rejects the "only source of sanity and health" in Denmark (121). As an outsider, Desdemona, like Othello, disbelieves that her mate could love her. In a perversion of the patterns of comedy, Lady Macbeth, like the comic heroines, attempts to challenge and change her man, but she only leads him to a more horrific code of destructive manhood. While the comic heroines temporarily adopt male disguises, Lady Macbeth wants to throw off her femininity permanently. In offering the mutuality lacking in the other tragedies, *AC* creates a different tragic pattern. But the lovers' "claims are ... suspect" (125) since they are guilty of self-dramatization and they "define a union" which is clearly "denied by the play's action." The romances "redeem the tragic pattern" by having offending husbands and fathers reunited with their wives and daughters. Unlike the tragedies where the daughters suffer a divided duty, the daughters of romance (Perdita, Marina, Imogen) help to repudiate the "destructive emotional logic of patriarchy" (127). Although Prospero does not regain his daughter as the other romance fathers do, his giving Miranda to Ferdinand results in "loss ... transformed into a gain."

192. Kimbrough, Robert. "Androgyny Seen through Shakespeare's Disguise." *Shakespeare Quarterly* 33 (1982): 17-33.

It is misleading to see only literal comedy behind girl-as-boy disguises in Shakespeare. Renaissance Humanism saw androgyny as an "ideal goal, a secular dream" (19) because it allowed the individual to express "the wholeness and unity" of "personhood" and thereby escape "gender stereotyping" (25). Man in Renaissance England was ready "philosophically, theologically, practically, and psychologically to accept woman as a composite of all her historical and social 'roles'" (20). "Transsexual disguises" in Shakespeare offer a "laboratory testing-ground" (21) for these ideas. Of the seven examples of girl-into-boy, Imogen "makes no significant reference to her new sex" (21), and Portia is not an androgynous justice figure since female compassion does not triumph in *MV*. On the other hand, Rosalind "grows into a fuller human self" (23) because of her disguise; her wit is "indivisibly both masculine and feminine" (25). She is a giddy girl, a saucy lackey, and a magician, roles which allow Orlando to be more open and honest and Rosalind to challenge, through her anti-feminine barbs, "attributes created for women by society" (25). The boy actor who speaks the Epilogue emphasizes our need to accept our sex–and our common humanity--"instead of hiding behind the disguise of gender" (27). *TN* is Shakespeare's "furthest venture into androgyny" (29). Viola, who is far more troubled by the "sex of her sex" than is Rosalind, must learn that androgyny is "not a physical state, but a state of mind" (28). Assisted in this because she is a twin, Viola through her disguise makes Orsino more "confessional," freeing her as a "prisoner of gender," and teaching us that "many apparent differences between men and women are dissolvable" (30).

193. Klein, Joan Larsen. "Women and Marriage in Renaissance England: Male Perspectives." *Topic* [Washington and Jefferson College] 36 (Fall 1982): 20-37.

Because of religious and political censorship, works that ran contrary to the accepted notions of women and marriage were rarely published. Women themselves were hindered from publishing their own works. "Between 1475 and 1640 women could read very little about themselves that was not written from a male perspective" (21). Women's vocation was marriage, and those living alone were open to charges of witchcraft. Thus women were dependent on men because they were created for men. Men turned to adultery because they could only perform the sexual act with their spouse if it was in order to beget a child. A woman conceiving out of wedlock was ostracized from society because her child would not be blessed by God. Seduction and rape irreparably damaged a woman because it soiled her chastity. Jacques Du Bosc's *The Compleat Woman* advocated the education of women because knowledge, not ignorance, leads a woman to chastity. His book was criticized, however, because it ignored scripture.

194. McFeely, Maureen Connolly. "Elizabethan Views of Women and Shakespeare's Comic Heroines." *DAI* 42 (1982): 4009A. CUNY. [Esp. *AYL*, *MM*, and *TGV*.]

195. McGuire, Jerry L. "Shakespeare's *Tempest*: Rhetoric and Poetics." *American Imago* 39 (1982): 219-37.

Throughout his career, Shakespeare was concerned with the ambiguities and questions of gender. In *Tem*, gender "affirms patriarchal authority." Behind the play lies the pre-oedipal theme of infant binding with the mother, then (for males) breaking away to join the fathers, and occasionally regressing. The maternal is represented by poetry, metaphor, silence, and mutuality; the paternal is associated with language, rhetoric, and law. As a "maternal father," Prospero merges these opposites through his own fictions. In the "central paradox of the play," Prospero possesses the "metaphoricity" and nurturing of the female while still preserving the authorial goals of patriarchy. Prospero makes the audience partners with him. Ariel "represents Prospero's poetic function" (229) while Caliban is a "creature of earth and rhetoric" (230). Miranda, who is "the purity of maternal metaphor" (231), must learn to avoid the bog of Caliban's rhetoric while at the same time play the male game of chess. In her marriage to an African, Claribel becomes the "perfect female ... lost to the darkness of a stranger" (235). She is replaced by her opposite Sycorax, appropriately named for the "father of rhetoric" and a sow of the earth. In revealing his fantasies in two parallel stories (Acts 1.2.53-186; 1.2.252-94) about Sycorax replacing Miranda's mother, Prospero wants to "provide Miranda with such a rhetoric–to usurp her perfect, insular, idealized femininity, [and] to transform her to the masculinized, chess-playing verbal strategist of the play's end" (237).

196. McLuskie, Kate. "Feminist Deconstruction: The Example of Shakespeare's *Taming of the Shrew*." *Red Letters: Communist Party Literature Journal* [London] 12 (1982): 33-40.

Historical criticism of Shakespeare incorrectly assumes "a permanent and unshifting audience position" and that the plays demonstrate a "transcending truth" (34). But a radical reading of culture can deconstruct a liberal democratic expression of love and marriage to arrive at a more fruitful understanding of the plays. Though the tone and structure of *TSh* are comic, the ideological assumptions behind the play are based on female submission. Women are regarded as "commodities within a pattern of luxury consumption and aristocratic life style" (36). Yet, it is the political context of these assumptions which is more at issue than Petruchio's cruelty or kindness. *TSh* is more than a relic which critics try to explain away. There is a clear analogy between sexual and power relations, and the "connections between private life and public policies, obscured by later capitalist culture, are made explicit" in Kate's final speech (38). Love is a cash transaction in *TSh*, admirably portrayed in Michael Bogdanov's 1978 production with Baptista figuring the dowry on an adding machine and the men playing poker in the last scene. Though the product of a different culture's sexual politics, the sexism in *TSh*, as Bogdanov showed, is deeply buried in "the metaphors of ideological assumptions." The ideological positioning of a work of art "is not fixed by its explicit statements" (39). A feminist aesthetic cannot be developed by rejecting works by a male culture or privileging works by women; it must reject the notion that "pre-existing meaning" is automatically created by "assuming the audience is male" (39).

197. Muslin, Hyman L. "Romeo and Juliet: The Tragic Self in Adolescence." *Adolescent Psychiatry* 10 (1982): 106-17.

When Juliet is urged by her mother to consider the prospect of marriage, Lady Capulet denies her daughter's self-development. After Juliet refuses to marry Paris, Father Capulet's rage is fueled by the tensions of losing his daughter to another man, which is a sign of his defeat to a younger man. Romeo is vulnerable from being spurned by Rosaline. In psychoanalytic terms, he tries to fulfill his oedipal urges through Juliet, a forbidden woman from a rival family. Their secret marriage will give the couple an autonomy that could never be achieved from succumbing to the wishes of their parents. *RJ* dramatizes the predicament of "self-absorbed parents unable to respond to their children's striving for greater selfhood" (113).

198. Norvell, Betty G. "'O Mother, Mother: What Have You Done?' Shakespeare's Mothers in Relation to Catastrophe." *DAI* 43 (1982): 812A. West Virginia U. [*Cor, Ham, 2H6, 3H6, R3, TA,* and *WT*.]

199. Parten, Anne. "Re-Establishing Sexual Order: The Ring Episode in *The Merchant of Venice*." *Women's Studies* 9 (1982): 145-55.

Accustomed to happy resolutions in comedies where the wife is submissive to her husband, an Elizabethan audience might find Portia's triumph over the masculine world "faintly disturbing" (153). She is an intimidating figure because of her wealth, power, and likely "feminine ascendancy" (150) in marriage. Shakespeare uses the ring episode to explore and solve these major problems in the relationships between the sexes. More than just a source of "ready laughter," the ring business exorcises men's fears of being cuckolded as when Portia threatens Bassanio in her "two sexed figure" of Balthasar and Portia. (152). The ring episode is a "comic re-enactment of the casket trial," but Bassanio fails this second test. Giving away Portia's ring, he gives away his wife, for the ring symbolized a woman's "independent power and physical love" (152). Women who made cuckolds of their husbands were traditionally thought to dominate marriage. Removing that threat through her "game" and by giving Bassanio his ring, Portia reasserts "her return to unthreatening femininity" (153).

200. Perret, Marion D. "Of Sex and the Shrew." *Ariel: A Review of International English Literature* 13 (1982): 3-20.

The emphasis in *TSh* is "on the relationship of the sexes rather than sexual relations" (3). In *TSh*, one of Shakespeare's "less indecent works," bawdy puns and sexual innuendo are "morally instructive," suggesting virtue by their opposites. The bawdy of the Induction contrasts with Petruchio's behavior. While the Lord promotes Sly's lust for a mock wife, Petruchio refrains from sex on his wedding night (a traditional way to tame a shrew) to make Kate "appreciate spiritual values she has neglected, [and] so she can become a wife who will be a friend and companion rather than a mere sexual convenience" (6). The theme of sexual desire in the Induction is mirrored in the subplot. Shakespeare often associates sensuality with shrewishness in his female characters. Thus Kate "speaks bawdily when she is a shrew; Bianca does not speak bawdily until she shows herself a shrew" (9). That Kate and Petruchio speak in bawdy puns in Acts 2 and 3 proves that she is destined to be a wife and mother and he will be "her equal." Unlike the Richard Burton/Elizabeth Taylor film of *TSh*, where Petruchio arouses Kate's sexual desire only to make her submissive, Shakespeare's Petruchio reveals "moral awareness and sensitivity" in wanting to join their hearts and minds, not just their bodies. Unquestionably, Kate and Petruchio are lusty, not lustful. Shakespeare in *TSh* "uses sex as a touchstone for character and values" (18).

201. Ranald, Margaret Loftus. "Women and Political Power in Shakespeare's English Histories." *Topic* [Washington and Jefferson College] 36 (Fall 1982): 54-65.

The motto "deeds are for men, words for women" generally characterizes the role of women in the English history plays. Yet Margaret of Anjou, Constance of Brittany, and Katherine of Aragon "offer interesting variations" on this theme as they "exemplify the roles and problems of women on the historical stage" (54). All are victims of the "masculine drive to power." The termagant, unfaithful wife, Margaret is the masculine, Amazonian woman who shrewdly manipulates with her words. Unlike the *Chronicles*, Shakespeare displays "no such antifeminist attitude" toward her (55). He portrays her as a mother incensed at her son's disinheritance who later becomes "deficient in all womanliness" and shows "a cruelty impossible even for Lady Macbeth" (57). Casting her as both victim and Nemesis, Shakespeare arouses no sympathy for Margaret in *R3*. Unlike Margaret, Constance is entirely maternal, a faithful wife. Her only weapons are her words and, adopting a technique of the powerless, she "picks up a word introduced by others and rings changes upon it" (59). No match for Elinor, Constance is a figure of lamentation. Like Constance, Katherine is a victim and a voice of conscience against political expediency. "After *King John*, women have no real place in the second tetralogy," yet only in *H8* does Shakespeare "do real justice to a historical lady" (60). In fact, Shakespeare "does more justice to her than to any other woman in the genre" (64). Katherine is closer to the women of the late romances; like Hermione she is a loyal wife and a figure of sacrifice. Katherine wins a moral victory over the cardinals who visit her, a domestic scene of Shakespeare's invention, as she barbs her words "with quiet irony" (63). Katherine's words are not just the weapons of the weak; they have "the strength of redemption" (64).

202. Rosenberg, Marvin. "Macbeth and Lady Macbeth in the Eighteenth and Nineteenth Centuries." In *Focus on Macbeth*. Ed. John Russell Brown. London: Routledge, 1982. 73-86.

Comic, singing witches and Garrick's noble Macbeth required
Hannah Pritchard's fearsome Lady Macbeth to spur Macbeth on
to murder. Pritchard evidently felt no remorse in the sleepwalking scene. Sarrah Siddons and John Philip Kemble carried on
the tradition of playing Lady Macbeth as the "fierce, eagerly
murderous wife" and Macbeth as the "noble, reluctantly
murderous husband" (76). Kemble's "gentlemanly" Macbeth was
"inevitably smothered" by Siddons's power. Edmund Kean took
away some of Lady Macbeth's burden of guilt with his "self-
generated criminality." With the German actress Rosalie Nouseul
there started a gradual softening of the character of Lady
Macbeth with more attention given to her feminine side. Helen
Faucit, who was a "transitional figure between Siddons and post-
Siddons characterizations" (81), conveyed a sense of Lady
Macbeth's vulnerability, femininity, care, and wifely devotion. To
Henry Irving's villainous, hypocritical Macbeth, Ellen Terry
offered a soft interpretation in the late nineteenth century. Terry
believed that femininity was "the true core" of Lady Macbeth's
character. Unlike earlier Macbeths who needed external
compulsion, Irving's Macbeth provoked Terry's Lady Macbeth to
"urge him to the crimes he had already thought of" (85).

203. Sinfield, Alan. "Kinds of Loving: Women in the Plays." In *Self and
Society in Shakespeare's Troilus and Cressida and Measure for
Measure*. Ed. J.A. Jowitt and R.K.S. Taylor. Bradford: U of
Leeds Centre for Adult Education, 1982. 27-44.

Elizabethan ideology, as portrayed in Hector's speech in Act
2.2 of *TrC*, supported patriarchy by insisting that "woman is
subordinate and sexual indulgence is sinful" (27). Two love modes
collide, scramble, and are readjusted in *TrC*. The Ovidian lover
saw woman as a sexual target; his "aggressive masculinity" agreed
with the Church's asceticism which also subordinated women.
Romanticism worshipped women, focusing on the rituals of
courtship rather than sexual fulfillment. Yet both modes, though
contrary, "extended the emotional range of patriarchy without
challenging it fundamentally" (29). Beginning as a romantic,
Troilus moves to being an Ovidian desiring sexual union with
Cressida. Yet when she leaves for the Greek camp, he protests

like a romantic, though later rejects her fickleness like an Ovidian. Trojan council and Greek camp alike use women as "props in the male action" (33). Diomedes, "the most thorough-going Ovidian" (34), demonstrates how society breaks such "face-saving ... love codes." Protestantism disrupted these codes of love by rejuvenating marriage as a mutual union and by asserting the value of sex in re-evaluating chastity as marital fidelity. Shakespeare, too, "often present[s] marriage as the virtuous resolution of problems" created by these codes (36). Even though Protestantism enhanced the status of women, they still were regarded as inferior and subordinate to men. A disconcerting contradiction erupted between mutual love and authority (patriarchy). As a function of the state, marriage is controlled by the Duke in *MM* who forces Lucio, Angelo (Ovidian turned Christian), and even Isabel into matrimony. The conventional "processes of marriage" fail in *MM*, which offers the "form of a happy ending, but not its content." Consequently *MM* offers a critique of the orthodox doctrine of marriage. The real problem of the play resides in the "structure of Shakespeare's society," not in whether Isabel is "right" to plot in the bed trick (42).

204. Splitter, Randolph. "Language, Sexual Conflict and 'Symbiosis Anxiety' in *Othello*." *Mosaic* 15.3 (1982): 17-26.

Oth reveals a "fundamental 'preoedipal' uncertainty about (sexual) identity, the boundaries of self, and the interpenetration of inner and outer worlds" (17). Violently destroying Othello's self, Iago wants himself rather than Desdemona or Cassio to be loved by the Moor, as is seen in Iago's interpretation of dreams. Because of his hatred of women, whom he regards as whores, Iago places them in "wrong roles in the wrong situations." He tries to convince Othello that a woman's honor (a word that has a different meaning when applied to men) is an ambiguous, "unseen essence" that is easily lost (like a good name) without a husband knowing it. And in doing so Iago raises questions about honor as Falstaff does over the word and its referents. Iago links a woman's virginity (her honor) to a purse, since for him "putting money in a purse is an economic, bourgeois metaphor for sexual intercourse" (22) in which men and women lose by spending. Iago dismisses a woman's virginity as trash, "something, nothing"; he treats women as a commodity. According to Iago's "fantasy of sexual violence," men lose their manliness and self-control when they engage in effeminate passion. Othello regards killing as a "substitute for sex" and the only way he can preserve Desdemona's virginity. Through his poisonous words, Iago "impregnates" Othello, penetrating the Moor's mind, creating a "kind of symbiosis anxiety" (24) and breaking down the integrity and autonomy of Othello's self. Iago's words become not healthy pharmakon (as in Derrida) but "destructive pharmaka," or the "false 'conceits' of female honor and purity, the whole social code of masculinity and femininity, which reinforces and revives early childhood fears of betrayal, loss, and contamination" (25).

205. Stallybrass, Peter. *"Macbeth* and Witchcraft." In *Focus on Macbeth*. Ed. John Russell Brown. London: Routledge, 1982. 189-209.

Charges of witchcraft, which reveal more about the accuser than the accused, were directed against the outsider, the rival, old, poor women. Fears about witchcraft helped James I to establish the opposite analogies; because James was God's anointed, he was under demonic attack. Such a view serves as the "ideological terrain" of *Mac* (192). Witchcraft stood for the antitheses of "the order of monarchy, patriarchy, and reason." It was associated with feminine rule and the womanish killing of Duncan (201) and was antifamily, antisovereignty. The ambiguity of the witches in *Mac*, who were like English widows yet more mysterious, provides a double perspective on evil. Private scenes with women championing evil alternate with public, male ones. Lady Macbeth is structurally associated with the witches in establishing "the relation between women, witchcraft and the undermining of patriarchal authority and sterility" (197). Although Lady Macduff represents the ideal family and vindicates women, there are also womanless, virtuous families of men (Duncan, Banquo). Both Lady Macbeth and the witches manifest their antitheses; she becomes a solicitous wife in Act 5 and they are transformed from equivocal to clear speakers. In Act 4.1, the "emblematic centre" of the play, the witches' dance can be seen as the "systematic undoing of the hierarchal ceremonies of speech, cooking, and dancing" (200). The father is established through Macduff, a father born not of woman, though. Even though *Mac* ultimately attributes witchcraft to women who challenge the powerful patrilineal, patrilocal society, *Mac* does "not analyze the position of women; rather, it mobilizes the patriarchal fear of unsubordinated woman ... " (205).

206. Taylor, Mark. *Shakespeare's Darker Purpose: A Question of Incest.* New York: AMS P, 1982. Esp. Chapter One, "A Kind of Incest," 1-23; and Chapter Three, "Mother, Wife, and Yet His Child," 49-83.

Early in the *WT,* Antigonus defends Hermione's chastity by vowing that if she prove false, he'll geld his own daughters. Although his comments are part of the general context which supports Hermione's innocence, the violence of the threat underscores his own fears of his daughters. "If he can conceive, however remotely, of a situation in which he would desire to eradicate their sexual identity, it is because that identity is to him a dangerous and unacceptable fact" (17). Gratiano expresses a similar fear when he threatens to geld "the clerk" when Nerissa threatens infidelity. The chief difference, however, is that wives are frequently sexually faithful to their husbands; daughters seldom forego sexual maturity to remain faithful to their fathers. In *MM* Isabella chooses celibacy so that she may remain faithful to her father. In an unconscious acknowledgement of his latent incestuous desire, Antigonus threatens also to geld himself rather than have his daughters bear illegitimate heirs: he "cannot entertain the notion of his little girls going to someone else; he would rather deprive them altogether of their sexual identities; but as if he recognizes that his preference is a revelation of sublimated incestuous feelings, a taboo that his conscious, civilized mind cannot accept, he violently reacts to it by hypothetically inflicting self-mutilation" (20-21). Before his death, Antigonus concedes that Hermione is guilty. His death is necessary not only as punishment but also as prevention against his incestuous threats.

Shakespeare dramatizes the reunion between Leontes and
Hermione, but his decision to narrate rather than dramatize the
reunion between Leontes and Perdita seems unsatisfying. The
king's banishment of his infant daughter is the most serious crime
he commits because it removes from Sicily "the female principle
of fecundity" (51), thus leaving him without an heir and his
kingdom sterile. His action resembles Antigonus's threat against
his own daughters. A happy resolution of the play depends on the
daughter's restoration. Cordelia in *Lear* and Marina are two other
daughters separated from fathers, although for vastly different
reasons. While Lear and Pericles show the effects of this
separation, they, too, are renewed by restorations brought about
by their daughters. In *WT,* the expectations set up early in the
play suggest that the prime reunion should be between father and
daughter, but it is actually between husband and wife. In
Pandosto, Shakespeare's source, the father's incestuous desire for
his daughter (although he does not recognize her) is not
sublimated. His suicide at the end is an acknowledgement of his
unnatural desire, a consequence of his earlier unnatural rejection
of her. Shakespeare diverts the sequence of events leading to
incest by "keeping Hermione alive and forcing his drama to move
toward her reunion with Leontes" (67).

The potential threat of incest in the restored daughter plays is
developed through other characters. In *Per*, Antiochus and his
daughter share an actual unlawful relationship. In *WT*, Polixenes,
a father figure, desires Perdita, and interferes in his son's plans to
marry her. Borrowing heavily from the actual father/daughter
meeting in *Pandosto*, this scenario dramatizes in a less tragic way
the possible consequences of reuniting with a once rejected and
now unrecognized daughter.

Reviews: Maguin, Jean-Marie, *Cahiers Elisabethains* 24 (Oct.
1983): 130-32; Traister, Daniel, *Shakespeare Bulletin* 1 (Nov.
1983): 22-24.

207. Tennenhouse, Leonard. "Representing Power: *Measure for
      Measure* in Its Time." *Genre* 15.2-3 (1982): 139-56.

The trickster figure, who is also a monarch, "observes the state
and witnesses both sexual misconduct and the abuses of political

power" (139). His disguise and the adoption and discarding of it bring reform to the social order. *MM* differs from the romantic comedies by emphasizing the need for regulation of the law instead of trying to loosen and humanize it. The state has become separated from the monarch because he adopts a disguise to look at the court from a distance, leaving his kingdom to be run by deputies. The law is transformed from serving personal interests to upholding traditional values. Also, the regulation of sexual behavior is needed through the protection of marriage. In the romantic comedies, marriage was one of the few ways for a man to gain power in society. However, the erotic desire of the earlier comedies is questioned in the later plays. The language of desire is no longer linked to chastity, the former being politically dangerous. Chastity "is idealized while erotic desire is debased"; it has become diseased sexuality and must be banished by the disguised ruler. "These plays portray the power of the monarch as that of the patriarch" (149) who makes sure that the women marry suitable mates to ensure the male distribution of wealth and power.

208. Thomas, Paul R. "The Marriage of True Minds–Ideal Friendship in *Two Gentlemen of Verona." Iowa State Journal of Research* 57 (1982): 187-92.

Ideal male friendship ("amitie") helps to explain the way Proteus and Valentine act toward each other and the way Julia and Silvia are characterized. Valentine and Proteus's friendship is analogous to David and Jonathan's in 1 Samuel and Palamon and Arcite's in Chaucer's *Knight's Tale* where male friendship is a higher order than a man's love for a woman. According to the code of ideal friendship, "a woman fit to be wife to one should be quite acceptable to the other" (92). True friends must be constant and liberal to one another. Inconstant Proteus is dominated by passion and so "has become effeminate." A "Proteus" herself because she changes shapes, Julia "becomes masculine to aid her beloved Proteus in achieving the proper balance–reason dominating will and desire" (91). Julia is Proteus's constant guide. "Perhaps the greatest paradox of *Two Gentlemen of Verona* is that by 'losing' Silvia, Valentine 'finds' her" (190). As a sign of his liberality, Valentine gives Silvia to Proteus who gives her back and returns to Julia as a sign of his cure.

209. Wildermuth, Catherine T. "Rings Around Venice: Love in *The Merchant of Venice*." *Proceedings of Conference of College Teachers of English of Texas* 47 (Sept. 1982): 6-13.

The central event in *MV* is not the trial but Portia's marriage. Though she regrets her inability to control her own body, Portia nonetheless "speaks and acts as if she were under the power of her own control" (7). The ring is not a sign of Bassanio's control of her but a symbol of mutual obligation. Portia's "father has given her a husband, but Portia herself retains the power to give her husband a loving wife" (8). But the marriage cannot be consummated until Bassanio's bond is paid to Antonio who "unconsciously" and selfishly wants to disrupt the marriage. Antonio's love is "death-producing" (13). The ring business indicates how great Bassanio's and Antonio's debts are to Portia. Though the ring business initially shows Antonio winning in a test of loyalties, it is Portia who is in complete control in Act 5 because of the rings. She "symbolically destroys and renews her marriage vows to make her husband much more aware of the value of his wife and much more intent on keeping faith" (11). The resolution of *MV* is not on masculine cruelty but on the redeeming and "life-producing powers of love."

210. Williamson, Marilyn L. "Doubling, Women's Anger, and Genre." *Women's Studies* 9 (1982): 107-19.

Shakespeare frequently uses dramatic "psychic doubles," the wronged, docile heroine and her assertive and angry "socially inferior" companion. Three such pairs–Hero/Beatrice in *Ado*; Desdemona/Emilia in *Oth*; and Hermione/Paulina in *WT*–show that Shakespeare "can express both the bitter resentment of women about their oppression and, at the same time, the socializing power of society" (109). Although Beatrice comes to Hero's defense in a lively attack on the "public wrong" and so blasts male society in Messina, the "pressure of genre" finds women "eagerly accepting their place in a patriarchy ... " (111). An outspoken critic like Beatrice, Emilia has much in common with Desdemona. But contrary to what recent critics say about Desdemona as assertive, she is punished by Othello for the behavior she demonstrates early in the play and thus becomes a passive, obedient wife. Through her words, Emilia is able to influence both the audience and Othello. A bitter critic of men, Emilia offers a "voice of judgment which her silenced mistress could not raise" (114). Paulina helps to right the wrongs done to Hermione who like Desdemona cannot defend herself; and in blistering Leontes, Paulina helps to purge him. She is an "anomaly in English literature" as Leontes's counselor (116); her actions are "possibly a sign of [Shakespeare's] personal growth toward a more androgynous vision" (117). Genre plays a major role in the way these pairs function in male society. Beyond doubt, these doubles have tremendous implications for feminist criticism. Such doubling "allows a patriarchal society to retain the traditional ideal of womanhood and to ratify the socialization of women to convention ... " (117). Women, therefore, can give vent to their hostility while at the same time society can control such anger.

211. Wolf, William D. "'New Heaven, New Earth': The Escape from Mutability in *Antony and Cleopatra*." *Shakespeare Quarterly* 33 (1982): 328-35.

Although Rome (power) and Egypt (life force) have been contrasted, there is a "subtle yet important similarity" between them. Both Rome and Egypt repeatedly illustrate the "principle of fluctuation" (329). Politics change in Rome as Cleopatra's moods do in Alexandria. Antony fluctuates "wildly" between love and valor, reflected in both the visual and verbal imagery of *AC*. Antony's sword "represents both sexuality and martial valor" (330). As he does elsewhere, Shakespeare explores the conflict of mutability and permanence, both frequently presented as "the material versus the non-material" (331). Antony and Cleopatra triumph over mutability ("earthly love and duty") as they do through death. When he arrives at Cleopatra's monument, a "new Antony" is "purged of sexual desire and stripped of temporal power" (333). Escaping his body, he escapes the earth. Although Cleopatra first expresses her vision in sensual terms, she undergoes the "same transformation" as Antony does through her death. Her worm "replaces the sword as the symbol of sexual pleasure" (335).

212. Ziegler, Georgianna. "A Supplement to the Lenz-Greene-Neely Bibliography on 'Women and Men in Shakespeare' Based on the Collections of the Furness University of Pennsylvania Shakespeare Library." *Women's Studies* 9 (1982): 203-13.

This unannotated bibliography is divided into six sections: "Books–Pre 1900"; "Books–1900 and After"; "Recent Works About Women in Early Drama Including Shakespeare"; "Women Playwrights Whose Works Are Represented in the Collection"; "Prompt-Books Belonging to the Following Actresses"; and "Collection of Books About the Following Actresses."

1983

213. Araki, Masazumi. "A Fantastical Perspective of the Suppressed 'Incest' Theme in *Twelfth Night*." *Shakespeare Studies* [Japan] 18 (1983): 29-56.

   TN represents an epiphany. The number twelve comes from an Old English word meaning "two left behind after counting ten," while the number ten is a symbol of unity. Hence, two is the "centering code" for the reading of the play and can be seen as a symbol of androgyny. In the end, all characters' desires, except those of Andrew and Malvolio, are fulfilled. Sebastian and Viola could be seen as doubles of Orsino and Olivia; but as counterparts, they must have a brother-sister relationship, a twin relationship, an incestuous relationship. Olivia's mourning requires her to be chaste, yet her imposed chastity suggests incestuous desires. If she accepts Orsino's love, she would be unchaste to her brother. Viola as Cesario is androgynous, aptly described by Malvolio as a "peascod" and "codling." The dolphin is also a symbol of the feminine principle and the womb. As both a solar and lunar symbol, it represents androgyny. "Perfection is the state in which antagonistic elements are integrated into one....One is not purity but confusion ... or chaos" (54). The night of *TN* provides secrecy for the sexual implications of oneness.

214. Bromley, Laura G. "Lucrece's Re-Creation." *Shakespeare Quarterly* 34 (1983): 200-11.

Many critical readings of *RL* fail to recognize Lucrece's definition of herself in terms of her culture and in terms of the poem. "Far from being a mere mouthpiece for the rhetorical embellishment of an abstract ideal, Lucrece is a complex character who engages in a moral struggle and finds a way to oppose and overcome the evil that entraps her" (201). According to the Renaissance perception of the world as a set of polarities, Lucrece's suicide restores the order disrupted by the evil and corruption of the rape. The evil of Tarquin's lust is infectious. He ignores signs of it, rationalizing rather than recognizing it. When he rapes Lucrece, he passes his pollution on to her. Unlike Tarquin, Lucrece sees the evil for what it is; she comes to see herself "as a victim of circumstance, subject to the forces of Time and Opportunity" (204), which are beyond the male order. Once defiled, she regains control and consciously chooses to restore her purity and end the spread of corruption. She understands that "private sin" can become "public plague" (207), if she does not stop it. By staging a public suicide, she can oppose and resist corruption.

215. Colley, Scott. "Leontes' Search for Wisdom in *The Winter's Tale*." *South Atlantic Review* 48 (1983): 43-53.

Leontes's deliverance from jealous torments depends upon his "prolonged education about the nature of time, change, and sexual maturity" (43). In the comedies, wisdom is as much a goal as is marriage with the women serving as teachers. In the romances, Shakespeare explores how the marriages from the comedies turned out emphasizing that "love must be learned again and again" (45). Leontes must learn from Hermione and Paulina, the "surrogate-teacher." His jealous rage is the result of associating sexuality with sin; he is repelled by Hermione's femininity which once "led him out of the garden of youth and innocence" (46). Before Leontes discovered sex, he and Polixenes "shared a masculine paradise, an asexual Eden" (47). Suspecting Hermione, Leontes denounces her as a "devil" who has made him commit an offense, forcing him to surrender his Edenic innocence because of sexuality. Having to grow up and "become sexually mature necessarily leads Leontes to confront disability and death" (48). Hermione, his first teacher, shows him the "ways of natural knowledge and natural sexuality." But clinging to the past, Leontes finds such knowledge poison. Though we do not see him during Hermione's sixteen-year absence, Leontes comes to accept the "complexities and contradictions" of love, change, and growth that provide parallels to his life in the "Bohemian adventures" of *WT*. To possess knowledge of love, Leontes must learn about the "responsibilities to married love" magically represented in Hermione's statue.

216. Dusinberre, Juliet. "*Troilus and Cressida* and the Definition of Beauty." *Shakespeare Survey* 36 (1983): 85-95.

In the world of *TrC*, beauty is defined by the beautiful woman, whether it is Helen or Cressida. The opening scene of the play sets up a competition between the beauty of Cressida and of Helen. Troilus, like Pandarus, measures Cressida's beauty by Helen's, which is defined by what it costs. Therefore, to deny Helen's worth is to deny Cressida's, for in the mercantile world of Troy, both women are weighed in the same scale. Beauty is also defined by its sweetness and through its sight and sound. The eyes and ears persuade the will about the form of physical beauty, but mislead the judgment about its relation to goodness. There is no consciousness of beauty in the mind. In this play, the Renaissance image of the mirror "betrays men and women into narcissism." *TrC* dramatizes the inseparability of the fair and the foul in human experience. The whore thus becomes the physical emblem of the barrenness of beauty.

217. Greene, Gayle. "Feminist Criticism and Marilyn French: With Such Friends, Who Needs Enemies?" *Shakespeare Quarterly* 34 (1983): 479-86.

Marilyn French's *Shakespeare's Division of Experience* (item 155) has "done feminist criticism an enormous disservice" (486). She imposes her theories of gender (e.g., male/female, inlaw/outlaw feminine) "mindlessly" and inconsistently on the plays and without regard to cultural or critical contexts. She defines male and female "loosely" and contradictorily; Richard III is both an example of the outlaw feminine principle and the "unmitigated masculine" one for French. Gender is not ahistorical, as French assumes. By arguing that males can embody the female and vice versa, French contradicts her own "division of experience into masculine and feminine" (482). She fails to recognize that Isabella's devotion to chastity, the constant of the feminine inlaw, is flawed because of its uncharitable rigor. Shakespeare "perhaps" saw feminine virtue as a "more broadly 'human' quality." French is again wrong to claim that Shakespeare grew fearful of female sexuality as he got older, while at the same time arguing that he idolized women in the late romances. It could be argued that *Tem* has the "most thoroughly 'masculine' resolution of any play in the canon" (484) because of its rules and insistence on hierarchy. A better approach is to study Miranda's role in its historical context. French ignores social and family histories as well as recent feminist criticism. Her approach is not "typical" or "predictable" of feminist criticism, as many of her reviewers protested, but, rather, a throwback to more traditional assumptions about Shakespeare and his female characters.

218. Hartman, Vicki Shahly. "*A Midsummer Night's Dream*: A Gentle Concord to the Oedipal Problem." *American Imago* 40 (1983): 355-69.

In *MND*, Shakespeare dramatizes every variety of oedipal conflict to show the necessity of acquiring proper gender identity and heterosexual love. The impossible love relationships in *MND* are the result of forbidden oedipal fantasies. When the woodland lovers pursue the wrong mates, they illustrate "the systematic self-defeating oedipal-type fascination with unobtainable partnership" (361). Suffering from castration anxiety, Bottom exemplifies another "tabooed" love affair. Titania is his "mother figure" who has two changeling sons, Bottom and the Indian boy. Oberon is the absent father who upon his return finds the child, Bottom, "asexual" (363). Titania and Egeus, the two wayward parents, are suitably admonished. It is only "oedipal intent to which the play concedes, not oedipal behavior" (364). Shakespeare defuses the oedipal problem by having the action take place in a "guilt-free environment"; the woods are "inverted and splintered to avoid anxiety." At the end of *MND*, there is a return to the daylight world of reason where oedipal fantasies are renounced and where the characters find the "consolation of a more appropriate but still contrasexual love" (365). Puck's ironic Epilogue addresses the audience's own oedipal fantasies by inviting both men and women to personalize imaginatively the experience of the play.

219. Hogan, Patrick Colm. "*Macbeth*: Authority and Progenitorship." *American Imago* 40 (1983): 385-95.

The narrative structure of *Mac* is based on oedipal crimes and appropriate punishments. The characters are "strictly defined in gender and kinship terms" (386). Banquo and Duncan double as fathers and progenitors, as do Macduff and the King of England. Phallic women, the witches and Lady Macbeth, double as mothers who seduce their son (Macbeth) "into violating the law of the father" (386) for which he is annihilated and castrated by Macduff, the punishing father. Contrasting with these seductive mothers are the benevolent ones–Lady Macduff, Lady Duncan, and Scotland. Macbeth's oedipal pattern of repeated seductions robs innocence and conformity from the law of the father, leaving only illegitimate authority and violations of progenitorship. His murderous associations with mothers (Lady Macduff, Scotland, Lady Macbeth) lead to his sterility and death, "correlates of castration and annihilation as well as seduction and incorporation" (390). Filled with an abundance of grace, the innocent son Malcolm has a different relationship with his mother Scotland; unlike the seductive mothers, she does not kill herself but retreats from the evils of the world. True to the oedipal pattern, Macbeth as the guilty son must die. The imagery of growth, planting, and nurturing reinforces oedipal fantasies. Macbeth is associated with imagery of "death and decay behind a facade of growth and fertility" (392). Unlike the good mothers, Lady Macbeth and the witches are linked to the imagery of "poisonous nurturance" (393).

220. Holmberg, Arthur. "*The Two Gentlemen of Verona*: Shakespearean Comedy as a Rite of Passage." *Queen's Quarterly* 90.1 (1983): 33-44.

Since "there has probably never been a visually more acute audience in history" than ours (39), the image of the actor and actress playing Shakespeare's adolescents must be believable. Many modern productions are visually ineffective and inaccurate because of miscasting. In a Stratford-upon-Avon misguided production of *LLL*, the Princess of France "lumbered about the stage barefoot ... and proceeded to pare carrots" (38). Shakespeare's adolescents in the comedies require actors and actresses who are young and beautiful. An ungainly actress should never play Miranda. Having "undeniable comeliness," actors and actresses give directors room to experiment in developing the romantic leads. Such casting is essential in *TGV*, which represents a "symbolic rite of passage from adolescence into adulthood" (42). Shakespeare's adolescent courtiers and ladies experience "the opposing pulls of human love: a desire to lose the self and a desire to reaffirm the self" (40). Good-looking adolescents help to represent visually and accurately the key themes of *TGV*–"vocational anxiety, intimacy, and the dual problem of competition and complacency" (44). Moreover, such physical grace and beauty is mandatory for Julia's disguise as Proteus's page, which "raises the question of sexual ambiguity and gender identification" (40). With marriage the lovers in *TGV* enter society as adults.

221. Hurst, Mary L. "Shakespeare, Chaucer, and 'False Cressida': A Reinterpretation." *Selected Papers from the West Virginia Shakespeare and Renaissance Association* 8 (1983): 1-8.

Though Shakespeare's literary legacy encouraged him to present Cressida as an Eve figure, a temptress false and dangerous, he wisely chose to make her much more complex than her detractors allowed. In fact, he "seems to be on her side, aware of her position and doing his best to set the record straight" (6). For Shakespeare, Cressida is an "embryonic feminist" (7), a woman who uses her wit and courage to survive in a cruel, masculine world. In essence, "Shakespeare's Cressida is neither Mary nor Eve, neither Desdemona nor the 'cunning whore' of Troy, but the product of sixteenth-century creative imagination, Criseyde's sister over time" (2). Like Chaucer's lady, Shakespeare's Cressida is "alone in a male-dominated world." In *TrC*, she is not to blame for the problems of love; time and society are against her. In a male world at war, women are pulled away "at a moment's notice," indicating Cressida's "helplessness" (6). Since she does not have years in which to court, as does Chaucer's character, Cressida's "verbal fencing with Troilus should not be censured" but seen as her means of self-protection. She is as concerned with modesty as Chaucer's Criseyde; she has been secret, though others have betrayed her. It is not her fault that Troilus is weak, impotent, and indiscreet. Both Chaucer's and Shakespeare's Troiluses are egocentric. Cressida is not to be faulted for kissing the Greeks or seeking a guardian in Diomedes; she is, after all, at the mercy of her captors. The "final vindication" of Shakespeare's heroine is that he refuses "to condemn Cressida by punishing her in any way" (7).

222. Iannone, Carol. "Feminist Literary Criticism: At War with Itself." *CEA Critic* 45 (1983): 11-19.

Realistic and self-conscious, feminist critics are dissatisfied with their own criticism. It is "fatally flawed" (11) in part since it uses "variants" of older criticism and relies on the "male-dominated" cultural theory. The publication of the special Shakespeare issue of *Women's Studies* in 1981 "serves as a conscious gloss" on previous feminist work. Two theoretical essays in that collection even "dismantle any need for feminist criticism" (12). Carol Thomas Neely (item 164) argues that feminists are "trapped by the very language of their revolution"; and in maintaining the necessity of a binary opposition (men/women), Neely actually perpetuates the stereotypes feminists fight against. Neely's attempts to establish a transformational criticism that empowers critics does not release feminism from its "theoretical bankruptcy" (14). Similarly, when Marianne Novy (item 163) admits that

women in love willingly subordinate themselves to men, she
concedes the power of patriarchy. The essays in *Women's Part*
(item 126) substantiate Richard Levin's *(New Readings vs.*
Old Plays: Recent Trends in the Reinterpretation of English Renaissance
Drama [Chicago: U of Chicago P, 1979]) charge that feminism is
guilty of thematic readings that are "selective," "out of context,"
and that are "sustained by systematic omission of contrary
evidence" (15). The essays in *Women's Studies* violate Shakespeare
and hinder the cause of feminism. Feminists themselves recognize
that they are at a dead end and so have gone to the social
sciences for support. Yet their aesthetic ground is collapsing. They
are misguided in insisting on the connection between "literature
and life" or the strict dichotomy between man and woman; female
readers can identify with male characters and vice versa. Male
readers can find parallels with Ophelia; Hamlet's dilemma is "a
common human dilemma" (17).

223. Jagendorf, Zvi. "Strangers in the Night: Sexual Encounters in
     Religious and Secular Texts." *University of Toronto Quarterly* 53
     (1983/84): 135-48.

     The bed-trick, or substitution of one woman for another in the
dark, is found in Genesis (Jacob and Leah), Terence's *Hecyra*, the
Reeve's Tale, *MM*, *AWW*, and Moliere's *Amphitryon*. Shakespeare
reverses the Biblical archetype that man gains knowledge from
such encounters, i.e., he knows woman as the patriarch Jacob did.
Instead, for Shakespeare such sexual tricks are "a stage for the
dramatization of illusion and error in the guise of knowledge"
(136). Man is stripped bare and cast in a dialectic of doubt,
caught in a paradox of love and lust, knowledge and ignorance,
salvation and damnation. The bed-trick is "a quintessential
tragicomic device" (142). *MM* concentrates on the male (Angelo's)
"burden of conscience," not the woman's (Mariana's) who is
regarded only as an instrument. *MM* explores "the paradox of
male sexuality, its perverse blindness, which in spite of itself is
turned into fruitful ends" (143). But in *AWW*, Helena's "articulate
awareness" is of primary concern. Unlike Leah or Mariana,
Helena is "her own mistress" who, through a combination of

feminine passivity and male-like aggression, will "use Bertram not as he uses her ... " (144). Helena must bear the "ordeal of consciousness," the pleasure and disgust of her actions. Yet true to comedy, she harbors no revenge against Bertram. Guilty of blind lust, Bertram does not know himself and requests knowledge from Helena who becomes the source of his love. Shakespeare's "cheating women" ultimately tame their lustful men (Angelo, Bertram) who "plant their seeds in supposedly forbidden wombs" (147). The bed-trick, therefore, symbolizes the tensions between male and female sexuality.

224. Jardine, Lisa. *Still Harping on Daughters: Women and Drama in the Age of Shakespeare*. Sussex: Harvester; Totowa, NJ: Barnes, 1983. Esp. 3-5, 12-15, 18-20, 29-36, 44-46, 58-61, 70-75, 80-82, 85-86, 92-100, 108-14, 117-24, 127-36, 184-95.

Shakespeare entertains a modestly enlightened view of "the woman's place" as illustrated by Kate's final speech in support of wifely deference in *TSh* and in Portia's abdication of her hereditary independence to Bassanio in *MV*. These speeches are seen in terms of good-humored comedy, for where women "have no social freedom, comedy is absent" (59). Kate's words bear no relation to the preceding action. In fact, if obedience goes with financial support, then it is Petruchio who should kneel to Kate. Portia converts her hard financial currency into "virtues, beauties, [and] friends." In *CE*, Adriana faces "husbandly schizophrenia" as a passive victim of Antipholus of Ephesus. At no point does she deliberately oppose her husband's behavior. Presenting a travesty of ordinary domestic relations, the play ironically underlines the acceptability of a double standard applied to male and female marital fidelity.

Hamlet's confrontation with his mother converts her so-called "lascivious waywardness" into "emblematic chaste resignation." Ironically, it is a male character who perceives free choice on the part of the female character as the inevitable sign of irrational lust. Gertrude has also cut off Hamlet from his "hereditary entitlement." Furthermore, her sexual relationship with Claudius may likely produce a new heir to the kingdom of Denmark.

Ophelia is either honest or a bawd, depending on how Hamlet chooses to describe his own behavior toward her. In *TA*, after Lavinia has been the victim of rape and mutilation, it is she who must atone for the crime. Such a combination of sexual frailty and spiritual strength characterizes the female heroine. A pervasive misogynistic tradition is thus behind the representation of female figures like Lady Macbeth, Reagan and Goneril, and Tamora in *TA* as "not-woman." And affirming such a tradition, these female anti-heroes regularly compare themselves to the ultimate in "not-womanhood"–Medea.

Reviews: Ashley, Leonard R.N., *Bibliotheque d'Humanisme et Renaissance* 47 (1985): 443-44; Barton, Anne, *London Review of Books* 18-31 Aug. 1983: 18-19; Blaisdell, Charmarie J., *Sixteenth Century Journal* 15 (1984): 514; Ewbank, Inga-Stina, *Times Literary Supplement* 2 Sept. 1983: 934; Gibbons, Brian, *Shakespeare Survey* 38 (1985): 224; Helton, Tinsley, *Seventeenth-Century News* 42 (1984): 40-41; Kahn, Coppelia, *Shakespeare Quarterly* 35 (1984): 489-91; Kermode, Frank, *New York Review of Books* 28 April 1983: 30-33; Knapp, Margaret, *Educational Theatre Journal* 36 (1984): 281-82; Schabert, Ina, *Shakespeare Jahrbuch* 121 (1986): 223-29.

225. Kestenbaum, Clarice J. "Fathers and Daughters: The Father's Contribution to Feminine Identification in Girls as Depicted in Fairy Tales and Myths." *American Journal of Psychoanalysis* 43 (1983): 119-27.

Fathers play an important role in their daughters' development, often serving as a "model for identification and superego formation" (119). One group of fairy tales treats the disastrous triangle of father, daughter, and mother. Another group deals with "a daughter's purposely provoking an overly attentive father so that he becomes angry with her and sends her away" (122). Shakespeare's play about Cordelia and King Lear is best seen as a version of the tale of "who loves father best."

226. Kimbrough, Robert. "Macbeth: The Prisoner of Gender." *Shakespeare Studies* 16 (1983): 175-90.

In *Mac*, as in *TrC* or *RJ*, Shakespeare criticizes the "personal and social destructiveness of [a] polarized masculinity and femininity" (177) that portrays manliness as cruel, bold, and without compassion, and the womanly as weak, cowardly, and pitiable. Macduff's resolve to combine "bravery and compassion" illustrates the ideal, "fully-realized" human (androgynous) response. Lady Macbeth and Macbeth suffer from society's view of gender which separates and divides. Macbeth's tragedy is that he gradually represses the better part of his manhood for its "merely tough part" (185) in his pursuit of a "chauvinistic war ethic" (177). Falling into Lady Macbeth's trap of what she thinks is manly, Macbeth violates nature and the virtues associated with the feminine. He renounces the compunctious virtues, including the milk of human kindness, aptly expressed in feminine terms.

Rejecting what she thinks is feminine and weak, Lady Macbeth confuses "womanhood and humanhood" (181) and embraces the diabolic. Her "unsex me" speech, which really means "ungender me" (187), expresses her wish to "uncultivate" (182) her feminine self. But Macbeth still feels the pangs of conscience in the banquet scene (Act 3.4), appropriately rendered in feminine terms. Although she attacks him for these "feminine flaws," it is these feelings that could "redeem, restore, or remake Macbeth" (185). Yet we do not hate the Macbeths because Shakespeare "appeals to our shared humanity" which must "rise above our gender division" (186). The "humanizing" touches of Lady Macbeth's suicide (which partakes of the feminine), Macbeth's ability to see a better life, and their love for each other all prove that the couple cannot deny their humanity.

227. Kleinberg, Seymour. "*The Merchant of Venice*: The Homosexual as Anti-Semite in Nascent Capitalism." *Journal of Homosexuality* 8.3-4 (1983): 113-26.

MV is about the complexities of sexual rivalry, about "homosexual eroticism in conflict with heterosexual marriage" (113). Shakespeare's sonnets and other plays are also filled with homoeroticism. Shakespeare was fond of using "debt and usury as metaphors for sexual longing" (117), and in *MV* love is inseparable from money. In selecting the right casket, Bassanio chooses life, generation, and marriage. Yet the "fate of Leah's ring casts a shadow" over Belmont (118). Portia shares Shylock's vulgarity and "confusions of feelings and money" (119). She is as ignorant of male affection as she is of marriage. Elizabethan law equated sodomites and Jews as heretics. "Shylock, the Jewish dog, already a heretic, is also a symbol for the sodomite; conversely, Antonio the sodomite with his heretical desires is linked to the other alien in Venice, the not quite human Jew" (121). Shylock is Antonio, and the Venetian's sexual guilt translates into ethnic hatred. Portia has to rescue Bassanio from Antonio's homoerotic love so he can enter into marriage freely. With Antonio and Bassanio, she forms an emotional triangle. She does "succumb" to ethnic hatred, jealousy, and revenge in the courtroom. Because Bassanio gives the ring away, he voids the terms of their marriage. Portia is thus "free to negotiate for her freedom" (123) and will never yield to man again. She freely gives herself to Bassanio. A conservative, Shakespeare does not have his melancholiacs (Jaques, Antonio) marry and shows the triumph of "heterosexual marriage and the promise of generation over the romantic but sterile infatuation of homoeroticism" (124).

228. McAvey, Marion Sheila. "'Tis Pity She's a Woman: Image and Identity for the Female Protagonist in Jacobean Comedy." *DAI* 44 (1983): 1093A. U of Massachusetts.

229. McPherson, David. "The Attack on Stage in Shakespeare's Time: An International Affair." *Comparative Literature Studies* 20 (1983): 168-82.

There are a number of significant parallels in the anti-theatrical prejudice in the age of Shakespeare and Lope de Vega. As the sixteenth century "was drawing to a close neither Philip II nor Elizabeth had the zest for amusements which they had when young" (171). The stage's attackers were "most concerned" about sex, thinking that "chastity was the major issue." Spain allowed women to play parts on the stage, whereas England in having men play women's parts violated Deuteronomy 22:5. Even so, Juan de

Mariana, a Spanish Jesuit, believed that "female actresses were worse ... because more men are heterosexual than homosexual" (174). William Prynne's *Histriomastix* (1633) echoes Mariana's sentiments about women and even quotes him. It may be surprising to find the English moralist citing a Spaniard "on the sexual evils promoted by plays," but Prynne may have liked the idea "that if even the wicked Papists hate plays, Protestants must go beyond them in zeal" (175).

230. McQuain, Jeffrey Hunter. "'The Authority of Her Merit': Virtue and Women in Chaucer and Shakespeare." *DAI* 44 (1983): 761A. American U.

231. Montrose, Louis Adrian. "Shaping Fantasies: Figurations of Gender and Power in Elizabethan Culture." *Representations* 1.2 (1983): 61-94.

The harmony arising from marital union in *MND* implies a wife's obedience to her husband as specified by the patriarchal hierarchy. The maidens, Hermia and Helena, remain constant to their men at the cost of inconstancy to each other. Tensions in the patriarchal society arise because of a female ruler. Bottom's dream is an experience of "fleeting intimacy with a powerful female," who is at once a mother, a lover, and a queen. Titania is extremely possessive of Bottom, commanding him not to leave the wood. Both Theseus and Oberon are preoccupied with the fulfillment of their desires to possess or repossess a wife. Happiness can only be achieved when the wayward wife has been mastered. In devising Hermia's punishment for refusing to marry the man of her father's choosing, Theseus parodies the very condition the Amazons built their society upon–the rejection of male society. In the argument over the changeling boy, Titania also upholds Amazon ideals. "By emphasizing her own role as a foster mother to her gossip's offspring, Titania links the biological and social aspects of parenthood together within a wholly maternal world, a world in which the relationship between women has displaced the relationship between wife and husband" (72). By the end of the play, the wedding transforms the maidens into wives; through defloration the husband takes physical and symbolic possession of the bride.

232. Nelson, T.G.A., and Charles Haines. "Othello's Unconsummated Marriage." *Essays in Criticism* 33 (1983): 1-18.

In light of Renaissance marriage customs, *Oth* offers verbal and nonverbal evidence to prove that Othello never consummated his marriage to Desdemona. By not doing so, Othello's jealousy, his "neurotic suggestibility" (3), becomes more creditable and the tragedy more plausible. Not following a double time pattern, *Oth* presents a swift dramatic narrative in which Othello and Desdemona either do not have the time to consummate their marriage or are interrupted from doing so in Act 2. The music Cassio arranges at the beginning of Act 3 mocks Othello's "ill fated union" as in the tradition of the charivari. The Moor, as Iago wants to show, is seen as the old dotard coupled with a young wanton. The handkerchief, idealized as the longed-for virgin-stained bedsheets, becomes a "talisman ... of the taking of Desdemona's virginity" (9). Seeing the handkerchief in Cassio's possession leads Othello to believe that there's none of her virginity left for him. Iago, of course, wants Othello to think Desdemona played the whore in her father's house before she married him. In their pleas before the Senate, Desdemona acknowledges the significance of "the 'rites' of the bridal night" while Othello betrays his fear of uxoriousness and his rash belief that the consummation can wait upon his military, heroic duties. Iago's test (which Othello fails) is to see that the Moor can live up to that standard. Othello fails as soldier and husband. However, it is Othello's denial of his "sexual nature" that marks his true hubris (14).

233. Norvell, Betty G. "The Dramatic Portrait of Margaret in Shakespeare's Henry VI Plays." *Bulletin of the West Virginia Association of College English Teachers* 8 (Spring 1983): 38-44.

Margaret is not the stereotype of "unmitigated villainess," since she capably plays "a constellation of roles including lover,

Machiavellian, military leader, mother, debater, and avenger" (38), some of them simultaneously. With Suffolk, Margaret is "strong, witty and charming." Though she alienates the audience as a "Machiavellian tigress" (39) and shocks them with her bestial treatment of York, Margaret does win sympathy as a mother defending her son against disinheritance. Unlike Henry, who is indecisive and self-indulgent, Margaret has a remarkable resiliency and as an orator in the French king's court can change from "fury to silver-tongued femininity" (42). She certainly captures Shakespeare's understanding in large part because she adapts so well to diverse situations with "brains and guts" (44).

234. O'Connell, Margaret Ellen. "The Motif of the Woman Disguised as a Man in Shakespeare and Some Siglo de Oro Spanish Dramatists: The Portia Figure." *DAI* 44 (1983): 1081A. Princeton U.

235. Pearson, D'Orsay W. "Renaissance Adolescent Marriage: Another Look at Hymen." *Cithara* 23 (1983): 17-27.

In Renaissance England, marriage was divided into the stages of the exchange of vows, *desponsatio*, and *commixito sexum*. Though Elizabethan law set the age of 12 for girls and 14 for boys to wed, social custom often extended the time for those wanting to marry. When a young bride and groom were married, it was a widespread practice to delay their sexual union. An exchange of vows did not mean a consummation. Because of their physical and emotional immaturity, young (early teens) brides and grooms were often separated and prevented from having intercourse. Enjoying the "fruits" of marriage thus does not point to the violence and pain stressed by some feminists. Of his five teenage heroines, Marina, Perdita, and Miranda are betrothed, not wed, and have to wait for the final ceremony, usually after a sea voyage. *RJ* offers a "two-generation perspective of marriage" (23). Though Father Capulet's request to Paris to postpone his marriage to Juliet for a couple of years until she is "ripe" (sexually ready) upholds the English custom, the views of Paris and Lady Capulet counter this opinion. "Neither Juliet's early exchange of

vows nor the subsequent consummation by carnal knowledge
seems to violate Veronese practice–only English ones" (24). Cook
(item 35) on young marriages is right but her views must be
expanded. Portraying an erotic Italy, Shakespeare pits "the English
norm" against "Veronese practice." Shakespeare often condemns
the erotic world of Italy. Though Anne Page's elopement with
Fenton in *MWW* violates English law and social custom, the
undesirability of her suitors would "mitigate audience response"
(25). Moreover, unlike Juliet, Anne Page is "a 'ripe' bride whose
age falls within limits of social practice" (25).

236. Perret, Marion D. "Petruchio: The Model Wife." *Studies in
English Literature, 1500-1900* 23 (1983): 223-35.

   In violation of Renaissance conduct books, Kate and Petruchio
reverse "male and female domestic roles in Act 4" (232).
Assuming the woman's role, Petruchio both tells and shows Kate
how to be a good wife, acting like a model "as well as a mirror for
her bad behavior." Petruchio as good wife is dietician, physician,
manager of household affairs, and an example to servants. Yet he
cannot make Kate a model wife, "for that is the woman's job"
(229). A comparison of Petruchio's exaggerated behavior in Acts
3 and 4 with Kate's in Act 5 shows her intellectual and emotional
growth. In asking for a second proof of Kate's obedience (i.e., a
kiss in public) in Act 5, Petruchio is not uxorious, but by "putting
his pride as a man into her hands" (233), he finds that her
agreement is an act of love revealing her "understanding of their
right relationship." Kate's exaggeration in Act 5.2, in her lecture
to the other wives, is another reversal of roles, since the wife did
not defend the husband's honor. All of this proves that Kate "is as
good at Petruchio's game as he." By following the spirit, if not the
letter, of Renaissance domestic law, Kate and Petruchio
"transcend the limitations of traditional male and female
propriety" (234).

237. Rackin, Phyllis. "*Coriolanus*: Shakespeare's Anatomy of *Virtus*."
Modern Language Studies 13 (1983): 68-79.

Tragedy arises when Coriolanus is incapable of rule and there is no better alternative. He is the ultimate expression of *virtus* in a society that values *virtus* above all other things. Valor in this society is what distinguishes a man from a boy or a woman, and hence the only rites of passage are battles. Such a view neglects the positive nurturing values associated with femininity. Coriolanus is opposed to the plebeians and their demands for food and, therefore, seems to oppose life itself. He prefers killing to harvesting. Ironically, Volumnia has taught Coriolanus these values. "The nurse neglects her occupation to praise the warrior: idolatry of *virtus* leaves no place for maternal solicitude, even in women" (72). Volumnia is a manly woman who has taught Coriolanus to fear everything feminine; his exaggerated devotion to *virtus* leaves him with no capacity for rational control. The ideal of *virtus* is essentially solitary, for it fails to recognize any of the bonds that unite the human community. "In the Rome of *Coriolanus*, the characters, like their society, remain fragmented" (77). It is the body politic without head or heart.

238. Schore, George Robin. "'Incest? Tush!': Jacobean Incest Tragedy and Jacobean England." *DAI* 43 (1983): 3608A. SUNY, Stoneybrook.

239. Silver, Donald, M.D. "The Dark Lady: Sibling Loss and Mourning in the Shakespearean Sonnets." *Psychoanalytic Inquiry* 3 (1983): 513-27.

Shakespeare's psychobiography, as well as his mother's, illuminates the portrayal of women in the plays and the ambivalence toward the Dark Lady in the sonnets. Mary Arden Shakespeare lost three children, a sister, and her father before Shakespeare was born and consequently he became a "replacement child, i.e., a child replacing a dead sibling" (513). Within this "maternal environment," Shakespeare was scared, feeling anger at his mother for not being able to conquer her heart and yet identifying with her reaction to death. Mary Arden Shakespeare predisposed the playwright to future loss. In this light, mourning and death recur in the plays; Mary Arden

Shakespeare may be the model for Constance in *KJ*. In general, mothers are not presented sympathetically in Shakespeare–Lady Macbeth, Gertrude, Richard III's mother–as they were in Elizabethan literature (520). This negative attitude can be traced to Shakespeare's reactions to his mother. The Dark Lady was also influenced by Shakespeare's relationship with his mother. In studying the Dark Lady's face, the way a child would his mother, Shakespeare identifies her with death to get her attention; Shakespeare's association is "reminiscent of the distorted mentality of the replacement child" (522). Trapped in such a relationship, Shakespeare exhibits childhood sadness. In Sonnet 143, Shakespeare "the boy" speaks "poignantly from within himself to the mother of his past" (525). We see Mary Arden seeking the children lost to her in the past here, too.

240. Singh, Sarup. *Family Relationships in Shakespeare and the Restoration Comedy of Manners*. Delhi: Oxford UP, 1983.

Although written under different social environments, the family relationships shown in Restoration comedy owe a debt to the treatment of families in Shakespeare's plays. While Restoration dramatists directly attack untenable social realities, Shakespeare indirectly uses the ideal to expose the real. Although accepting patriarchal society, Shakespeare in his plays reflects the inherent tensions which, by the Restoration, led to a crumbling of patriarchal authority. Parental authority in Shakespeare often breaks down due to poor communication between parent and child, as with Desdemona, Hermia, and Romeo and Juliet. While our sympathy goes to the children who disobey, the parents are seldom held exclusively to blame.

In Restoration comedy, marriage is a battlefield of the sexes. "The impression that one gathers from Shakespeare's plays is that it is his constant endeavor to reconcile love and marriage" (103). The rivalry between Beatrice and Benedick is merely a pose; both readily give in once their love is disclosed. In *TSh* the struggle is a learning experience for Petruchio as well as for Katherine. "By the time the play ends, the husband and wife have come to realize that there can be no rivalry between them nor any exploitation of one by the other" (108). Throughout the plays, Shakespeare presents the ideals of marriage. Marital fidelity is exalted; he expects his heroes to be as pure as his heroines. There are no rakes; lecherous men are comic, contemptible, or pitiable. Shakespeare opposes arranged marriages, opting for ones based on companionship.

Shakespeare's women strive for a basis of compatibility, rejecting romantic love and, in the case of Rosalind and Beatrice, refusing to be docile, subservient wives. In order to determine compatibility, Shakespeare's women often resort to sex-reversal techniques–most notably, male disguise–as Rosalind and Viola do. Shakespeare accepts the notion of wifely obedience, but insists that this obedience depends on husbandly love. Husbands who treat their wives as property are usually condemned, as Othello and Posthumus certainly are.

Reviews: *Choice* 21 (1984): 1138; *Shakespeare Newsletter* 33 (1983): 46; Ashley, Leonard R.N., *Bibliotheque d'Humanisme et Renaissance* 47 (1985): 435-36; ---. *Bibliotheque d'Humanisme et Renaissance* 49 (1987): 679; Gibbons, Brian, *Shakespeare Survey* 39 (1986): 212-13; Kaufman, A., *The Eighteenth Century: A Current Bibliography* 9 (1988 for 1983): 486; Raja, P., *Indian Literature* 28 (Mar.-Apr. 1984): 195-204; Rose, Mary Beth, *Review* 7 (1985): 19; Stathis, J.J., *Shakespeare Quarterly* 37 (1986): 265.

241. Sundelson, David. *Shakespeare's Restorations of the Father.* New Brunswick: Rutgers UP, 1983.

Chapter One on "Shakespeare's Psychological Themes" finds a "robust, protective father ... indispensable for Shakespeare's comic resolutions" (18). Yet in the early history plays, women are portrayed as destructive and dangerous–Margaret, Joan, Margery Jourdain–because of their magic, witchcraft, but most of all because of their "castrating and infantilizing" (21). Women do not nurse lovingly but instead do the sucking, destroying the men whose "mode of attachment to women is infantile" (23). Men like Joan's father try to turn "the maternal poison back against the women who betray them" (23). Marriage is successful when it "connects a man less to a woman than to a benign and truly commanding father" (25). The only way for men and women to be neither submissive to nor dominant over each other is to have a "relationship [that] is play" (25). Yet play is absent in the early comedies like *TSh* where it "falls victim to masculine insecurity" but present in *Mac's* "harrowing ... playfulness" (25).

Chapter Two deals with "Fathers, Sons, and Brothers in *The Henriad*," and Chapter Three focuses on "Community in *The Henriad*." Hotspur may be afraid of the "infantile passivity" of his brother Mortimer toward his Welsh wife, but Hotspur and Lady Hotspur "seem to be trying hard–too hard perhaps–to respond to each other playfully without quite managing to find the proper voice" (45).

Chapter Four concentrates on "Fathers and Daughters in *Merchant of Venice*." Unlike history, which is "almost exclusively a male affair" for Shakespeare, the comedies explore women's nature, "their search for selfhood and attachment" (72). Prominence is given to the tensions between fathers and daughters in the comedies. Yet in contrast to the "easy compromises" with the fathers in *AYL* and *Ado*, "patriarchy provokes a powerful and pervasive ambivalence" (74-75) in *MV*, where the fathers are "ambiguous figures." Shakespeare is "clearly of two minds about the nature of fathers and their need to control their children" (72). While Jessica breaks away from her tyrannical father, Portia cannot break away from the benevolent protectiveness of her father. Her struggle is best seen in terms of the mourning process. Like Hamlet, she "lives in the shadow of a dead father" (75) with whom she has a "psychological kinship." Bound by her father's will, she sees her suitors derisively through her father's eyes. When she cannot find "paternal qualities" in either Antonio, whose nurturing is feminine, or Bassanio, Portia "discovers [them] in herself" (82). *MV* expresses a "fearfulness about women," an anxiety about marriage and "uneasy joking" about sexuality. "Fathers dominated the play's old order, and Portia embodies some of their authority, but her own command seems primarily maternal" (85); Portia is a menacing mother. Like Leontes, Bassanio, through his spider imagery (Act 3.2.120-23), fears female power. The wrong choice of a casket leads to metaphoric castration and female engulfment. Yet "anxieties about such a mother are present but contained, just as the fantasy of woman as monster occasionally breaks through the celebration of femininity in the other comedies" (86). Shylock, too, is more than the castrating father; he is turned into the "devouring mother" whose presence "serves as a screen for the misogyny" in *MV* (88). Chapter Five, "Misogyny and Rule in *Measure for Measure*," focuses on the ways in which sexual and political fears are fused in this problem play. *MM's* "considerable misogyny" can be traced to men's "grave fears" about their own "precarious" identity and the "destructive power of women" (89). Fearing female power, men turn violence into a defense. Angelo is worried about who is the weaker sex in his confrontations with Isabella; her "growing female potency" can not only humiliate him but also lead him to question whether he is a woman. His own "sexuality is inseparable from his wish to annihilate women." Thus, the patriarchal system of Vienna reins in female initiative and turns women into whores. The Duke's cruel lie about Isabella's brother, "perhaps the central irony of the play" (93), allows him to tame and control her, "precluding any marriage of true minds." Isabella is forced to exchange one convent for another. No true "altruist," the Duke "serves only himself," for his piety is "questionable." Having Angelo to act out fantasies and to play the unjust deputy, the Duke is "free to define his own identity in safer terms." Striving for power not available to other men, the Duke becomes a voyeur, enabling him to "be everywhere and nowhere, powerful and passive" (98). He "seeks to rise above the messy domains of human sexuality and power" (98).

Chapter Six, "Shakespeare's Restoration of the Father," finds that dramatic conflict is absent from *Tem* where "real fellowship is elusive" (103); the play "belongs to Prospero in a way that seems downright un-Shakespearean" (104). Dissent is confined to the "discredited"–Caliban, Antonio, and Sebastian. Like King Lear, Prospero wants to be both the father and the child; his "language hints at sexual uncertainties that underlie the conflict about power, at a fantasy that Duke Prospero was both mother and father, but doubly vulnerable rather than doubly strong" (105-106). His departure from Milan is really an escape from shame and weakness, reflecting his "half suppressed doubts about his wife's chastity" (106). He flees the demands of being a duke as well as those of a wife. Because Miranda does exactly what her father wants, she contributes to his "paternal narcissism: the prevailing sense that there is no worthiness like a father's ... " (108). Prospero acts like a midwife when he saves Ariel from Sycorax; in fact, his art "enables him to implement Ariel's rebirth" (110). Ariel, who represents a "sexuality ... completely stripped of physical grossness" (115), acknowledges Prospero's supreme paternal authority and, for that reason, Prospero feels more comfortable with Ariel than with Miranda. Caliban subversively reminds us of the similarities between man and monster; paternity for Caliban is "an infinite multiplication of himself" (113). *Tem* refines the "psychological material" Shakespeare earlier presented in *TA*; the later play is much more complex than the earlier in expressing "sexual ambivalence" (125).

Reviews: Choice 21 (1984): 1310; *Shakespeare Newsletter* 33 (1983): 46; Abrams, R., *Kritikon Litterarum* 1-4 (1984): 84-86; Ashley, Leonard R.N., *Bibliotheque d'Humanisme et Renaissance* 47 (1985): 193-94; Candido, Joseph, *Shakespeare Studies* 20 (1988): 323; Evans, Maurice, *Renaissance Quarterly* 38 (1985): 172; Keyishian, Harry, *Shakespeare Bulletin* 3 (May-June 1985): 26-27; Willbern, David, *Shakespeare Quarterly* 37 (1986): 126.

242. Taylor, Michael. "The Pastoral Reckoning in *Cymbeline.*" *Shakespeare Survey* 36 (1983): 97-106.

Imogen's "grotesque experience" (98) in Act 4.2–lying with the headless Cloten in a "coital sequence" (99) and smearing his blood on her face–marks a turning point toward grace in the play. Her "operatic role" is a "mad burlesque of sexual passion" and shows "shattered idyllic expectations" (99). Unlike the other romances, *Cym* "makes much of the treacherous eroticism of its lovers' innocence with Imogen cast as the play's Isabella ... " (101). But there is a significant reason for Posthumus's prurience and Imogen's sexual behavior preparatory to their fruitful union. In *Cym*, Shakespeare shows that "the lovers' renewal of innocence is completed only after a rigorous purging of their sensual frailty" (105).

243. Wilson, Douglas B. "The Commerce of Desire: Freudian Narcissism in Chaucer's *Troilus and Criseyde* and Shakespeare's *Troilus and Cressida.*" *English Language Notes* 21 (1983): 11-22.

Chaucer's Criseyde and Shakespeare's Cressida offer "radically different versions of desire and the Troilus legend" itself (11-12). Seen in light of Rene Girard's negative assessment of Freud's theory of narcissism ("Individual Psychology," *Denver Quarterly* 14 [1979]: 3-19), Shakespeare's Cressida is the model of Freud's narcissistic woman whose "resurgent narcissism" outweighs her need to love another. She progresses through the "barren cycle of narcissistic desire" from self back to self. Pretending to fulfill "an incompleteness" (13) in Troilus, Cressida uses narcissism as a strategy; it is "partly an illusion" so she can trade in the male marketplace of desire. Hence, she "invites [the] disdain of a feminist critique" (14). Diminishing "her intrinsic worth," Cressida coquettishly caters to male desire and so differs from Portia and Bassanio in using metaphors from love and business to express a mutual love affair. In *TrC*, "love and war are demystified by the imagery of tainted vendibles" (15). When Cressida betrays Troilus, she reverts to "predominant narcissism" (16). In loving Cressida, Troilus, too, is guilty of worshipping "an idolatrous image of his own need." Unlike Shakespeare's couple, Chaucer's "lovers escape the entrapment of Freudian narcissism ... in progressing toward mutual caring and respect for themselves" (22).

1984

244. Bevington, David. "Shakespeare's Development: *Measure for Measure* and *Othello*." In *Psychoanalysis: The Vital Issues*. Vol. 1 of *Psychoanalysis as an Intellectual Discipline*. Ed. John E. Gedo and George H. Pollock. New York: International UP, 1984. 277-96.

Marriage is important in Shakespeare's drama "as the relation that at once perpetuates the family and exists in ineradicable tension with familial bonds" (282). The strong woman figure of the festive comedies is an ideal and beloved mother. Yet the action of the plays arises through "truncated and disguised oedipal situations" (284). The sonnets dwell on friendship and sexual relations rather than marriage. *MM* is the key play because it is a comedy written during the period of Shakespeare's great tragedies. Sexual conflict lies at its heart. Shakespeare's "ideal of feminine purity and his equation of sexuality with evil originate together; they are polarized derivatives of the preoedipal union of infantile sexual desire and tender regard" (288). Othello has as a model for his happy marriage the relationship he had with his mother and so he tries to capture the "primary narcissism of childhood" (291) in his marriage to Desdemona. Iago leads Othello to believe that he is unlovable by having the Moor re-enact "the painful separation from the mother" (292). Cassio idealizes Desdemona, but only has a sexual liaison with a whore.

245. Burt, Richard A. "Charisma, Coercion, and Comic Form in *The Taming of the Shrew*." *Criticism* 26 (1984): 295-311.

The resolutions of Shakespearean comedy are problematic; conflicts are not solved by ending but by controlling them. *TSh* is "paradigmatic of Shakespearean comedy" (296). Novy (item 262) wrongly separates Petruchio's coercion from his game playing by arguing that his wit frees him and Kate from the tyranny of patriarchy. On the contrary, Petruchio's role-playing "does not oppose patriarchy but relocates and reinforces it within a domestic relationship; the husband increases his authority over his wife by gaining her love" (297). Petruchio's role-playing and his charismatic authority are "in the service of a new kind" of patriarchy where the husband must be able to "display" his wife's obedience. Thus Kate must display an ongoing performance. Their relationship is closer, more intimate whenever they have a scapegoat toward which they can direct their aggression, e.g., Vincentio, the other women whom Kate chastises.

This "scapegoat mechanism," which is at the "heart of the social order" (306), lies behind the resolution of *TSh*. That resolution is subversive by replacing a husband's authority with a father's over the daughter; yet it also reinforces the social order by using women, the new victims, as the "socially accepted target of aggression" (302). Petruchio's games with Kate provide "domestic intimacy" by separating the couple from Paduan society. Though disguised, Petruchio's coercion is necessary to that harmony. "Love can never conclusively be separated from coercion because romantic love is not natural ... " (305). Because closure is at odds with domestic harmony, *TSh* does not end with the frame device so that Petruchio's relationship with Kate will seem natural. Thus, "Shakespeare does not stage the subversion of patriarchy but stages a subversive threat to patriarchy–the unruly and insubordinate woman–in order to contain it" (307).

246. Calderwood, James. "'More Than What You Were': Augmentation and Increase in *Macbeth*." *English Literary Renaissance* 14 (1984): 70-82.

Shakespeare's comparison of murderous Macbeth with Tarquin, who raped Lucrece, is not inappropriate. Macbeth's "self-negating desire" (71) makes him want excess which is really a growing lack. Seen from the perspective of augmentation ("associated with meaningless repetition" [76]) found in *RL* and Sonnet 129, Macbeth's ambition is like lust as his murderous deeds become like "the repetition of sexual doing." This repetition is illustrated through the triplicity found in *Mac*; there are not three witches, though, but "simply one witch repeated three times" (75). Macbeth's desire for power is unfulfilling; he has no progeny or increase, and his sterile "self-love" contrasts with the procreative gains of Malcolm and Banquo. The movement of the play toward the fulfillment of Shakespeare's own theatrical presence shows a "procreativity" that contrasts with Macbeth's barren experience.

247. Carney, Jo Eldridge. "Female Friendship in Elizabethan Literature." *DAI* 44 (1984): 2151A. U of Iowa.

248. Daniell, David. "The Good Marriage of Katherine and Petruchio." *Shakespeare Survey* 37 (1984): 23-31.

Critics must move beyond explanations of Kate's relationship with Petruchio based on "sustained irony." The cruelties found in folk tales of shrew taming are also at odds with the tone of the play. Moreover, though parallels in language and situation exist between *TSh* and the early history plays, there is more at work than simple comparisons of order in the state and in marriage. In terms of its multiple "removes" of illusion, *TSh* is more like a "set of Chinese boxes" (25). Hence, acting is one of the play's "chief concerns." As actors with many voices who create worlds for each other, Kate and Petruchio acquire a "special quality of mutuality" (28), invisible to the other characters, to "enhance and give form to violence." In their preparation for a serious marriage, they learn about, and become more real because of, their multiple roles in their "play-world." It is wrong to see Kate at the end as a "female wimp" (30). Using the language of "an imaginary history play," Kate's last speech tells Petruchio that "the civil war in her is over, and she will not fight her rescuer. Partly she is rejoicing in their new world" (30). Yet her language of "a dramatized civil war" is appropriately incongruous because their war, their play, and their marriage are only now beginning. *TSh*, like *MV* and *Ado*, is not limited by a "firmly closed ending."

249. Gall, John. "'You panderly rascals': Plot and Characterization in *The Merry Wives of Windsor*." *Selected Papers from the West Virginia Shakespeare and Renaissance Association* 9 (1984): 1-7.

Many characters in *MWW* are panders and recruit others as panders. Page is a pander for Master Brooke; Mistress Quickly (seemingly "the most active pander") and Falstaff are the chief panders in *MWW*. The play links lust and greed. Love, or *caritas*, is the opposite of lust, or *cupiditas*. As a lover/suitor, Fenton displays true *caritas* toward Anne while Falstaff and Quickly represent *cupiditas*. The love of Fenton and Anne contrasts with Falstaff's sensuality and his "adulterous attempts" to seduce the wives. The garden setting of the last act suggests the relationship of the two sexes, idolatrous for Falstaff and rewarding for the young lovers.

250. Garner, Shirley Nelson. "His stones, his daughter, and his ducats.'" *The Upstart Crow* 5 (1984): 35-49.

The chief conflict in *MV* is sexual as Antonio and Shylock try to "destroy each other's manliness" (35). By being spit upon, Shylock is "symbolically castrated" in a Christian society that brands him a coward. Forbidden by the law to retaliate, Shylock creates the bond to degrade Antonio as a prostitute, thus allowing the Jew to castrate him. Antonio acts not out of generosity but to manipulate Bassanio. The castration theme continues in Shylock losing his daughter and his stones. In eloping with Lorenzo, Jessica robs her father of his wealth, and consequently "diminishes his source of power" (40). Yet Jessica's actions create sympathy for Shylock, for "None of Shakespeare's disobedient daughters leaves her father so coolly ..." (41-42). Antonio, who does not act out of *caritas*, unmercifully deprives Shylock of the right to disinherit his daughter. Not offering a celebration, the ending of *MV* shows that the "pairing of lovers is tenuous" (46).

251. Geary, Keith. "The Nature of Portia's Victory: Turning to Men in *The Merchant of Venice*." *Shakespeare Survey* 37 (1984): 55-68.

Portia's sexual disguise differs greatly from those used by Julia, Viola, or Rosalind. As Balthasar, Portia is "wholly masculine" (58), establishing an "absolute distinction" between herself and the lawyer. Like the other characters in *MV*, Portia has a double self. Her "resilient femininity" observed in the "pre-disguise scenes," more than for any of the other disguised heroines (57), clearly shows she is ready to be the lawyer. Through Portia's disguise as Balthasar, Shakespeare "adapts the *debate* theme framework to dramatize the struggle between heterosexual and homosexual love in the triangle of Portia, Bassanio, and Antonio" (58). *MV* hinges on the conflict between Portia and Antonio for Bassanio's love. In not consummating his marriage, Bassanio places friendship before Portia; yet by sending him to Venice she asserts her legal claim to him. As Antonio's letter indicates, the bond is his attempt to hold on to Bassanio in opposition to Portia's claims to him through marriage. Through his sacrifice, Antonio wants to show the "final grand proof" of his love and so prove "Bassanio's debt of love."

Acting in her own best interest, Portia must dress as a man to "get her husband into bed" and to "displace" Antonio's hold on him. In true "Shylockian fashion," Portia protects her interests in Bassanio when she insists on the terms of her marriage to him, figuratively cutting "Bassanio out of Antonio's heart" (66). The only reason for Act 5, "almost a re-enactment of the trial itself," is for Portia to assert her right to Bassanio. The tactics she uses as Balthasar in court she uses as Portia in Belmont. To complete her judgment of Antonio, Portia employs a "dual sexuality," allowing her to fasten "the homoerotic tendency of Bassanio's sexuality" and the "obligations of masculine friendship" (67) onto herself as Balthasar and Portia. Antonio, like Shylock, is left with nothing.

252. Geckle, George L. "Politics and Sexuality in Shakespeare's Second Tetralogy." In *Romanticism and Culture: A Tribute to Morse Peckham and A Bibliography of His Work*. Ed. H.W. Matalene. Columbia, SC: Camden House, 1984. 117-32.

Shakespeare's plays frequently intertwine sex and politics as, for example, in *MM*, "generally considered to be Shakespeare's most sexual play." A similar connection occurs in *TrC* and *Ham*, where the Prince's tragedy "derives from his inability to come to terms with either sex or politics, each dependent on the other ..." (118). The second tetralogy also illustrates the sex/politics nexus. Eric Partridge (*Shakespeare's Bawdy* [1947]) aptly observed that *R2* is the "cleanest" Shakespeare play while *H5* is the "obscenest." Morse Peckham's theory (*Art and Pornography: An Experiment in Explanation* [New York: Basic Books, 1969]) that society, confronting stability and innovation, polices such trivial matters as sex and costume to support larger, more vital ones such as economics and order, verifies Partridge's observation. More's theory helps to explain sex and politics in the second tetralogy.

R2 is the cleanest play because Shakespeare "probably" felt that the audience would not be "interested in such trivial matters as sex and bawdy dialogue" (125) in the serious business of revolution. Shakespeare introduced sex in *1H4* and *2H4* as part of Hal's "education and maturation." Though far more rigid than Hal, Hotspur is overtly sexual in the two scenes with his wife (Acts 2.3 and 3.1), mixing military language and sexual context. Because of his social station, Hal cannot have the sexual involvement with the tavern women that Falstaff has, showing that the Prince must risk exposure to the trivial to transcend it. For this reason, there is an "increasing amount of sexual action and dialogue the closer we get to Hal's reign" (128). In wooing Katherine, Henry has an opportunity to validate his manhood and his love, but "sounds suspiciously like Hotspur" (130). Henry brings "order out of disorder and sexual union out of an aggressive courtship" (131); his courtship represents English masculinity and Katherine's response signals "French feminine passivity" (130). Because of its necessity to Hal's development, the forbidden sexual license of Eastcheap is "at the same time acceptable and unacceptable" (131).

253. Gossett, Suzanne. "Best Men Are Molded Out of Faults: Marrying the Rapist in Jacobean Drama." *English Literary Renaissance* 14 (1984): 305-27.

TA, Tourneur's *The Revenger's Tragedy,* Heywood's *Rape of Lucrece,* and Fletcher's *Valentinian* demonstrate the existence of a norm for the dramatic depiction of rape. In all four plays, the woman is married, virtuous, chaste, and religious (306). All use classical models–the raped woman is avenged by her husband or father; the rapists are seen as having committed an unforgivable crime; and all four heroines die. The rapes are primarily for sexual purposes, although political motives cannot be ruled out, and each rape is seen as a wicked attack on virtue. The women of these plays accept the patriarchal system of society, and although they are victims, they accept death readily rather than being guilty of the crime themselves. In *AYL*, rape is seen as a natural instinct which must be brought under control by marriage, a notion supported by contemporary views of rape and the laxity with which courts treated the offenders.

254. Greene, James J. "*Macbeth*: Masculinity as Murder." *American Imago* 41 (1984): 155-80.

Mac "vibrates with a variety of sexual meanings" (156). In their sexually confused world, Macbeth and Lady Macbeth equate manhood with murder, and murder with sex. For them, Duncan's murder is a "surrogate act of copulation" (156) in which Lady Macbeth's words encouraging her husband (*performance, desire, deed, attempt*) resonate with a perverse sexuality. The murder of Duncan, a "slain fertility god" (172), also suggests the "ritual murder" of Lady Macbeth's father and the resolution of her oedipal conflicts. The Porter scene, with its explicit sexual references, is a "comically garbled echo" of Lady Macbeth's words at the start of Act 2.2. After Macbeth murders Duncan, Lady Macbeth "for the first time" bestows "full sexual status" on her husband (166). The four visions presented by the witches, figures of twisted sexuality, contrast sterility (first two) with fertility (last two through Lady Macduff and Macduff). Shakespeare questions and subtly undermines the traditional sex roles assigned to men as the "sword wielder" and women as "the compassionate weeper" (176). As the Macbeths demonstrate in their adherence to sterility and death, such cultural preconceptions about male and female principles threaten "not only individual psyches" but also "the delicate balance of civilization itself" (179).

255. Hannaford, Stephen. "'My Money Is My Daughter': Sexual and Financial Possession in English Renaissance Comedy." *Shakespeare Jahrbuch* 119 (1984): 93-110.

Three "basic characters" (the woman, the lover, and the senex) appear along with three major elements (the treasure, a set of closed doors or chest, and a key) in English Renaissance comedy. In a variety of Shakespearean plays, including *AWW, Cym, MWW, MV,* and *TGV,* the "theme of sexual possession is at issue in each case" (110). These plays have eleven points in common: (1) the woman is seen as a treasure; (2) chastity is regarded as a jewel; (3) the loss of a jewel is the loss of virtue, with *MV* presenting a "clever reversal, for it is the men who must defend their loss" (99); (4) when a jewel is the price of chastity, "sexual traffic then becomes the commerce of jewels" (100); (5) the senex guards the treasure illustrating that "he who enjoys fortune rarely enjoys sex" (102); (6) the senex keeps the woman locked in a closed space; (7) the lover gets the key (that is, the woman) and enters the closed space; (8) the lover is locked or hidden in the closed space; (9) the senex is diverted from his treasure in the hopes of multiplying it; (10) taking the woman is theft; and (11) when the woman is taken, the senex cries for both woman and treasure.

256. Hoover, Claudette. "Goneril and Regan: 'So Horrid as in Woman.'" *San Jose Studies* 10.3 (1984): 49-65.

The text of *Lear* "teases us with explanations" of Goneril and Regan's actions in terms of the myths and stereotypes of women that "constantly prove inadequate to our questions" (62). By rejecting traditional antifeminist stereotypes and motivations of greed, jealousy, and revenge, all found in the *True Chronicle Historie of King Leir,* Shakespeare creates a Goneril and Regan who "inspire metaphysical questions" (50). The classical models of masculine women, which Goneril and Regan seem to imitate but which are only a "false analogy" (57), do not offer a satisfactory interpretation of their conduct. Unlike Antigone or Clytemnestra,

Lear's older daughters lack the "possibility for heroism." They
remain "unknowable." Another "especially puzzling" feature is that
their desire for Edmund is not a question of simple lust; they
reassuringly want to possess him for reasons of power. Thus their
motivation does not derive from the "insatiable strumpet
stereotype." Symbolic readings of these sisters as evil simplify
rather than clarify. We respond to them as women whose
motivation is gender-based; Lear attacks them as unnatural
daughters and women. Yet, again, their actions are not in keeping
with what violent women in other plays do. Goneril and Regan's
"violence is sometimes arbitrary and sadistic." Like Lear, we want
to find reasons for Goneril and Regan's brutality in the hope of
having something familiar to hang on to.

257. La Guardia, Eric. "Bawdy Night." *Shakespeare Bulletin* 2.10
     (July-Aug. 1984): 15-19.

TN dramatically projects the "pathology of obstructed or
deferred desire" (16). In the sexual metaphorics of the play, the
characters who reveal dual sexual identities show that such
blockages are "self-willed." The primary conceit of the play is "the
doomed sexual project" (17), with Olivia being the central sexual
object. The "language of sexual infirmity surrounds Viola in terms
of her dual and therefore suspended sexual identity" (17). She and
Olivia share a sisterhood of grief. As in *TrC*, the language of *TN*
reveals sexual ambitions and inadequacies.   Malvolio is
characterized by bawdy language and by a "thwarted phallic
ambition." Toby, Maria, and Feste are the "lords of mis-rule in
this carnival of sexual tumescence" (18). The ending of *TN*, where
"impotency is eroticized," is artificial, showing that reason
triumphs over the "complexity of desire" (18).

258. Latimer, Kathleen. "The Communal Action of *The Winter's Tale*."
     In *The Terrain of Comedy*. Ed. Louise Cowan. Dallas: Dallas
     Institute of Humanities and Culture, 1984. 125-42.

Potentially tragic, *WT* is enclosed "within an ultimate comic
pattern" (139). A community of Pauline, Camillo, Antigonus, and
Hermione seeks to save Leontes from his own destructive fury.

Only Leontes is sick, not the court as in *Ham*; none of the community shares Leontes's doubts. The "comic action" of this community "unifies the entire play" (127). Paulina and Camillo stage a drama of "evasive delay, deceit ... and disguise" for Leontes (139). As long as he is isolated from their community, he cannot be regenerated. Hermione's trial is also Leontes's for his "guilt and purgation." Hermione is symbolically present through Perdita who sums up the values of *communitas*–"love, trust, good fellowship, harmony with nature, and enjoyment of sensual pleasure" (135). For their regeneration, Leontes and Polixenes "must regain" this sense of community. Protesting the union of Perdita and Florizel, Polixenes is "unwilling to relinquish the sense of immortality ... [that] comes through one's posterity for the greater sense achieved through the oneness with the cycles of nature found in *communitas*" (137). Paulina's art provides the opportunity for Leontes to join the community; his accepting Hermione "in whatever terms she has returned" proves he has rejoined humanity and society. The couple's joyful reunion "completes the fusion of social structures and *communitas*, of law and love ... " (139). The audience, too, can join the harmonious community on stage by accepting Hermione's awakening.

259. Lynch, Stephen L. "Shakespeare's Cressida: 'A Woman of Quick Sense.'" *Philological Quarterly* 63 (1984): 357-68.

Though Cressida's sensuality has often been commented on, her wit has not received proper attention. As the "singular introspective character" in *TrC*, she sees clearly and is a "trustworthy commentator" (357). Though she herself does not "rise above the contaminated values that engulf her world" (359), her cynicism is on target, for she humorously and skillfully debunks male heroism and lovers. Unlike Troilus, she has "few illusions about the quality of their love." While she is more aware of her own nature than Troilus is of his, she suppresses her awareness of her "folly" by being seduced by Troilus, who fashions her into quite a different kind of woman. She moves from cynicism to idealism. It is wrong to characterize her as a "daughter of the game," for this designation is "an expression of Greek psychology more than an accurate or final assessment." Both the

Trojans and Greeks "use women to gratify their lust, but the Trojans do so with poetic delusions, the Greeks with animal aggression" (364). In the Greek camp, Cressida is defiled, "caught in the perennial instability of Ulyssean philosophy" (365). She wisely chooses to submit to Diomedes, for if she did not have his protection, she would have to submit to the entire Greek camp. Because she is aware of the consequences of her vile act, Cressida "stands out in the play as the one character who perceives her own weaknesses" (366).

260. McGuire, Susan Bassnett. "An Ill Marriage in An Ill Government: Patterns of Unresolved Conflict in *All's Well That Ends Well*." *Shakespeare Jahrbuch* 120 (1984): 97-102.

The relationship of marriage contracts to those made with the state constitutes a "major structural feature" (100) in *AWW*. Oaths affecting husbands and wives present similar problems to those involving subjects and rulers. However, in "the decaying courtly world" of *AWW*, the entire matter of "public and private contract is thrown into confusion" (101). The ending of the play offers only ineffective compromises. Bertram tries to "reject feudal authority" in his private life, yet he is forced to accept both a wife and an heir. In replacing the "idealization of virginity" with a socially profitable marriage, Helena loses the commitment from a partner she needs and thereby "is as far away from a marriage as a union of equal minds as she has ever been" (101).

261. Mercer, John Moore. "Sibling Relationships in Shakespeare's Plays: Course, Quality, and Function." *DAI* 45 (1984): 530A. U of Missouri-Columbia.

262. Novy, Marianne. *Love's Argument: Gender Relations in Shakespeare*. Chapel Hill: U of North Carolina P, 1984.

Chapter One focuses on "Patriarchy and Mutuality, Control and Emotion." Shakespeare's plays resolve the conflicts between these opposites. Marriage in Elizabethan England strove for the ideals of patriarchy and mutuality, advocated by many preachers. Shakespeare's plays represent these social tensions, but cannot be considered realistic portrayals of contemporary society. In the comedies, the women control the games, and though women are active, their relationships with men develop in the spirit of mutuality. The masculine disguises provide freedom and emotional distance as does the state of courtship as opposed to the restrictions of marriage, but, ultimately, disguises control women's behavior. The combination of patriarchy and mutuality in the tragedies proves destructive. Lady Macbeth and Volumnia, for example, live vicariously through the men in their lives, enjoying the violence they cannot commit themselves. The romances present women's vulnerability in conjunction with their resilience. "Coriolanus is the tragic hero whose behavior Shakespeare most explicitly links to child-rearing ideals of emotional distance" (11).

Chapter Two, "'An You Smile Not, He's Gagged': Mutuality in Shakespearean Comedy," explores the ways mutuality, often on a continuum, is threatened or achieved. Analogies between jester/listener, man/woman, and actor/audience illustrate Shakespeare's "emphasis on mutual dependence" (22). Shakespearean comedy transcends patriarchal models from the classical world where women were excluded and Petrarchianism where women were idealized into silence. Comedies such as *LLL* and *TGV* do not achieve mutuality, but "the failure is sometimes part of the point" (24). *Ado* offers two kinds of mutuality; one type separates the lovers into different partners and the other distinguishes them into Anteros/Eros leading to a "more complete sharing" (28). In *AYL*, Orlando's Petrarchianism "makes mutuality more difficult" by keeping Rosalind at a distance, but thanks to her "supportive conversation" he replaces idealization with reciprocity. Rosalind is both gift and giver in the last scene where Hymen's masque becomes "an ideal of mutual relationship between man and woman" (31). In *TN*, the "idealization of one's feelings" (32) is an even greater obstacle to mutuality than Petrarchianism. Indulging in self-love, Orsino has to learn that Viola is "equally capable of devotion" (34). The "most emblematic celebration of mutuality" in *TN*, however, is between Viola and Sebastian, reminiscent of two lovers united but offering a still higher union since the two share one experience. Isolated from love, Malvolio cannot progress beyond "self-enclosure" (40). It is wrong to see the endings of these comedies as a "return to a hierarchy made more stable by its temporary inversion" (42). Women and men are joined in gestures of submission at the end. In Chapter Three, "Patriarchy and Play in *The Taming of the Shrew*," analogies between "the social order and a game" permit us to see how Kate and Petruchio create a new world that acknowledges patriarchy while magically dissolving its dangers. Joining the role of player and patriarch, Petruchio challenges the social order through the games he plays involving language (especially with Kate's puns) and his subordination of women. He involves Kate in his games (she is "gamesome") to make her his partner. Together they replace the values of an external world with newer, better ones of an internal world. As in a game, Petruchio and Kate define their "relationship as an enclosed sphere where imagination can re-create the universe" (54), promising them a new independence from a patriarchal society. Significantly, Kate joins Petruchio in confusing the old patriarch Vincentio. The younger characters may use respectful language in seeking pardon from the fathers, but this is just a pretext for their own ends, and "it is against this background that we must see" the final scene. There Kate seemingly affirms the strict "sexual and social roles" mandated by society, but in reality through her performance, her "improvisation," she "reconciles patriarchy and mutuality" (59). Her "socially approved language corresponds to a new command of social convention" (60).

Chapter Four, "Giving and Taking in *The Merchant of Venice*," situates Shakespeare's play against the "struggle between two types of giving" central to "the historical, religious, and psychological conflicts of Renaissance Europe" (62). *MV* illustrates the transition from feudal self-sacrifice to Renaissance self-assertiveness. Portia triumphs over the rival representatives of different kinds of giving and taking. Her "accepting sexuality" (62) and mutuality show how unfavorable Antonio's position is. Of all Shakespeare's major characters, Antonio is the one "least given to talking about sex in any way" (69); his self-denying and sacrificial deeds admit no mutuality, unlike Portia's commitment to Bassanio. Psychologically, Antonio's self-sacrifice (Act 4.1. 114-116) and depression are a result of idealism. As an outsider and a representative of the flesh, Portia is linked with Shylock and in fact uses some of his ploys of "self-assertion and demand for his rights" (77) in Belmont in Act 5. But her generosity and love separate her from him. Through her witty language and keen awareness, Portia "finds a way to force them [Antonio and Shylock] out of their extreme positions" (75) at the trial by getting Antonio to take and Shylock to give. Demonstrating the need for mutuality in marriage, Portia presents a vision of "a sexual relationship in which both partners can maintain their own identity" (79) and so transcends the rivalries of "passion and asceticism." Portia combines Antonio's "self surrender," Shylock's aggression, and Bassanio's "responsiveness" to "finish the play bound in love and friendship with the representatives of the two attitudes," Antonio's and Bassanio's, Shakespeare's audience "honored most" (81).

Chapter Five, "Tragic Women as Actors and Audience," explores how a number of Shakespeare's tragic female characters assume roles as actors (both in terms of "pretense" and "doing") and as "onstage audiences responding with sympathy" to the men (83-84). Ophelia is a "mediator" between Hamlet and the "offstage audience" while Desdemona assumes the role of audience "trying to understand Othello, sympathizing with him, imagining him in pain" (85). Lady Macbeth and Desdemona use "pretense" which "stirs their resourcefulness in crises." Both women as actors, though, fail to win the cooperation of their spouses. Cordelia and Lear, on the other hand, "can be moved by each other, like an audience, and can express feelings, like an actor, in a kind of mutual dependence" (90). *AC* is the "only Shakespearean tragedy that focuses on and indeed glorifies the woman as actor ... " (91), thus forging an equal partnership between the Egyptian queen and her Roman general. The similarities between actors and women establish both groups as minorities, "separate and alien," and force them to please people. Women–like actors–were suspected of being the "Other." This anti-theatrical bias with its emphasis on the negative side of acting is "a part of the world view of the typical Shakespearean tragic hero, actor though he is. He tries to be an actor-as-doer; he feels sullied by the necessity of pretending. He hates female pretense ... " (95). Yet women and actors are strongly "associated with one quality that tragedy values–concern for feeling" which makes them, more than the men, "sympathetic audiences" (95). Women as actors/audience are far more easily accepted in comedy than in tragedy. "This difference is clearly related not only to the genre but also to gender; women in the tragedies have no obsessive suspicion about men as actors" (92). Chapter Six on "Violence, Love, and Gender in *Romeo and Juliet* and *Troilus and Cressida*" investigates problems of gender polarization in these two plays. In both, though, "the women maintain or increase their ability to pretend" while they keep their love affair secret in a private though precarious world (123). Romeo and Juliet transcend traditional stereotypes of male aggression and female weakness in their asymmetrical imagery of finance (where women are not a commodity) and by their mutual expression of love. "The servants, Friar, and Nurse, uphold the conventional views of women as weak"; and the lovers keep their love a secret to protect it from Verona's code of "the manhood of violence" (107). By slaying Tybalt, Romeo accepts that code, and when Juliet follows the Nurse and Friar's advice "of pretense and mock death" the "failure to transcend the gender polarizations of their society makes disaster inevitable" (108). In professing absolute trust in each other, Romeo and Juliet demonstrate the "extreme purity that gives their love its special tragedy" (109). In contrast to *RJ*, the lovers' world in *TrC* is the same as their outer world. *TrC* is "one of the most devastating pictures in the Shakespeare canon ... of the gender relations consequent on the treatment of women primarily as property" (110). Sexual politics (lust) mirrors military strategy. Armies and lovers use pretense and are self-centered. Like Achilles and Hector, Troilus rejects the feminine. Like Helen, Cressida is a male pawn. Troilus moves from idolizing women to abandoning the "woman-like" delay to violence in himself. Unlike Romeo and Juliet, Troilus and Cressida experience no mutuality; theirs is a "bond chiefly of unintegrated sexuality" (115). Unlike Juliet, Desdemona, or Cleopatra, Cressida cannot even choose her relationships with men.

Chapter Seven, "Marriage and Mutuality in *Othello,*" identifies "the vulnerability of the combination of patriarchy and mutuality" (130). Desdemona and Othello, however, transcend female and male stereotypes; she is courageous and direct, he loves deeply.

Yet Othello feels guilty about sex and fears the loss of control. The tension in the play results from the conflict between his passionate love and the restraints he places on it. In his relationship with Desdemona, Othello engenders a "fantasy of love as fusion with a woman both maternal and virginal" (137), a belief reinforced by the symbolic associations of the handkerchief. Othello wants Desdemona to be totally fused with him to escape his fear of separation; he sees himself as an infant and her as a nurturing mother. Using a "latent masculine alliance," Iago manipulates Othello's strangeness to offer him the mutuality the Moor seeks with Desdemona. Under Iago's control, Othello treats Desdemona in ways befitting "the harshest potential" of a patriarchal marriage (137). Having his love "contaminated by the masculine code of revenge by murder" (145), Othello cannot understand her forgiveness. Men pervert love by seeing control as union. Dorothy Dinnerstein's *The Mermaid and the Minotaur* (1977) sheds light on the "symbiosis" between men and women in terms of control, female empathy, and the rejection of women by men bound to their destructive culture.

Chapter Eight concentrates on "Patriarchy, Mutuality, and Forgiveness in *Lear.*" The domineering father in a patriarchal society, Lear frustrates mutuality by coercing his daughters. Because of his "illusory omnipotence as head of the family" (152), he is like a husband in having his daughters depend on him. Lear is guilty of using women as scapegoats and projecting his own faults (lust) on them. Unlike Goneril and Regan, who act like bad mothers to Lear, Cordelia offers her father mutuality through the "creative power" (152) of her tears and compassion. When Lear begs his daughter's forgiveness, he inverts the patriarchal pattern of a child doing that to a parent. His "need for forgiveness reverses hierarchies of both age and sex and suggests their limitations" (159). Because men through their power abuse women, Lear must seek "forgiveness and repentance" to restore mutuality. Thanks to Cordelia, the audience feels sympathy for Lear who, in caring for her in prison, acts like a woman expressing nurturing mutuality. Though the "issue of sexuality" may be submerged, *Lear* does reveal "the vulnerabilities to each other that the contrasting social roles of men and women intensify" (163).

Chapter Nine on the "Transformed Images of Manhood in the
Romances" argues that unlike tragic heroes, romance heroes are
more willing to "express their sense of insecurity and vulnerability"
and to "take on the occupations usually held by women" (164).
The standard masculine dichotomy between control and emotion
dissolves. Men in the romances are resigned to being passive,
accept penance, display patience and endurance, and value other
people rather than relying on unilateral action. Masculine violence
in *Cym*, for example, is parodied through Cloten, and masculine
valor is a "triffle" (168) compared to Posthumus's marriage to
Imogen. Concerned with "generativity" (178), the romances
emphasize the imagery of biological ties and fertility. Since
childbearing is envied, Cymbeline and Pericles use cross-gender
imagery to describe themselves as mothers and thus share in
women's pain. The romances focus on men's development rather
than women's (excluding Imogen's) after marriage. Because there
is a "reversal of the suspicion of them" (181), women are different
in the romances, too. They bear more children, have stronger
mother-daughter ties, and, as Hermione attests, can be the equal
of a man who is a tyrant. In short, the romances are less about
mutuality between young lovers, or relationships being developed,
than about mutuality between repentance and forgiveness (178).
Challenging "the patriarchal world view," the romances (even
Tem) take place in the family sphere rather than in the military
or political arena.

Chapter Ten, "Shakespeare's Imagery of Gender and Gender
Crossing," recapitulates and further develops ideas presented in
earlier chapters. Shakespeare's presentation of gender "changes
significantly" from the comedies to the tragedies. In the tragedies,
notions of manhood, defined by violence, are rigid and destructive.
Gender transcendence is attacked. The feminine is seen as weak,
as in *RJ* and *Ham*. Cross-sexual imagery does not help
Desdemona or Lady Macbeth from being denied partnership with
their husbands. In the comedies, however, men transcend "a
narrow masculinity" by not struggling for power. The rich
ambiguity of having boy actors play women, with whom they
psychically associated themselves, offered Shakespeare an
opportunity to comment on gender stereotyping. In *AYL*, for
example, gender is a "role," not a "biological given" (193). Unlike

the comedies, gender is not polarized in the romances; women are primary by virtue of their generative power. Cross-gender, "visual and verbal," is not simply a result of "the requirements of stage conditions" but occurs because Shakespeare saw through the "limitations of conventional gender expectations" (200). His own biography–as grandfather and father–also explains changes in gender in the plays.

Reviews: Ashley, Leonard R.N., *Bibliotheque d'Humanisme et Renaissance* 48 (1986): 172-73; Belsey, Catherine, *Renaissance Quarterly* 39 (1986): 806-08; Burt, Richard A., *Shakespeare Studies* 19 (1987): 324-28; Espey, John, *Los Angeles Times Book Review* 14 Apr. 1985: 10; Gibbons, Brian, *Shakespeare Survey* 39 (1986): 207-23; Greene, Gayle, *Shakespeare Quarterly* 37 (1986): 128-32; Harris, Laurilyn J., *Theatre History Studies* 5 (1985): 133-35; Hatlen, B., *Review* 8 (1986): 241-64; Neely, Carol Thomas, *Modern Philology* 84 (1987): 314-16; Swift, Carolyn Ruth, *Signs: Journal of Women in Culture and Society* 12 (1986): 167-68; Thompson, Ann, *English* 34 (1985): 251-55; Watterson, W.C., *Choice* 22 (1985): 1494-95; Widmann, R.L., *English Language Notes* 25 (1988): 82.

263. Paris, Bernard J. "'His Scorn I Approve': The Self-Effacing Desdemona." *American Journal of Psychoanalysis* 44 (1984): 413-24.

The "central puzzle" of *Oth* is that Desdemona is assertive at the start of the play yet unable to defend herself at the end. One of Shakespeare's "most complex psychological portrait[s]," Desdemona suffers from an inner conflict because of the conventional role forced upon her by Venetian society. Consequently, she has an aversion to marriage to any of Venice's curled darlings. But in marrying Othello, she shares vicariously in his exotic past, fulfilling her own romantic fantasies even if she is mocked for them. True to Karen Horney's theory of self-effacing persons, Desdemona submerges her self in Othello, who is an expansive person, in a union that initially brings pleasure but later leads to self-destructive guilt. When Desdemona pleads for Cassio, she is not being aggressive but is "engaged in the typical self-effacing project of fighting for someone else" (417). Iago recognizes Desdemona's compulsive devotion and excessive generosity, marks of the self-effacing person, and manipulates them to Desdemona's own undoing. In Horney's terms, Cassio and Desdemona have a "morbid dependency" on Othello. Desdemona's aggressive generosity reverts to passivity when she is threatened which causes her to assume unwarranted blame for Othello's anger, "displacing his irritation onto her" (419). Her passivity results from self-contempt and guilt at deceiving her father and not pleasing her husband. Such guilt is compensatory and helps expiate for her sins. Rejected by Othello, she loses pride. Yet even in death she must preserve "her idealized picture of him in order to protect her investment" (422).

264. Parker, R.B. "War and Sex in *All's Well That Ends Well.*" *Shakespeare Survey* 37 (1984): 99-113.

G. Wilson Knight's view of the play ("The Triple Eye," in *The Sovereign Flower* [1958]: 93-160) as a battle between masculine war and feminine chastity is misleading. In *AWW* war and love modify each other "so that the conclusion takes the form of a wry accommodation between them..." (99). Bertram has to be educated to accept sexuality and the responsibility that goes with it. Helena has to "abandon the false religion of self-abnegation in sexual love" (100) and become deliberately more aggressive. For Bertram, war stands for male honor, bravery, companionship, a "deflection of sexuality" (102). The point is forced home by the King who believes that war is "a rival, or substitute, for sexuality" (101). Consistent with his view of war, Bertram regards sex as the taking of female spoils and promiscuity as normal male aggression; he has no responsibility to the woman. Just as Bertram must learn about sex, Helena has to "fight for her love even at some sacrifice of self-respect" (107).

265. Parten, Anne. "Beatrice's Horns: A Note on *Much Ado About Nothing*, II.i. 25-27." *Shakespeare Quarterly* 35 (1984): 201-02.

As Beatrice's retort makes clear, women as well as men could fall victim to the cuckold's horns, not an "inherent incompatibility between femininity" and masculinity for Shakespeare's audience. Beatrice shares this fear with Benedick.

266. ---. "Cuckoldry in Shakespeare." *DAI* 44 (1984): 2775A. Yale U.

267. ---. "Masculine Adultery and Feminine Rejoinders in Shakespeare, Dekker and Sharpham." *Mosaic* 17 (1984): 9-18. Rpt. in *"For Better or Worse": Attitudes Toward Marriage in Literature*. Ed. Evelyn J. Hinz. Winnipeg: U of Manitoba P, 1985. 9-18.

Though the Renaissance held that women were subordinate to men, questions about the equality of the sexes in matters of adultery–guilt and redress–are raised in the drama. Traditionally, women were more harshly blamed for such transgressions than men. Since women were inferior, men had nonreciprocal property rights over their wives. Though Adriana in *CE* may have been "on firm doctrinal ground" (1 Corinthians 7) to reproach her offending husband, her protests for sexual parity would have branded her "as a woman on the verge of falling into the heresy of rejecting the divine law of sexual subordination" (11). Unlike Dekker in *The Honest Whore, Part 2* or Edward Sharpham in *Cupid's Whirligig,* who approved the wronged wife's demands for sexual equality, Shakespeare fostered the more conservative ideal of wifely inequality and obedient chastity even when her husband committed adultery. Shakespearean wives followed a "higher truth" to duty. It is wrong, therefore, to interpret Emilia's words to Desdemona in *Oth* (Act 4.3.93-95) as a legitimate feminist cry for egalitarianism in marriage; Desdemona, the ideal Shakespearean wife, rejects Emilia's "catechism." Faced with the "greatest temptation" to fall from wifely virtue, Imogen refuses to throw off wifely submission, condemn all men, or seek revenge (16). Even though Shakespeare shows an "apparent consistency" in his plays to a wife devoting herself to "inequality" in the face of masculine adultery, there is a "steadily growing sensitivity" to the husband's marital obligations and appreciation of the wife's hallowed gifts.

268. Pugh, Elaine Upton. "The Art Itself is Nature: The Fashioning of Shakespeare's Heroines." *DAI* 44 (1984): 2775A. Ohio State U.

269. Reifer, Marcia. "'Instruments of some more mightier member':
      The Constriction of Female Power in *Measure for Measure*."
      Shakespeare Quarterly 35 (1984): 157-69.

      Isabella is a "pivotal female figure," linking the early comic
      heroines with the "victimized tragic women" (169). Unlike the
      female heroines before her, Isabella is a powerless victim of Duke
      Vincentio and gradually loses her voice and her autonomy.
      Isabella has no green world or cloister to retreat to. She also loses
      her place as a controlling playwright, a role vigorously enacted by
      the women in the comedies, to the Duke who "perverts
      Shakespeare's established comic paradigm" (159). A "model third-
      rate playwright" (168), the Duke is not well-intentioned in his
      dramaturgy. He is insensitive, selfish, betrays the public trust,
      imposes sexual restrictions (as the blocking figures in the
      comedies do), and "replicates the indifference" of Angelo and
      Claudio to Isabella's mortal plight. In Vienna, dominated by
      manipulative men, female sexuality is rendered unhealthy. Isabella
      becomes a silent actor in the Duke's cruel play, suffering as male
      characters do not. Her final speech does not show growth of
      character but only her twisted logic and justice. *MM* is "Isabella's
      tragedy" (167). Shakespeare's relationship to the Duke in handling
      women characters is "murky" and possibly unethical. "As Vincentio
      'drains' life out of Isabella and Mariana, so Shakespeare drains
      life out of Gertrude and Ophelia giving them scarcely any
      character at all" (168). *MM* proves that an unrelenting, triumphant
      patriarchy is at odds with "comic structures."

270. Rose, Mary Beth. "Moral Conceptions of Sexual Love in
      Elizabethan Comedy." *Renaissance Drama* 15 (1984): 1-29.

      See item 431.

271. Sturrock, June. "*Othello*: Women and 'Woman.'" *Atlantis* 9.2
      (1984): 1-8.

      Despite the "glorification" of Queen Elizabeth, a strong current
      of antifeminism runs throughout the age. Shakespeare uses
      conventional satire against women dramatically and ironically in

Oth; the loyalty and love of the women in the play counterpoint the savage attacks on them. Expressing his misogyny in different ways to the men, Iago employs commonplaces denouncing women for their faithlessness and pride. Falling victim to Iago's tactic of "grouping and labeling" all women, Othello "loses sight of the actual Desdemona ... [and] sees instead only the sexual generalization" (3). Desdemona's "instinctive charity" and deep love, Emilia's humane action, and Bianca's love for Cassio challenge Iago's generalizations. Emilia, whose faults in a twisted way show her protecting her husband, "provides a kind of release for the audience by voicing its ordinary and spontaneous 'low' reactions to the speech and actions of the major characters" (5). While Othello's jealousy is destructive, Bianca's is protective. Unlike the men, the women remain loyal. While Othello follows the old covenant based on justice, Desdemona pursues the new one based on love. Contrasts between Desdemona's and Emilia's marriages are illuminating. Iago leads Othello away from his wife into "corruption and folly" while Desdemona forces Emilia to abandon her harmful trust in Iago. The ultimate truth in *Oth* is that "man gravitates toward man destructively, woman toward woman redemptively" (7).

272. Woodbridge, Linda. *Women and the English Renaissance: Literature and the Nature of Womankind, 1540-1620.* Urbana: U of Illinois P, 1984.

Shakespeare's women characters have "muscular personalities" (214). Lady Macbeth's behavior does not really raise questions about women's tenderheartedness; she has to be unsexed before she can divest herself of tenderness. Lear's imagery makes monsters out of Regan and Goneril. In *2H6*, Queen Margaret is "inhuman." Steering away from female stereotypes, these women's behavior is seen as unnatural. Shakespeare compares Queen Margaret and Joan of Arc with the Amazons; these female leaders in Shakespeare are unhappy examples of womanhood. One is an adulteress, the other a witch. In the case of shrewishness, there is power to be gained from women, though sometimes it is unscrupulous power; for example, Lady Macbeth talks her husband into regicide. When Fulvia makes war on

Caesar, Antony apologizes by claiming she has always been an uncontrollable shrew. Antony is not dominated by Cleopatra, but she exercises her manipulative powers over him. Enobarbus, the misogynist of *AC*, has a soldier's contempt for women, and the woman he dislikes most is Cleopatra. He sees her relationship with Antony as destructive, even feminizing. In *AC*, military action climaxes with a great military leader's leaving the battle to follow a woman. Troilus loses his military courage because loving a woman has made him effeminate. However, Shakespeare mainly limits contempt for male effeminacy to the battlefield, valuing tenderheartedness regardless of gender. The power Shakespeare invests in his female characters is great.

1985

273. Abrams, Richard. "Gender Confusion and Sexual Politics in *The Two Noble Kinsmen*." In *Drama, Sex, and Politics*. Ed. James Redmond. Cambridge: Cambridge UP, 1985. 69-76.

Unlike *MND*, where identities change but not genders, in *TNK* "strict differentiation of sexual kind breaks down ... " (69). Palamon and Arcite's declaration of Platonic love is like a marriage vow. Given new identities as Emilia's lovers, the two men acquire different gender traits. The "Narcissus of Emilia's complaint," Palamon fantasizes being "ravaged by his manly lady" (71). Emilia's "sapphic orientation" is reflected in her description of the rose as the very emblem of a maid. In battle, Palamon and Arcite "represent almost heraldically the male and female principle" (73). Yet their vanity and "lack of curiosity" about Emilia reveal their "fear of sensual awakening," and so they "turn back to each other conflictually" (75). The deepest conflict in *TNK*, however, is between Theseus, the misogynist who represents destructive chivalry, and Emilia who stands for women's power, healing, and nurturing. The "sexual-political" content of *TNK* moves "beyond the cruelly patripotestal worlds" of *Tem* and *H8* (75).

274. Adelman, Janet. "Male Bonding in Shakespeare's Comedies." In Erickson and Kahn, item 286. 73-103.

Problems with male bonding in the comedies are absent in the tragedies but resurface in the romances. Early comedies such as *CE*, *TGV*, and *LLL* are not primarily concerned with marriage but with male identities, bonding, and friendships, all threatened by women and marriage. In *TGV*, the conflict between male friendship ("a mirroring bond") and women is "less resolved than wished away" (79). Women's autonomy is sacrificed for male bonds which are magically restored at the end of the play. This "final fantasy ... works to establish not the heterosexual but the same-sex bond" (79). In *MV*, that "fantasy solution is impossible" since Bassanio is returned to his rightful owner, Portia. The middle comedies–*MND*, *AYL*, *TN*–"explore the complications of heterosexual love in the absence of strong male bonds" (81). Male bonds are insignificant while the female ones are comic in *MND*. *AYL* "neglects" problems with female bonds (Celia is not pained at Rosalind's loving Orlando); the male relationships "seem to deny the possibility of such a conflict" (84). Women's absence in the forest suggests an all-male Eden; yet it is only through marriage to Rosalind that Orlando can be "restored to his rightful place in the male order of things" (85). The fantasy solution in *TGV* is replaced in *AYL* by Rosalind's disguise which ensures that "same-sex bonding can be maintained at the same time that heterosexual relationships are achieved in fact" (85). This "fantasy of simultaneity" allows Rosalind to be both male friend and female lover. Offering a "darker exploration" of the same fantasies, *TN*, which does not protect male bonding from women, "mourns" the loss of "sexual indeterminacy" at the same time it promotes it through fantasy. In *WT*, the marriage at the end unites male friends Polixenes and Leontes, yet it is only the "healing presence of the wife-mother" (93) that can make this possible. In *CE* as in *WT*, the "search for a twin self is partly a search for a safe mother" (95), a simultaneous discovery. In the comedies, the male bonds can be protected since "mothers themselves are banished" (96).

275. Belsey, Catherine. "Disrupting Sexual Difference: Meaning And Gender in the Comedies." In Drakakis, item 282. 166-90.

By challenging the sexual polarity of male/female, we can escape a suffocating ideology which fixes meaning. Instead, we need to see the plurality of selves inherent in Shakespeare's comic heroines. The idea of family (including the role of women and marriage) underwent a major change in the sixteenth century from a dynastic unit where women were excluded to the affected family, the self-contained unit "where the wife was seen as the husband's companion, though she was banished to the domestic sphere away from the center of power." Patriarchy was, of course, asserted in both family units, but "radical discontinuity in the meaning of the family, which is not in any sense an evolution, produces a gap in which definitions of other modes of being for women are momentarily visible" (178). These "modes" included Amazons, roaring girls, and "women disguised as pages."

Female transvestism in Shakespeare's plays "throws into relief patriarchal assumptions"; ironically, Portia has authority and wisdom only because she appears to be a man. Such transvestism challenges patriarchy by "unsettling the categories which legitimate it" (180). When Shakespeare's heroines dress like men, there is a comedy of uncertainty complicated by the "extra-textual sex of the actor" as well as "the gender of the protagonist" (181). "Who is speaking?"–a man or a woman. Misled by contemporary criticism and acting traditions, we cannot assume that it is just Rosalind speaking. Rosalind/Ganymede is sometimes feminine, sometimes masculine. Ganymede, who has "a certain autonomy," offers "the escape from the limitations of Rosalind's femininity" (182). Rosalind/Ganymede can "speak from antithetical positions [which] transgress the norms of sexual differences" (184). By being both male and female, this central character "celebrates the plurality" the role releases.

In other texts, the woman disguised as a man is in danger, and in this light perhaps *TN*, "of all of Shakespeare's comedies ... takes the most remarkable risks with the identity of the central figure" (185). These risks lead to the plurality of selves. While Julia in *TGV* "simultaneously occupied" the identities of Julia and Sebastian, Viola becomes herself, Cesario as well as a third speaker–the Viola of whom Viola speaks but who is not identical to her. This third speaker is "not precisely masculine or feminine" but projects an identity that displays "a difference within subjectivity, and the singularity which resides in *this* difference" (187).

276. Berggren, Paula S. "'From a God to a Bull': Shakespeare's Slumming Jove." *Classical and Modern Literature* 5 (1985): 277-91.

From the *H6* plays through the comedies of the late 1590s, the myth of Jove disguised as a bull to rape Europa was "ever an appealing presence" (289) in Shakespeare. But Shakespeare was more concerned about the moral stigma of Jove's behavior than about erotic responses or sympathy for Europa. Portrayed as a victim who fittingly represented jealous husbands and lovers, Jove's horns thus symbolized male "self deceit and indulgence" (29). In his "career as bull Jove," the *MWW* Falstaff is more accurately described in terms reserved for Jove's victims–Semele, Danae–than an overpowering god. Disguises in the last comedies (*MWW*, *Ado*) do not solve problems. Beatrice, who is "bitterly alert to infractions of sexual decorum" (284), alludes to Jove's horns to discredit men. The metaphoric associations of Jove as bull allow Benedick to insult Claudio's ancestry and to mock Don John as a "convenient scapegoat" for the dishonored god. In *WT*, Florizel's reference to the bull distances him from the sexual "exploitation" such myth involved. The myth also helps to clarify the "powerful incognito" of male characters in *MM*, *Ham*, and *Mac*. Shakespeare clearly departed from the Christian interpretation of the myth as the descent of "the son of God into human form."

277. Burt, Richard Alan. "Gender, Genre, and Scapegoats: Essays on the Social Function of Shakespeare's Comic Form." *DAI* 46 (1985): 976A. U of California, Berkeley.

278. Clark, Sandra. "*Hic Mulier, Haec Vir*, and the Controversy over Masculine Women." *Studies in Philology* 82 (1985): 157-83.

Women's clothing for the Renaissance portrayed the lustful nature of females and the extravagant demands they enjoyed imposing on their husbands. Toward the end of the reign of King

James, women were accused of dressing and behaving like men. Two pamphlets of 1620, *Hic Mulier* (mannish woman) and *Haec Vir* (her consort) show women as objects of satire. A woman dressed as a man was a common literary figure; Portia assumes a male professional role. In Shakespeare, "the hero is attracted to the disguised heroine because of the feminine attributes intuitively perceived behind the disguise" (164). Such attributes assure the audience of the hero's heterosexuality. Misogynist literature argued that women dressed as men have loose morals and lack the idealized womanly virtues of chastity and modesty. To dress like the opposite sex went against the natural order of society.

279. Coursen, H.R. "A Jungian Approach to Characterization: *Macbeth*." In Erickson and Kahn, item 286. 230-44.

A Jungian approach helps to define Macbeth and Lady Macbeth "in the context of the world they inhabit" (230) and to explain the dynamics of change in a character. Characters can be classified as introverts and extroverts; they conduct themselves through thinking and feeling, intuition and sensation. One of these functions is dominant in each individual. Desdemona has extroverted intuition; Othello has introverted sensation; and Iago is the extroverted thinker. Initially, Macbeth and Lady Macbeth incorporate the opposite character types of the introvert and extrovert, although they have a common goal. Few women in Shakespeare belong to the extroverted thinker category, a type usually reserved for men. However, Portia and Lady Macbeth, the latter an extreme example, fit this type. Lady Macbeth uses both masculinity and feminine weapons to achieve her goals through her husband. Shakespeare reveals a familiar pattern of "a husband and wife entangling themselves in self-woven webs of misunderstanding" (243) that is central to their tragedy.

280. Crawford, Kathleen V. "The Transvestite Heroine in Seventeenth-Century Popular Literature." *DAI* 45 (1985): 2109A. Harvard U.

281. Delbaere-Garant, Jeanne. "Prospero Today: Magus, Monster, or Patriarch?" In *Communiquer et traduire: Hommages a Jean*

Dierickx/Communicating and Translating: Essays in Honor of Jean Dierickx. Ed. Gilbert Debusscher and Jean-Perre Van Noppen. Bruxelles: Ed. de l U de Bruxelles, 1985. 293-302.

Three culturally diverse responses to *Tem* are present in the works of John Fowles (England), Georges Lamming (Barbados), and Margaret Laurence (Canada). In her *Side Jordan* and *The Diviners*, Laurence portrays the Miranda figure as wanting to liberate herself from Prospero's paternal authority in order to live in Caliban's world. Prospero's values are obsolete and need to be fused with Caliban's in order to become effective again. In *The Diviners*, Morag, like Miranda, is naive and depends on the experience and wisdom of an older man. Both Brooke and Prospero assume the role of teacher for their women. Morag's marriage to Brooke is as sterile as Prospero's island. She rejects everything she has learned from her husband. For a woman to be her own person, she must break away from masculine authority and take up temporary union with Caliban in order to re-establish her identity.

282. Drakakis, John. *Alternative Shakespeares*. London and New York: Methuen, 1985.

Reviews: *Times Educational Supplement* 6 June 1986: 29; Ashley, L.R.N., *Bibliotheque d' Humanisme et Renaissance* 49 (1987): 158-60; Berry, R., *Queen's Quarterly* 93 (1986): 423; Burt, Richard Alan, *Review* 9 (1987): 95; Erickson, Peter, *Shakespeare Quarterly* 37 (1986): 516; Ewbank, Inga-Stina, *Times Literary Supplement* 25 Apr. 1986: 451; Fitter, C., *Notes & Queries* 34 (1987): 113; Norbrook, D., *London Review of Books* 18 July 1985: 3; Payne, Deborah C., *Theatre Journal* 39 (1987): 113; Pfister, Manfred, *Shakespeare Jarhbuch* (1988): 235; Rabey, D.I., *Theatre Research International* 11 (1986): 167; Smith, N., *English* 35 (1986): 57; Todd, R., *Dutch Quarterly Review of Anglo-American Letters* 17 (1987): 262-82; Walch, G., *Shakespeare Jahrbuch* 123 (1987): 176-77; Watterson, W.C., *Choice* 23 (Mar. 1986): 1059; Wilson, R., *Literature and History* 14 (1988): 211.

283. Du Bois, Page. "A Disturbance of Syntax at the Gates of Rome."
     Stanford Literature Review 2 (1985): 185-208.

   In *Cor*, Shakespeare "reads the world" through the paradigm of
the relationship of mother to son. When Coriolanus breaks the
matriarchal line from mother to daughter, his speech is broken,
and the surface of his body is broken with wounds. Coriolanus
must be "both male and female in his mother's closed world." He
is driven to schizophrenic language, to broken syntax, to silence,
to psychic or physical death. Coriolanus is not schizophrenic but
suffers from disturbed communication with his mother. Volumnia
gives him the paradoxical command that requires him to be a man
like her. But she is a woman. Suppressing her husband's existence,
Volumnia suggests that she is the only one who gives Coriolanus
life. She is what Freud calls the phallic mother. Coriolanus's
identity depends on her definition of him, and she projects her
own narcissistic needs on her son. Her wounded vanity castrates
him, leaving him as wounded and bleeding as she is. The
homoerotic dimension of Coriolanus's military life is very
prominent, for Volumnia "finds martial intercourse with men to
be the most gratifying physical experience available" (195).
Ultimately, the play rejects matriarchal power because of the
"perversity of a world controlled by mothers."

284. Erickson, Peter. *Patriarchal Structures in Shakespeare's Drama*.
     Berkeley: U of California P, 1985.

   Chapter One, "Sexual Politics and Social Structure in *As You
Like It*," argues that concentrating on Rosalind "to the neglect of
other issues distorts the overall design of *AYL*, one that is
governed by male ends" (16). Orlando's political education and his
relationship with Rosalind's father is of crucial importance. Unlike
LLL, *AYL* does not take place in a static environment lacking
feminine energy; Rosalind validates a "benevolent patriarchy" by
harmoniously submitting to male control. She clearly learns a
"double lesson" (21) in the forest–to beware of the "Phebe in her"
and to teach Orlando not to belittle himself in love. Idolizing
women in love leads to making men slaves; both "male
subservience" and "female omnipotence," present in *LLL*, are

equally misguided. Rosalind's disguise as Ganymede is not
androgynous; she keeps the genders "distinct and separable" (23).
Though she is vulnerable, she does "gain access to masculine
virtues of strength and control" (31). It is men who reap most of
the benefits of androgyny, not women. *AYL* shows how to make
patriarchy and androgyny compatible. Rosalind approves
patriarchy by giving in to Duke Senior and Orlando who have
previously made peace in the forest. Love thus occurs in a positive
"paternal context" in which male bonds and nurturing are seen as
benevolent forces, and masculine aggression is condemned. In the
forest, "an idealized male enclave" (29), Orlando learns the
"traditional female attributes of compassion and nurturance" (31).
Men must acknowledge their "feminine self" and transcend
"narrow masculinity" (34), a process replicated by the boy actor
who makes that discovery for himself. The "phasing out" of
Rosalind in the Epilogue eliminates female dominance yet allows
the men to experience womanhood vicariously. *AYL* is "primarily
a defensive action against female power rather than a celebration
of it." Through marriage, patriarchal institutions are made loving.

According to Chapter Two, "Fathers, Sons, and Brothers in
Henry the Fifth," it is wrong to see the man "squeezed out of
Henry V" (40). There is a strain in his rhetoric; and the father-son
relationships account for this strain. The only way Hal/Henry V
can shape his own identity is through an "incisive encounter with
his father" (63). Incorporating his father, Hal inherits a "burdened"
blessing of heroic purification and guilty conscience. Hal is unable
to "scapegoat" his father (51) by confining the blame and
responsibility to Bolingbroke. Hal has to grapple with his own
conscience and confront the "paternal sin." In Act 4.1, Henry V's
own "heroic faith remains problematic" (52) and his male bonding
with his soldiers, whom he terms his brothers, does take "the
pressure off the father-son tension in Act 4.1" (52). The York-
Suffolk story of Act 4.6 idealizes "male comradeship" based on a
military view of masculinity, illustrating the masculine dream of
purity. The story allows sentimentality–"men's quasi-maternal
cherishing of one another" (54). The honest manliness of Henry
V and his English soldiers contrasts with the false virility of the
French, especially the Dauphin who, as Henry's rival, travesties
masculinity and represents "the corrupted negative version of the

bond between Henry IV and Hal" (57). Henry V's wooing of Katherine, though seemingly comic, portrays women as pawns, and sexuality as "a form of military aggression and conquest" (6). In the second tetralogy, women are marginalized, illustrated by Hal's need to bypass women to serve his commitment to male bonding based upon a military definition of masculinity. Henry V can be linked to Hamlet as sons who must reject false fathers, seek male bonding at the expense of their relations with women, and confront the tensions imposed by problematic father-son relationships.

Chapter Three is entitled "Maternal Images and Male Bonds in *Hamlet, Othello*, and *King Lear*." Providing Hamlet with an alternative to the ghost, Horatio offers the Prince constancy and intimacy allowing him to express his independence and true self. Asking Horatio to tell his story, Hamlet "preserves an alternate legacy of nonviolent fraternal cherishing" (72). Hamlet's relationship to Horatio is inseparable from his relationship with Gertrude and Ophelia. Transferring his adoration of Ophelia to Horatio, Hamlet also turns to Horatio as a maternal substitute for Gertrude, who made him a bastard by disinheriting him. But this male bonding sometimes produces misogyny and is not a suitable alternative to women. The "redemptive spirit" at the end of *Ham* is achieved by Hamlet's "enclosing himself in male fellowship" (79). Yet that relationship does not relieve Hamlet of the responsibility for his share in his "disastrous relations" with women.

Rejecting the "indulgent sentimentality surrounding male bonds" in *Ham, Oth* offers the paired friends, Othello and Iago. Othello has to confront two male authorities–Brabantio and the state. He allies himself with the male state as its "proper son." In fact, the state becomes Othello's "superego" (102), but by striving to serve the state, Othello reduces sexuality to "incapacitation and emasculation" (88). A gender reversal can be seen in Desdemona, the "fair warrior," seizing power through Othello's stories. The handkerchief dooms her because it prophetically associates "female chastity with dead maidens" (94). Offering male constancy, Iago supplants Desdemona and Cassio ("chaste wife" and best friend); it is Iago whom Othello loves wisely but not well. Othello adopts two extreme versions of women (saints or whores) and of himself (defender of the state and infidel). He deceives himself, yet that self-deception is not cause for censuring the tragedy, if T.S. Eliot is read correctly, but for deepening it and our engagement with Othello.

In *Lear*, the comfort of nurturing male bonds (through Kent, Edgar, and Gloucester) gives Lear a temporary rescue and contrasts with the evil feminine plots of Goneril and Regan. Yet "male bounty, independent of women, cannot be sustained" (112). Such male bonds as in *Ham* have a "misogynist edge" (107) and encourage distrust of women and disdain for their sexuality. When Lear gives up his authority, he dismantles "the patriarchal order" and reinstates "maternal power" (111). Moreover, by not having authentic communication with Cordelia and being "subsumed in his escapist vision" (114), Lear repeats the first scene of the play. His own "self-evasion" and lack of understanding compels him to tragedy. In terms of the sequence of these three plays, the "power of male bonding is diminished" (116), and in later plays (*AC*, *Cor*, *Mac*), the bonds with women (especially in their maternal roles) are strengthened.

The thesis of Chapter Four, "Identification with the Maternal in *Antony and Cleopatra*," is that the play is an experiment in the "reformulation of masculine identity in the context of sustainable androgynous heterosexuality" (144). A different kind of tragedy from *Lear* or *Oth*, *AC* presents a Cleopatra who reverses and transcends tragic feminine stereotypes and an Antony who deliberately loosens male bonds. *AC* is not a classical, orthodox tragedy where Antony's effeminacy and military losses are regarded as mistakes. Labeling Antony a failed soldier only blurs "the subject of gender so that it becomes impossible to analyze" (130). Instead, a dual vision of gender as both "reversal and exchange" demonstrates how Antony and Cleopatra can cross gender boundaries without losing their sex roles as man or woman. Striving for an "alternative masculinity," Antony imitates "maternal bounty" (134) and, like Cleopatra, plays a nurturing mother (with Enobarbus, Scarus, Cleopatra) to "find the maternal within himself" (135). Parallels between the sonnets, especially Sonnet 143, and Antony emphasize the forcefulness of maternal bounty and the association of food and sex, and Cleopatra as the Dark Lady. Through his liberality, which promises him the loss he seeks, Antony re-allocates gender roles to reach a reciprocal relationship with Cleopatra whom he rivals in gifting. But the pair is not completely successful "in fashioning a new, wholly positive model of relationship between men and women"; they evoke a "painfully divided response" (145). Though Caesar may be cynical about women and calculating, he helps Shakespeare as playwright to keep "his distance and ambivalence" regarding the lovers (145).

Chapter Five, "The Limitations of Reformed Masculinity in *The Winter's Tale*," maintains that Shakespeare's late romance "enacts the disruption and revival of patriarchy." The "fashioning [of] a benign patriarchy" must ultimately be "founded on the female body" (164), though. The challenges patriarchy faces in Sicilia stem from Leontes being threatened by Hermione in her role as mother. In the ideal patriarchal state, mothers would be "unnecessary" (157). The connection between female bounty and entertainment is at the heart of the crisis. Giving as practiced in male institutions is corrupted, and the "concept of entertainment through festive occasions" must center on women and "serve as analogues of maternal nurturance" for the "eventual return of entertainment to male control" (154). Paulina's mother-child imagery and her own nurturance are poison to Leontes. Perdita is the most positive representative of a feminine image, "congenial to patriarchal expectations" (160). Perdita, Paulina, and Hermione function as one character–the woman who gives birth and suck to her baby (161). In *WT* caring for children is "extrapolated to include caring for men" (161). Even though the last scene of *WT* "celebrates the nurturant life that Cleopatra in her final performance is forced to relinquish," the romance pays the price by returning to "polarized sexual roles" (172), situating women as either above or below men.

Reviews: Ashley, L.R.N., *Bibliotheque d'Humanisme et Renaissance* 48 (1986): 163; Bement, Peter, *Review of English Studies* 38 (1987): 555-60; Cerny, Lothar, *Shakespeare Jahrbuch* (1986): 230-38; Ewbank, Inga-Stina, *Times Literary Supplement* 25 Apr. 1986: 451-52; Garner, Shirley N., *Shakespeare Studies* 18 (1986): 293-99; Greene, Gayle, *Shakespeare Quarterly* 37 (1986): 128-32; Hatlen, Burton, *Review* 8 (1986): 241-64; Kahn, Coppelia, *Women's Studies* 13 (1987): 396-98; Rackin, Phyllis, *Theatre Journal* 38 (1986): 498; Rudnytsky, Peter L., *Renaissance Quarterly*

39 (1987): 819-20; Sedgwick, Eve Kosofsky, *Amherst* 39 (1986): 36-38; Shapiro, M., *Modern Language Review* 83 (1988): 945; Swift, Carolyn Ruth, *Signs* 12 (1986): 167-68; Thompson, Ann, *English* (1985): 251-55; Williamson, Marilyn, *Journal of English and Germanic Philology* 86 (1987): 108-10.

285. ---. "Shakespeare and the "Author-Function." In Erickson and Kahn, item 286. 245-55.

There is a sense of taboo in critical scholarship attached to any mention of the author of a text. In part, this arises from the fear of reducing the stature of an author like Shakespeare to a size manageable to the reader. The "figure of the author ... [should] emerge from the work itself" (245-6), to establish a balance between the integrity of author and reader. There are four representative approaches to the authorial problem in the case of Shakespeare. (1) It is either impossible or inappropriate to assess Shakespeare's views because he is detached from his work. Yet it is more profitable to look at "Shakespeare's temperament as embodied in his art" (249) rather than through mere biographical speculation. (2) Shakespeare has an "ideological investment" in his work, because he is conventional and represents the views of his age. However, this approach ignores the fact that "Shakespeare's drama has an extraordinary power to raise and probe difficult issues which it cannot fully resolve" (250). (3) Shakespeare is critical of the views of his age. (4) Relations between Shakespeare and his reader are richer when they become fluid, and the two sides are not always in agreement. Shakespeare presents no definitive philosophy of gender running throughout his work.

286. Erickson, Peter, and Coppelia Kahn, eds. *Shakespeare's "Rough Magic": Renaissance Essays in Honor of C.L. Barber*. Newark: U of Delaware P, 1985.

Reviews: Cartelli, T., *Shakespeare Studies* 20 (1988): 283-88; Ewbank, Inga-Stina, *Times Literary Supplement* 25 Apr. 1986: 451-52; Frey, Charles, *Studies in English Literature, 1500-1900* 26 (1986): 384-86; Hatlen, Burton, *Review* 8 (1986): 241-46; Hyman,

L.W., *Psychoanalytic Review* 76 (1989): 452; Watson, R.N., *Shakespeare Quarterly* 38 (1987): 249-53.

287. Fineman, Joel. "The Turn of the Shrew." In Parker and Hartman, item 303. 138-59.

TSh contains the "master plot of the relationship between language and desire" (155), showing the connections between rhetoric and gender. The play illustrates the arguments between Lacanian psychoanalytic patriarchalism and Derridean "antipatriarchal gender deconstructions," the battle between "the determinate, literal language traditionally spoken by men and the figurative, indeterminate language traditionally spoken by women" (143). Yet *TSh* "speaks neither for the language of woman nor against the authority of man" (138). Instead, it is based upon an orthodox paradox that feminine subversive tactics actually "resecure ... the very order" to which they are opposed. Petruchio is never so patriarchal as when, in his lunacy, he "bespeaks the language of woman" to silence Kate (142). *TSh* thereby validates an "erotic paradox"; the orthodox views about the battle of the sexes are "reconfirmed" by "madly translating a man into a mad woman" (144). Two different female voices in the play–Bianca's and Kate's–"elicit two different kinds of male desire" (148). Bianca's visionary language of silence is opposed to Kate's vocal, verbal language; this opposition "runs throughout the play governing its largest dramatic as well as thematic movements" (148).

The contradictory status of women is best documented through Robert Fludd's iconographic depiction of a hierarchical cosmos. As both "the object and the motive of desire," woman is subordinate to man, a "likeness of a likeness"; she is also a radical sub-version of man claiming her own identity. Fludd's work posits a "universe of logical sameness" that is "built up *on* its logical contra-diction, e.g., the language of woman because it is the very lunacy of discourse that returns both man and woman to the golden, solar order of the patriarchal Word [sic]" (154). Thus Petruchio "re-establishes the differences between the sexes by speaking lunatic language of woman." No sooner, though, is Kate tamed and made silent than two quiet women (Bianca, the

Widow) become shrews to show that the subversive language that
opened the play must point the way forward to "a repetition of the
same old story." Thus with Fludd's cosmos as a model reflected
in *TSh*, Shakespeare's play presents a "logic and a logos whose
internal disruption forever defers, even as this deferment elicits a
desire for, a summary conclusion" (155).

288. Gardiner, Judith Kegan. "The Marriage of Male Minds in
     Shakespeare's Sonnets." *Journal of English and Germanic
     Philology* 84 (1985): 328-47.

The "complex emotional texture of the sonnets" comes from
the "contrast between [Shakespeare's] ideology of marriage and
the difficulties of applying that ideology to an idealized passion
between men ... " (330). According to that ideology, marriage was
instituted for procreation, companionship, and "relief of
concupiscence." The sonnets reflect, reinforce, and use the
imagery of that ideology; in fact, Shakespeare helped to shape
Renaissance views of marriage. The sonnet sequence "moves like
a comedy from courtship to marriage; like a tragedy from
marriage to adultery, absence, and death; like a romance from
death to Christian transcendence" (332). Shakespeare violates
gender roles in seeing the poet's relationship to the young man in
conjugal terms. The first 17 sonnets deal with the traditional
theme of "wife-choosing" and generation; Shakespeare does not
explore the other reasons–companionship or relief from
concupiscence–for matrimony. The middle sonnets (18-126)
concern the "intense, ambivalent relationship between the poet
and his male beloved," and since there is no "recognizable
institution" providing an ideal model, Shakespeare uses marriage
which "validates and unifies body and soul, self and other" (335).
    The sonnets should not be de-eroticized by limiting them to
expressions of friendship. The poet's relationship with the young
man is portrayed with the generational, social, legal, and
economic images found in the Renaissance ideology of courtship
and marriage. But "the poet seeks his love's commitment; not
consummation" (339). Sonnet 116 is the "finest expression of this
union" (340). Adultery and unfaithful minds threaten the
relationship in the next sequence (Sonnets 127-52). The lover's

triangle (poet, young man, Dark Lady) "raise[s] traditional, husband-like complaints." Like a betrayed husband, the poet presents the Dark Lady as a cuckolder; she is a "female version of Persephone's ravisher" taking the young man away to hell (343). In the sonnets, Shakespeare "translates marriage into an ideal literary coupling," masking his desire for patronage through "the vicarious transports of sublimated heterosexual courtship" of the young man.

289. Girard, Rene. "The Politics of Desire in *Troilus and Cressida*." In Parker and Hartman, item 303. 188-209.

Shakespeare presents two messages in *TrC*, one conventional and the other subtle. Conventionally, critics have selectively read the play inventing a positive hero in Troilus. In a superficial reading, Cressida's falseness and infidelity alone are deplorable. Yet in terms of Shakespeare's subtle message, Troilus's fidelity "means nothing" (192), since he never had time to be unfaithful. Admittedly, Troilus is not a hero and Cressida is not a heroine, but she is "more likable" (193) than Troilus and the other men. Troilus's sins include male vanity, selfishness, and, most of all, indifference. At first his "self confidence" about Cressida is "boundless" (194). But complacency gives way to jealousy. "Just as she knew possession kills desire, Cressida seems to know the one efficient method for reviving a dead desire: jealousy" (196). Troilus's betrayal of Cressida leads to her betrayal of him, "an imitation of what Troilus has done to her" (197).

One desire triggers another, duplicating the first; desire "can only result from an imitation of it, a kind of copy," or mimetic desire (198) which is a "pervasive and unifying power" in *TrC*. As the "inspirer of desire," Helen is a "magnet for countless desires" (200) responsible for the "vicious circle of mimetic desire." Political strategies of indifference and jealousy mirror erotic ones; in fact, they are "really one and the same" (206). Ulysses is a "political Pandarus" (208) who manipulates Ajax as a rival model for Achilles in the same way Cressida invokes the "merry Greeks" to control Troilus. Ulysses and Cressida "shatter" a "rebellious partner by persuading him that the desire upon which he counts as a model for self-love is now denied him, either because it is

focused on someone else, a more successful rival, or ... no one but
the desiring subject himself, which amounts to the same thing"
(206). In *TrC*, mimesis is desire and desire is mimesis.

290. Goldberg, Jonathan. "Shakespearean Inscriptions: The Voicing of
      Power." In Parker and Hartman, item 303. 116-37

Linda Bamber's *Comic Women, Tragic Men* (item 175) errs
because "the rigidity that she brings to the Shakespearean text is
her own; her categories do not correspond to the historical
specificity of the Shakespearean text" (117). Our notions of
male/female, gender/genre were not necessarily Shakespeare's,
and his culture did not automatically validate sexism and
patriarchalism. It is "not necessarily a sign of power to have a
voice, not necessarily a sign of subjection to lose it" (130). Portia
is silenced by the law (will) of her father, yet she "becomes the
father" (law) through Bellario's letter about her as Balthasar. Yet
that letter "equivocates"; carrying it, she makes "two wills one,
binding father and daughter, male and female, inner and outer"
(124). Portia's voice is, therefore, neither male nor in "the realm
of feminine discourse." She passes through the text, "affirming the
meeting of, the suspension of, difference" (125). In *MM*, Isabella's
silence does not spell defeat; the Duke asks for her voice to
"ratify" his work. Portia's silence in *JC* is "not the result of her
exclusion" from the male world of power; to the contrary, it points
to "the constitutive alienation of her participation in the plot" with
Brutus (128). Speaking with two voices, Portia becomes one with
her husband, marrying "the self to its otherness" (130). There is
"power in inarticulation" in *Oth*, as Iago as well as Desdemona
prove. Similarly, Cordelia's silence in *Lear* reveals her refusal to
betray her inferiority and contrasts with Lear's "megalomanic
acquisitiveness" (133). Hippolyta's speech in Act 5 of *MND*
counterpoints Hermia and Helena's "knowing silence."
Voices–speaking or silent–in the text alert us to the slippages that
challenge simplistic readings of "hegemonic power" in
Shakespeare.

291. Heffernan, Carol F. "*The Taming of the Shrew*: The Bourgeoisie
      in Love." *Essays in Literature* 12 (1985): 3-14.

Shakespeare attacks the bourgeois abuses of marriage and women in *TSh*. Against the background of Elizabethan marriage manuals as well as in contrast with the possible source/parallel play *The Taming of a Shrew*, Shakespeare expanded "the burgher aspect" of *TSh* by emphasizing "the explicit obviousness with property" (5) the middle class attached to marriage. Being a wealthy merchant's son wins Lucentio's favor with Baptista; and Petruchio, too, is a moneyed man, possibly one of "the new gentry" as well as a fortune hunter. Baptista violates the injunctions found in the marriage manuals by not being concerned with whether or not Kate loves Petruchio; he is so eager to rid himself of his shrewish daughter that he does not even "haggle" with Petruchio. Baptista acts otherwise with Bianca whom he will greedily sell off to the highest bidder, again giving "no thought to the compatibility of marriage partners" (9). Though Lucentio evades "ordinary bourgeoisie expectation" by eloping, Kate and Petruchio "rise above the middle class commercialism of their marital agreement even more dramatically" (9). Following Myles Coverdale's *Christian State of Matrimony,* Petruchio does not allow fine dress and pomp to displace the wedding ceremony. He uses the taming of Kate to "attack middle class values and connections" while winning a handsome dowry at the same time.

292. Henderson, Katherine Usher, and Barbara F. McManus. *Half Humankind: Contexts and Texts of the Controversy About Women in England, 1540-1640.* Urbana: U of Illinois P, 1985. Esp. 114-119.

The stereotypes about women found in the drama mirror those in the feminist and anti-feminist pamphlets of the period. Though there were no actresses on the Renaissance stage, the "prominence of women's roles constitutes an irony best explained in terms of the period's passionate interest in women" (114). The "source of dramatic tension" in many of Shakespeare's plays is having the heroes cast women as seductresses and shrews, though "in most cases" the women are vindicated. Iago's false charges against Desdemona demand comparison with antifeminist treatises; "Desdemona's innocence is mute testimony to the falseness of Iago's stereotype of women" (115). Emilia's defense of her mistress's sexual behavior employs the "same arguments used by Mary Tattlewell (*The Women's Sharp Revenge* [1640]) in defending adulterous women" (115). Hamlet also projects the stereotype of the lustful woman on Ophelia and sees her use of cosmetics as a sign of her "sexual looseness"; ironically, Hamlet himself is earlier characterized as a seducer by Polonius. Leontes, too, "casts two women in the negative stereotypes found in the antifeminist pamphlets"; Paulina, however, is hardly a shrew but a "complex character with a capacity for deep loyalty and enduring love as well as righteous indignation. Part of her complexity is ambivalence at her own assertiveness ... " (119).

293. Kahn, Coppelia. "The Cuckoo's Note: Male Friendship and Cuckoldry in *The Merchant of Venice*." In Erickson and Kahn, item 286. 104-12.

Shakespeare undercuts the marriage ideal in *MV* with the ring plot which places male friendship and marriage in conflict. Portia gives the ring to Bassanio to point out the primacy of marital obligations over male bonds. The suggestion is that if men do not renounce or even betray their male friends after marriage, their wives will betray them. Portia and Antonio do not seem competitive in the beginning; however, conflict arises when Antonio's letter about his lost ships prevents the consummation of his friend's marriage. The conflict is intensified when Antonio urges Bassanio to give Portia's ring away. Portia's power over Bassanio is based on cuckoldry. Bassanio's faithfulness is a condition for Portia's love. In Portia, Shakespeare presents a view of women suggesting that they are not fickle but that they use the threat of betrayal as a defense. The ring plot emphasizes sexual differences rather than harmonies.

294. Lecercle, Ann. "Anatomy of a Fistula, Anomaly of a Drama." In *All's Well That Ends Well: Nouvelles Perspectives Critiques*. Ed. Jean Fuzier and Francois Laroque. Collection Astrea 1. Montpellier: Pubs. de l'Universite Paul Valery, 1985. 105-24.

AWW is informed by a fistuline logic which is at the center of desire in the play. The fistula, which is the "quintessential syntax of the enigma" in *AWW* (109), is a conjunction of opposites–a wound or hole (castration)/the "short-circuiting" of castration, repulsion/desire, lust/love, and separation/marriage–the displacement of the erotic and a rapport with the flesh (118). The play is saturated with poisons–both of the word and the eye (or invidia)–including the phylaxy, phallic eye. Since it takes an enigma to cure an enigma, Helen, the physician's daughter, participates in the wounding and the less than virtuous cure. Her conduct with the King is shadowy, and Bertram rejects her because he knows of her deeds. The play is filled with compulsive repetitions, subversions, inversions. "What we see in *AWW* is a St. Vitus dance of desire where all change places and roles, dramatic and sexual, active and passive; all are doubles and masks" (121). Laveche, for example, is the male cow, the "inverse" and complement of the "phallic virgin," Helen. *AWW* is a "fully-fledged comedy of the Fall" (122) where Helen/Helena has little to do with the ideals of chastity. As the fallen woman, she is Helena Invida (poison), a "Britomartis seen through the prism of the sonnets" (123).

295. McLuskie, Kathleen. "The Patriarchal Bard: Feminist Criticism and Shakespeare: *King Lear* and *Measure for Measure*." In *Political Shakespeare: New Essays in Cultural Materialism*. Ed. Jonathan Dollimore and Alan Sinfield. Manchester: U of Manchester P, 1985. 88-108.

Rather than co-opting Shakespeare and privileging his female characters, feminists should subvert his text. The "mimetic, essentialist models of feminist criticism" (91), illustrated by Juliet Dusinberre (item 6), Linda Bamber (item 175), and Marilyn French (item 155), wrongly assume that the relationship between drama and society is static in representing women. More complex social forces were at work in determining the nature of women, which was under severe ideological pressure. Feminists should not simply construct an author ("Shakespeare as a feminist") behind the plays, which really were "products of an entertainment industry" (92) excluding women. Instead, feminists should understand and explore the textual strategies that circumscribed the ways in which "women characters are 'seen' in the action"

(95). These strategies–narrative, structural, and rhetorical–privilege men and deny an "autonomous position for the female viewer of the action." Radical feminist productions of *MM* might celebrate Isabella's chastity; yet Isabella and Mariana are "defined theatrically by the men around [them] for the men in the audience" (96). Isabella's speeches are sexualized, and she (like Mariana) is physically framed by men–Angelo and Lucio–who control her destiny. Since women's roles are limited in *MM*, feminist criticism of the play "is restricted to exposing its own exclusion from the text" (97).

The strategy of tragedy, too, implies maleness. In *Lear*, the "narrative and its dramatization present a connection between sexual insubordination and explicitly misogynist emphasis" (98). Woman's own lust is linked to chaos. The "saving love" of Cordelia is less "a redemption for womankind than ... an example of patriarchy restored" (99). By pitying Lear we accept his patriarchal ideology. To deny his suffering is unthinkable. "Feminism cannot simply take 'the woman's part' that has been so morally loaded and theatrically circumscribed" through Goneril and Regan. The way for feminist criticism to enter the play more satisfactorily is to deconstruct the conflict between "affective relations and contractual agreements" (104), emphasizing that Lear, like the women, can be deprived of male power. Goneril and Regan's power over him is "the obverse of his power over them" (105).

296. McPherson, David. "Three Charges Against Sixteenth- and Seventeenth-Century Playwrights: Libel, Bawdy, and Blasphemy." *Medieval and Renaissance Drama in England* 2 (1985): 269-82.

To those opposed to the theatre, no amount of reforming scripts could make the stage acceptable. Yet when the specific charges of libel, blasphemy, and bawdiness were leveled against the theatres, the scripts came under attack. Those who assaulted the plays "reached white heat in their denunciation of sexual and scatological references ... " (273). Not having a Scriptural text to support their attack of the theatre, moralists based their opposition on the Seventh Commandment. They, therefore, vilified the unchaste behavior of the players for engaging in sodomy and for corrupting the audience's morals with lustful shows. Moralists did invoke Deuteronomy 22:5, which prohibited crossdressing, to lash out at men playing women's parts on stage. Yet one moralist in particular, William Prynne, was "particularly bothered by the question of whether it was worse for boys to act the women's roles or for women to act them" (275). Deciding it was morally worse for spectators to see women on the stage, Prynne thereby demonstrated "considerable independence from biblical justification because such a view renders Deuteronomy 22:5 largely irrelevant" (276).

297. Murray, Timothy. "Othello's Foul Generic Thoughts and Methods." In *Persons in Groups: Social Behavior as Identity Formation in Medieval and Renaissance Europe. Papers of the Sixteenth Annual Conference for the Center for Medieval and Renaissance Studies.* Binghamton, NY: Medieval & Renaissance Texts & Studies, 1985. 67-77.

In striving for man's vision of truth, generic modes neglect women. A *"genderic"* study ("in view of genre as well as gender" [68]) of *Oth* shows how Thomas Rymer's objections to the play–it aroused horror rather than pity–were "endemic" to Renaissance theatre. Mimesis as well as women are threatened in *Oth.* Opponents of the theatre condemned the stage for its mimesis ("the source of male fear" [69]) and associated mimesis with feminine weaknesses and presentations–feminine self-fashioning, passion, seduction, and other vices which "were interpreted with suspicion by the cultural codes of men" (74). Desdemona's inconstancy and her theatrical performance show her representations before "desirous beholders." Her performance reflects back on Othello, his erratic turnings, seizures, and loss of self-control exemplifying the "antitheatrical fears of dramatic mimesis" (70). Women were thought to be more susceptible to mimesis than were men because they were less capable of distinguishing between "a theatrical sign and its counterfeit signified" and also because of their trust in the fixed representations of patriarchy. Desdemona and Othello react differently to theatrical puzzles such as the handkerchief.

As a "female worker of words," she outmaneuvers Iago while her method ironically enacts his words. She tries to "reorder the linguistic play of her house." Othello "confuses Desdemona's generic method with his belief in her genderic fickleness" (75). Desdemona may be thought of as a "female scapegoat who is sacrificed by an antitheatrical and misogynous society for being a visible woman exercising flexible and rational methods contrary to the fearful norms of patriarchy" (75). Yet *Oth* offers a "concealed but radical woman's vision of things" through Bianca's assertion of her own space and her discovery of herself as a female with an honest life. Though Bianca is the only woman in the play to "proclaim openly and publicly her indifference to patriarchal beds and the webbing of heroic representation," she is forced by Iago to lie in a "bed of patriarchy" at the end.

298. Neely, Carol Thomas. *Broken Nuptials in Shakespeare's Plays.* New Haven: Yale UP, 1985.

The "Introduction: Wooing, Wedding, and Repenting" finds that marriage in Shakespeare is a focus for tensions and reconciliations between the sexes. "The broken nuptials express the anxieties, desires, and conflicts of the couples who enter into marital unions as well as the external pressures placed on these unions by parents, rulers, the community" (1). Marriage defines female characters in terms of their position in society and the way women define themselves in relationship to men. Even Cleopatra and Lady Macbeth are subject to the confines of patriarchy. The mending of ruptured nuptials in *Ado*, *AC*, *Oth*, and *WT* is achieved through the women's actual or apparent deaths. The women in Shakespeare's plays expose the emptiness of Petrarchianism and male idealization as well as the unreliability of male vows of undying love. Both cuckoldry and misogyny are expressions of anxiety about or hostility toward marital sexuality.

Chapter One, "Broken Nuptials in Shakespeare's Comedies: *Much Ado About Nothing*," emphasizes that in broken nuptials Shakespeare finds the sources for his comedies while weddings reconcile romance and desire. Male resistance to marriage is different from women's because conflicting bonds are male, not familial. Instead of withdrawing, men defend themselves against women and protect their self-esteem by "aggressive misogyny" or "witty idealization" which in turn are met with "parodic ceremonies" imposed by the women on the men they love. While women fear submission, men fear sexual betrayal. *Ado* contains the most clear-cut example of broken nuptials with Claudio's interruption of his wedding ceremony to accuse Hero of infidelity. The Hero/Claudio and Beatrice/Benedick plots maintain an equilibrium between male control and female initiative. Beatrice's mockery of marriage and men only shows her desire for both. She is anxious about remaining unmarried, but fears the social and sexual power marriage grants men. "Throughout the comedies broken nuptials, even when initiated by men, give women the power to resist, control, or alter the movement of courtship" (56). But with the completed nuptials, male control is reestablished.

Chapter Two focuses on "Power and Virginity in the Problem Comedies: *All's Well That Ends Well*." These plays are connected with their concern about sexuality and its strained relation to social authority. Marriages at the end of the dramas are formed under pressure. Unlike the festive comedies, in *AWW* sex, love, and marriage are deliberately problematic. Sexuality is frequently separated from marriage and procreation. Romantic love is easily manipulated and easily shattered. "As sexuality becomes more central and more debased in the problem plays and as marriage becomes legally and socially more difficult, the protection of virginity, an underlying assumption in the festive comedies, becomes a matter for debate" (63). Virginity becomes at once a virtue and a commodity for exchange; it can be seductive power, but when lost, the woman loses her ability to inspire male adoration. It also signals a change of status from beloved to wife. Helen and Bertram are isolated from each other because they associate with separate male and female communities. Their marriage and Helen's subsequent pregnancy reunite sexuality with family. All three women in *AWW* use the image of the thorn in the flower to express the mingled pain and pleasure of sexual experience. In *AWW* marriage does not promise a happy ending but an open-ended beginning; in *MM*, marriage is a social punishment for sexual sins.

The subject of Chapter Three is "Women and Men in *Othello*." An "Emilia critic" can take issue with the Othello and Iago critics who misrepresent the women in the play in part by viewing the conflict in *Oth* as good versus evil. The "play's central theme is ... marital love ... and [its sources] quite as illuminating as the tragedies ... Cinthio, and especially Shakespeare's preceding comedies" (108). *Oth* resembles these comedies in the attempts (doomed in the tragedy) by the women to turn "men from foolish lovers" into "sensible husbands." Yet the play is "a terrifying completion of the comedies" (110). A comparison of *Oth* with the comedies reveals significant differences between men and the women. The men in *Oth* "darken the anxieties of the comedy heroes"; Othello cannot accept the "cuckoldry and sexuality found in the comedies" (111), and Iago, like a Jaques, is the "victim" of his own manipulations (113). The women, on the other hand, resemble comic heroines in combining "realism with romance, mockery with affection" (114). Bianca in jealousy does not seek revenge from Cassio; "sharp-tongued" Emilia understands "but tolerates male fancy" (115). In courtship and marriage, Desdemona views "love as risk and challenge" (125-26), tempering it "by realism ... like that of the comedy heroines" (115). She is neither "the saint extolled by the critics" nor the passive bungler. Her indirection in wooing Othello is "not unlike Rosalind's" (115), and her friendship with Emilia is "reminiscent of the generous, witty female friendship in the comedies" (123). While the women do not worry about reputation and are "partially free of vanity, jealousy, and competitiveness," the men are vain, preoccupied with "rank and reputation, and their cowardice render[s] them as incapable of friendship as they are of love" (122). A symbol of "women's loving, civilizing, sexual power" (128), the handkerchief initially "represents women's ability to moderate men's erratic (and erotic) 'fancies'"; it then reflects "the failure of Desdemona's power" (130); and it ultimately, in Emilia's confession about its theft, "becomes the vehicle through which civilizing control is returned to the women" (131). While the ending of *Oth*, as in the comedies, has "most of the characters remain where they started" (134), there is no "comic resolution of male with female, idealism with realism, wit with sex" (135).

Chapter Four on "Gender and Genre in *Antony and Cleopatra*" argues that *AC* does not eliminate gender distinctions; it shows them in greater variety by exploring, magnifying, and ratifying

them. Female and male "roles are not equal–not even here" (165).
Mocking Antony so she can acquire a more realistic view of
heroism, Cleopatra wants him to enter into a sexual intimacy
without conventionalizing or idealizing their relationship. Octavia's
timorousness contrasts with Cleopatra's self-assertiveness and thus
legitimizes Antony's return to Egypt. When Antony is freed from
the roles of romantic lover and soldier and Cleopatra is released
from being the exasperated heroine, the two can play more
mutual roles. Their union defies the antithesis of love (passion)
and honor (male codes) found in *Oth*, *Mac*, *Lear*, and *AWW*. At
the midpoint of the play, the antitheses of soft/hard, sexual
passion/heroism merge. Passion becomes heroism for Antony and
heroism becomes passion for Cleopatra. Yet this new union
threatens both of them. Antony experiences a "double
defeat"–sexual in thinking Cleopatra is unfaithful and political in
thinking she betrayed him. Yet Cleopatra is only trying to absorb
his losses through her mock death which is both "active and
defensive, both for her own sake and his" (150). Unlike other
tragic heroes, Antony does not assume a "feminine role"; he can
"accept more fully Cleopatra's sexuality, duplicity, and difference
from him and find them compatible with his manhood" (150).
Enobarbus's ambivalence toward Cleopatra reflects the play's
central conflicts; his death foreshadows the "accommodation of
male bonds to heterosexual union" (153). Armed by Cleopatra and
Eros (in place of Enobarbus), Antony "takes on a fuller identity
without discarding the virtues of the old" (156). To escape
Caesar's debasing her sexuality, Cleopatra enacts her own
stagings. Her death, the "fullest expression of her sexuality in the
play" (161), complements and completes Antony's vision of her.
In *AC* the symbolic marriage of Antony and Cleopatra "is a
liberation of sexuality from family, society, and history, a
consummation in death" (163). No dynastic family emerges
triumphant in *AC* as in the history plays, and victory does not
wipe out the great sense of loss as in the tragedies. *AC* "holds in
solution" the elements of comedy, history, and tragedy.

According to Chapter Five, "Incest and Issue in the Romances;
The Winter's Tale," the "excessive power of men is expressed,
blunted and transmuted into benign forms, while threatening
female sexuality is chastened through women's defended chastity,

disguise, separation, confinement, or death" (167). The absence of mothers causes broken nuptials in the older generation. Mothers die in childbirth or following the birth of a child. The death of bad mothers protects fathers and children from their destructive power while the death of good mothers idealizes their sexual and procreative powers. The mother's sexuality is eliminated from the romances until the moment it can be passed on to the marriageable daughter who must obtain the father's approval for her marriage. The possessive misogyny behind Leontes's jealousy stems from bitter memories of his courtship of Hermione. He creates the object of jealousy as the comic lover created the object of his love. Leontes wrongly divorces sexuality from love. The three women in the play are at ease with sex, while the two kings are uneasy about it. Paulina effects the reunion because she assumes an unthreatening asexual role. As "Hermione's double," Perdita is important for her role in healthy relationships. The final scene is symbolic of Leontes's acceptance of Hermione as his wife again. Paulina's marriage to Camillo reflects the equality and mutuality of Leontes and Paulina. In *WT* marriage is not a punishment or a convention but a hard-earned fulfillment.

Reviews: Ashley, L.R.N., *Bibliotheque d'Humanisme et Renaissance* 49 (1987): 161-62; Bevington, David, *Journal of English and Germanic Philology* 86 (1987): 405-07; Clerici, M.E.S., *Notes & Queries* 34 (1987): 376-77; Ewbank, Inga-Stina, *Times Literary Supplement* 25 Apr. 1986: 451-52; Kahn, Coppelia, *Shakespeare Quarterly* 38 (1987): 368-71; Kirsch, Arthur, *Renaissance Quarterly* 40 (1987): 171-72; McEachern, Claire, *Shakespeare Studies* 20 (1987): 306-310; Motte-Sherman, Brunhilde de la, *Shakespeare Jahrbuch* 123 (1987): 180-82; Peake, R.H., *Choice* 23 (1986): 743; Shapiro, Michael, *Modern Language Review* 83 (1988): 945; Shulman, J., *Sixteenth Century Journal* 17 (1986): 548; Thompson, Ann, *Times Higher Education Supplement* 25 Apr. 1986: 18; Williams, Jimmy, *South Central Review* 3 (1986): 105-06.

299. ---. "Feminist Criticism in Motion." In *For Alma Mater: Theory and Practice in Feminist Scholarship*. Ed. Paula A Treichler, Cheris Kramarae, and Beth Stafford. Urbana: U of Illinois P, 1985. 69-90.

See item 298.

300. ---. "Broken Nuptials in Shakespeare's Comedies: *Much Ado About Nothing*." In Erickson and Kahn, item 286.

See item 298.

301. Nelson, T.G.A. "'Bad Commodity' or 'Fair Posterity'? The Ambivalence of Issue in English Renaissance Comedy." *English Literary Renaissance* 15 (1985): 195-224.

The treatment of childbearing and child raising in Renaissance and Shakespearean comedy does not project unmitigated joy over fecundity but an "ambivalence, with embarrassment, foreboding, and resentment often predominating over acceptance and affection" (196). Tragedy, too, certainly shows a rift between parents and children but unlike comedy presents "positive feelings toward children" as a sign of "goodness or mental health as negative ones are of wickedness or derangement" (198). Shakespeare's romantic comedies, especially *MND*, *CE*, *MM*, are "particularly rich in references to labor pains, death in childbed" and deformed and illegitimate issue (204). Shakespeare's "low and cynical" characters frequently speak of pregnancy and childbearing with "calculated disrespect"; *MM* "seems to go out of its way" to attack fertility, for pregnancy and childbearing are stigmatized as "embarrassing, and often sordid or ludicrous consequences of sexual activity" (207). The shepherd's kindly treatment of Perdita in *WT* is more a sign of the demands of the pastoral genre than a reflection of the "social facts" of Shakespeare's age. Childbearing "carries with it disturbing associations that cluster around sexuality in general" (222).

302. Noling, Kim Hunter. "The Self-Dramatizing Matron in Shakespeare's Romances." *DAI* 46 (1985): 159A. Cornell U.

303. Parker, Patricia, and Geoffrey Hartman, eds. *Shakespeare and the Question of Theory*. New York: Metheun, 1985.

Reviews: British Book News June 1986: 366; *Poetics Today* 8 (1987): 468; *Times Educational Supplement* 6 June 1986: 25; Adams, R.M., *New York Review of Books* 6 Nov. 1986: 50; Ashley, L.R.N., *Bibliotheque d'Humanisme et Renaissance* 49 (1987): 675; Brown, Keith, *Times Literary Supplement* 22 Aug. 1986: 917-18; Burt, Richard Alan, *Review of English Studies* 38 (1987): 553-55; Dodsworth, M., *English* [London] 35 (1986): 188-96; Drakakis, John, *Notes & Queries* 35 (1988): 369-71; Erickson, Peter, *Shakespeare Quarterly* 37 (1986): 516-20; Howard, Jean E., *Studies in English Literature, to 1500-1900* 27 (1987): 357-58; Keefer, M.H., *University of Toronto Quarterly* 57 (1987): 109-11; Kernan, Alvin, *Yale Review* 77 (1987): 86; Riese, U., *Shakespeare-Jahrbuch* 124 (1988): 263-64; Semple, H., *Journal of Literary Studies* 2 (1986): 71-76; Storfer, P., *Drama: The Quarterly Theatre Review* No. 162 (1986): 48-49; Strier, Richard, *Modern Philology* 86 (1988): 56; Thompson, Ann, *Times Higher Education Supplement* 25 Apr. 1986: 18; Todd, R., *Dutch Quarterly Review of Anglo-American Letters* 17 (1987): 262-82; Wenzel, P., *Anglia* 106 (1988): 529-34; White, R.S., *Shakespeare Survey* 40 (1988): 189-90; Wilson, R., *Hamlet Studies* 9 (1987): 118-25.

304. Parten, Anne. "Falstaff's Horns: Masculine Inadequacy and Feminine Mirth in *The Merry Wives of Windsor*." *Studies in Philology* 82 (1985): 184-99.

Falstaff's folly and punishments can be seen in light of the skimmington, the ritual in which a man is shamed for his "distasteful or disruptive" sexual behavior. The victim of the skimmington, to which *MWW* has a strong "thematic affinity" (187), had to ride behind a woman "mounted ahead of him on the same horse," hold a distaff, and be pummeled with a skimming-ladle, revealing that his "masculine ineffectuality [was] equated with cuckoldom" (187). The merry wives demonstrate that their mirth did not signal a compromised chastity, thus challenging the Elizabethan belief that feminine mirth was associated with loose moral behavior. Despite the justification of their wit, the wives doubtless aroused anxiety in the audience because of their domination of men. Yet Falstaff and Ford are "analogous exemplars" of the corrupt and weak men who fell victims to an "ascendant arch-wife." "Brothers in error" (191), who share the role of "villain-victim" (192), Falstaff and Ford see adultery as "exclusively a matter of competition between men," love as a "business transaction," and combine the jealous-husband and the "would-be adulterer" of contemporary narratives. John Steadman ("Falstaff as Actaeon: A Dramatic Emblem," *Shakespeare Quarterly* 14 [1963]: 231-44) incorrectly links Falstaff and Actaeon as victims of lust. It was more likely that for Elizabethan audiences horns suggested cuckoldry, that the roles of the cuckold and jealous husband were not mutually exclusive, and that Falstaff and Ford were converted into "symbolic cuckold[s]" (193), through the skimmington punishment. A parallel for the wives' punishment of Falstaff as a cuckold is the deer-slaying scene of *LLL*. A woman can cuckold a man through her wit; in doing so, the wives call attention "to the vain old knight's condition as a diminished male" and consequently "affirm the community's support for the normal sexual order" (199).

305. Rackin, Phyllis. "Anti-Historians: Women's Roles in Shakespeare's Histories." *Theatre Journal* 37 (1985): 329-44.

In Shakespeare's English history plays, women are "never the central actors" (343). They are suppressed and alien, subverting the patriarchal myths by which men immortalize themselves. Denied a place in that history, women become anti-historians. In *1H6*, Joan tries to discredit the historical record that Talbot wants to enshrine in a battle between the masculine and feminine, chivalry and pragmatism, fame and physical reality. Like Joan, the Countess of Auvergne insists on Talbot's physical presence, but since he is only a "shadow" in her castle, her version of him is "vulnerable to metadramatic attack" (333). Masculine realism (feudalism) overcomes feminine nominalism (individualism). The "subversive female voice is never allowed to prevail for more than a moment" in *1H6*; even Margaret's adultery has no impact on the action. However, in *KJ* women's "sexual transgressions" significantly disrupt male-written history. In this most troubling history play, women are "for the first time sharply individualized" (338), particularly Constance, the spokesperson for "the anti-historical forces," and Eleanor. Adultery, a central issue in *KJ*, calls into question male history which depends on genealogies (narratives of succession) to preserve the male legacy. Two key disputes in *KJ* involve questions of motherhood–Arthur/John and the Bastard/Robert Faulconbridge. In giving his decision for the Bastard, John "demythologizes the record" and turns the principle of "patriarchal succession" into a "legal fiction." Revealingly, women (Eleanor and Lady Faulconbridge) supply the Bastard with his patriarchy. Incorporating women into history shows that the "words of the historical [male] text" can never fully represent actuality.

306. Rogers, Katharine M. "Masculine and Feminine Values in Restoration Drama: The Distinctive Power of *Venice Preserved*." *Texas Studies in Literature and Language* 27 (1985): 390-404.

Shakespearean tragedy presents conflicting values within the ambiguity of life itself, whereas Restoration tragedy oversimplifies conflict, even favoring one value above the other. While both Dryden and Shakespeare emphasize the irrationality of Antony and Cleopatra's love, Shakespeare's play "neither holds up reason as the highest human standard nor identifies it with values such as manly honor and military glory."

307. Rose, Jacqueline. "Sexuality in the Reading of Shakespeare: *Hamlet* and *Measure for Measure*." In Drakakis, item 282. 95-118.

The question of female sexuality and meaning is inseparable in much criticism of *Ham* and *MM*. Female desire is the main offense that critics believe leads to moral uncertainty. Women embody fantasies yet they are expected to uphold order. Gertrude and Isabella are held accountable for the aesthetic and ethical problems in their respective plays. In T.S. Eliot's normative criticism of *Ham*, Gertrude is the "cause of the excess and deficiency" as well as the object which does not match the emotion it should properly elicit. Isabella's "sexual identity" arouses critics' anxiety which in turn develops into a sexual reproach of women for excess. Ernest Jones's psychoanalytical interpretation of *Ham*, emphasizing Hamlet's oedipal problems, demands comparison with Eliot's reading of the play. The unknown, the disorder in the text, is traced to Gertrude again. In lusting after his mother, Hamlet is guilty of desire which is associated with the feminine side of his nature; the woman in him explains "the impasse or impossibility of resolution" (113). At the root of this psychoanalytical interpretation, as in Eliot's moral one, is the belief that "feminine fantasy as excess" is responsible for the critical dilemma the play creates. Andre Green believes that in *Ham* good feminism is the source of Shakespeare's aesthetic power because it allows him to triumph over the bad feminism found in the character of Hamlet. But such an interpretation only brings us back full circle, for feminism is split "between a degradation and an idealization" (115). Woman is wrongly held up as "enigma and source" of the problem rather than "a failure of integration within language and subjectivity itself" (118).

308. Showalter, Elaine. "Representing Ophelia: Women, Madness, and the Responsibilities of Feminist Criticism." In Parker and Hartman, item 303. 77-94.

The iconography of Ophelia can be traced "in English and French painting, photography, psychiatry, and literature, as well as in theatrical production" (80) to explore how the representations of women and madness reflect the ideological views of their times. Although valuable, some contemporary feminist readings of Ophelia marginalize her by seeing her "as the female subtext" of Hamlet or by describing her in a patriarchal discourse that dismisses her as lack, negative, or absent. Actresses as well as critics provide a useful feminist interpretation of the role. During the seventeenth century and Restoration, Ophelia was portrayed as a victim of erotomania; her sensuality was emphasized in her white dress and garland. Eighteenth-century Ophelias, more subdued because of censorship, "made female insanity a pretty stimulant to male sensibility" (82). The romantic Ophelia, especially as portrayed by Harriet Smithson, "feels too much"; this female sexuality was intensely foregrounded in paintings of the mad Ophelia. By Victorian times, "the

iconography of the romantic Ophelia had begun to infiltrate
reality" (86); physicians used Ophelia as a clinical model and even
coached their patients to adopt Ophelia-like gestures and props.
Ellen Terry on stage and Mary Cowden Clarke in her *The
Girlhood of Shakespeare's Heroines* ("a pre-Freudian speculation
on the traumatic sources of female sexual identity" [89]) rebelled
against the dominant, male-controlled representation and
interpretation of Ophelia.

In the first part of the twentieth century, Freudian-colored
Ophelias, especially as depicted by Ernest Jones, were seen as
loose women suffering from guilt because of their incest with (or
desire for) Laertes or Polonius. This Ophelia suffers a breakdown
because she "fails in the female developmental task of shifting her
sexual attachment" from Polonius to a proper husband (90). Since
the 1960s, "antipsychiatry" presents a schizophrenic Ophelia who,
in the theories of R.D. Laing, is deprived of her selfhood
altogether. Radical feminist representations of Ophelia cast her as
a rebel; in Melissa Murray's agitprop play she "becomes a lesbian
and runs off" with a female servant.

309. Simonds, Peggy Munoz. "*Coriolanus* and the Myth of Juno and
      Mars." *Mosaic* 18.2 (1985): 33-50.

The archetypical elements of *Cor* are overlooked in discussions
that stress political aspects, Roman history, and the relationship
between the hero and his mother. "The myth of Coriolanus
originally concerned the relationship between two major Roman
deities: Juno, patroness of Rome ... and her chthonic son, Mars,
protective god of the city's outermost boundaries" (35). There is
no mention of Coriolanus's father in the play; and it was well
known in the Renaissance that Mars was not conceived by a man.
Volumnia, like Juno, is jealous and angry. Plutarch's Volumnia is
human and womanly whereas Shakespeare created a more
masculine character, a "bloodthirsty Roman mother" (37). The
gentler characteristics of Plutarch's Volumnia are inherited by
Shakespeare's Virgilia. The dominant motif of the play is of three
women saving Rome from the terrible son. The Indo-European
Triple Goddess is parallel to the Roman Juno. This Feminine
Principle is embodied in Virgilia, Valeria, and Volumnia, who

personifies the darker side of the trio as mother, warrior and
purification. "Thus as the Feminine Principle incarnate, she is for
her warrior son the source of both birth and death; she is also the
city which he has been trained to defend and which he must not
enter as an aggressor" (39). Valeria represents Diana, the warrior,
huntress, and the new moon. Virgilia, as Coriolanus's wife and
mother of his son, becomes Venus, goddess of love, sexual
attraction and fertility, and the full moon. Coriolanus plays a
sacrificial role in terms of the Feminine Principle. Volumnia is
unable to transform her son from warrior to politician during
times of peace because of the "dehumanizing rigidity of his
character" (45). What remains mysterious is the "true relationship"
between Coriolanus and Volumnia.

310. Snow, Edward. "Language and Sexual Difference in *Romeo and
Juliet*." In Erickson and Kahn, item 286. 168-92.

RJ emphasizes the opposition between the imaginative vision
of the two lovers and "the truth of a world whose order must be
enforced at passion's expense" (168). Transgressing sexual
difference and social opposition, Romeo and Juliet mirror their
relationship in language of elaborately matched images and turns
of phrase that link their separate speeches. Their level of
communication is "beyond the conscious level and reflects two
imaginations working in the same idiom, both having similar
experiences of self and the world." The language of the play is
more concerned with sexual differentiation than social
consequences. Romeo's desire is dominated by eyesight; his
language makes him an onlooker in the world whereas the plot
stresses his involvement. Like other Shakespearean males, Romeo
experiences love as "a moment of satisfaction, feeling a loss after
the event." Romeo's imagination is limited by his gender. Juliet,
on the other hand, is the center of affirmative energies because
her imagination is informed by all her senses. Although her
freedom in the actual world is severely limited, her imagination
places her in a dynamic world. Of all Shakespeare's romantic or
tragic heroes, Romeo is the one "least inhibited by male bonding
and the cultural values that reinforce them and denigrate women."

311. Sproat, Kezia Vanmeter. "Rereading *Othello*, II, 1." *Kenyon Review* 7.3 (1985): 44-51.

   Although the wit-combat between Desdemona and Iago has been disparaged as "one of the most unsatisfactory passages in Shakespeare," the scene is "a necessary and well-fitted part" of *Oth* (45) and summarizes "the theme of the play" in a variety of ways. It fuels Iago's hatred of Desdemona who "thwarts Iago by stopping his verbal attack on Emilia"; it also establishes "woman-hating as orthodox in the play's culture" (45), as practiced in Venice and Cyprus. Calling Iago a "slanderer" early in *Oth*, Desdemona "gives us the entire plot in one word," thus increasing dramatic tension (47). As she "tries to educate [Iago], to mitigate his hostility," Desdemona only beguiles herself, though. Even Cassio is tarnished in this wit-combat; he is far "less honorable and less innocent than he is usually portrayed" (51), demonstrably cynical about women. "As Iago derides Emilia in [Act 2.1], so Cassio will soon deride Bianca behind her back ... " (49). The fact that Cassio tolerates Iago's scurrilous attack on women "makes plausible Othello's belief that Desdemona is an adulteress" (50).

312. Stockholder, Kay. "Sex and Authority in *Hamlet, King Lear*, and *Pericles*." *Mosaic* 18 (1985): 17-29.

   The last plays reveal that Shakespeare "was entrapped in the attitudes toward sexuality and women with which his protagonists struggle" (17). Parallels in action, characterization, and language between *Ham* and *Per* emphasize the problematic roles of women stereotyped as good or evil, the issue of incest, and the association of incest with "corrupt authority." Both Hamlet and Pericles are disgusted by incest, filled with melancholy, and challenged to receive paternal approval. Parallels and differences between these two princes, especially between the gravedigger scene in *Ham* and the fishermen one in *Per*, show Pericles winning victory by following a paternal model and Hamlet losing a wife and inheriting only Yorick's skull from his father's realm. In dealing with women, both men have to "disentangle sexuality from incest" (23). Additional parallels between the women of the two plays occur in the sexual ambiguity of Hamlet's "nunnery speech" which is externalized and split in *Per* between Marina (in the bawdy house she purifies) and Thaisa (as the priestess). However, while women can cleanse Pericles's world, Ophelia and Gertrude, "Shakespeare's most ordinary women" (23), cannot in Hamlet's. The females in *Per* have more in common with the women in *Lear*, especially Marina with Cordelia, who demonstrate that "the association of women with cruelty, obvious in the action and imagery of *Lear*, is present, though submerged, in the later play" (25). When they lose women, Lear and Pericles suffer similar fates, though the action in *Lear* is "softened" in *Per*. Even so, the "psychological dynamics" behind these three plays clearly underscore "the emotional costs for men by making women symbols of good and evil" (28).

313. Vickers, Nancy. "'The blazon of sweet beauty's best': Shakespeare's *Lucrece*." In Parker and Hartman, item 303. 95-115.

The term "blazon" has a variety of meanings–to proclaim or celebrate; it can also refer to an heraldic description of a shield or a "conventional poetic description of an object praised or blamed by a rhetorician-poet" (95). In *RL,* the use of "blazon" marks a descriptive occasion. Praise of beauty is shaped and controlled by the male imagination. Praising women constitutes male rivalry where the female body is on display. Heraldry expresses and is tied to a "patriarchal system of entitlement." Acting in both praise and blame of women, the shield is a male trap constructed to ensnare women. Shakespeare returns to the dangers of falling victim to the manipulation of descriptive rhetoric about women in his characterization of Iago, who manipulates Othello.

314. Wayne, Valerie. "Refashioning the Shrew." *Shakespeare Studies* 17 (1985): 159-87.

The Wakefield Master and Shakespeare "transform the shrew from the unregenerate agent of discord," characterized by her abusive scolding, to a "regenerate agent for concord" by permitting her to "upset the marital hierarchy" (182). In *The*

Second Shepherds' Play, discord disappears when Gill is assisted
by Mak in her deception, which parallels the Wakefield Master's
own creative manipulations. Adriana in *CE* is a shrew who is
"denigrated," but she is not at fault for violating "any preordained
harmonious system of degree" (169). Even so, "unresolved
marriage problems" do not thwart the outcome of *CE* because
they "never were the primary problem" (170). With *TSh*,
Shakespeare departs greatly from conventional views of the shrew.
Kate feigns excessive obedience, thus "shattering the facade of
female hypocrisy" advocated by Luis Vives in *The Instruction of a
Christian Woman*. Exaggerating her dependence to "prove herself"
Petruchio's "equal in parodic performance" (173), Kate learns the
role from Petruchio who is "in on the joke." While such feigning
will not solve the problems of marriage or patriarchy, Shakespeare
managed "to devise a more humane and artistic way to 'tame' a
shrew than any previous writer" (174). Discord in *Oth* "is caused
not by a shrew but by a husband who charges his wife with being
a shrew" (177). Although Desdemona threatens to be a shrew to
help Cassio, she obeys her husband. Emilia, on the other hand,
ironically will follow her husband's instruction even if she must
abandon her conscience to "uphold marital hierarchy." When
Emilia acts like a shrew, berating her husband in Act 5.2, she
shows that obedience to Iago is inappropriate and, moreover, that
her shrewish conduct is as "ironic as it is necessary" (179). In
killing her marriage "with words," she affirms Desdemona's
innocence. Paulina's shrewish speech in *WT* serves a "purgative
function" by keeping Hermione alive.

315. Wheeler, Richard P. "'... And my loud crying still': *The Sonnets,
     The Merchant of Venice*, and *Othello*." In Erickson and Kahn,
     item 286. 193-209.

     Each of these problematic works "dramatizes conflicts that
emerge within and between bonds of man to man in friendship
and sexual bonds of man to woman" (193). Inherent in these
conflicts are three key ideas that help to explain the stress on
their genre boundaries: masculine autonomy, feminine sexuality,
and nurturant maternity. In the sonnets and *MV*, masculine
independence and sexuality are subdued or suppressed. The poet

of the sonnets is forced to surrender his selfhood when his male friend bonds with a woman. In *MV*, Portia achieves what is only poetically wished for in the sonnets; she becomes Bassanio's Dark Lady and "master-mistress" controlling his "masculine assertiveness." For reasons of comedy, such assertiveness is displaced onto Shylock who, like the sonnets poet and Antonio, suffers "shame and self-laceration" (200) through feminine betrayals. Suspended male sexuality and autonomy "reappear comprehensively" (201) in *Oth*, where the Moor's heroic quest is at odds with marriage commitments. To become Othello's partner in his marriage bed, Desdemona must "unwittingly undermine the very heroic identity he has invested in her ... " (204). As happens in *MV* and the sonnets, Othello seeks a "pre-oedipal experience with the nurturant mother" (203). Through death *Oth* integrates the conflicting values of male autonomy, female sexuality, and nurturing. Shakespeare's later works use death to reach the "inclusiveness" of these three concepts. Murdering Desdemona and himself, Othello is able to reconstruct "his self-image into a tender, sexual bond with his wife" (206).

316. Wickenden, Dorothy. "How to Protect Your Kids from Shakespeare: Bowdlerizing the Bard." *New Republic* 3 June 1985: 16-19.

As in the nineteenth century, textbooks for high school classes delete or adapt Shakespearean language perceived as objectionable. *RJ* has been a "perfect candidate" for such "excisions," especially the "impassioned words" of the young Juliet referring to female anatomy, childbearing, and "sexual desire or activity." Such censorship is doomed.

317. Wilcox, Lance. "Katherine of France as Victim and Bride." *Shakespeare Studies* 17 (1985): 61-76.

Shakespeare uses Katherine in *H5* to "control the audience's reaction to Henry himself" (73). Not an aesthetic or moral presence, Katherine's thematic function associates her, as one of the victims of war, with the comparisons made between military invasion and a "sexual violation," or rape. In his grisly address to the citizens of Harfleur, Henry appears as the King of Rape and so is morally responsible for his men's actions. Katherine represents the brutalized civilians besieged by Henry's army. Shakespeare has to reconcile the image of Henry the sexual assailant with Henry the hero while Katherine must be transformed from her image as the pristine virgin so that Henry is not "trapped in his role as sexual aggressor" (71). To accomplish this, Shakespeare charts Katherine's growing sexual maturity. In Act 3.4, she acknowledges her sexuality by learning English words for her own body parts. The erotic puns in this scene soften the "ferocious sexual themes" of Henry's Harfleur speech and show the couple moving away from roles as prey and predator and toward mature lovers. But it is the "coarse bawdy between Burgundy and Henry [in Act 5.2] that proclaims most bluntly Katherine's sexual potential" (71). In his presentation of Katherine being wooed by Henry, Shakespeare attempts to mitigate "a tale of military and sexual conquest with the colors and trappings of romantic comedy and ends the play, like any good Elizabethan love story, with a marriage" (73). In the final analysis, however, Shakespeare's attempt to "whitewash" Henry is not successful because the gory scenes with his brutal speeches dominate.

318. Williams, Mary C. "Much Ado About Chastity in *Much Ado About Nothing.*" *Renaissance Papers 1984* (1985): 37-45.

Ado incorporates a "great tension" between regarding a woman's chastity as a moral ideal and appreciating her as a frankly sexual human being. Though the men in *Ado* want a woman who is both chaste and sexually responsive, they still fear and mistrust female sexuality. This ambivalence about a woman's chastity is set against the "overwhelming sexuality and physicality of the whole world of the play" (38). The "elemental quality" of *Ado* is countered by "embellishments of civility," though none of the lovers can be called Petrarchan. Beatrice and Benedick parody Petrarchan love conventions; and the downright bawdiness of the play counters the "decorative effect of Petrarchianism." Images of eating, trapping, bulls, cows, and other beasts transform the characters into animals, though not savages, and reflect their "anger, sexual desire, and sexual jealousy." Having acknowledged the ambivalence about a woman's chastity, Beatrice and Benedick as well as Hero (who has been held to a severe standard of chastity in the play) and Claudio learn to trust each other. The ending of *Ado*, therefore, must be seen as optimistic. The contradiction "present all through the play" (that a woman should be both chaste and "light") proves that "chastity is everything, yet nothing" (45).

319. Willinsky, John. "From Feminist Literary Criticism Certain Classroom Splendours." *English Quarterly* 18.3 (1985): 35-43.

Feminist criticism, which began as a "revolt against the privilege of an academic and authoritive reading" (35), offers many lively benefits for the high school classroom. Though feminist critics share the common goal of providing an alternative to "misogynous conceptions in writing and criticism," they take diverse approaches, using Marxism, reader-response criticism, etc. In looking at Shakespeare's women, feminist critics "dispel" stereotypical notions, study "overlooked relationships between women," and examine the impact of patriarchy and genre on women's actions. Alternative readings open new possibilities. Rather than seeing Gertrude as a "self-centered temptress," she might be examined (as J. Karen Ray does in "The Ethics of Feminism in the Literature Classroom," *English Journal* 74 [1985]: 57) as a woman and a queen in her forties looking to have her attractiveness confirmed. Marilyn French's (item 155) point about the male double standard (the crime of murder is matched with "incest and sexuality of women") is well taken. Alternative feminist readings can "cover the greater range of experience represented in Shakespeare" (39).

1986

320. Aquino, Deborah T. Curren. "Toward A Star That Danced: Woman As Survivor in Shakespeare's Early Comedies." *Selected Papers from the West Virginia Shakespeare and Renaissance Association* 11 (1986): 50-61.

Contrary to some critical opinion (e.g., Bamber, item 175), the women in the early comedies cannot be dismissed as shrews who do not have significant choices to make. While the women before *Ado* may not yet be the dominant force in their plays, they nonetheless have highly developed survival skills that make them adapt far better than the men to shifting domestic and public situations. In terms of their facility in action, language, and psychology, the women in *LLL*, *CE*, *TGV*, and *MND* outsmart and outmaneuver the men. While the men's facility is "passive, derivative, and self preserving," the women's is "active, creative, and heteronomous" (50). Men in these early plays "depend on female efficiency, practicality, and resourcefulness for survival." As Aemilia, Adriana, and even Kate attest, women are responsive to men's needs and have far more adaptable verbal skills. The men in these comedies are "awed by the female's gift for the spoken word" (55); the women's discourse is discreet and subtle, attuned to the "propriety of the moment" (57) while the men's is cunning and blatant. The men, not the women, are given to outbursts. Unlike Antipholus of Ephesus, whose complaints to the Duke are pathetic and egocentric, Adriana reasons logically like a civic-minded citizen. Psychologically, Hippolita, Kate, and the ladies in

LLL "put the men on the defensive" (57), undermining them. Journeying to find their men, Aemilia, Silvia, and Julia are prudent and practical.

321. Asp, Carolyn. "'The Clamor of Eros': Freud, Aging, and *King Lear*." In *Memory and Desire: Aging, Literature, Psychoanalysis*. Ed. Kathleen Woodward and Murray M. Schwartz. Bloomington: Indiana UP, 1986. 192-204.

The aging patriarch, Lear, allows himself to become dependent on family bonds. Tension exists between generations resulting from paternal demands and rejection by the children. Freud saw *Lear* in terms of the "illusory nature of choice, symbolization of death as love, and the ... myth of female power" (193). A man chooses a woman, unaware that he is choosing death. Wisdom is acquired in the acceptance of death; *Lear* explores how this is achieved. Giving up responsibilities to perpetuate his daughters' love for him, Lear looks for a mother to nurture him during his second childhood, unaware that mothers teach their children to resign themselves to death. Cordelia's rejection brings on the death he is trying to avoid.

Instead of the nurturing he anticipated, Lear is faced with narcissistic and indifferent female company. "As rejecting mothers, Goneril and Regan remind him of his need and dependence, but they will do nothing to alleviate it" (195). What results for Lear is the "enigmatic indifference and self-sufficiency" of Goneril and Regan, not the idealistic "maternal nurturance" he expects from Cordelia. Their desire to destroy their father is insatiable, forcing "upon him the reality of his age and weakness, stripping him down to symbolic zero" (196). This symbolic stripping reduces Lear to using feminine tactics such as crying, and his inability to accept his new feminine position–"marginal, cast out, and powerless"–reduces him to madness. Lear also represses his sexual desires for Cordelia, in whom he sees incest and death. Yet in the early scenes, Cordelia rejects the role as "Goddess of Death." Lear wins the battle between father and husband and thereby gains license to destroy Cordelia. Her death has nothing to do with fate; it defies all natural law. It represents the castration of Lear and ultimately leads to his tragic destiny.

322. Bensel-Meyers, Linda Diane. "A 'Figure Cut in Alabaster': The Paradoxical Widow of Renaissance Drama." *DAI* 46 (1986): 1945A. U of Oregon.

323. Bono, Barbara J. "Mixed Gender, Mixed Genre in Shakespeare's *As You Like It.*" In *Renaissance Genres: Essays on Theory, History, and Interpretation.* Ed. Barbara Kiefer Lewalski. Harvard English Studies 14. Cambridge, Mass.: Harvard UP, 1986. 189-212.

In Shakespeare "both the explicitly threatening women of the tragedies and the seemingly benevolent women of the comedies operate within a 'universe of masculinist assumptions' about the nature of women" (193). The purpose of Rosalind's disguise is to transform Petrarchan views of women into those advocating companionship within marriage. Ambiguities arise when the ideas of women presented onstage are determined by a male acting company where even Rosalind is played by a boy. Before he can turn to love, Orlando has to establish his male identity and relieve his fear of maternal engulfment. He first finds himself in conflict with paternal figures, but is ultimately rescued from a consuming Mother Nature by a kind father. Rosalind assumes a masculine disguise to safeguard against female vulnerability in the absence of a male protector. She maintains the disguise to test Orlando, to have him revise his idealized picture of women, and to accommodate herself to the idea of love. Rosalind throws off her disguise when her fear of men has been put to rest, thus accommodating herself to both father and lover. Accepting society's demands on women, Rosalind becomes a submissive wife.

324. Boose, Lynda E. "An Approach through Theme: Marriage and the Family." In *Approaches to Teaching Shakespeare's King Lear.* Ed. Robert H. Ray. New York: Modern Language Association, 1986. 59-68.

Student problems with *Lear* can be resolved by seeing the play in terms of the inversions of marriage and family "rituals, taboos, distributions, and hierarchies ... that depend on age, positional relationships, and gender" (60). In the patrilineal and patriarchal world of *Lear*, sons seek independence from the father yet return to the family to claim the father's name and inheritance. No so with the daughter who, as the "transitory" member of the family, "exists only to be lost" (62) from the father's control through marriage. Lear's demand for complete love must be seen within the context of his wanting to frustrate the traditional rite of passage for his daughters in marriage. The demands Lear places upon receiving the dowry (something he has predetermined) would nullify the daughter's necessary separation by constituting a return to him. Hence, Cordelia must refuse Lear in Act 1. If she vowed to love her father unqualifyingly, she would violate the chief marital condition to give all her love to her spouse. Lear wants to retain his daughters "within the psychic territory of paternal rule" so that he will not be alone on his journey toward death. But by not relinquishing his daughters, Lear tries to unmarry Goneril and Regan and prevent Cordelia from marrying. Through such circularity symbolized in Act 1, Lear would keep his daughters in bondage. Yet since Cordelia spends her life with France in tears, Lear succeeds in thwarting the "natural pattern" of Cordelia's release by enclosing her in the "sterile cipher of 'Nothing.'" The maternal is absent in *Lear* because maternal pity is missing in the brutal world of the play. However, in our capacity as readers to feel, the maternal is located in our hearts.

325. Carducci, Jane Shook. "'Our Hearts You See Not': Shakespeare's Roman Men." *DAI* 46 (1986): 1946A. U of Nevada, Reno.

326. Cook, Carol. "'The Sign and Semblance of Her Honor': Reading Gender Difference in *Much Ado About Nothing.*" *PMLA* 101 (1986): 186-202.

Ado does not show "humane feminine qualities" triumphing over "inadequate masculine values" (186). Messina's "masculine ethos survives" (200) through the male defense strategies found in the play, the most notable being the male process of representation. Reading others means emasculating them. Language in *Ado* is phallic, male-dominated, violent. The cuckold jokes, which reveal the male fear of castration and female sexuality, actually "restore the male prerogative" by privileging the [male] third party and by "silencing women." Both men and women in *Ado* "brandish phallic wit"; and having women mirror "masculine identity by their own lack" rules out the possibility of a "feminine alternative" (190). Messina is threatened more by Hero than by Beatrice. By usurping masculine behavior, Beatrice flouts conventional sex roles only to concede them and regards male behavior as "the only defense against feminine weakness." Beatrice is as aggressive as the men because she fears being read, being exposed.

Hero, on the other hand, is "the 'nothing' that generates so much ado" (192). Claudio thinks he can read Hero, who on the surface seems comely but deeper down manifests the female sexuality that betrays men. Yet, ironically, in "thinking they have exposed the 'proper nakedness' of Hero's sin, her accusers only expose themselves" (195). The Friar's counsel and attention to Hero seemingly place him outside of Messina's masculine code, but he believes the charges against her are true, reinforcing "the assumptions of which Hero is a victim" (197). The "circularity" of the final act shows that the conflicts of the play go unresolved. The shift toward ritual, the deflection of Claudio's guilt onto Borachio and Don John, and Hero's symbolic sacrifice (which leaves her still "dead") prove that the patriarchal heritage of Messina continues. In parodying masculine control, Dogberry is mastered by a language that undercuts his attempts.

327. Dalsimer, Katherine. *Female Adolescence: Psychoanalytic Reflections on Works of Literature.* New Haven: Yale UP, 1986. Esp. "Middle Adolescence: *Romeo and Juliet*": 77-112.

RJ brings to light the psychological conflict of adolescent love. An individual's first love is inevitably the enemy of one's family because it is through this love that the power of early ties is diminished, just as Romeo and Juliet must transcend the family feud that makes their love forbidden. Juliet gradually breaks away from parental figures—her mother, her father, her nurse, Friar Laurence. By the end of the play, she has severed childhood ties to her family to become independent and loyal to another party. Going through middle adolescence, Romeo has withdrawn from family and is more intimate with friends. His attention also turns to the opposite sex, first of all to a deliberately chosen elusive figure, and then to Juliet (110-11). His commitment to her allows Romeo to grow enough to break his parental ties.

328. Davies, Stevie. *The Feminine Reclaimed: The Idea of Woman in Spenser, Shakespeare and Milton.* Lexington: UP of Kentucky, 1986. Esp. 105-74.

In five sections on Shakespeare, Davies explores the following topics:

Hamnet and Judith
The theme of twins, or androgyny, stems from Shakespeare's own family history. He is interested in feminine sources of masculine identity, the consequences of males being severed from those sources, and a final recreation of "the bond of trust" in the feminine principle. The values of the family within a traditional hierarchical structure, especially in *Lear* and *WT*, reflect the nature of feminine power. "The history plays concern a male world in eternal feud with itself, where a woman plays a negligible or debased role" (110). The comedies are set apart as an exploration of the feminine world, where men are in turmoil because they repudiate the feminine. The comedies, which portray a more hopeful world, are resolved through the actions of strong, wise and loving women such as Portia and Rosalind.
Isis and Ceres
The dreaming in *MND* is an alternative feminine reality. All events take place within the transforming medium of moonlight, a life-giving force. The conflict between Oberon and Titania is over the primacy of male and female principles. Oberon wants the boy initiated into an adult male world rather than into a repressive female one. Oberon's primary motive is jealousy while Titania's is a love bond with the boy's mother.
Marina and Eleusis
In the last plays, the sea is archetypally feminine representing death and rebirth. In *Per*, political life is referred throughout in terms of the feminine principle, the mother-daughter relationship. Having a feminine rather than a military approach to adversity,

Pericles displays a sustained evasion of action, and when he does act, his behavior suggests a feminine role. The act of incest is not an isolated event in his personal world; it is symptomatic of the state of society as well as a state of mind.

The Temple of Demeter Hermione
WT has its roots in the grave, something that even Mother Nature cannot avoid. In this framework, Shakespeare presents the breaking of the most sacred taboos of human life as they relate to women, children, and the mother-culture. In the Hermione-Mamillius relationship, the inner and feminine world declares itself in snatches of simple, apparently insignificant conversation, which are debased by Leontes. Mamillius dies because of the lack of motherly nurturing.

Woman as Magus
In Paulina, Shakespeare has created the unprecedented figure of the woman magus, complete with the power of white magic and connected to the female mythology of Eleusis. She channels a holy element into the play, for, as magus, Paulina retards the revelation process to curtail Leontes's affections until the right moment. Seeing *WT* as the imitation of life by art is looking at the play from a masculine perspective. From the feminine viewpoint, "in life there is one artistic process which fulfills all the metaphorical requirements of the raising of the statue: birth itself, the whitest magic" (166) which Paulina possesses.

329. Dollimore, Jonathan. "Subjectivity, Sexuality, and Transgression: The Jacobean Connection." *Renaissance Drama* 17 (1986): 53–81.

The Renaissance view of identity also involved social integration: a person's metaphysical position was also his/her social position. A man was seen in relationship to his king, and the woman was seen in terms of the man. These identities were fixed. Actors were seen as undermining God-given identity. "It was not so much that the player disguised his real self in playing; rather he had no self apart from that which he was playing" (63). The actors' crossdressing transgressed the natural and fixed order of things, especially in plays such as *The Roaring Girl*. That boys dressed as women onstage supposedly incited the male audience

to perverse heterosexual and homosexual acts. The pamphlet
Haec Vir insisted that gender differences were a result of mere
custom and concluded that women have become more masculine
because the men are effeminate. Renaissance women had to look
to male rules in order to be free. In John Fletcher's *Love's Cure*,
a girl has been brought up as a boy and wants to remain one.
What is at stake here is the legitimacy of the entire social order.
"Masculine sexuality is shown to be complex and unstably
implicated within the whole social domain" (73). Male sexuality in
the Renaissance was supported passively by women and actively
by men.

330. Dreher, Diane Elizabeth. *Domination and Defiance: Fathers and
Daughters in Shakespeare*. Lexington: UP of Kentucky, 1986.

Chapter One, "A Psychological Perspective," maintains that
Shakespeare frequently depicts middle-aged fathers hesitant to
release their young adult daughters into marriage. "The passionate
conflicts, fears, and insecurities as each faces a crucial challenge
of adulthood cast new light on questions of moral development,
male and female sex roles, traditional and progressive social
norms" (1). Anticipating Freudian and Jungian psychology,
Shakespeare's aging fathers attempt to ward off the weaknesses
and impotency of old age by exercising control over their
daughters. The daughters, reaching sexual maturity, ultimately
challenge the fathers' control. Each father-daughter conflict
becomes "an inevitable drama of domination and defiance, born
of the clashing demands of youth and age, a developmental
struggle as certain as the seasons themselves" (2). The challenge
confronting these middle-aged men is individuation, or reconciling
the anima and animus within themselves. For Prospero these two
sides are represented by Miranda and Caliban. Misogyny results
when these sides are not united. Possessive fathers in Shakespeare
do not acknowledge their daughters' adulthood; and mercenary
fathers see their daughters as an investment, an extension of their
own anima. Although Shakespeare does not deal directly with
incest (except in *Per*), many of the daughters in the plays show the
effects of pseudo-incest: they either forego independence to serve
their father or they transfer obedience to a surrogate father.

Shakespeare's plays, however, condemn patriarchal domination. Daughters who follow traditional female submissive roles, such as Desdemona, fall victim to masochism and self-effacement. Daughters who rebel, such as Jessica, earn independence and respect.

Chapter Two, "The Renaissance Background," surveys primary sources–tracts, manuals–on marriage and the role of women. During Shakespeare's lifetime traditional views based on hierarchy clashed with progressive ones strongly influenced by Puritanism. Shakespeare was doubtless influenced by these Puritan views of love and marriage. Traditionally, women were to be submissive and obedient in all things to their fathers and then to their husbands. Children had to profess an unconditional love that "would probably have contented King Lear" (22). Marriage was less a "personal relationship" than a political and financial arrangement. Challenging these traditional views, Puritans "placed emphasis on conscience and individual responsibility" (30). A "new kind of woman" was created, better educated, having more freedom, and acquiring a "growing assertiveness in marriage" (32). In a "new marriage pattern," love was not an act of concupiscence or a duty but an "integral part of God's plan"; a wife was not an "obedient subject" but a companion, a partner. Conflicting critical opinions (Dusinberre, item 6 vs. Stone, item 54) have been voiced about whether Shakespeare's plays mirrored the prevailing (traditional) marriage beliefs. Elizabethans themselves held divided opinions accounting for the "dynamism" of the age (38).

Chapter Three, "The Paternal Role in Transition," explores reasons why fathers had trouble letting daughters go. As daughters do in marriage, fathers must go through a rite of passage reflecting a crucial stage in their development toward old age and death. Shakespearean fathers cannot easily do this because of their possessiveness which falls into a number of categories. *Reactionary* fathers like Brabantio, Cymbeline, and Polonius refuse to let their daughters grow up, which would threaten their masculine authority, and brand the daughters' actions as "terribly wrong" (47). Yet it "is not tradition and hierarchical obedience but personal loyalty, trust, and commitment that Shakespeare upholds as the basis for human relationships" (47). *Mercenary* fathers like Egeus, Shylock, Capulet, and Portia's father regard their daughters as valuable property and possess them "to assuage their egos" (51) or, worse yet, to make a profit. Polonius is "the most reprehensible father" (52), blatantly selling Ophelia in his crass world of "power and profit." *Egocentric* fathers–Leontes, Lear–see their children as part of themselves; even Prospero, "certainly the wisest of Shakespeare's fathers" (56), refers to Miranda as "my foot." *Jealous* fathers, particularly Cymbeline, Capulet, the Duke in *TGV*, cannot accept "their daughters' emerging sexuality" (56) and believe they are bewitched for wanting a suitor. "Incestuous undercurrents" run throughout most of the plays. Withholding their blessings, these fathers distort the marriage rites. In the tragedies the daughter is doomed; yet in the comedies a triumph over the *senex iratus* signals a healthy reincorporation. King Lear incorporates all four fatherly vices. As a reactionary father, he wants to keep his daughters children. He views love as mercenary, not realizing that it cannot be measured as a commodity. He egocentrically identifies with his daughters. His jealousy for Cordelia casts him as her lover and her as his mother. Lear violates the Renaissance rules of primogeniture, regresses toward infantilism, and fails to trust. What he wants from Cordelia, "he must ultimately find for himself" (72).

Chapter Four on "Dominated Daughters" concentrates on Ophelia, Hero, and Desdemona. Following conventional patterns of behavior for wives and daughters, these women lose their autonomy, intimacy, and do not achieve adulthood. As a "vessel of procreation" (79), Ophelia is taught that men's sensual aggression turns them into beasts. Therefore, she is forced by Polonius and Laertes to uphold the static virtue of chastity upon which patriarchy rests. Yet patriarchy imposes a "false self" on her, obliterating her psyche and her identity. Unlike the women in comedies, Ophelia has no sure moral guide, model, or friend. She succumbs to a fatal guilt for having caused Hamlet's madness (transforming him into a beast by her love) and for her father's death. The betrayed Hero is seen as a model Renaissance woman–submissive and not in control of her fate. Her predicament proves that nothing a woman can do will change the male perception of her. Through Hero, Shakespeare criticizes the Renaissance feminine stereotype which "represses women and makes them far too vulnerable to the oft-observed antimony between appearance and reality" (87). Desdemona is a "tragic paradox" (88) being painted as a saint or a lustful manipulator. Before marriage she is "androgynous," combining "feminine compassion" and "masculine courage" (89) when she defies conventions in Act 1.3. Yet after marriage she adopts the conventional role of a submissive wife (as suitably described by Elizabethan writer William Gouge) and through her "excess of self altruism" loses her self. In their roles as heroic husband and passive wife, Othello and Desdemona do not really know who they are. Desdemona's love for Othello forces her into a "closed-image syndrome" (94). She "fails herself."

Chapter Five is concerned with "Defiant Daughters." Seventeen of Shakespeare's plays deal with daughters who establish new identities as they leave their fathers for marriage. The daughter's revolt is also "the structural core at least" for nine tragedies. Progressive comic heroines such as Helena (*MND*) and Sylvia (*TGV*) and tragic ones such as Juliet and Desdemona reject filial obedience for love. Romantic love in the comedies reflects the Puritan view of love as "a gift of God, a force of inspiration and renewal" (101), thus explaining women's following their conscience in choosing their spouses. Jessica, however, wrongly steals from Shylock in an act of selfish, adolescent revenge that would be condemned by Renaissance commentators on marriage. Her conversion to Christianity is shallow and her rebellion "antisocial and destructive" (104). Sociopathic and animalistic, Goneril and Regan, motivated by appetite, show the "devastating effect of relationships based only on hierarchal power" (104). Abandoning her husband to return to Lear, Cordelia would have been criticized by Shakespeare's contemporaries who saw a wife's first obligations to her husband. Like Lear, Cordelia shows immaturity and like her father, too, she must "regress in time to amend the mistake" (108). In *TSh*, Bianca is "a shrew in sheep's clothing" (109); her seeming feminine weakness, though, is an example of oppressive female stereotyping by men. Lacking intimacy with Lucentio, Bianca plays a game that Kate sees through and rebels against. Attacking her sister and her father, Kate is "locked into a self-perpetuating cycle" (111) and wants to escape domination and manipulation. A rebel and a shrew like Kate, Petruchio "mirrors her extreme choleric behavior to demonstrate its destructiveness" (113). Kate acquires a new identity and Petruchio a new partner. Both of them reject "patriarchal domination" through a "dynamic relationship" (114).

The "Androgynous Daughters" in Chapter Six are liberated from male stereotypes through their disguises and so can represent the balance and harmony of marriage. The most androgynous women in Shakespeare are fatherless daughters who have not been "traumatized" by a father's loss and who often perform his functions in society. In her disguise and her same-sex friendships, Julia in *TGV* foreshadows the androgyny of later comedies. As other androgynous heroines, Rosalind through her disguise examines Orlando's motifs, sheds feminine stereotypes, and enters into a new kind of partnership. "Realistic and romantic," Rosalind arranges her own marriage, unites "the forces of romance and friendship," and restores harmony. Androgynous Viola offers an optimistic "dynamic balance" that contrasts with Olivia's coldness. Viola's friendship with sexist Orsino liberates him from his "Petrarchianism and sexual fantasies" (127). Yet it takes a crisis for Beatrice and Benedick to learn to trust members of the opposite sex. Beneath their "defensive facades" lies love. Portia, the "most androgynous of Shakespeare's women" (129), confronts the traditional dilemma women face of "love and duty"; she regards her marriage as a partnership. "Assertive" Portia assumes her father's role as Bassanio's teacher. In the "world of men," Portia's brilliant courtroom performance threatens the "validity of gender stereotypes" (134) that cast men as wise and women as soft. The ring is a symbol of completeness and harmony that Portia promises. Bassanio "weds Portia twice: first as her feminine self (in Act 3) and then as friend and partner" (135). The "most problematic woman hero" (136) in the plays, Helena reverses sex roles in wooing Bertram as Shakespeare tests his audience's gender notions. Yet even though Helena uses all gender means (from being a "knight errant" to a "clever Griselda"), she cannot get Bertram to see her as anything except a conventional, subjugated woman. Thus "the conclusion of the play is imperfect" (147).

Chapter Seven, "Redemptive Love and Wisdom," argues that "paternal love informs the romances" (161) rather than romantic love. The men in the romances struggle to come to terms with the

woman, or anima, within themselves. Denying that feminine
principle, they castigate women as the malefic anima, deceiver and
whore, and so reside in an "anti-androgynous world" (145). These
fathers are brought to wholeness by their daughters who are more
like icons than characters and so lack the "troublesome sexuality"
of tragic women. Banishing his daughter and wife, Pericles rejects
the "responsibilities of parenthood [and] ... the images of birth and
death" and so renounces "his feminine side completely" (149). His
suffering restores his balance. Like Pericles, Leontes cannot come
to terms with his sexuality and is "unable to trust or respect
Hermione"; it is only through Paulina's instruction that he learns
"penance, patience, and passivity." Perdita also helps to restore her
father to "emotional wholeness" (152). At the end of the play,
Hermione's statue symbolizes Leontes's own "spiritual rebirth in
the regeneration of the anima, his acceptance of the life-giving
woman's part in himself" (153). Posthumus and Cymbeline must
learn to accept the anima within themselves. Posthumus becomes
a misogynist, and only when he seeks family bonds and trust can
he find the woman in himself. Similarly, Cymbeline through his
maternal imagery and seeing Imogen as the "benevolent anima"
achieves a psychic wholeness. In *Tem*, "the themes of domination
and defiance, integration and personal growth are brought to a
conclusion" (157). Moving from an imbalanced life because of his
"excessive intellectualism," Prospero achieves an "internal balance"
(158). Feigning domination over Miranda and Ferdinand,
Prospero asks them to undergo "an educational process" to
prepare them for marriage. Unlike other fathers, Prospero does
not wish to "possess and dominate" but reconciles his masculine
and feminine sides to attain power.

Chapter Eight, the last chapter, "Beyond Domination and
Defiance," asserts that "the majority of fathers in Shakespeare"
demand compliance from their daughters and "fail to respect their
daughters' needs" (166). Yet in "exposing the limits of traditional
sex roles" (167), Shakespeare's plays deny "patriarchal norms,"
assault male aggression, and call for "the need for personal
integration." (169). Shakespeare advocates and shows "balanced
characters" becoming part of one family. In reaching this goal,
they "bring the harmony of androgyny and individuation to their
world" (170).

Reviews: Baines, Barbara J., *South Atlantic Quarterly* 86 (1987): 198-200; Brophy, J.D., *Choice* 24 (1986): 120; Dash, Irene, *Journal of English and Germanic Philology* 86 (1987): 553-54; Howard, Jean E., *Studies in English Literature, 1500-1900* 27 (1987): 349; Krantz, Susan E., *South Atlantic Review* 52 (1987): 103-05; Novy, Marianne, *Renaissance Quarterly* 41 (1988): 167; Rackin, Phyllis, *Theatre Journal* 38 (1986): 498-99; White, R.S., *Shakespeare Survey* 40 (1987): 191-92.

331. Eaton, Sara Joan. "The Rhetoric of Sexual Revenge in Jacobean Drama." *DAI* 46 (1986): 3724A. U of Minnesota.

332. Farnsworth, Jane Elizabeth. "Intimate Relationships between Women in English Renaissance Literature, 1558-1642." *DAI* 46 (1986): 2299A. Queen's U, Kingston, Canada.

333. Ferguson, Margaret W., Maureen Quilligan, and Nancy J. Vickers. Ed. *Rewriting the Renaissance: The Discourse of Sexual Difference in Early Modern Europe*. U of Chicago P, 1986.

Reviews: *History: Reviews of New Books* 16 (1988): 123; Ashley, L.R.N., *Bibliotheque d'Humanisme et Renaissance* 50 (1988): 153-54; Attridge, D., *Renaissance Quarterly* 40 (1987): 810; Conley, V.A., *L'Esprit Createur* 28 (1988): 99; DeNeef, A. Leigh, *Studies in English Literature, 1500-1900* 27 (1987): 143-44; Hageman, Elizabeth H., *Shakespeare Quarterly* 39 (1988): 247; Harris, J., *Choice* 24 (1987): 923; Kernan, Alvin, *Yale Review* 77 (1987): 86; McLean, A.M., *Moreana* 24 (June 1987): 57-59; Smith, H.L., *American Historical Review* 93 (1988): 407-8; Warnicke, R., *Journal of the Rocky Mountain Medieval* and *Renaissance Association* 8 (1987): 209-10; Wynne-Davies, M., *Renaissance Studies* 2 (1988): 105-9.

334. Free, Mary. "Shakespeare's Comedic Heroines: Protofeminists or Conformers to Patriarchy?" *Shakespeare Bulletin* 4 (Sept.-Oct. 1986): 23-25.

Feminist readings are in error by seeing Shakespeare's comic heroines as iconoclastic individuals created by a playwright who was "the woman's champion." A "post-revisionist perspective" is needed. "Society, rather than the individual, is the heart of the comedies," and it is a male-dominated society that "defines woman and her role." Consequently, it is misleading to see Kate's Act 5 speech as a parody of patriarchal rule; it is an echo of "the gender based Renaissance arguments on women's subjection as part of natural order." Kate, Rosalind, and other comic heroines speak in accord with the "patriarchal point of view" laid down in Renaissance manuals and marriage treatises (24). The boy actors' disguise did not allow these heroines to voice sentiments that went against male customs. "Despite their garb, these boy-heroines remain feminine" and are part of the comic rituals, like the Boy Bishop, created by men, and they "react to masculine dictates." The "allure" of Shakespeare's heroines "arises from their femininity, not their feminism" (25).

335. Froula, Christine. "The Daughter's Seduction: Sexual Violence and Literary History." *Signs* 11 (1986): 621-44.

The literary relations of daughters and fathers "resemble in some important ways the model developed by Judith Herman and Lisa Hirschman to describe the family situations of incest victims" (622). Daughters are silenced by fathers who are threatened by the daughters' revelations, their "hysterical cultural script" (623). In her *I Know Why the Caged Bird Sings,* Maya Angelou expresses her interest in Shakespeare who, though he was white, made a big impact on her through his line "When in disgrace with fortune and men's eyes." Angelou wrote: "It was a state with which I felt myself most familiar" (634).

336. Garber, Marjorie. "The Education of Orlando." In *Comedy from Shakespeare to Sheridan: Change and Continuity in the English and European Dramatic Tradition.* Ed. A.R. Braunmuller and J.C. Bulman. Newark: U of Delaware P, 1986. 102-112.

Unlike Portia, Julia, or Imogen, who need to retain their male disguises "because of the exigencies of the plot" (103), Rosalind does not need to keep hers after Act 2, for she is in no danger in the forest and has the assurance of Orlando's love. She does not retain the disguise for herself but to educate Orlando "about himself, about her, and about the nature of love" (104). As other Shakespearean comic heroines, Rosalind is superior to the men in her knowledge of human nature. She and Orlando are forced to leave court because for Rosalind "falling in love is itself a rebellion against patriarchal domination and the filial bond" (105). In the forest, she maintains her disguise to make the tongue-tied Orlando of Act 1 feel less ill at ease and to give him time to develop from an adolescent to a mature lover. Though Orlando's language to Rosalind/Ganymede (e.g., "pretty youth") gives "clues to her real identity," he is too dense to follow up (108). But such clues are "dramaturgically helpful" to an audience trying to keep up with the "fictive courtship." When Orlando gives Rosalind the bloody napkin, equivalent to "showing the sheets," he shows how far he has matured from the foolish poet. Celia and Oliver's hasty courtship serves as a catalyst for the marriage of Rosalind and Orlando. Rosalind prefigures Prospero.

337. Hawkes, Terence. "Feminism." In *The Cambridge Companion to Shakespeare Studies.* Ed. Stanley Wells. Cambridge: Cambridge UP, 1986. 296-97.

Feminism radically transforms our reading of Shakespeare by using "two fundamental strategies." The first examines the roles women play or that are enforced upon them; unfortunately such studies "reinforce the male or phallocentric status quo" feminism deplores, as in *TSh* and *AYL*. The second strategy examines Shakespeare from a woman's point of view and, using *Mac* as an example, makes Lady Macbeth the central murderer/homicide. The witches project the "crisis felt by society in respect to the role it assigned to women, with its consequent suppression of their counter-claims to a different degree and level of involvement" (297).

338. Hill, James L. "'What, are they children?': Shakespeare's Tragic Women and the Boy Actors." *Studies in English Literature, 1500-1900* 26 (1986): 235-58.

Feminist readings of Shakespeare need to take into account that Shakespeare used different methods of characterization for boy actors playing women's roles than he did for adult male actors. Concerned about the demands placed upon boy actors, Shakespeare made sure they were not "overwhelmed" (251). Unlike the "complex and multileveled roles" of Hamlet and Claudius, "boy actresses" playing Ophelia and Gertrude have fewer lines, do not initiate or control the "blocks" they are in, nor do they have to make difficult transitions within a scene. The boy playing Ophelia uses song, not words, to present his madness, though the range of Gertrude's responses is more extensive than Ophelia's. Shakespeare employs the same strategy by having Hamlet take the offensive with the boy actor. The boy playing Lady Macbeth is spared a sense of struggle as Macbeth is not. Having a "one dimensional and non-developing" (244) character, Lady Macbeth is not called on to dominate in any scene and her motivation is single-minded.

Volumnia, who has the "longest speech by any female character in the tragedies" (245), dominates, but it is over younger boy actors playing Valeria and Virgilia. It is the audience, though, that assembles her character. Unquestionably having the "most complex female role" (246), Cleopatra is developed through comic techniques of split characterization, witty retorts, and pacing. Cleopatra is a performer who, in the comic structure up to Act 4, deals with messengers, confidants, and Antony briefly. In her last two scenes, "the most difficult ... for a boy actor in any of the plays" (250), Cleopatra uses eloquence and rhythms in a series of straightforward beats, so that the boy actor is "not forced to go through a continuous complex developmental change" (252). We sense Cleopatra's plight from her speeches, not from her motivational changes. Set against the tragic heroes, the tragic women do not let us see "their inner lives" or their "inner conflicts" (253). Whether Shakespeare's portrait of female characters is "a response to the limitations of boy actors" or "his conception of women" cannot be proved, though the "limiting filter" of the boy actors must be considered in any discussion of Shakespeare's women in relationship to the men.

339. Hodgdon, Barbara. "The Making of Virgins and Mothers: Sexual Signs, Substitute Scenes and Doubled Presences in *All's Well That Ends Well*." *Philological Quarterly* 66 (1986): 47-71.

Like Rosalind, Helena hides her sexuality in the guise of a male to gain or preserve love. Her virginity and the use she makes of it reveal her "sexual awareness, her obsessive desire" (48). Yet Helena's language highlights her fear of sexuality while her actions move her toward a husband and sexual experience. In her capacity as healer, she is a "minister of grace," a virtuous miracle worker. By being linked idealistically to Diana, Helena still loses her virginity though she preserves the chastity of the literal Diana. By not accepting Helena's aid until she offers both her help and her life in the name of heaven, the King forces Helena to equate love, sex and death. The Clown is Helena's double by offering sexual healing as "an answer [that] will serve all men" (53). Providing a dowry like a father, the King makes Helena marriageable and "transforms her virginity into a medium of exchange" (55).

At midpoint in the play, Helena is both wife and virgin; she is nothing. Helena views the consummation with Bertram as not mutually pleasurable, but as pure gratification for her husband. Confusion about sex puts Helena in a kind of limbo. By winning her husband back, she endorses "Diana's" chastity, resulting in the King giving her a dowry and a husband. Thus, "*AWW* positions women either as virgins ready for marriage or as mothers. Implicitly and explicitly, the woman who acknowledges her own sexual desire becomes transformed into one or the other" (65). Through Bertram's acceptance of her, Helena is transformed into both wife and mother, no longer equating love and death. A woman, proving herself to be a virgin, touches on the possibilities of female power in a patriarchal system.

340. Howard, Jean E. "The Difficulties of Closure: An Approach to the Problematic in Shakespearian Comedy." In *Comedy from Shakespeare to Sheridan: Change and Continuity in the English and European Dramatic Tradition*. Ed. A.R. Braunmuller and J.C. Bulman. Newark: U of Delaware P, 1986. 113-28.

The comedies do not project "images of harmony" and mythic timelessness as C.L. Barber and Northrop Frye have claimed. These plays are "inextricably bound up with the contradictions and discontinuities" of Elizabethan culture (114). In light of Wolfgang Iser's theories, the comedies frustrate an audience's "desire to 'close the gestalt,' to bring all the pieces of the text to a satisfying configuration" (115). *TSh* destabilizes an audience's comic assumptions by suggesting that shrews may be more worth winning than "good girls" while still not romanticizing shrews. Neither a straight (traditional) nor ironic reading of Kate's final speech is satisfying. The one turns her into a "reciter" of conventional sayings, and the other deprives us of knowing her true feelings. Her speech is problematic, deliberately contradictory, and hard for an audience to "create a final synthetic gestalt" (118). The speech establishes the gap between seeing a speaker as "a serious or rhetorical being" (125). *MM* "much more profoundly" is "resistant to harmonious totalization" (121), since the comic forms it uses cannot resolve problems. Set up as the "play's regenerative healer," the Duke and his marriage proposal (and Isabella's silence) work to "undermine that comic perspective." In *MV*, neither the "celebratory" nor "the cynical" (122) releases an audience from anxiety; either view does not "fit into a developing gestalt." Differences in *MV* are turned into sameness. Characters become one another. Like Antonio, Portia binds Bassanio to herself through her bounty. The "fallen Venice and the graced Belmont" (124) are both mercantile, legalistic. Comic formulas are dangerous in Shakespeare because they make "closure difficult" (125).

341. Kahn, Coppelia. "The Absent Mother in *King Lear*." In Ferguson, Quilligan, and Vickers, item 333. 33-48.

No literal mother exists in *Lear*; "we are shown only fathers and their godlike capacity to make or mar their children" (35). The role of mother in this patriarchal society is subverted to elevate male power, yet *Lear* shows the failure of a father to command love in a male-dominated arena, and the emotional price Lear has to pay. The marriage ceremony traditionally excludes the mother as the father settles the dowry, gives his daughter away, and assures the future husband of her virginity. By asking that she love him more than her spouse, Lear tries to hold onto Cordelia as well as give her away, thus revealing his "frustrated incestuous desire for his daughter" (39). In Freudian terms, Lear will shortly be returning to Mother Earth and so feels the need to be childlike again and to have a mother-figure.

Desiring absolute control over his daughters, he wants to be absolutely dependent on them as well. Goneril and Regan prove to be bad mothers. "Lear's madness is essentially his rage at being deprived of the maternal presence" (41). Regressing into infantile modes of behavior, Lear resorts to feminine weapons, such as hysteria. The storm symbolizes Lear's breaking heart, floods of tears and fantasies about the universal persecution of men by women. Lear monopolizes patriarchal ideology to claim a blood tie to his daughters, excluding the mother and reducing her to a mere sexual partner. Cordelia's good qualities derive from himself whereas Goneril and Regan act as though they had another father. Re-entering the play in tears of power, not surrender, Cordelia like the Virgin Mary is full of mercy and pity. Understanding his maleness and Cordelia's femaleness, Lear realizes that paternal authority is bypassed for equality and mutual love. Cordelia's death leaves only men, proving to Lear that a daughter cannot be her father's mother.

342. Lowe, Lisa. "'Say I play the man I am': Gender and Politics in *Coriolanus." Kenyon Review* 8.4 (1986): 86-95.

Cor clearly reveals the "coexistence of political and gender dramas ... " (86). Interpretations of the play as a "dramatic metaphor for English politics" miss the mark as much as those psychoanalytic readings that "locate the mother-son Dyad" (94) at the heart of the problem. Despite interpretations of Volumnia as a non-nurturing mother who associates oral needs with warfare and maternal dependence, she is not responsible for inculcating the notions of violence and manhood in Coriolanus. The connection between "parental love and violence," found earlier in Act 1, can be attributed to "civic fatherhood" (90), illustrated in the conflict between the patricians and the plebeians. Coriolanus repeatedly associates wounds with manhood. Naming, or the identification of manhood, is a central element in *Cor.* The only way Caius Martius can gain the name Coriolanus is to show his wounds, "reveal his lack of male genealogy" (93), to be unmanned, in short. He rebels against this Roman patriarchal "system" which confers gender only through "emasculation and submission" (94). Harboring a "fantasy of absolute unsocial identity," Coriolanus goes to his banishment and death. Gender, therefore, is not restricted to psychological relationships but is also a part of the male structure of domination.

343. Mead, Stephen X. "Shakespeare's Concept of Chastity: A Study of the Problem Plays." *DAI* 47 (1986): 1735A. Indiana U.

344. Montrose, Louis Adrian. "*A Midsummer Night's Dream* and the Shaping Fantasies of Elizabethan Culture: Gender, Power, Form." In Ferguson, Quilligan, and Vickers, item 333. 65-87.

Like other Renaissance texts and courtly performances, *MND* figures "the Elizabethan sex/gender system and the queen's place in it" (70). Elizabeth's sexual politics inform the dialectic pull between honoring a woman monarch and representing male power. Borrowing from the Marian cult, the cult of Elizabeth represented her as a virgin, mother, and monarch, erotic and spiritual simultaneously. Her metamorphic presence is crucial to the cultural fictions of *MND*. In having women rule and even kill men, Amazons (like Hippolita) inverted European patriarchy. Yet *MND* "eventually restores the inverted system of gender and nurture to a patriarchal norm" (72). Defeating Hippolita, Theseus appropriates control of a woman's body (i.e., Hermia's) as if it were a piece of property. In terms of "embryological notions," Shakespeare is "distinctly phallocentric" (75), reversing the Amazonian practice of using men only for women's power. Yet while the "dramatic structure" of *MND* "articulates a patriarchal ideology," it also "undermines" such an ideology by "evoking precisely what it seeks to suppress" (76-77). Legitimizing the authority of husbands sanctions the presence of unruly wives. Moreover, Hippolytus's birth, predicted and blessed by the fairies at the end of *MND*, led to incest and civil disruption.

Disapproving of the Amazon image, Elizabeth saw herself as androgynous. She transformed her virginity into a religious cult making her uniquely qualified to rule without "undermining the male hegemony of her culture" (81). By splitting the "triune queen" into Titania, unruly wife, and the vestal maiden who escapes Cupid's bow, and by portraying the male prerogatives of Oberon and Theseus, *MND* "symbolically neutralizes the royal power to which it ostensibly pays homage" (84). Invoking Elizabeth's virginal power without offering her invulnerable control, Shakespeare's play almost depends "upon her absence, her exclusion" to represent the cultural fantasies about gender, theatre, and political power essential to Elizabethan rule. Shakespeare "re-mythologizes" the cult of Elizabeth.

345. Orgel, Stephen. "Prospero's Wife." In Ferguson, Quilligan, and Vickers, item 333. 50-64.

The absent wife in *Tem* is crucial psychoanalytically and biographically. Treating the play as a case history, not as an objective account, is to see *Tem* as a series of "collaborative fantasies" (52) between Shakespeare and the audience. Central to these fantasies is the family. Prospero creates his own surrogate family on the island, a bad child Caliban, the "good child/wife" Miranda. Caliban derives his ownership of the island from his mother Sycorax who represents the negative side of women, and so Prospero dismisses Caliban as a bastard. Yet the opposite is true, too. If women are whores, then "all men at heart are rapists–Caliban, Ferdinand, and of course ... Prospero, too" (55). The family paradigm in Shakespeare is unstable; we do not get complete families but rather a "chiastic relationship–father and daughter, mother and son" (56). The emphasis on parents and siblings reinforces biographical parallels with Shakespeare and his daughters. Because of his early marriage, "we should see as much of Shakespeare in Miranda and Ariel as in Prospero" (57).

Seen from the "realities of contemporary kingship" (Elizabeth as well as James), Prospero's art/magic and Caliban's maternal inheritance embody the ways in which royal authority was conceived. Prospero's source of power, like King James', is "rigidly paternalistic" but also incorporates the maternal (59). Like

Prospero, James thought of himself as the head of a single-parent family. Thus "all the dangers of promiscuity and bastardy are resolved ... unless, of course, the parent is a woman" (59). Prospero's magic intentionally disallows the possibility of Antonio's reconciliation. Through Miranda's marriage, Milan is turned into a "Neapolitan fiefdom," effectively excluding Antonio from power. Consequently, Prospero's authority is preserved rather than relinquished.

346. Roberts, Jeanne Addison. "Making a Woman and Other Institutionalized Diversions." *Shakespeare Quarterly* 37 (1986): 366-69.

Shakespeare needs to be de-institutionalized in secondary schools (and elsewhere) so that the plays will not be seen from an exclusive male perspective of patriarchy and from the tradition of male critics. Shakespeare cannot be blamed since "he could have known only a patriarchal society" (367). To establish women's importance and to expand female roles, more comedies (where women even dominate) need to be taught, and critical approaches concerned with gender need to be taken. Recent critics scrutinize Shakespeare's ideologies to "challenge and illuminate our own" (368). For example, Novy (item 262) and Erickson (item 284) look at the plays in terms of patriarchal structures; Kahn (item 160) "explores the pattern of male development"; Montrose (item 344) studies representations of Queen Elizabeth; and Bamber (item 175) focuses on "women as male fantasies." The making of a woman needs to be given as much attention as the making of a man.

347. Scoble, Fran Norris. "In Search of the Female Hero." *English Journal* 75 (1986): 85-87.

To provide a balanced curriculum means moving away from the tradition of "equating the male questing" experience with all human experience. The female voice and experience must also be presented by including alternate texts and by "turning the lens" on traditional ones. In teaching *RJ*, for example, instructors must emphasize Juliet's "capacity to choose" and act on the consequences of those choices. She is witty, resourceful, and courageous. While Romeo "becomes dramatically secondary, even a passive figure because he is banished" (86), Juliet has to remain behind to confront and act on the decisions the young lovers have made. Female students can identify with her.

348. Stallybrass, Peter. "Patriarchal Territories: The Body Enclosed." In Ferguson, Quilligan, and Vickers, item 333. 123-42.

Women in the Renaissance were considered to be naturally grotesque, possessing openness of the body. Patriarchal society held these natural tendencies in control. The three areas of control entrusted to women were the mouth, chastity, and the household. The family was created within an enclosed area of private property under the absolute control of the father. The natural and imposed tendencies of women translated into class ideas. Categorized according to class, women of the closed body were in control of the three important female assets; others argued that women should be classified as open in terms of gender, "daughters of Eve" (136). Male social climbers needed some higher class to aspire to and saw women as sometimes open and sometimes closed. Othello, who belongs in this ambivalent category, is a Venetian by virtue of his marriage to Desdemona. He is the possessor of the possessed, Desdemona, but the threat of loss from Iago makes his position tenuous. Hence, the possessor does not have a "cultural entitlement" to Desdemona. As a Moor, he has married well above his rank, making him virtuous and a Venetian, but "the very fact that Desdemona was 'open' to him endangers her status as his spiritual enclosure, the impermeable container of his honor" (136). Searching for his wife between the two extremes, Othello has equated the handkerchief, a symbol of his family's honor and Desdemona's chastity, with bodily functions, making it a symbol of both private and public actions. Iago recognizes this and similarly transforms Cassio's public displays into private acts to suggest sexual promiscuity. According to Iago, Desdemona has either returned to her class by taking Cassio as a lover, or she is merely assuming her natural role. Opposing Emilia's view that adultery is a "small vice,"

Desdemona represents the virtues of the closed classical body,
while Emilia validates the grotesque and open body.

349. Waller, Marguerite. "Usurpation, Seduction, and the Problematics
of the Proper: A 'Deconstructive,' 'Feminist' Rereading of the
Seductions of Richard and Anne in Shakespeare's *Richard III*."
In Ferguson, Quilligan, and Vickers, item 333. 159-74.

Feminism and deconstructionism should not triumph over each
other. Even if they are not consistent, they offer a "totalizing
discourse" (174) asynchronously. As Jacques Derrida points out,
language causes violence; women in particular are the victims of
such subversive violence. In light of Derrida's theory, the
characters in and critics of *R3* have seduced themselves into
deception through naming. Richard is not manipulative or vital
but a self-deceived dupe. Critics are wrong to react to the
seduction scene (Act 1.2) by saying it is shocking and by asking
how can Anne be so weak and Richard so persuasive. Miner
(item 131) and Dash (item 152) attribute too much to the "male-
authored performances and commentaries of *R3*" (164) by seeing
women as completely subordinated to men. Similarly, Kahn (item
160) errs in believing that the "male characters know and define
themselves."

Unaware of the rhetorical structures of their own language
that they use to talk about themselves, Richard and Anne have a
problematic status. Confounded by his illusory rhetoric, Richard
believes he possesses an autonomous, sovereign selfhood. Yet he
and Anne are not "independent subjects" (170) but exhibit a
paradoxical, mutual dependence. Richard is less the initiator in
Act 1.2 than a self-serving victim. He does not view his theoretical
position with the irony that he applies to others. Establishing the
terms of discourse Richard will employ, Anne is in a stronger
position than she had been in before. Richard is dependent on
"Anne's continuing sense of authorship." And to remain the author
of her own terms, Anne must remain in conversation with
Richard. As elsewhere in *R3*, opposite terms employed by
enemies seemingly confer the "stability" of identity on individuals.
Richard is tricked by his own "shady rhetorical blindness" (173),
and Anne has "no habitual or social alternative" (172).

Interestingly, by giving Anne a ring Richard becomes her
ornament. Yet both Richard and Anne are attached to
"rhetorically impossible ideals of selfhood" (174).

350. White, R.S. *Innocent Victims: Poetic Injustice in Shakespearean
    Tragedy.* Newcastle-Upon-Tyne: Tyneside Free P, 1982; 2nd
    ed., 1986.

"This book ... is partly about the outrage stirred in us when we
feelingly watch the perpetuation of an injustice and partly about
the perception for potential peace, harmony, and justice which is
displayed in our shared recognition of injustice" (3).
    Shakespeare was "constantly and uniquely" concerned with
victims from his earliest tragedies. These victims are mostly
women but also children. Each tragedy offers "an innocent victim
who is accorded neither justice in her own world, nor poetic
justice in the work of art" (90). Nor have they received justice
from the critics who have explained away their moral function and
have concentrated their attention on male heroes. Shakespeare's
victims are martyrs who reveal justice, truth, and beauty in their
lives and in their dealings with others.
    In the brutal world of *TA*, Lavinia as victim arouses pathos.
Though "hardly given enough lines to establish a fully developed
personality" (23), Lavinia looks forward to Ophelia as a daughter
obeying her father and Cordelia in her eloquent though silent
suffering. Lavinia arouses in us intense feelings that "the violation
is not only directed at the body of a woman, but at the whole
ethic of goodness and love."
    Shakespeare's innocent victims have this common
characteristic–"an eloquent silence about their own feelings" (31).
Even in his early poem Shakespeare shows Lucrece suffering in
silence; she is "seen only from the inside," unable to respond as
Brutus does. Her suicide is a "paradox of innocence acquiring
shame." Ophelia is victimized by her father in particular, by
Denmark society in general. She is oblivious, though, to her own
loneliness. The audience feels protective toward her, guided by
Gertrude's pity, but we are helpless. Ophelia is silent, lost to the
cruel machinations all around her.

Desdemona, too, lives in a male world of storms and battles,
quarrels over reputations, in a society that has a "vested interest
in ignoring or covering up injustice" (61). Othello and Iago may
have different attitudes toward justice, but their views determine
the way they regard Desdemona. Othello thinks her marriage to
him was a "reward for his virtue"; she is a hero-worshipper, and
he is fascinated by her domestic, conciliatory life, something alien
to him. For Iago, marriage is physical and sexual; women are
obligated to satisfy men's lusts or be "denounced like Emilia as a
shrew." Iago challenges Othello's assumptions about marriage on
rational grounds. Desdemona's "central trait" is to cover up her
feelings in public; she has a strong desire for peace. Yet she does
not generalize. Like Ophelia, she "is forced to speak her feelings
obliquely" (72). Still, it is wrong to see her as a "stereotype of
femininity" (71). The world around her forces her to "prevaricate."
Othello should be neither condemned nor condoned; his
repentance "should give us some relief" (74). Othello, Iago, and
Desdemona die in character. Desdemona dies for others; Othello
"regains sufficient objectivity" to assess his condition; and Iago
survives without accepting moral justice.

Lear is not Lear's tragedy but Cordelia's. It is the "tragedy *par
excellence* of the innocent victim" (79). But Cordelia does not die
in vain; her message is spoken by survivors. Unlike Ophelia, she
is a remote figure, "confiding no vulnerability." Although a truth-
teller, Cordelia speaks her selfless compassion through silence. As
Cordelia shows, words fail to communicate in *Lear*. She is the
"raw and disturbing voice that asserts no relationship is worth
losing faith with oneself, for to do so would be to negate love
itself" (83). Critics who fault Cordelia's obstinacy fail to see the
social and political context of the play. The Fool drops out of the
play into total silence.

Reviews: First Edition (1982)–*British Book News* Aug. 1982:
508; Dodsworth, Martin, *English* [London] 31 (1982): 191-96;
Palven, Paul, *Shakespeare Bulletin* 2 (Nov.-Dec. 1983): 13; von
Rosador, Tetzeli, *Shakespeare Jahrbuch* (1985): 230; Wilcher,
Robert, *Cahiers Elisabethains* 22 (Oct. 1982): 127-29. Second
Edition (1986)–Champion, Larry S., *Shakespeare Quarterly* 38
(1987): 379-81; Hawkes, Terence, *Times Literary Supplement* 10
Apr. 1987: 390; Hillman, R., *Renaissance and*

Reformation/Renaissance et Reforme 12 (1988): 315; Weis, Rene
J.A., *Times Higher Education Supplement* 19 Sept. 1986: 20.

351. Wikander, Matthew H. "'As secret as maidenhead': The
Profession of the Boy-Actress in *Twelfth Night*." *Comparative
Drama* 20 (1986): 349-62.

The key to Viola's virgin mystery is that she is wearing
inappropriate clothing for a woman. As she grows to perfection,
her disguise is removed. Such removal is complicated by the male
actor playing the part. "Viola remains trapped in her boy's clothes;
the boy-actress remains trapped in the role" (351). This confusion
can also be interpreted as a rite of passage from childhood to
maturity; the boy-actress would neither be male nor female. "The
searching and uncertainty of Viola are those of the boy-actress at
the height of his career, wondering whether his next part will be
male or female ... " (354). So, by seeing the world of the play as
theatre, Viola in the part of Cesario appears as a great comedian
and improviser. The sexual rivalry in the play could be construed
as the professional rivalry of a theatre company, with the dialogue
between Viola and Feste displaying the actors' improvisational
skills. Yet Malvolio and Viola are actors without freedom.
Malvolio loses the audience that he had rehearsed for; Viola's
part is limited because of her feminine/adolescent passivity.
Aware of the hollowness beneath the clothing, she does not have
the male power to accompany the disguise. The status of women
is thus linked in *TN* with the status of apprentice actor. Just as
the maid dies when a woman gets married, the apprentice-actor
disappears when brought to perfection. As the actor fears being
miscast, Viola risks making the wrong choice of husbands.

352. Williamson, Marilyn L. *The Patriarchy of Shakespeare's Comedies.*
Detroit: Wayne State UP, 1986.

Chapter One focuses on "The Comedies of Courtship: Men's
Profit, Women's Power." Women had power in the courtship
phase; and, in fact, Elizabeth's own "supreme power in a
hierarchical society made almost inevitable that Elizabethan
fictions of love [would] ascribe great power to the women" (29).

The middle comedies, *AYL*, *MV*, and *TN*, deal with the marriage of a socially superior woman and a lower class man. The man gains financial profit or social advancement while the woman is forced into subordination. "Marriage was a particularly appropriate metaphor of establishing a man's worth because in the Elizabethan world it signified his entry into full membership within society" (37). A married woman was legally "no person"; the social class into which she was born became irrelevant as soon as she married.

Yet the husband acquired a new identity–cuckold. But while marriage to a superior lady brings both her and her property to the husband, these benefits become the "basis of cuckoldry and the fact it most frequently protests" (53). The cuckoldry theme begins before the marriage has begun, and is the one power women retain. The jokes men make about cuckoldry act as a defense against this threat. Shakespeare also uses them to re-affirm the status quo, by making patriarchal marriage the norm. Therefore, any deviant behavior can be scorned. Cuckoldry depends on three factors–misogyny, a double standard, and patriarchal marriage. Cuckold jokes emphasize feminine sexuality and paint the wife as a disruptive woman. *MV*, *AYL*, and *Ado* all show how Shakespeare incorporated the "complex code" (45) of cuckoldry, seen as a crime that is presented or "an affair between men." Rosalind's threats are temporary. The threat of cuckoldry in *Ado* strengthens male bonds yet ostracizes women. Perhaps Portia is powerful in *MV* because in Venice wealth transcends social boundaries. Olivia and Viola in *TN* have the capacity to be as strong as Portia, but neither chooses to exercise her potential.

In Chapter Two, "The Problem Plays: Social Regulation of Desire," *AWW* and *MM* are part of a wider discourse about patriarchal authority. The plays, written under the rule of King James, deal with the relation of a father to his children. The ruler of the country is represented as a parent. Both plays use sexuality and the making of marriages as the central conflict in dissecting patriarchal authority. This authority involves and sanctions enforced marriage and the bed trick. *AWW* deals with the abuse of wardship when the King forces his ward to marry. In all the plays of enforced marriage, the husband's prodigality expresses his rebellion at the world of property, which has "bought him and sold him like chattel" (65). By deserting Helena, Bertram follows the "prodigal pattern." Shakespeare complicates and makes problematical the patient wife of the enforced marriage by making her also a "clever wench whose motives are ambitious and overly sexual." In *AWW*, the bed trick is not just the consummation of a marriage, complete with a wedding ring; it is also "an act of procreation." In *MM*, Shakespeare devotes an entire subplot to the topical issue of bastardy. While desire is a problem in the play, the laws, too, are problematic since they have not been enforced by the duke's rule. "Laxity is replaced by tyranny, disrupting the social order." However, the bed trick is "the most disturbing element" in *MM* because the state intrudes directly in the act of sexual intercourse.

Chapter Three concentrates on "The Romances: Patriarchy, Pure and Simple." Shakespeare's last plays–*Per*, *Cym*, *WT*, and *Tem*–are related to the political discourse of Jacobean England. These plays reproduce the history of their times. By employing the genre of romance, Shakespeare mythologizes patriarchal power. The father's natural authority within the family becomes the inevitable model for political power and license to control the lives of others. While the most immediate threat to society is the abuse of power by the ruler or his counterparts, the threats hovering at the center of these plays are the destruction of the family, sexual infidelity, and loss of heirs. Evil in *Per* and *Cym* is connected to bad relations with women. Along with *WT*, the plays "depoliticize their patriarchal structures by presenting their conflicts in sexual relationships," especially infidelity and marriage choice. Although women in *WT* are no longer a source of evil, relations with them define the tyranny of both kings. In all of the plays, "these rulers must rise above the impulse to revenge, which ties one inevitably to the past. Instead of repeating the past, the romances present it as a prologue to a hopeful future in the younger generation, whose succession to the power of the father is the life stream of the patriarchy" (157). Motherhood is also essential to succession, which ultimately depends upon the female generative power. Yet the patriarchal system tries to control reproduction.

Reviews: Ashley, L.R.N., *Bibliotheque d'Humanisme et Renaissance* 50 (1988): 420-21; Charney, Maurice, *Renaissance*

Quarterly 41 (1988): 529; Demetrakopoulos, S., *Comparative Drama* 22 (1988): 89; Howard, Jean E., *Studies in English Literature, 1500-1900* 27 (1987): 324-26; Rackin, Phyllis, *Shakespeare Quarterly* 38 (1987): 524; Thompson, Ann, *The Yearbook of English Studies* 19 (1988): 316; Vaughn, V.M., *Choice* 24 (1987): 1068.

1987

353. Adelman, Janet. "'Born of Woman': Fantasies of Maternal Power in *Macbeth*." In *Cannibals, Witches, and Divorce: Estranging the Renaissance*. Ed. Marjorie Garber. *Selected Papers from the English Institute*. 1985. New Series 11. Baltimore: Johns-Hopkins UP, 1987. 90-121.

The two "psychological fantasies" of *Mac* contradictorily deal with an "absolute and destructive maternal power" and an "absolute escape from this power" (90). Maternal power is "diffused" in *Mac* through the witches and Lady Macbeth who try to reduce Macbeth to a vulnerable infant. Like Richard III, Macbeth wields a bloody masculine axe to escape the maternal presence. Duncan, the "androgynous parent" (94) who is "idealized for his nurturing paternity ... [yet] is killed for his womanish softness" (95), is powerless to protect his son. Duncan's androgyny is "ambivalent," and in his absence "male and female break apart" (94). Consequently, Macbeth is at the mercy of "maternal malevolence"–the witches and Lady Macbeth are "persistently" identified/fused as one (97). The female in *Mac* coerces male Macbeth and equates his manhood with murder. Lady Macbeth's power over him is "more absolute than the witches can achieve" (102). The fantasy of escaping their female power is "centrally invested" (103) in Macbeth, but the ending of the play reveals "the dual process of repudiation and enactment of the fantasy" (103). The witches punish Macbeth through equivocation, yet the female is punished and eliminated. Macduff is "deprived of a nurturing female presence" (108) and the traitor Macdonaldwald's body (like Fortune whom he served) is feminized and conquered by an "all-male erotic" (106). Ultimately, *Mac* is a "recuperative consolidation of male power" and the feminine is far more "contained" than in *Ham* or *Lear*. The "purely male realm" of *Mac* looks toward Prospero's island.

354. Bergeron, David M., and Geraldo U. De Sousa. *Shakespeare: A Study and Research Guide.* 2nd. ed. Lawrence: UP of Kansas, 1987. Esp. "Feminism and Gender Studies," 137-45.

Assessing the importance of feminist criticism, this section of the *Guide* provides brief overviews of *The Woman's Part* (item 126); Dusinberre (item 6); Jardine (item 224); Dash (item 152); Garber (item 156); French (item 155); Pitt (item 165); Cook (item 108); Bamber (item 175); Novy (item 262); Kahn (item 160); Erickson (item 284); Neely (item 298); Sundelson (item 241); and Dreher (item 330).

355. Boose, Lynda E. "The Family in Shakespeare Studies; or–Studies in the Family of Shakespeareans; or–The Politics of Politics." *Renaissance Quarterly* 40 (1987): 707-42.

The tradition which feminist scholarship has challenged is typified by E.M.W. Tillyard and others who regarded the family and gender as givens since they upheld the "ideology of a father-headed, father-named nuclear family" (711), a position that went unchanged for almost 400 years. Women's roles were also unquestioned except when, like Cleopatra, they broke away from male-ordered bounds. But the emergence of Shakespearean feminism in the mid-1970s turned to non-Freudian psychoanalysis to find out about gender and locate the "missing maternal role" (715). Feminists found it "self-annihilating," however, to restrict their study to nonexistent women writers of the Renaissance, for they would then have to relinquish their claims to interpret the most sacrosanct canonical writer, Shakespeare. Feminist work "opened up what we might call a new, scholarly mother-lode" (716) in which the feminine side/identity of masculinity was explored and created a "newly enfranchised space for latter-day

Renaissance man" (717). Moving from character analysis to a scrutiny of social institutions, Shakespearean feminism identified the conflict that existed between the patriarchy and a "model of feminine fulfillment" (720). The question of Shakespeare's own views of patriarchy and "its institutional subordination of women" threatens to become "some sort of oath of allegiance upon which feminist critics are compelled to swear" (721). Some critics have seen "gender reversal and female power" in the plays as a way of consolidating "the status quo of male hierarchy" (721). Erickson's view (item 284) that Shakespeare attacks tyrannical patriarchy but affirms its benevolence contrasts with McLuskie's Marxist reading (item 295) that the plays offer "so totally masculinized a perspective that the only possible position open to feminist readers is radical resistance" (723).

Feminist scholarship "right now stands at a crossroads" (726). An incipient "schism" (727) has taken place, squaring off the new historicists with feminists. New historicism, which has displaced and erased women in its consideration of male power, projects a "single gendered body" of plays. The family is replaced by the court. Feminists have maintained a healthy skepticism toward valorizing a history that was male written and transmitted and that marginalized women. The historic critic wrongly assumes the role of patriarch by making Shakespeare "a co-opted servant of state orthodoxies" (741); new historicism, which privileges history to control subversive resistance, has its roots in male experience confronting authority.

356. Carducci, Jane S. "Shakespeare's *Titus Andronicus*: An Experiment in Expression." *Cahiers Elisabethains* 31 (1987): 1-9.

TA is not untypical of Shakespeare's Roman world, also exemplified in *JC*, *AC*, and *Cor*, that boasts "military prowess and [is] bathed in oratory" (1). *TA* embodies Rome's male political institutions. Lavinia's mute silence represents the failure of her family to find adequate words to express their violent emotions. In the wilderness where Lavinia is raped, Roman oratory is worthless. Marcus's description of Lavinia after she has been mutilated is more appropriate to a painting or tapestry than to a woman. Titus also formalizes his grief in words that do not fit the reality of his daughter's rape. Like Lear, Titus turns to madness because he is unable to vent his grief. His unexpressed emotions lead Titus to revenge his daughter's mutilation by violating the laws of hospitality. The language of Roman men is limited to externals; it reflects the failure of the Roman masculine ideal.

357. Carlson, Susan. "Women in *As You Like It*: Community, Change, and Choice." *Essays in Literature* 14 (1987): 151-69.

While there is "invigorating freedom" and "serious consideration of that power and community" (166) in *AYL*, female power is nonetheless restricted through limitations placed on women's language and friendships. Erickson (item 284) is right that androgyny does not help women but supports male-imposed norms. Women's gains are temporary in Arden, which is only a "different sort of man's world" (161). *AYL* displays an "encoded sexism" (167). Though Rosalind displays great ingenuity and freedom in the middle of the play, she is finally left with no choices save marriage as Shakespeare seemingly battles against conventions but ends up affirming them. Rosalind's witty language is undercut by female stereotypes and linguistic patterns ("indirection and inversions" [155]) which she herself typifies and attacks. As Ganymede, Rosalind "doubts," "disdains," and "blames" women. Her linguistic freedom, her comic power for lies, implies betrayal and at the end of the play she is silent as the men recapture a "playful language" (159). Celia and Rosalind are drawn apart, separated by Rosalind's male disguise. Also showing "restrictions on female community" (162) are Phebe and Audrey who emphasize the "isolation of women in the play," thus defusing female threats. Optimistic readings by French (item 155), McKewin (item 130), and Belsey (item 275) are unfounded. Rather than offering reconciliation and comedic joy, marriage in *AYL* is "more an assumption than a visible institution"; even Rosalind's view of matrimony is "mockingly brutal" (165). Rosalind does not change society but has surrendered the power of choice.

358. Chojnacki, Stanley. "Comments: Blurring Genders." *Renaissance Quarterly* 40 (1987): 743-51.

Responding to discussions of gender by Lynda Boose (item 355) and to papers by historian Barbara Diefendorf and art historian Rona Goffen (*Renaissance Quarterly* 40 [1987]: 661-81), Chojnacki believes that these scholars raise important questions, "the very posing of which calls for a less sharply defined approach to gender" (749). Although patriarchy is regarded as a truism, a more enveloping concept of gender with "flexible categories, with permeable boundaries and overlapping parameters" (751) better accounts for historical events. Men (younger, unmarried, unpropertied sons) as well as women were subject to patriarchal structures. Moreover, though Boose sees women confined to the private sphere, they also played a part in the public arena in "ostensibly male, 'patriarchal' roles" (747). Boose discusses not a scholarly field but a "battlefield" of competing criticisms; recent scholarship on gender emphasizing "contacts and overlaps" can modulate the new historicist's concern with power and the feminist's approach to women's roles in the household and the state.

359. Clark, Sandra. "'Wives May be Merry and Yet Honest Too': Women and Wit in *The Merry Wives of Windsor* and Some Other Plays." In *"Fanned and Winnowed Opinions"*: *Shakespearean Essays Presented to Harold Jenkins*. Ed. John W. Mahon and Thomas A. Pendleton. London: Methuen, 1987. 249-67.

Women in the comedies possess an "alternative wit exhibited in cleverness of action rather than of speech" (249) that often stigmatizes them as shrews. Though Shakespeare's sources may celebrate women deceiving their husbands, the English tradition did not and in fact expressed a strong misogyny. From the male perspective, a woman's wit (tongue) was associated with scolding and lust; however, wit is not a "gender related quality" in the comedies. Possessing a greater understanding of the constraints of wit, the ladies in *LLL* attack the men "rather than the other way round" (252). Displaying a "wider range of wit" than Orlando,

Rosalind as Ganymede can distance herself from the image of a shrew while still offering the possibility of shrewishness. While Beatrice's wit has a "dangerous affinity with shrewishness," Bertram's is praised as "part of his repertoire of charms." The wives, who are cunning and down to earth in *MWW*, are not subversive females but "share fully in the men's attitudes toward property and self preservation" (258). The wives protect their reputations which from a male perspective are more easily sullied than a man's for a sexual offense. Knowing that Falstaff's lust like Ford's jealousy is a "masculine voice" (276), the wives improvise punishments and in the last scene are joined by others to make it a public punishment. Mistress Page's wit, however, must "misfire" when she backs Dr. Caius as Anne's suitor because "her husband's discomfiture is not compatible with the play's final re-establishment of social order" (264). *MWW* is the "comic obverse" of *Oth*, yet the wives' wit, unlike Iago's, effects a cure. Emilia's wit defends Desdemona in Act 5.2 when she refuses to "muster the same spirit for herself," thus vindicating the "strength of the women's bond" (267).

360. Cohen, Derek. "Patriarchy and Jealousy in *Othello* and *The Winter's Tale*." *Modern Language Quarterly* 48 (1987): 207-23.

Othello and Leontes illustrate that in a patriarchy "the fidelity of wives is the major prop and condition of social order" (207) and that when wives are unfaithful the husbands' control is threatened. Sexually jealous husbands, Othello and Leontes imagine their wives with the other (arch-sexual rivals Cassio and Polixenes) who usurps their place. Othello and Leontes hallucinate many small "erotic details" to help them avoid "confusion" while they control their wives. Their certain knowledge of the wives' infidelity is tied to the distorted views of themselves. Othello's confident public self is at odds with his unworthy private one. Like Othello, Leontes is "caught by a compulsive need to interpret what he sees, to decode the evidence of his eyes into terrible visions the details make real" (212). Victims of their own "pornographic imaginations," these tragic heroes compulsively "anatomize" their wives sexually in precise images (lips, thighs, sheets, kisses, smiles) that turn Othello into a "willing voyeur"

(215) and Leontes into a cruel abuser. By reducing their wives to "sexual objects," the men show that "evil is distilled into the single idea of female infidelity." Portraying Hermione as a "nothing" (slang for vagina), Leontes is "effectively describing himself." In the brothel scene, Othello tries to "regain his status through abuse"; his distorted justice is, despite the beauty of its music, a "huge self aggrandizing lie" (223). Displaying their patriarchal intentions, both men want to remain in control by sacrificing their wives.

361. Cook, Carol Jane. "Imagining the Other: Reading Gender Difference in Shakespeare." *DAI* 47 (1987): 259A. Cornell U.

362. Cotton, Nancy. "Castrating (W)itches: Impotence and Magic in *The Merry Wives of Windsor*." *Shakespeare Quarterly* 38 (1987): 320-26.

Witches were believed to have the power to castrate men, taking away their "instruments of venerie." Ford associates his wife's cuckolding him with witchcraft. Beating Falstaff as Mother Prat, Ford "projects" his wife's infidelity onto Falstaff the witch. *MWW* contains numerous illustrations of Ford's phobia about being unmanned, especially his jealousy of Page for having offspring. Like Ford, Falstaff and the other foolish suitors "experience impotence in the face of magical female powers" (323). They all suffer symbolic emasculation. Though the last scene may present the wives as witches, these "evil and lustful wives exist only in masculine imagination" (325). The women, all of whom are Mother Prats ("tricky women"), actually "restore potency to the husband Ford" through healing, comic punishments.

363. Desmet, Christy. "Speaking Sensibly: Feminine Rhetoric in *Measure for Measure* and *All's Well That Ends Well*." *Renaissance Papers 1986* (1987): 43-51.

Rhetoric in the Renaissance was seen as either an ornate entrapment or a means to express civil responsibility. This ambivalence toward rhetoric, often personified in terms of a woman's virtues or vices, lies behind Shakespeare's presentation of Helena and Isabella. A "clever rhetorician" (49), Helena's behavior is at times "inscrutable" and her motives "ambiguous." She is both "the perfect female speaker" (48) with the king, yet she arouses his senses through her pleasing words, one of rhetoric's most feared vices. Similarly, Isabella in *MM* "rejects rhetorical ornaments" while adopting "her opponent's style" of using analogies to which Angelo erotically responds. Ultimately "uneasy" about the power of rhetoric, Shakespeare consigns these women, and their "feminine rhetoric," to silence in a male world, a "particularly ironic fate" since Helena and Isabella had to "lie and flatter skeptical judges for a good cause" (51).

364. Dubrow, Heather. *Captive Victors: Shakespeare's Narrative Poems and Sonnets*. Ithaca: Cornell UP, 1987.

Shakespeare uses rhetorical tropes–particularly *syneciosis*–to show character development in his narrative poems and sonnets. In both *VA* and *RL*, a "central character connects passion and power; in both the conventions of love poetry express–and, more disturbingly, perhaps encourage–that connection" (27). Venus is both a symbolic and mimetic character. She equates love with control; speaking of her relationship with Mars, she tells of "Leading him prisoner in a red-rose chain" (*VA*, line 110). She tells Adonis, "But if thou needs wilt hunt, be rul'd by me" (line 673). Her attempts to assert power over Adonis through language often show that she herself is imprisoned by language. Her elegy on Adonis echoes the language of the Petrarchan lover–"with the important difference, of course, that the sex roles are reversed" (31).

The sexual politics of *VA*–woman appropriating the sexually aggressive behavior of man–may reflect an ambivalence toward Queen Elizabeth, an aggressive female monarch. The female who tries to take charge of her own destiny is a figure who obviously intrigued Shakespeare, since she appears in many other of his works. *VA* goes further than other Ovidian mythological narratives in rejecting the Petrarchan ideal of woman: "if other authors in the genre insistently demonstrated that women feel desire, Shakespeare renders that desire even more comic, less dignified"

(69). By reversing traditional sexual roles of pursuer and pursued, Shakespeare forces readers to examine their own attitudes and behavior through unexpected and unfamiliar identification with the characters.

In *RL,* "*syneciosis* describes–and evokes–tension" (81). The setting for the poem is a distrustful, Roman society, dominated by male competitiveness. This competition, not lust, leads to the rape. "Even inanimate objects and abstract ideas compete with each other in the milieu the poem evokes" (87). The description of colors in Lucrece's face, the rivalry over who has the most right to mourn her death, and the implication that Collatine, not Lucrece, is the victim, all point up the competitive elements of Roman society. The comparison of rape to a siege and attack of a city is clearly not unique to *RL*, but here it is important because Tarquin's attack may be termed "acquaintance rape" and not "rape by a stranger" (95). Rome is destroyed internally by the competition of those, such as a king's son, who are sworn to protect her. "Lucrece is the victim not only of her attacker but also of a society that defines women in terms of their relationships to men and, in particular, assumes that their worth resides in the chastity enjoined by those relationships" (101).

But the poem goes on to assert that Lucrece is not completely conditioned; she is an individual who has options and "her responses to the rape are but one of the many ways a Roman woman might have behaved" (101). In a reversal of the typical Petrarchan love poem, the innocence of the woman does not protect her; her unavailability arouses the lust of her attacker and her naivete does not permit her to recognize, and thus resist, evil. Lucrece's reaction to the rape is written in the traditional rhetoric of poetry, but Shakespeare accurately conveys the psychological state of mind of a rape victim. Lucrece's speeches are monologues, showing her unwillingness to talk to others about the rape. She wonders if she is at fault, but simultaneously maintains her innocence. She dwells on how it could have been prevented. "Above all, however, it is in her loss of identity ... that Lucrece exemplifies the patterns charted by rape students" (107). Ironically, she begins to identify with her attacker.

In his narrative poems, Shakespeare reveals the latent danger in poetic imagery. "Much as *Venus and Adonis* reminds us that the Petrarchan metaphor of the hunt may reflect real pain and much as other passages in *Rape of Lucrece* imply that the treasure hunt may not be a happy experience for its object, so Shakespeare is demonstrating [in Tarquin's military metaphors] that the conventional literary linkage between warring and loving may conceal–and at the same time reveal–destructive urges" (121). As the emphasis on martial maneuvers shows, Tarquin's attack is a power rape, an attempt to assert his masculinity in answer to the challenge he hears in Collatine's boast.

In the sonnets, "Shakespeare continues the exploration of sexual politics" (204); the speaker "moves from master to servant, a translation of the physiological facts of sexuality into the imperatives of power" (205). In the sonnets on the Dark Lady, Shakespeare participates in and even glorifies anti-Petrarchan conventions, but still consciously demonstrates that the speaker cannot fully break from the traditions. "Though the Dark Lady does not look or behave like a Petrarchan mistress in some of the more important ways, she indulges in certain forms of Petrarchan behavior, notably tyranny, and her lover is trapped into behaving like a Petrarchan sonneteer" (242). Thus in the sonnets as in *VA* and *RL*, Shakespeare explores the ways in which men and women strive for power.

Reviews: *Philological Quarterly* 68 (1989): 443; Ashley, L.R.N., *Bibliotheque d'Humanisme et Renaissance* 50 (1988): 748; Cheney, D., *Studies in English Literature, 1500-1900* 28 (1988): 175-76; Hallissy, M., *Library Journal* 112 (1 Feb. 1987): 78; Keach, W., *Renaissance Quarterly* 41 (1988): 752; Spiller, M.R.G., *Durham University Journal* 80 (1988): 344-45.

365. Erickson, Peter. "The Order of the Garter, the Cult of Elizabeth, and Class-Gender Tension in *The Merry Wives of Windsor*." In Howard and O'Connor, item 376. 116-40.

Patriarchy is not a monolithic doctrine but involves pressures, changes, and subversions. *MWW* reveals some of these tensions confronting patriarchy in the conflicts between class and gender. *MWW* does not celebrate "female, middle class power" (118); instead the play testifies to the stressful conflicts feminine power creates. It is wrong to take a sentimental view of *MWW* and see events there as harmless, farcical. Conflicts are avoided or postponed by characters through "diversionary" plot making, generating new conflicts to evade old problems. Evans, the Host, Caius, Ford, and even the wives engage in manipulative plotting to achieve temporary reconciliation. Fenton's success in winning Anne may show the "revitalization of the aristocratic class" and involve the transfer of power from the women to men, but even though he may limit the wives' power, his actions do not establish a "clear-cut restoration of male control." The institution of the Garter established a link between Queen Elizabeth and the wives, particularly in the shared ways in which their wielding power creates cultural tensions. "The Queen's presence doubles the effect of female domination in the play, and the impression of the Queen and the wives as strong women is further amplified because their power comes from a similar source–the culture-specific Elizabethan ideology of 'political Petrarchianism'" (129). According to this ideology, Elizabeth used her sexuality/virginity for patriotic ends to control ruthless men around her. Her sexuality aroused and contained male desire; yet her virginity, "deferred sexuality," allowed her to postpone marriage and with it male control.

Like the aging Queen, the wives "use love as a political device to shape, contain, and deny male desire" (130). Falstaff and Ford (as Master Brooke) act like disappointed Petrarchan lovers in a "game controlled by women" (131). But the humor of the ending reveals a troublesome paradox that "the play cannot reaffirm class hierarchy without also affirming female power in the Queen" (132). However, the Queen's power/political strategy, like the wives', depends on chastity which derives its meaning and strength from the male discourse of gender. Thus, Shakespeare "brings women's power back within reach of a patriarchally inflicted framework, albeit as an expression of patriarchal anxiety rather than of decisive male control" (135).

366.   ---. "Rewriting the Renaissance, Rewriting Ourselves." *Shakespeare Quarterly* 38 (1987): 327-37.

Stephen Orgel (item 345) claims that in looking at Shakespeare psychoanalytically critics are being subjective and reflect their own views. This subjectivity is part of the conflict between new historicist and feminist critics. Feminists see gender as a central issue whereas new historicists view it as one of many cultural forces at work. Feminists have different, flexible perceptions of the structure of Renaissance culture; new historicism is well-defined but unbending.

For example, Jonathan Goldberg is willing to embrace history but not politics, hence feminism. Though he claims that *Mac* voices "anxiety about women," he does admit (item 290) that "women may be denied a voice in patriarchal theory but actually voice power in theatrical practice" (334). Attempting to combine new historicism with feminism, Montrose (item 344) recognizes that the violence used for masculine self-definition is directed against the female. More importantly, Montrose's work reflects one of the primary tensions between the two critical approaches to Shakespeare. New historicism sees the present as a force to neutralize or negate whereas feminists find the present a source of power. The past must be seen through the perceptions of the present; it can make the difference between looking at a dead Shakespeare, as do the new historicists, or live playwright as feminists see Shakespeare.

367. Fiske, Martha. "What Happened to Mrs. Lear?–or, Students Force a Fresh View of *King Lear.*" *English Journal* 76 (1987): 82-85.

Traditional views of Lear as a tragic protagonist need to be rethought thanks to students' perception of his sexist behavior. Lear never reaches the heroic heights for students who abhor his anti-feminine behavior, especially his constant comparison of women with evil, lecherous beasts and monsters. The students do not buy the "fusion" of females with seduction and the "loss of property or love" (83), though they comically refer to Goneril and Regan as "the Social Disease Sisters." Even Gloucester and Edgar are attacked for sexist attitudes. Students denounce Edgar's perception that "Bad guys come from whores and bitches; fathers are just genetic bystanders." Lear's "ultimate insult to women" can be found in his sulphurous pit comparison which is an expression of his double standard. "What happens to the classics if ... hubris is just another word for *macho*?" (85).

368. Fontana, Ernest. "Shakespeare's Sonnet 55." *The Explicator* 45
(1987): 6-8.

Shakespeare's use of "sluttish time" in Sonnet 55 personifies a
feminine time that can destroy a stone statue of the young man
with decay the way a whore might infect him with syphilis. A
corresponding use of "sluts" can be found in *Tim*, Act 4.3. 136-37.
Thus while the "enchantments" of female time deface, the "male
voice" of the poet is "generative and vivifying" (7).

369. Freedman, Barbara. "Separation and Fusion in *Twelfth Night*." In
Psychoanalytic Approaches to Literature and Film. Ed. Maurice
Charney and Joseph Reppen. London: Associated UP;
Rutherford, NJ: Fairleigh Dickinson UP, 1987. 96-119.

As with the fairy tale "Snow White," *TN* focuses on conflicts of
separation and fusion between the sexes and similarly shuts out
the audience by artificial conventions. "The aware audience
vaguely senses that it is being placated with the mere facsimile of
the comic form" (97). The play employs masks, secrets, and
unknown countries as if to ensure the audience's status as
outsiders. The audience is thus denied knowledge of the series of
events that make the action onstage plausible. Each character in
TN is faced with the threat of abandonment, loss, and
disillusionment in a sexual relationship and is forced to come to
terms with that experience. The nature of the play encourages
both audience and character to see what they will, yet reminds
them of the reality that is, thus allowing them to accept
disillusionment gradually. Viola unmasks all the major characters
revealing them for what they are.

370. Grennan, Eamon. "The Women's Voices in *Othello*: Speech, Song,
and Silence." *Shakespeare Quarterly* 38 (1987): 275-92.

The voices of the women in *Oth* stand for morality which is
"implicitly identified...with honest feeling and plain speech" (285).
Desdemona's speech in fact "must serve as the moral measure
necessary to any comprehensive understanding of the play" (288).
In Act 4.3, a "protected enclosure" in which men are absent,

Desdemona and Emilia confidently and freely discuss sex,
regardless of their differences of opinion; the scene "composes a
spectrum of female sexuality–including worldly innocence and
experience, extravagant passion, all forgiving love ... " (282). In
"many ways the most outspoken character" in the play, Bianca
uses direct and simple language to tell Cassio of her jealousy
which contrasts with Othello's "convoluted responses to his own
jealousy" (283). Similarly, Emilia's speech is direct and honest in
defending Desdemona, even though her silence about the
handkerchief provokes tragic consequences. Desdemona's speech
is perfectly balanced between reason and passion, logic and
feeling, showing that she is not the naive innocent. Her speech,
"itself the moral act of her identity" (287), asserts her freedom to
love. Unlike Othello's fantasies about her adultery, Desdemona's
speech is anchored in reality, the physical present. Though Othello
extinguishes her speech, Desdemona is protective and generous
even in silence. Because of Emilia's revelations, the last scene,
like Act 1.3, reveals the "public world waiting upon a woman's
word" (291).

371. Grubb, Shirley Carr. "Women, Rhetoric, and Power: The Women
of Shakespeare's *Richard III* as Collective Antagonist." *DAI* 48
(1987): 1058A. U of Colorado, Boulder.

372. Hinely, Jan Lawson. "Expounding the Dream: Shaping Fantasies
in *A Midsummer Night's Dream*." In *Psychoanalytic Approaches
to Literature and Film*. Ed. Maurice Charney and Joseph
Reppen. London: Associated UP; Rutherford, NJ: Fairleigh
Dickinson UP, 1987. 120-38.

Through the dreams of the play, individual sexual anxieties are
released and transformed and social harmony is reestablished.
MND begins in a male-dominated society, with struggles between
male and female–Theseus and Hippolyta–and between rivals for
the same women–Demetrius and Lysander. Denied the right to
choose for herself, Hermia is forced to allow her father to decide
who will receive her sexual favors as wife. Fleeing Athens, the
lovers move "from waking to dream, from reason to imagination,
from sanity to madness, from limitation to freedom, and from

order to anarchy" (121). The unfinished fight in the woods between Demetrius and Lysander is a substitute for the sexual consummation that has not been achieved. Masculinity is proved through a violent act instead of a sexual one. Jan Kott says that Oberon's dream of Titania falling in love with a foul beast is an essentially brutal fantasy of male wish-fulfillment arousing disgust and abhorrence. Yet Titania's love for Bottom is transfigured into something touching, far different from Oberon's fantasy of revenge. Oberon's fantasy of erotic savagery has been recreated by Titania's maternal tenderness, thus curing Oberon's jealousy. The new roles the characters assume at the end of the play do not challenge the old patriarchal order but transform it. The movement of *MND* goes from "the narcissistic and injurious love characteristic of courtship to the reciprocal and trusting love necessary for harmonious marriage" (137).

373. Hooks, Roberta M. "Shakespeare's *Antony and Cleopatra*: Power and Submission." *American Imago* 44 (1987): 37-49.

In Shakespeare's *AC* "the psychosis at the core of the play involves issues of differentiation from a maternal environment and the difficulties of maintaining an integrated, reality-oriented perspective toward the love object" (37). Both Antony and Cleopatra have trouble recognizing the boundaries between themselves and external objects, a trait generally learned in the weaning process. In Antony's rejection of the political scene and declaration of devotion to Cleopatra he claims his omnipotence, but this omnipotence is established within the maternal sphere created with Cleopatra. Antony's vacillations between Rome and Egypt reflect his contrary desires for the maternal safe zone ("Here is my space" [Act 1.1.34]) and autonomy ("These strong Egyptian fetters I must break,/Or lose myself in dotage" [Act 1.1.120]). Through his suicide, "Antony conceives of death as an extension of the transcendence and stability he has sought in Cleopatra" (46), a recapturing of the pre-oedipal union.

374. Horowitz, Maryanne Cline. "The Woman Question in Renaissance Texts." *History of European Ideas* 8. 4-5 (1987): 587-95.

Renaissance women's etiquette books reveal that
"'womanliness' and 'manliness' are social constructs" (587).
Scholars have been misguided in analyzing fictional female
characters and then trying to apply their findings to the actual
historical situation. In Renaissance texts woman is "an artificial
cultural construct containing intertextual echoes of earlier texts,
both Judaeo-Christian and classical" (589). Gender studies and
theories should be applied to male and female subjects alike; and
other areas of discourse, such as theology and law, should be re-
evaluated. "There were multiple, often conflicting images and
ideas of 'women' afloat in the years of the Continental and
English Renaissance" (589). No ultimate definition of the
Renaissance idea of woman exists because there were too many
diverse individualities involved. Women should be viewed not only
in terms of their social setting, but also within a medical, legal
and religious context.

375. Howard, Jean E. "Renaissance Antitheatricality and the Politics
      of Gender and Rank in *Much Ado About Nothing*." In Howard
      and O'Connor, item 376. 163-87.

Elizabethan theatre upheld the status quo through legislation
and thus served the interests of the powerful. Antitheatrical tracts
claimed that theatre threatened social stability. Plays lied about
present reality, with no real images of truth; actors committed the
unforgivable act of transgressing gender boundaries. Sir Philip
Sidney presents the image of popular theatre as a wayward
woman. Filled with playlets, staged shows, actors, and interior
dramatists, *Ado* dramatizes a world permeated with theatrical
practices; eventually this world regains control over this
theatricality. *Ado* also speaks against itself in regard to its
presentation between truth and illusion by dramatizing the social
consequences of staging lies. Don John's trick at the window
assumes and supports the idea that women are universally prone
to deception. As a bastard, Don John testifies to a woman's
weakness and his role as outsider. Women and bastards are the
natural and inevitable source of social disruption and evil in this
play. The ending of *Ado* proves that "while illusion is everywhere,
good fictions merely reveal a pre-existent truth of nature ... while

evil fictions ... which distort nature melt like manna in the sun and their perpetrators disappear" (182).

376. Howard, Jean E., and Marion F. O'Connor, eds. *Shakespeare Reproduced: The Text in History and Ideology.* New York: Methuen, 1987.

Reviews: British Book News Oct. 1987: 700; *Minnesota Review* (Spring 1988): 238; Barlow, Richard G., *Theatre Journal* 41 (1989): 575-77; Drakakis, John, *Shakespeare Quarterly* 40 (1989): 342-45; Griffin, R.P., *Choice* 25 (1988): 1248; Holderness, Graham, *Modern Language Review* 85 (1990): 141-44; Porter, D., *Theatre Research International* 14 (1989): 88-90; Vickers, Brian, *Times Literary Supplement* 26 Aug. 1988: 933-35.

377. Jardine, Lisa. "Cultural Confusion and Shakespeare's Learned Heroines: 'These are old paradoxes.'" *Shakespeare Quarterly* 38 (1987): 1-18.

Reflecting a cultural ambivalence and tension, Renaissance treatises expressed contradictory attitudes toward the education of women. Paradoxically, learned women were emblematically chaste and wise; yet a "knowing" woman was feared as unruly and threatening for men because of her potentially dominating sexuality. The crux of the plots of *AWW* and *MV* depend on learned women, and the virtues and "forwardness" of their education "are reproduced in the plot strategies" (16). *AWW* emphasizes that Helena's male skills in medicine were sustained "only with difficulty," since they could "emasculate" men. Her knowledge is made public rather than remaining domestically secluded. Helena's "knowing" as demonstrated through folklore references, her jests with Parolles, and her tricking Bertram are feared as "sexually and socially disruptive" acts. Yet through her "chaste service" and atonement in the second part of the play, Helena reconciles "the paradox of the two-faced learned lady" (12) to the satisfaction of the male world. Unlike Helena, Portia is more unruly (she is always on top) and uses greater sophistry; yet her role has "social justification" (14). But like Helena, Portia borrows her knowledge from the male world, a "knowing" associated with "sexual unruliness." Though Portia (who has a "legitimate entitlement to rule") and Nerissa save their husbands, putting them in "positions of servitude," *MV* closes with the "husband's ownership and control of his wife's 'ring'" (17) and thus defuses the issue of women ruling men.

378. Kahn, Coppelia. "Magic of Bounty: *Timon of Athens*, Jacobean Patronage, and Maternal Power." *Shakespeare Quarterly* 38 (1987): 34-57.

Estranged from women and politics, *Tim* would seem to resist questions of gender and power. Yet the play has a psychological core of fantasies about maternal generosity and subsequent betrayal. The Poet's speech in the opening scene depicts Timon's rise and predicts his downfall by seeing the hero as an infant dependent on the Goddess Fortuna, who perpetuates his ruin by changing from mother to a fickle mistress who rejects him. In the first three acts, Timon himself plays the role of Fortuna, bestowing gifts on people and refusing repayment. This gift-giving serves Timon's emotional needs, but he pursues his philanthropy in a way that causes his downfall. Timon becomes dependent on the friends to whom he gave gifts to help him pay his debts. Fortuna has turned into the fickle mistress that the Poet promised; she alienates Timon from his friends. Timon no longer plays the bountiful mother; rather, he lashes out at Fortuna's betrayal. He seeks sustenance from Mother Earth, but she is no better than a whore. His death is described in terms of a maternal embrace. *Tim* gives a sense of women not only as inherently deceptive, but also as objects of erotic pleasure.

379. Kehler, Dorothea. "*The Comedy of Errors* as Problem Comedy." *Rocky Mountain Review of Language and Literature* 41 (1987): 229-40.

Containing an "admixture of genres," *CE* like *AWW* and *MM* ends with an "inconclusive" conclusion. Exploring the problems of marriage, the play focuses on the emotional divorce between spouses. Not a farcical character like her husband Antipholus of Ephesus, Adriana looks forward to Juliet and Desdemona. While she does not seek "sexual equality" or even question male supremacy, Adriana does feel powerless and revolts against a "lack of love" (233). *CE* in fact depicts "the almost inevitable imbalance of love between spouses–an imbalance often aggravated to the woman's disadvantage by societal conditions and restrictions ... " (231). Like her jealous husband, Adriana is guilty of incivility; yet she deserves sympathy. She does not know her husband any longer; he is literally a stranger to her while Antipholus of Syracuse becomes "the honeymoon-lover of her heart's desire" (234). She may abuse the liberty of her tongue, but Antipholus of Ephesus, by lusting after the courtesan, abuses the "liberty of his eyes" (235). Luciana's speech in favor of wifely servitude and male domination "misfires" (234), since it is undermined by Adriana's true love and since the male characters in *CE* are a powerless and, except for Egeon and Solinius, a "sorry lot." Suffering from "commitment phobia" (236), Luciana may later be cured of her matrimonial doubts. In creating a suffering and compassionate Adriana, Shakespeare departed from the traditional presentation of the shrew.

380. ---. "Echoes of the Induction in *The Taming of the Shrew*." *Renaissance Papers 1986* (1987): 31-42.

Renaissance women must have been "disturbed" by being treated like property. *TSh* contains a "subversive subtext" which appealed to these women and which "undercuts the manifest code-affirming surface of the drama" (32). Links between Sly and the Hostess in the Induction and Kate call attention to this subtext. Like the Hostess and Sly, Kate is denied sex. Petruchio deprives her of this benefit a spinster could legitimately seek in marriage. She is made to distort reality or suffer a worse fate in Petruchio's house than in her father's. Kate's having to mistake Vincentio for a young maid is "as disturbing as it is amusing" (36). Petruchio treats her like a beast or a child, and the last part of the play, filled with "dog/wife iterative imagery," (40) echoes the animal imagery of the Induction. "The difference of opinion over which of the three dogs is best foreshadows the bet over which of the three wives is best" (39). Whether Kate in surrendering to Petruchio is a hypocrite or brainwashed is not the point. He is her veterinarian, not her loving spouse, and "to regard Petruchio as the source of Kate's 'cure' is to avert attention from the cultural disease that has made her ill and to applaud her acceptance of that disease ... " (41). Kate has paid a high price for her "warm bed" by vindicating Petruchio's "methods of enforcing Renaissance ideology" (42). The subtext of *TSh* is a subversive parable, for Renaissance women to learn and from which to profit.

381. Lenta, Margaret. "*Othello* and the Tragic Heroine." *Crux: A Journal on the Teaching of English* 21.2 (1987): 26-35.

Shakespeare explores the "problems of being a woman" through Desdemona who "parallels the process" of Othello's breakdown and "in a way is more accessible" (26). A "free" (confident, generous) woman, Desdemona fulfills the role of a ruler's wife by begging for mercy for the guilty. She is also like the Madonna prayed to in the *Memorare*. Entering adulthood, she married Othello because he had the "energy and masculinity" (29) lacking in Venetian men. Though she can be outspoken and public, she is "too unselfconscious" (30). As Othello's jealousy grows more fatal, she loses her freedom. At first she is afraid and "ashamed of that fear"; sensing that Othello laid a trap for her by not telling her before about the magic of the handkerchief, she finally realizes that she cannot deceive herself about tolerating his behavior. Desdemona's naivete in talking with Emilia about adultery in Act 4.3 is strange in light of her earlier joking with Iago in Act 2.1; yet her disbelief signals her own "breakdown" and a "retreat into childishness of the moment, away from ghastly reality" (34). Choosing "heroism rather than strategy," Desdemona becomes vulnerable, though she is still the ideal Shakespeare makes her.

382. Levin, Carole. "'I trust I may not trust thee': Women's Visions of the World in Shakespeare's *King John*." In *Ambiguous Realities: Women in the Middle Ages and Renaissance*. Ed. Carole Levin and Jeanie Watson. Detroit: Wayne State UP, 1987. 219-34.

Though they are powerless in the male world, the three women characters in *KJ*–Eleanor, Constance, Blanche–are "far more insightful" (219) than the men. Eleanor, the "most unscrupulous of the three," would rule "more wisely" than her son, King John, in part because she is the better negotiator. Moreover, she is more clever and witty than her son, shares Queen Elizabeth's values, and astutely lets the Bastard join the royal household, perhaps her "wisest decision" (222). Her opposite in life as well as in death is Constance; the two women are "much fiercer enemies of each other than of their male counterparts" (224). They exchange bitter insults that actually undermine their interests. Less powerful than Eleanor, Constance has only words for her weapons; at the death of her son Arthur, she takes "refuge in a highly rhetorical form of grief." Yet her behavior is not "excessive," as Philip and Pandulph claim, for she displays true grief. A pawn in the male power struggle, Blanche is wooed for political reasons by Lewis who uses the insincere language of courtly love. As male corruption increases in *KJ*, the women's influence as well as their presence fades. King John does not confide in Eleanor about Arthur's murder, and after her death his character "begins to disintegrate" (231).

383. Logan, Robert A. "The Sexual Attitudes of Marlowe and Shakespeare." *Hartford Studies in Literature* 19 (1987): 1-23.

Romantic love for Shakespeare is a combination of passion, awe, and devotion. He uses sexual imagery that the audience will recognize to create "erotic appeal" (10). The forms of love among parents, children and friends were easier for Shakespeare to portray than more complicated sexual love. Making no distinction between homosexual and heterosexual love, the sonnets reveal the moral dilemma of love for the young man and the Dark Lady. Sexual jealousy in Shakespeare is destructive, throwing Hamlet into madness, destroying Othello, and almost doing the same to Leontes. Love, on the other hand, can restore and heal; Lear and Cordelia are reconciled by love. In the comedies, romantic illusions are stripped away to reveal that true love is attained by self-knowledge. Shakespeare's fullest portrayal of romantic and bonded love is through Antony and Cleopatra who realize that time is the enemy of their middle age, yet they rise above it to maintain their love. Throughout *AC* they move away from self-delusion toward self-knowledge. Shakespeare recognizes that although love is amoral, it needs to be governed by moral law.

384. Maus, Katharine Eisaman. "Horns of Dilemma: Gender, Jealousy, and Spectatorship in English Renaissance Drama." *ELH: Journal of Literary History* 54 (1987): 561-83.

The pathology of a jealous husband receives widespread representation in Renaissance drama, especially in Shakespeare and Jonson. Dramatists greatly expanded the brief attention a man's jealousy often receives in their sources. Sexual betrayals were popular because of the analogues between theatrical and sexual excitement which helped to explain the relationship of spectator to spectacle. In Renaissance theatre, the "generic spectator is male, the spectacle is female, and in some sense sexually available" (577). In this "fantasy of spectatorship" the jealous, eavesdropping husband is "not only the model for the Renaissance dramatic spectator, but he is in some respects the most disturbing" (578). Theatrical analogues to spying on one's wife are abundant in eavesdropping and deception scenes. Shakespeare's jealous husbands persistently identify with both the woman and the rival, confusing "heterosexual with homoerotic or homosocial bonds" (570).

According to the jealous husband, the transgressing wife has to be blind to the betrayer's faults, as Hamlet pounds home to Gertrude. The spying husband, like the "supervisor" Othello, has the "compensatory" advantage of seemingly omniscient knowledge and control. Yet caught by public revelation, the cuckold becomes a spectacle himself and is threatened by emasculation. Like the cuckold, the theatre audience has to rely on "inferential reasoning" (576) and is both aware and ignorant, powerful yet marginalized. The audience often does not know the character who exists in a "fictional world elsewhere," such as Gertrude in her relationship with Claudius. Eavesdropping scenes pinpoint the audience's dilemma; they may have paid for the performance but they "seem to be denied control over and knowledge of that which they seem to own" (578).

385. Micheli, Linda McJ. "'Sit by Us': Visual Imagery and the Two Queens in *Henry VIII*." *Shakespeare Quarterly* 38 (1987): 452-66.

The visual and nonverbal elements associated with the two queens in *H8* are contrasted and emphasized in parallel scenes. Anne and Katherine represent the opposing ideals of womanhood. Initially, Katherine is seen as a compassionate consort who observes the forms of protocol while maintaining her independence. Anne is portrayed as unimportant. The attraction between Anne and Henry is first established visually with a dance. She has beauty, intelligence, and virtue, but lacks deep feeling and self-knowledge. Katherine has been recognized for her patience in adversity, yet in the trial scene she is no passive victim but takes an active role in her defense. Katherine's gestures and movements confirm what is found in her words; in Anne's case, words and gestures are sometimes at odds, which makes Katherine more sympathetic.

386. Nakayama, Randall Shige. "Divided Duty: Gender, Identity, and Marriage in *Much Ado about Nothing, All's Well That Ends Well, Troilus and Cressida*, and *Othello*." *DAI* 48 (1987): 1211A. U of California, Berkeley.

387. Newman, Karen. "'And wash the Ethiop white': Femininity and the Monstrous in *Othello*." In Howard and O'Connor, item 376. 143-63.

The Elizabethans and Jacobeans displayed an "extraordinary fascination with and fear of racial and sexual differences" (157). These cultural prejudices wend their way through travel narratives, myths, and commentaries down to Thomas Rymer and even to M.R. Riddley whose Arden edition of *Oth* (1958) charts the Moor's "critical slippage ... from blackness to femininity" (155). Rather than being separated from Othello because of her color, Desdemona has been linked to him through her perceived sexual appetite; her oral greediness for his narratives shows her "blackened whiteness." Through their illicit union, both become the "other," aliens from the white establishment. Desdemona "forfeits" the "status and protection" of the white patriarchy. Critics have thus displaced "the struggle of white against black onto a cultural femininity" (145). Paradoxically, Othello in his own self-fashioning endorses the "dominant sex/gender system" by upholding its "rigorous sexual code" and ownership of wives; yet he is the black sexual monster feared by the white patriarchy. Act 4.1 demonstrates how the "male gaze is privileged" as Bianca represents Desdemona and Othello fulfills the "cultural prejudices" of the age (153). The handkerchief also links Desdemona's femininity and Othello's blackness; according to a culturally biased reading, the handkerchief associates Desdemona with deceit, witchcraft, motherhood, and sexual desire through the strawberries (a metonomy for her sexual parts). Othello's downfall is associated not with a great battle but with the handkerchief, "a trifle, a feminine toy" (156). Rereading *Oth* free from a biased historical discourse is a necessity, for the play "stands in a contestatory relation to the hegemonic ideologies of race and gender in early modern England" (157). By presenting Desdemona as virtuous and sympathetic and Othello as heroic and noble, Shakespeare "dislocates the conventional ideology of gender the play also enacts" (158).

388. --- . "Portia's Ring: Unruly Women and Structures of Exchange in *The Merchant of Venice.*" *Shakespeare Quarterly* 38 (1987): 19-33.

    MV can be read in light of Claude Levi-Strauss's theory that the exchange of women forges male bonds and supports male hegemony and also from Luce Irigaray's feminine perspective that Levi-Strauss's theory ultimately leads to homosexuality. In terms of Levi-Strauss's theory, Portia is a woman exchanged, commodified, and valued as capital. Elizabethan England followed a sex-gender system, like those described in Levi-Strauss's structures of exchange, which dictated that history was determined and commercial transactions were conducted by making women part of the contracts between men. Giving Bassanio her ring, Portia demonstrated the traditional role of a Renaissance woman acknowledging her husband as lord and master. But in giving more than can be returned (like Levi-Strauss's "Big-Man"), Portia "short-circuits the system of exchange and the male bonds it

creates, winning her husband away from the arms of Antonio"
(26). When Bassanio gives Portia's ring to Balthasar, the meaning
of the ring as a symbol of women's obedience is challenged. This
exchange signals the disruption of male hierarchy by admitting
Balthasar/Portia into the transaction. Thus Bassanio "opens his
marriage to forces of disorder, to bisexuality, equality between the
sexes ... " (28). Portia becomes the unruly woman who challenges
the sexual and political structures of a male society by subverting
its rules, by switching gender through a transvestite disguise, and
by her quibbling that associates her with the clown Launcelot
(who is also regarded as "the other").

389. Orgel, Stephen. "Shakespeare and the Cannibals." In *Cannibals,
      Witches, and Divorce: Estranging the Renaissance.* Ed. Marjorie
      Garber. *Selected Papers from the English Institute.* 1985. New
      Series 11. Baltimore: Johns-Hopkins UP, 1987. 41-66.

In *Tem* when Prospero reproaches Caliban for attempting to
rape Miranda, Caliban refuses to see the guilt in his action and
remains unrepentant. "This moment of sexual imperialism [serves]
as a locus of assumptions about exploration and empire" (40). The
Renaissance viewed the New World as cannibalistic, Utopian, and
sexually free. Free love among the natives was not interpreted as
lust, but as a condition of innocence, thus explaining why Caliban
lacks remorse for his attack. Another possible explanation lies in
inherited expansionist values. In history, Romulus encouraged the
rape of Sabine women as an act of political economy and Dido
supposedly kidnapped fifty women from Cyprus to people her
empire. Caliban would instinctively know to use sex to satisfy lust,
but when he complains, "Thou didst prevent me; I had peopled
else/This isle with Calibans" (Act 1.2 350-51), he demonstrates
knowledge of sex as geopolitical method. Undoubtedly, Prospero,
who has taught him everything, is his source of this knowledge.
Prospero's fear for Miranda's virginity supports such a reading,
and the betrothal masque also dramatizes these concerns. "It
invokes a myth in which the crucial act of destruction is the rape
of a daughter; it finds in the preservation of virginity the promise
of civilization and fecundity; and it presents as its patroness of

marriage not Hymen, but Juno, the goddess who symbolizes royal power as well" (65).

390. Parker, Patricia. *Literary Fat Ladies: Rhetoric, Gender, Property.* New York: Methuen, 1987. Esp. Chapter Five, "Transfigurations: Shakespeare and Rhetoric," 67-96; 22-25; and 132-39.

Shakespeare exploits rhetorical tropes beyond the level of pun or textual reference. Paying attention to rhetoric as structure, with its reversals, exchanges, duplications, transformations, and transpositions, helps readers to pose questions about gender and politics in the plays. Correspondences exist between various rhetorical figures and gender distinctions and stereotypes. The Renaissance adage "women are words, men deeds" stands behind the "male anxiety about the feminization of the verbal body" (22). Because of their wordiness (*copia*, or amplification), women are regarded as "fat," profusive. Yet the gender distinction is reversed in wordy men like the effeminate Osric or the bungling Polonius. Links between words and inactivity ("fatness") cause an impotent, feminized Hamlet to think all he can do is talk like a drab.

The rhetorical trope of *hysteron proteron* ("reversal of proper order") has implications for gender and genealogical hierarchies as when Lear makes his daughter his mother, or when Berowne, who must follow the women, becomes wordy in "visiting the speechless sick." *Dilation* and *delation* lie behind the larger context of delay, circumstance, and judicial accusations in *Oth*, where "this polarity of terms" is "relentlessly, subversively, exploited" (87). Desdemona becomes General Othello's "general" as well as his "addition" (particular), so that Othello descends to trifles. Through *antimetabole*, or reversal using the same or similar words, the characters and events in *Ham* are turned upside down, transformed into their opposites. The language of rhetoric usefully explains the gender politics of *Ham* and *Oth*, particularly in the ways women's secrets are revealed.

Reviews: Anderson, J.H., *Studies in English Literature, 1500-1900* 29 (1989): 163-64; Carpenter, M.W., *Queen's Quarterly* 96 (1989): 778-80; Correll, B., *Tulsa Studies in Women's Literature* 8 (1989): 321-27; Herz, J.S., *University of Toronto Quarterly* 59

(1989-1990): 115-16; Quilligan, Maureen, *Shakespeare Quarterly* 40 (1989): 369-71.

391. Paster, Gail Kern. "Leaky Vessels: The Incontinent Women of City Comedy." *Renaissance Drama* 18 (1987): 43-65.

What goes on in the privy–women's relieving themselves–can be used to see "how the ideological constructions of culture masquerade as 'the natural'" (43). In a powerful patriarchal society, the representation of women's "fluid expansiveness" (women as leaky vessels) is linked to their "excessive verbal fluency" and lack of self-control "as a function of gender" (44). Malvolio's "verbal trespass" against Olivia (Act 2.5.87) and Autolycus's more refined reference to excretion in *WT* (Act 4.4.826-28) illustrate the vulnerability of women as defined by their body functions by the patriarchy in city comedies such as Jonson's *Bartholomew Fair* and Middleton's *Chaste Maid in Cheapside.*

392. Pearson, D'Orsay. "Male Sovereignty, Harmony, and Irony in *A Midsummer Night's Dream*." *The Upstart Crow* 7 (1987): 24-35.

Shakespeare seems to uphold traditional male sovereignty in *MND* as outlined in the official "Sermon on the State of Matrimony" based on St. Paul, but Shakespeare "was not bound by that tradition" (33) and in fact presents a view of feminine duty and obedience that is strikingly modern. Like the "Sermon," *MND* presents an ironic, dualistic view of male domination. In both *MND* and "Sermon," male sovereignty does not automatically result from male superiority as much as it is a fiction that women concede. Numerous "disjunctive sovereignty-obedience relationships" (26) in Acts 1 and 2 of *MND* indicate that male dominance is tyranny and that "husband-wife power structures" are chaotic. Asserting their "ego-centered masculinity," Theseus, Oberon, and Egeus use power unjustly. Yet the structure of the play appears to confirm the "rightness of male sovereignty and its essential importance to harmony" (31). Masculine sovereignty, however, depends on "Machiavellian trickery" like that Oberon uses with Titania; authorial fiat as Theseus wields with Egeus and

Hermia; or the "gratification of female desire" when Lysander and Demetrius gain Hermia and Helena. As Theseus's wife, Hippolita characteristically offers a "*civil* form of rebellion to masculine superiority" (32); she contradicts him while appearing to comment objectively on events. Shakespeare concludes that harmony depends on tolerance and the "mutual vision of *duty*" (33).

393. Rackin, Phyllis. "Androgyny, Mimesis, and the Marriage of the Boy Heroine on the English Renaissance Stage." *PMLA* 102 (1987): 29-41.

The idea of gender is related to theatrical representation. The Renaissance theatre witnessed a world where ideas about gender and androgyny were changing. The seventeenth century was becoming "increasingly masculinized" in its thinking. Before the closing of the theatres, however, definitions of gender were "open to play" (38). Five plays–Lyly's *Galathea*, *AYL*, *MV*, *TN*, and Jonson's *Epicene*–illustrate "the changing conceptions of gender" and correspondingly "delineate a similar pattern of decline" of women's position in society resulting in "increasingly rigid and degraded conceptions of gender and femininity" (32). For Shakespeare (unlike Lyly or Jonson) the sexual ambiguity of his boy heroines in their transvestite disguises was "provisionally real" (31). Unlike Jonson, Lyly and Shakespeare saw life and art as complementary. Shakespeare gave female characters in art the power they lacked in reality and so reversed reality. A lowly member of the troupe, Shakespeare's boy actor, who was powerless as a woman, still exercised power, "thus inverting the offstage associations[;] stage illusion radically subverted gender divisions of the Elizabethan world" (38).

Shakespeare, like Lyly, celebrates androgyny and relies on its magic to resolve problems, as Rosalind proves. However, Jonson, who condemns fantastic plays and grotesque androgynes, championed "socially sanctioned gender divisions" (36) and by making all his major characters men he endorsed the "masculine reality principle" (37). In contrast, Shakespeare insisted on the ambivalence and attractiveness of sexual disguise; Rosalind combines Rosalind, Ganymede, and the boy actor. While Jonson and Lyly abolished sex distinctions to satisfy their audiences,

Shakespeare "implies that the relationship between the play and its audience is a kind of sexual transaction or marriage" (36). Mimesis invoking an iron-clad distinction between art and reality led to an "antithetical prejudice" and a rigid male hegemony.

394. Rovine, Harvey. *Silence in Shakespeare: Drama, Power, and Gender.* Ann Arbor: UMI, 1987. Esp. "Women and Silence," 37-51.

Women's silence in Shakespeare defines their obligations to family, husband/lover, and state/monarch. In the comedies, Shakespeare sets up contrastive female pairs, one talkative and assertive and the other quiet and reserved–Julia and Sylvia in *TGV*; Beatrice and Hero in *Ado*; Kate and Bianca in *TSh*. Oftentimes silence helps comic women gain what they want. Kate's silence points to her consent; at the end of the play she is a "woman transformed from a railing shrew to a sober spokeswoman for mutual dependence in marriage" (40). In the tragedies, however, silence is a "condition forced upon women" (41) who find that words are not sufficient to express their feelings. Since love cannot be easily expressed, Cordelia regards silence as "the only genuine response." Contrasting with Rome's "violent rhetoric" (42), Virgilia's lonely silence is a sign of her love for Coriolanus. Ophelia, Shakespeare's "most complex ... silent female character" (44), is compelled by father and king to be silent about Hamlet in public scenes and with him in private ones, too. Cordelia and Virgilia are "not forced to sink" to the level of Ophelia's humiliation, despair, and exploitation. A silent Ophelia (one of Claudius's decoys) present during Hamlet's "To be or not to be" soliloquy further convinces Hamlet that she is part of the plot against him. In a "mixed genre such as romance," Hermione's silence is a sign of her "tragic separation" and serves to "entice Leontes as it might in comedy" (50-51). Women's silence reflects society's gender distinctions.

395. Savers, Ann C. "The Elizabethan Shepherdess: Major Types and Variations." *DAI* 47 (1987): 2600A. U of California, Riverside.

396. Scheman, Naomi. "Othello's Doubt/Desdemona's Death: The
     Engendering of Skepticism." In *Power, Gender, and Values*. Ed.
     Judith Genova. Edmonton, Alberta: Academic Printing and
     Publishing, 1987. 113-33.

     The same impulse toward skepticism that leads Othello to
     adopt Iago's world view is at work in Descartes's *Meditations*.
     Othello's tragedy results from remembering an earlier maternal
     world which is breaking apart and which he must repudiate. Such
     male ambivalence toward women is inevitable. Men must feel that
     they control women, yet they recall their dependence on and
     intimacy with the mother. This anxiety "permeates" (117) *Oth* and
     Meditations. Othello's epistemological dependence was fixed on
     the magical world represented by Desdemona, yet Iago's
     "alternate metaphysics" and Cartesian epistemology (118) trap
     Othello into thinking he can have "greater clarity of dispassionate
     objectivity." Ironically, male bonding is not a threat to Othello but
     female connections are. Othello flees a comedic, or maternal,
     nature–characterized by "interdependency, trust, vulnerability, and
     epistemic reciprocity" (122)–for a paternalistic, or legalistic, one.
     The handkerchief, like Descartes's ball of wax, is a shifting
     signifier. At first symbolizing Desdemona's power over Othello,
     the handkerchief moves from being a maternal to a paternal sign
     in Act 5. Othello's "knowledge" of Desdemona goes through a
     similar change–from seeing her as a particular human being to
     regarding her in general terms as a contemptible female.
     Descartes and *Oth* address the issues of seeing, in both literal and
     metaphoric ways; Othello replaces Desdemona's transcendent
     vision with Iago's rational-empirical proofs. He accepts Iago's
     views of Desdemona because he fears being vulnerable to her,
     wants her to be an "autonomous desiring other" (125), and yet
     fears that by being so she will cuckold him. Most painfully,
     Desdemona offers Othello a world "far more real" than any Iago
     could promise (126).

397. Shiner, Roger A. "Masculinizing the Problem of Skepticism." In
     Power, Gender, and Values. Ed. Judith Genova. Edmonton,
     Alberta: Academic Printing and Publishing, 1987. 135-141.

Responding to Scheman (item 396), Shiner agrees with her about (a) the parallels between post-Cartesian epistemology and "the impulse that leads Othello to embrace Iago's view of the world" (135), (b) the destructive male ambivalence toward the "maternal element of female sexuality," and (c) the deplorable male perspective of sexuality (MPS) in terms of dominance. But a "central worry" about Scheman's thesis is that males as well as females can be deceived knowers. Both sexes exist in a community of knowers. Scheman's "MPS theme, then, amounts to a failure to acknowledge the distinction between features of the human condition as such and features of certain particular human situations" (138). Both men and women struggle for power in relationships. Being free and independent creatures, Desdemona and Othello are vulnerable. In a marriage both partners are jointly responsible for its maintenance. Scheman's claim that Othello's "avoidance of knowledge" is the result of his being typically male ("feeble and gullible") strips him of his tragic dimension, wrongly denies that males are incapable of sexual relations, and forgets that men as well as women need "liberation, enlightenment, re-education ... " (141).

398. Stapleton, Michael Lee. "The Lords and Owners of Their Faces: Shakespeare's Women and Power." *DAI* 48 (1987): 1462A. U of Michigan.

399. Stockholder, Kay. *Dream Works: Lovers and Families in Shakespeare's Plays*. Toronto: U of Toronto P, 1987.

In Shakespeare's plays about families and lovers, conscious and unconscious aims are often in conflict. Hamlet's stated purpose–avenging his father's death–is at odds with his unrecognized, inner desires, carried out through the words and actions of other characters. Claudius's murder of King Hamlet shows young Hamlet's unconscious wish to remove the obstacle to his assuming adult maturity and power. In his idealization of his father, Hamlet obscures his ambivalent sexual feelings. The pure marriage bed becomes the "incestuous sheets" of Gertrude and Claudius. "Male sexuality is associated with satyrlike lust and garbage, woman's with the diseased desire for it, and both with all that is rotten in Denmark" (45). However, Hamlet, as dreamer, has created the marriage of Claudius and Gertrude out of his own incestuous desires; he is able to watch and detach himself simultaneously from their "diseased passion."

In *TrC*, the mock-courtly stance of Troilus is shadowed by a cruder vision of love, expressed through both Diomedes and Helen. In *MM*, "Angelo generates Isabella, who as a novitiate represents chastity and purity, to force him to recognize his own sexual desires, and ... to protect him against the consequences of their illicit fulfillment" (78). Othello's unconscious urges are defined in part in the character of Iago and are revealed in his relationship to Desdemona. Iago's sexual and social sense of inferiority echo Othello's fears about his marriage. Desdemona, as dreamer, creates her unconscious desire for violence in the circumstances which lead to Othello's accusations. When Macbeth creates the witches, he is unconsciously recreating Lady Macbeth, a woman whose sexual identity is ambiguous. Furthermore, he plays out a deviant oedipal pattern in killing the father (Duncan) and converting his wife (who is childless) into a maternal figure.

In *Lear*, the protagonist "defines himself as both legitimate king and father, and generates a world in which familial and social authority function as analogues for each other" (118). Loss of kingly authority means loss of parental authority, and thus he becomes both maligned subject and abused child. Lear goes through various stages of identification so that he may "know himself as a man rather than as a king and father" (119) and so that he may reclaim Cordelia. Unlike these earlier protagonists, Antony is more consciously aware of the conflicting desires within himself. "However, his grasp on his freedom from the miasma that surrounds heterosexual love for other protagonists is tenuous, for ... the martial valour that allows him to define himself as a lover is undermined by his doing so" (149).

In Shakespeare's later romances, the quasi-magical (or in *Tem*, the truly magical) are the means to happy endings resembling daydreams, or wish fulfillment, more than actual dreams. "Therefore, their benign resolutions suggest the repression rather than dissolution of the conflicts that shape them" (170).

Reviews: Kahn, Coppelia, *Renaissance Quarterly* 41 (1988): 749-51; Levenson, Jill L., *Studies in English Literature, 1500-1900*

28 (1988): 351-53; Rubio, Gerald J., *Sidney Newsletter* 8.2 (1988): 38; Vickers, Brian, *Times Literary Supplement* 26 Aug.-1 Sept. 1988: 933-35.

400. Waller, Marguerite. "Academic Tootsie: The Denial of Difference and The Difference It Makes." *Diacritics* 17 (1987): 2-20.

Stephen Greenblatt's *Renaissance Self-Fashioning* (Chicago: U of Chicago P, 1980), like Sidney Pollack's movie *Tootsie*, suffers from the "discrepancy between old signifying habits and new thematic possibilities" (3). In Greenblatt's reading of *Oth*, the threatening "other," whether woman or outsider, consolidates the self-fashioned identity. However, Greenblatt's consideration of the "other" doubly denies difference: 1) by "privileging male interests, desires, and investments over those of the female" (14), he labels Desdemona "deviant" because she chooses to create a selfhood outside the hierarchical structure; 2) by projecting his own views on the excluded other, he fails "to see and hear that other in terms of the violence being done to her or him by that exclusion" (14). Actually, Desdemona is a potentially creative rather than a destructive force, offering alternatives to Othello's narrative identity.

Iago's motives stem from more than just a detached pleasure in unfashioning Othello. Iago's own selfhood is defined within the political constructs of Venice; his expected promotion is given to an outsider, a Florentine, by another outsider, a Moor. Desdemona's disobedience to her father and marriage to a black man further threatens the patriarchal hierarchy which has shaped Iago's identity. Iago's method is not to exploit Othello's sexual anxiety, as Greenblatt would have it. Sexual anxiety is a trait of "ordinary" Venetians. Rather, Iago gives Othello a chance to escape the role of "licentious and inferior" black man (13) and to "participate actively and passionately in the emotions, jealousies, and vengeances of full-fledged Venetian male selfhood" (18). The fatal consequences of the tragedy result because, in order for Othello to become a member of the existing patriarchal structure, Desdemona must conform to the prescribed female role, a role she has rejected when she first chose to be Othello's wife.

401. Williamson, Marilyn. "'When men are rul'd by women':
     Shakespeare's First Tetralogy." *Shakespeare Studies* 19 (1987):
     41-59.

   The first tetralogy presents a series of strong women.
Traditional traits of strong women are Amazonian prowess,
prophecy, witchcraft, unnatural ambition, and sexual freedom.
These women are hated because they represent deep male fears
of powerlessness and rebellion of the "weaker" sex. The Amazons
were admired for their strength and bravery, but were seen as
unnatural. Joan of Arc, who has the power of prophecy, is
portrayed this way. Because her sexuality is ambiguous, she is
turned into a witch. "Joan is a saint when the French are
victorious and a deceitful dame when they lose" (45). Joan is the
mirror of Talbot's weakness, which is why he and his son refuse
to fight with her. Margaret D'Anjou similarly becomes an
Amazon by fighting for Henry and Edward and is associated with
child killing and everything contrary to her gender. In *2H6*,
marriage becomes an emblem for the husband's public
deficiencies. The ambitions of Eleanor and Margaret contrast with
their husbands' patience. Richard III uses his deformity to reject
not only love of mother and kin but male bonds as well.

402. Wilson, Rob. "Othello: Jealousy as Mimetic Contagion." *American
     Imago* 44 (1987): 213-33.

   Applying Rene Girard's analysis of male jealousy as mimetic
desire (see item 289), "we can say that fraternal doubles such as
Iago and Othello can be appeased or reconciled only through the
sacrificial annihilation of their common female victim,
Desdemona, that *pharmakon* of difference who is both guilty
(poison) and guiltless (medicine) in arousing their initial desire in
a social situation where male jealousy induces the stigmata of
contagion itself" (215-16). Iago's manipulations serve to remove
the differences between himself and his stronger rival, Othello.
Iago's jealousy is a contagious agent which infects Othello who up
until then had not concerned himself with rivals. Mimetic desire,
or envy, is also present in females, as evidenced by Desdemona's
"rapt attention" to the tales of Othello's heroic exploits. With this

balance of female desire "we can more adequately see that the play is not only centered in the male will to power (Iago) but also in the female will to submit power to the more self-abnegating mandates of generous love (Emilia)" (228).

403. Woodbridge, Linda. "Black and White and Red All Over: The Sonnet Mistress Amongst the Ndembu." *Renaissance Quarterly* 40 (1987): 247-97.

In its use of ritualistic colors, Renaissance love poetry, including Shakespeare's sonnets, poems, and plays, has "roots in tribal rites of sexual maturity ... its delicate sighs and lovely languishings are somehow connected with circumcisions, animal masks, and smearings of the body with red ochre" (263) used by the African Ndembu. The color symbolism in the red/white/black triad is sex-linked indicating conflicts between the sexes as well as the opposition between the seasons. Red and white stand for love and sexuality, the return of the spring and resurrection. To suggest her resurrection, Hermione is appropriately a marble statue. Black is associated with lust and death. This red/white/black "imagery saturates Shakespeare's early poems. *Venus and Adonis* and *Rape of Lucrece* deal with sexual antagonism, female lusting after unwilling male in the one, and male lusting after unwilling female in the other, and both sexual poems culminating in death" (250). As fertility symbols, Venus and Adonis are described in terms of red and white; their colors conflicting with winter blackness. The beauty of the young man in the sonnets is immortalized through red and white; the mistress is associated with blackness. The color triad parallels the love triangles of two men (one a fool) and one woman in the plays. Foolish suitors include Roderigo, Thurio, and Cloten. The sequence of the sonnet cycle also "resolves itself into a love triangle of one woman and two men." The sonnet cycle, therefore, reveals a "connection between human wooing and crop fertility" (269).

1988

404. Bassnett, Susan. "Sexuality and Power in the Three Parts of *King Henry VI.*" *Shakespeare Jahrbuch* 124 (1988): 183-91.

Queen Elizabeth was a "split entity" (190), a sovereign and a woman, and her two roles were not easy to reconcile in the late sixteenth century. Portraits of Elizabeth reflected the ambiguity of her masculine and feminine traits. But society was moving away from the idealism of humanism, which advocated the education of women and acknowledged them as rulers, to the Enlightenment's skepticism about women who were perceived as irrational. Women were increasingly marginalized "in public life" (184) during the last part of Elizabeth's reign. Shakespeare's female protagonists in the three parts of *1H6* "typify the changed attitude to women and public power in an age of lost ideals" (190). These plays mirror the troubles of the early 1590s, and their popularity indicates that audiences "encoded" representations on stage into their awareness of events (186). Reflecting the age's worry, the three *H6* plays used "images of femininity as central metaphors" (187); in *Part 1*, the emphasis is on maidens (Joan, Countess of Auvergne); in *Part 2* wives (Eleanor, Margaret); and *Part 3* queens (Margaret, Elizabeth). Each of these women projected negative images of femininity, as deceitful, ruthless, and cruel. Margaret, who is "reminiscent of Lady Macbeth" (188), displays unnatural feminine feelings and uncharacteristically leads an army. These characters show the disorders that result when women enter public life; civil strife mirrors sexual problems. With *R3*, there is no doubt that the "age of warrior maidens and queens has very definitely ended ... " (189).

405. Berek, Peter. "Text, Gender, and Genre in *The Taming of the Shrew*." In *"Bad" Shakespeare: Revaluations of the Shakespeare Canon*. Ed. Maurice Charney. Rutherford, NJ: Fairleigh Dickinson UP, 1988. 91-104.

Though a sexist, Shakespeare was less so than his contemporaries, and his "attitudes toward gender may have been more supple and complex" (102) than theirs. The badness of the bad quarto of *TSh* and the genre of farce illuminate Shakespeare's views of patriarchy and women. *Taming of A Shrew*, the bad quarto, endorses the "Plain Man's Sexist Reading" in ways that *TSh* does not. Changes in characterization and ideology between the bad quarto and *TSh* show that Shakespeare made Kate more sympathetic and that her speech on obedience in Act 5 is much more personal and "grows out of the dramatic situation" (95). In the bad quarto, her speech is so impersonal that it could be spoken by a man as well as a woman. The bad quarto also displays a far more rigidly "theological antifeminism" than *TSh* which endorses patriarchy more for social reasons (97). Equally likely, the popularity of the bad quarto (as the pirated text of *TSh*) demonstrates that Elizabethan audiences approved the more sexist attitudes which they wrongly thought were in *TSh*. Any ironic reading of Kate's Act 5 speech, therefore, becomes "ahistorical" (98). As farce, *TSh* does more than provoke laughter; it does not lack meaning but denies it. But Petruchio and Kate "find ways of adapting while accepting all patriarchy's premises" (101). *TSh* confronts Shakespeare's likely distress with patriarchy through aggression and violence. These characteristics of badness at this stage of Shakespeare's career prove that he was dealing with "unassimilated conflict" without resolving it.

406. Bowers, A. Robin. "'The Merciful Construction of Good Women': Katherine of Aragon and Pity in Shakespeare's *King Henry VIII*." *Christianity & Literature* 37 (1988): 29-51.

Katherine's function in *H8* "points up the critical revisionism of the present century, in which female characters generally have been given short shrift" (30). A "figure of thematic as well as dramatic significance" (31), Katherine, who is the "symbolic paradigm" of rulers, elicits pity for others whose downfalls bracket hers–Buckingham, Wolsey, and Cranmer. Her tragedy is "critically located, explicitly dramatized to produce audience response of pity" (30). In the Renaissance, pity was not a passive but active virtue required of men as well as women. Katherine pleads "Desdemona-like" for Buckingham, urging pity for him from the audience. At Katherine's own trial, Anne Bullen "reinforces audience admiration and pity" for her (37). In Act 4, Katherine's dream is influenced by religious imagery associated with the Assumption; she is "apotheosized before our eyes." She has rejected despair and exhibits charity and forgiveness for Wolsey. There is an "iconographic bond" between Katherine and Elizabeth who is the "phoenix-like reincarnation" of the Spanish queen. Unlike the individual heroines of romance (e.g., Hermione), *H8* offers a "dual romance heroine" in Katherine and Elizabeth (44-45). While critics may proclaim that Henry towers over the play, Katherine reigns "spiritually over the inner turmoil which produces outward actions" (46).

407. Cacicedo, Alberto. "Forum: Shakespeare and Feminist Readings." *PMLA* 103 (1988): 817-18.

Although Richard Levin (item 421) accuses feminist critics of partial (incomplete, biased) readings, he himself is partial in not understanding *Oth*, which combines the unique with the physical. Levin's assertion that patriarchy is responsible for both tragedy and the happy endings of comedy ignores the protesting silence of the women at the end of *Ado*. The comedies pose "profound problems" for both sexes. Levin forgets that all power strategies, including the "malady" of masculinity, are problematic.

408. Cahn, Steven M. "The Wife of Lear." *Shakespeare Newsletter* 38 (Fall/Winter 1988): 51.

Cordelia is far more like her father–proud, faithful, and loving–than like her mother who must have influenced Goneril and Regan who knew her better and longer than Cordelia did. Lear's wife must have earlier duped him the way Goneril and Regan did.

409. Calderwood, James L. "Appalling Property in *Othello*." *University of Toronto Quarterly* 57 (1988): 353-75.

Desdemona is victimized by a "proprietary husband claiming absolute title to his wife's body" (370). Yet Desdemona refuses to allow herself to be a piece of property in Act 1 by standing up to her father and by choosing Othello for her husband. Her "distinctive identity," her own self as property, is threatened by the way Othello regards her. Still fashioning an identity for himself, Othello views Desdemona as an "external metaphor that reflects his inner parts" (358). Transforming her into an "aggrandized version of his own I," Othello robs Desdemona of her own I, her own identity. Because Othello possesses the only I, excluding Desdemona from the narrative and making her a third person, she "even more than Othello ... seems the outsider in the first act" (360). As Othello's "metaphorizing mirror," Desdemona looks through his blackness, scrubbing it away with her words. Reinforcing his sense of self at Desdemona's expense, Othello becomes obsessed with her surface appearance, denies her speech (she is a blank page as in Act 4.2.71-72), and does not listen to her when she talks about Cassio or herself. In death Desdemona remains silent.

In keeping with the male concept of property rights, unfaithful wives are whores; it is "merely a question of private versus public ownership" (366). Emilia, a "feminine Shylock" asking "Hath not women certain rights" and an analogue to the Nurse in *RJ*, attacks men who as property owners make arbitrary rules to control women. Although Desdemona is a victim of such property rights, she is "more, and less, than that" (369). Her death is neither a selfless surrender to patriarchal power, the "ultimate feminine fulfillment" (368), nor a challenge to such a code. Seen in light of her love for Othello rather than in terms of the "institution of marriage," Desdemona's death finds her retaining her identity as she purges "Othello's illusions, and beyond them, the illusions of masculine authority" (370). Truly, Desdemona is guilty of the sin of love, "absolute constancy."

410. Case, Sue-Ellen. *Feminism and Theatre.* New York: Methuen, 1988. Esp. 7; 21-27; 39; 117.

The cultural fiction of having boys play women in Shakespeare's theatre points to the patriarchal suppression of women. Having its roots in the Church's repression of the female body because of its sensuality, Shakespeare's celibate theatre used boys who were linked with women because both groups were "dependent on and inferior to the adult male" (22). Cross-gender casting, however, led to the stage being the "site for homoeroticism" (23), substantiated and denounced by the Puritan attacks on the theatre. Traditional, patriarchal critics such as Harley Granville-Barker used aesthetic arguments (boys were more artistic and better suited for stylized theatre) to legitimatize the exclusion of women. Even feminist critics such as Linda Bamber (item 175) and the editors of *The Women's Part* (item 126) ignore the "insidious implications for women" by "reading images of women in the text" (25) instead of deconstructing the texts to find the "power of misogyny" in cross-gender casting. Did women in Shakespeare's audience recognize this casting as a homoerotic game, or did they conclude that women "are only sexual as boys"? The "fictional female" in Shakespeare implies that woman is an object of exchange in a "homoerotic economy" (as in *MV*) and that such fiction is necessary to "negotiate the taboo against homosexuality" (26).

411. Cohen, Walter. "'None of woman born': Shakespeare, Women, and Revolution." *Shakespeare Jahrbuch* 124 (1988): 130-41.

Shakespeare's romantic comedies offer the ultimate vision of gender relations in realistic ways of providing pictures of female chastity and married love. The tragedies are misogynistic, portraying sexual betrayal, betrayal of trust, unnatural sexuality, and prostitution through transvestism. *Mac* is the most misogynistic of the tragedies. Opposed to the traditional reading of the play, where Lady Macbeth rejects her role as wife to push her husband toward an extreme masculinity, the misogynist approach necessitates the complete expulsion of women from a man's world. Female sexuality is metaphorically attacked. Indeed, "to be human is to be a man but not a woman ... to assert mastery over a woman" (135). Macbeth is defeated by Macduff because he is completely divorced from women by virtue of his Caesarian birth. *Mac* also reveals contemporary fear about female assertiveness, but ultimately supports the "blending of gender and class" that makes up a patriarchal hierarchy.

412. Daalder, Joost. "Shakespeare's Attitude to Gender in *Macbeth*." *Journal of the Australasian Universities Language and Literature Association* 70 (1988): 366-85.

Shakespeare's views on sex are complex, not simplistic. In the sonnets man is hermaphroditic; in the comedies woman rules. But it would be misleading to assume that Shakespeare automatically thought women were superior despite the exceptional accomplishments of his heroines. *Mac* makes a number of statements about gender. Arguing that *Mac* presents Shakespeare's "androgynous vision" where gender differences are only a matter of the mind, Robert Kimbrough (item 226) ignores the important fact that Shakespeare emphasized vital differences between the sexes in this play. Believing that women's desire for marriage–and childbearing–were "internal and innate" (370), Shakespeare presents Lady Macbeth violating her sex and denying "her deepest instincts to herself" (374). Male society does not deny/assign such maternal inclinations to her. Accordingly, it would be "inappropriate for Macbeth to be too full of the milk of human kindness, because he is a man" (372).

Unlike Lady Macbeth who rejects parenthood, Macbeth's preoccupation with children argues that Shakespeare "sees him as perverting his manhood less than Lady Macbeth does her womanhood" (376). It is not misogynistic to say Lady Macbeth has a "more restricted vision" than her husband who is "less likely to hide things from himself" (379). Though Macbeth is no less evil than his wife, he needs the witches more than she does to engender evil; and he "worries more abut the consequences" than she does. The Macduffs offer "healthier notions of manhood and womanhood" (381). *Mac* reveals that Shakespeare's "world is male-dominated," though he rejects macho images and violence. Shakespeare does not subscribe to a sexist view since he asks us to see "certain traits of mind and actions as 'male' and others as 'female'" (384).

413. Drakakis, John. "The Engendering of Toads: Patriarchy and the Problem of Subjectivity in Shakespeare's *Othello*." *Shakespeare Jahrbuch* 124 (1988): 62-80.

In *Oth,* Shakespeare's characters are inscribed in the images and myths of patriarchal order employing the political imagery of authority and subjection. Concepts of subjectivity, social status, and gender roles develop through a dialectical process. The tragic hero is displaced when Othello's dispensation of justice as governor and husband is challenged by Desdemona's innocence. "A compensatory authority can only be re-asserted through a revised inscription of the patriarchal subject as the 'self' which accepts full responsibility for its demonized 'other'" (71). The tragic human subject is constructed in part by its difference from female subjectivity, a potentially subversive element. Female thus becomes the "other" of patriarchy. Yet *Oth* questions gendered human subjects within dominant patriarchal discursive structures. Desdemona forsakes the patriarchal authority of her father but accepts subjection to her husband. Through the image of the cuckold, Othello inherits "the fear through which patriarchy registers its loss of possession, passed on to him by the dispossessed father" (74). Othello refers to Desdemona's body as "a storehouse, a geographical space, and finally as an aberration of nature" (74). Masculine identity and emotional life are derived from this "other." Through cultural stereotyping, sexual difference becomes gender ideology located in patriarchal morality. Othello accepts this stereotyping as a standard for judging Desdemona. The magic of the handkerchief reflects female honor, the means of preserving masculine fidelity. Its loss threatens the household. The women themselves contribute to the inscription of the female in patriarchal discourse, e.g., Emilia in Act 4.3 when she places the responsibility for women's behavior on men, without achieving

an independent identity in patriarchal discourse. Desdemona
becomes the "ideal," Emilia the "pragmatic," and Bianca the
"marginalized."

414. Garner, Shirley Nelson. *"The Taming of the Shrew:* Inside or
Outside the Joke?" In *"Bad" Shakespeare: Revaluations of the
Shakespeare Canon.* Ed. Maurice Charney. Rutherford, NJ:
Fairleigh Dickinson UP, 1988. 105-119.

TSh is a bad play because it depends on a sexist, humorless
joke which excludes women. Its assumptions about women and
sexuality are male dominated; in fact, *TSh* was "acted for the male
characters of the Induction" (108). Unlike Shakespeare's other
comedies, *TSh* offers no mutuality, nor does it radiate fear of
cuckoldry. Instead, it dramatizes the male need to dominate
women. Petruchio's taming Kate is to comfort other men in *TSh*
and was to be seen as acceptable, not cruel, since shrews were
treated like animals. *TSh* releases its misogyny in taming the way
Hamlet or Othello do through madness. Justifying *TSh* as farce,
critics wrongly dismiss the play's cruelty, which must be taken
seriously to "give credence to its misogyny" (109). Judging women
in terms of male desire makes Kate follow "patriarchal
prescriptions." Even though Kate and Petruchio are shrews (his
shrewishness is "latent"), they are not treated equally. His
overbearing behavior outweighs her words. Because *TSh* does not
present a fair contest and because Kate is threatened by isolation
and Petruchio's violence, the play lacks humor and suspense. Kate
is forced to surrender her reality (the true reality) and her high-
spirited voice. Silenced, she speaks someone else's words. Even if
we see Petruchio joining her in the joke, Kate is still the victim of
the assumptions of patriarchy. One of the "most difficult" aspects
of *TSh* is setting women against each other. More limited than
Shakespeare's other comedies, *TSh* reveals that the story of Kate
and Petruchio "did not quite work" for Shakespeare (118). He
never again showed women treated so harshly, except in the
tragedies.

415. Green, Douglas. "'The Unexpressive She': Is There Really a Rosalind?" *Journal of Dramatic Theory & Criticism* 2 (1988): 41-52.

Rosalind is not an independent woman; she has no identity besides the feminine "Other." She is "the periphery brought center-stage" (41). At the end of the play she follows the traditional role allowed her and gets married. Rosalind is the object of Orlando's desire and subject of his sonnets. Viewed from a modern perspective, she is unable to express herself. The boy actor who plays Rosalind also undermines the female character's apparent freedom. Shakespeare's women characters are the product of a male imagination. "Rosalind is a Shakespearean product exchanged between Ganymede and Orlando, between the boy actor and the adult male actor, and between Shakespeare, through the boy actor, and the Elizabethan audience" (42). The play thus exposes love as a creation of the male mind. "Such a beloved is the image of masculine desires, and nothing in herself" (43). Rosalind's real function is that of mediator, maintaining harmonious relationships. *AYL* shows male fear of Rosalind's female power, but such power is curtailed by the social act of marriage. "Even an artist as great as Shakespeare does not transcend the boundaries of his culture" (48).

416. Hamer, Mary. "Cleopatra: Housewife." *Textual Practice* [Cardiff] 2 (1988): 159-79.

The changing visual representations of Cleopatra from Boccaccio to de Braij signal "the reinforcing and renegotiation of gender differences that took place in early modern Europe" (160). In Boccaccio, Cleopatra at her banquet and with her asp challenged patriarchal power and male rule at home. Two hundred years later, Cleopatra was inscribed as a model of domestic concord, no doubt as a result of the changing attitudes toward marriage. For Rome, Cleopatra was more a "threat to the Law of the Fathers" than an "erotic symbol" (163). In the course of history she was defined as the "Other," her forbidden sexuality becoming subversive, as Shakespeare's Cleopatra appears. In light of Cleopatra's liabilities, Queen Elizabeth was keenly aware of the "anomalousness" of her position. By 1670, Cleopatra's appetites were transformed into duty (176).

417. Horwitz, Eve. "'The Truth of Your Own Seeming': Women and Language in *The Winter's Tale*." *Unisa English Studies* 26 (1988): 7-13.

WT contrasts male and female perceptions of language and time, reflecting "masculine and feminine visions of life" (9). As in *Oth*, words are related to reality in *WT*. Men's uncertainty about women "surround the meaning of woman." In Leontes's masculine world, "courtly antitheses and rational control" oppose a "feminine world of ... mutability and paradox" (9). The ambiguities of courtly language trigger Leontes's jealousy; male language with its binary opposites is associated with patriarchal control and death while the woman's language in *WT* is concerned with flux, fluidity, and creativity and helps to illustrate the theories of feminine language proposed by Julia Kristeva and Helene Cixous. But the feminine language of "natural flux" threatens disorder and uncertainty for Leontes. Unlike the female response to Hermione's pregnancy as a sign of growth and transcendence, Leontes judges it as grotesque. While Leontes's language degenerates into abuse, Hermione's "consistently statuesque and heroic diction confers a moral strength on her that contrasts strongly with her real powerlessness in the face of tyranny" (10). Yet in having to acknowledge Perdita, Leontes submits to the female (paradoxical) cycle of life and death. Perdita's creative imagination, her creative language, is not courtly; she "creates a fictive poetic world by re-incarnating nature into words" (12). Free from sexual ambiguities, Perdita's language unites the polarities that disrupted Leontes's court and marriage. Women have redemptive power and moral force through the fictions and silences associated with them. Through Hermione's statue "life is generated by death, speech by silence, and love restored by trust while the idealized image of the lost woman is recreated in the male imagination" (13).

418. Howard, Jean E. "Crossdressing, The Theatre, and Gender Struggle in Early Modern England." *Shakespeare Quarterly* 39 (1988): 418-40.

Shakespeare's age inveighed against crossdressing as a violation of the social and gender categories rigidly fixed by a patriarchal hierarchy. The fact that such attacks were made against crossdressing signals that it was a struggle to maintain such a patriarchal order. Men who crossdressed were shameful; women were masterless creatures usurping male power and guilty of sexual license. Social changes "produced sites of resistance and possibilities of new powers for women" (427). But crossdressing on the stage was "not a strong site of resistance to the period's patriarchal sex-gender system" (439). While plays expressed anxiety about female dominance and the "fragility of male rule," they did not do so uniformly (430). Three Shakespearean comedies where women dressed like men reflect a variety of responses to patriarchy. In *TN*, which treats gender conservatively, the crossdressed Viola, who announces a "properly feminine subjectivity" (432), is used to punish Olivia, an unruly, wealthy woman who is a greater threat to "masculine privilege and prerogatives." Viola does not crossdress to "protest gender iniquities" in order to survive.

In contrast, Portia's disguise in *MV* is a "vehicle for assuming power," and while she "hardly dismantle[s] the sex-gender system" (433) she demonstrates that a woman can assume a position of power as well as a man. She "rewrites her position within patriarchy even as she takes up the role of wife" (438). Rosalind actually confirms the gender system by acknowledging herself a lovesick maiden and thereby defuses an audience's fear of a threatening woman. Theatricalizing herself, Rosalind educates Orlando to acquire "more enabling" ideologies of gender. Overall, though, the theatre, which is a site of contradictory ideologies, recuperates threats to the sex-gender system. Because of their enhanced new freedoms, the citizen wives in the audience were more dangerous to hegemonic male power than Shakespeare's "fictions of crossdressings" (440).

419. Hunter, Dianne. "Doubling, Mythic Difference, and the Scapegoating of Female Power in *Macbeth*." *Psychoanalytic Review* 75 (1988): 129-152.

The ideology of succession in *Mac* requires an "oedipal scapegoat" in which female powers are seen in the form of demonized witchcraft. The political tensions between men and women result from women's power over childbirth and early infancy, and, therefore, over succession and continuity. The ambiguity lies in the fact that "man depends on woman for birth, but must rid himself of her in order to be re-born." Tension in *Mac* also exists between orderly succession through inheritance and unlawful seizure of power through regicide. The assassins are associated with the collapse of hierarchy; ironically enough, Malcolm wishes for the assassination, too. "Macbeth and the witches who announce his wishes are scapegoats to the legitimized masculine imagination of the play" (140). Female ascendancy is linked to disorder and excessive violence in the universe whereas the male ascendancy of Malcolm restores the realm of ordered differences. Asserting her own powers, Lady Macbeth becomes "unsexed," and in yielding to her feminine influence, Macbeth is "unmanned." In murdering Duncan, a figure of "benevolent androgyny," Macbeth symbolically castrates himself because he will not free himself from a female environment. All the women in the play are eliminated as a prelude to Macbeth's own death. The fact that Macduff had a mother "denies a fantasy of male self-generation; but contradictorily ... sustains the sense that violent separation from the mother is the mark of a successful man" (144). Masculine difference is achieved by canceling the feminine. The topical context of the play helps to signal the transition from female to male power, namely, from Elizabeth to James.

420. Jackson, Gabriele Bernhard. "Topical Ideology: Witches, Amazons, and Shakespeare's Joan of Arc." *English Literary Renaissance* 18 (1988): 40-65.

Although critics have consistently condemned Joan of Arc for her sexual and political crimes, she is not a consistent character with a coherent selfhood. She is a disjunctive figure who plays many contradictory roles reflecting the conflicting contemporary ideology that complicates *1H6*. Shakespeare "incorporates" an ambiguous ideology in *1H6* by establishing links between Talbot and Essex, Joan and Queen Elizabeth. But the "play can go both ways"–Shakespeare does not offer a clear-cut approval of Essex or a condemnation of Talbot. Similarly, Joan as the virago (woman with masculine spirit) is at first compared to virtuous women from the exempla tradition, an English military patriot (Penthesilea), and Amazons. Queen Elizabeth who dressed as an Amazon to visit her troops at Tilbury "is surely the shadowy double behind the sudden appearance in the French camp of Joan, the puzzlingly Astraea-connected Amazonian ... " (56). Dressing Joan in armor in 1589 "was a stunning *coup de theatre*" (54). But negative comparisons applied to Joan point to her self-contradiction as well as to the complicated ideology of *1H6*. Moving from her role as a female warrior (associated with the royal superiority of the virago [58]) in the first part of the play, she becomes a subversive woman who challenges masculine authority by crossdressing in the middle of *1H6*. The "popular strategy for neutralizing the manly woman was to feminize her" (59), and so at the end of the play Joan is portrayed as a witch, one of the "overwhelmingly female class of malefactors" (60). The witch is Joan's last "topical role." Even though she is "feminized and demonized," Joan still cannot relieve the "ideological discomfort" underlying *1H6*.

421. Levin, Richard. "Feminist Thematics and Shakespearean Tragedy." *PMLA* 103 (1988): 125-38.

While there are some benefits of feminist approaches to Shakespeare, the aims, methodology, and results of a number of earlier studies of the tragedies by Berger (item 80), Erickson (item 284), Greene (item 82), Gohlke (item 115), Kahn (item 160), Leverenz (item 128), Bamber (item 175), Novy (item 262), and others are flawed. Marilyn French (item 155), however, is the "worst offender" (130). These critics reduce the tragedies to a conflict between two abstractions (male and female), thus ignoring the complexities in characterization and tragic outcome. Guilty of "thematicism," these feminists remind us of the older theme and structure critics with whom they share many of the same sins. Feminists often do "theme stretching," making the "play fit the theme," leading to "arbitrary" or "absurd" results. The emphasis on patriarchy and gender force feminist critics to "omit a number of uncooperative facts" (129), such as Father Capulet's preventing stereotypical male violence by restraining Tybalt at the ball or Macbeth's being better off by banishing women (the witches and Lady Macbeth).

Homogenized by these critics, tragic heroes are reduced "to a sorry lot indeed" by failing to learn anything from their deeds (131). By depreciating men to appreciate women, the feminists "minimize [our] emotional involvement" with the heroes, "debasing them beyond tragic sympathy" (135). Nor are feminists able to find a tragic resolution because the problem for them is always seen in terms of patriarchy, not individual actions. Concentrating exclusively on theme (gender), feminist critics dissolve the difference between genres, seeing tragedy as comedy gone wrong, which in turn leads to the "diminution of the tragic genre in particular" (133). They fail to see that the conventions of tragedy determine the presentation of gender. In their intentionalist readings, feminists do not separate Shakespeare's views from their own, though they are moving in the right direction when they begin to discern gender assumptions inductively from the plays themselves. Finally, feminist psychoanalytical views of men as "unconscious misogynists" are distorted because "the conception does not fit the tragic heroes" and so "radically distorts their characters" (135). Feminists dangerously misrepresent the concept of masculinity.

422. ---. "Reply." *PMLA* 103 (1988): 818-19.

In response to Alberto Cacidedo (item 407), Levin maintains that Othello and Desdemona's marriage is not presented as a typical patriarchal marriage. As for the endings of the comedies, Shakespeare meant them that way even if the critics do not. The question is "not whether we can find such problems but whether the ending calls attention to them and so undercuts its own 'closure'" (819). The achievements of feminist criticism are still impressive, even though feminist revisionists are wrong to suggest that they possess the magic key to the plays.

423. Marsh, Derick R.C. "*Othello* Re-read." *Sydney Studies in English* 14 (1988-89): 3-12.

Contemporary critics, including feminists, misrepresent *Oth* by forcing the play into an ideological mold. Interpreting the play sexually, as against male chauvinism, only continues the F.R. Leavis approach of finding ways to make the tragedy less painful ("Diabolical Intellect and the Noble Hero," *Scrutiny* 6 [1937]). Denying Othello dignity and refusing to be upset by his distress turns the play into a "less agonizing experience than it is usually found to be" (8). Feminist critics have misguidedly elevated Desdemona to the role of the "central tragic figure" (7). Using *Oth* to indict the institution of marriage, Irene Dash (item 152) makes us feel that "There's nothing much wrong" in *Oth* "that a few sessions with a marriage counsellor wouldn't put right" (8). The real tragedy of *Oth* is that the couple's relationship is "founded on mutual love" that "cannot protect itself" (9). Feminist explanations of *Oth*, such as Kahn's (item 160), based on "fear of female sexuality," or Jardine's (item 224), focusing on "Desdemona's refusal to accept her place in a male-dominated society," reduce the "human condition to the level of triviality" (10). Interpretations of *Oth* based on "sexual politics" ignore Desdemona's defiance of her father, her spirited defense of Othello before the senate, and our caring for and being so passionately moved by the lovers. Exploring the great imponderable, love, *Oth* resists "simple ideological explanations" (12).

424. Mathis, Mary S. "Portia's Role-Playing in *The Merchant of Venice*: Yes, Nerrisa, We Shall Turn to Men." *Conference of College Teachers of English Studies* [Texas] 53 (Sept. 1988): 42-51.

The "most adept role-player" in *MV*, Portia moves with ease in her roles as dutiful daughter, lady of the green world, "professional man," and subordinate wife. Yet her "strength as a role-player is undermined by the power of a patriarchal order which ultimately benefits from her role-playing" (42). Although Portia may help Bassanio choose the leaden casket, she nonetheless validates her dead father's right to select her husband. Shylock's greed contrasts with Portia's father's humility to mitigate the "oppressive nature of the filial bond" (45). In the green world of Belmont, Portia is free to display her feminine wit. Even though she is qualified by that "incisive wit" to play the young braggart, she imitates the best of manhood in her courtroom performance as a lawyer, saving her criticism of men for Narissa's company. Her courtroom triumph is "diminished," however, because of the "low social stature of her opponent," Shylock, and because her female crossdressing would have been scorned by Elizabethan society, though the audience's "revulsion" would have been "blunted" (47) by Portia's achievement. She keeps the court in suspense about her solution to teach a moral lesson and to give Shylock three opportunities for mercy. Ultimately, she pays the price for her victory; she "sacrifices her claim to Bassanio's exclusive attention" since he gives Antonio her ring (48). Her male disguise upholds "the same patriarchal social order that confines both Jews and women to subordinate roles" (49). The audience knows at the end that she will return to Bassanio as his dutiful wife.

425. McEachern, Claire. "Fathering Herself: A Source Study of Shakespeare's Feminism." *Shakespeare Quarterly* 39 (1988): 269-90.

Proto-feminists discovered in Shakespeare's plays portrayals of women who were "strong and liberated in voice and action." Other feminists have concentrated on exposing the patriarchal assumptions and structures in his drama. Both feminism and new historicism see literature as a social text, but while feminists see politics extending into the family, new historicists limit the question of politics to larger issues of power. Shakespeare through his drama questions the dominant patriarchal system of his society by demystifying the role of the father. Because the marriage of a daughter entailed a loss of paternal authority demanding compensation, the father had the right to choose his daughter's husband.

Yet fathers must sacrifice their paternal authority to uphold the larger system of patriarchy. In *Ado*, Leonato realizes the implications of disowning his daughter in terms of the conflict between fatherly love and the social need for male honor. The conflict is revealed in Hero's physical appearance. Hero's physical resemblance to her father guarantees her mother's fidelity and her father's honor. Lear tries to fuse filial patriarchy with his social and political responsibilities, with devastating results. Driven by the urge to preserve his authority over both family and kingdom, Lear experiences the tension from which Cordelia's marriage signifies the final dissolution of his family and empire. "The ceremony of the division of the kingdom may be a way for Lear to formalize his loss and thereby minimize his pain" (284). Lear wants Cordelia to buy her right to marry, thus reversing the accepted transaction of marriage where the father pays for a husband for his daughter. One of the great strengths of feminist criticism is its ability to locate and analyze power structures that define the roles of women in a culture.

426. McLuskie, Kathleen. "'The Emperor of Russia Was My Father': Gender and Theatrical Power." In *Images of Shakespeare: Proceedings of the Third Congress of the International Shakespeare Association, 1986.* Ed. Werner Habicht, D.J. Palmer, and Roger Pringle. Newark, U of Delaware P, 1988. 174-87.

Shakespeare's plays illustrate the "conflict over reading woman as a sign" (182) to determine the meaning of women. Critics must make the "crucial difference between 'woman' and 'women' ... " (186). The question of a woman's identity in Shakespeare, as in other dramatic representations, is linked, "locked," into stories about her, usually stories about her sexuality. While these stories provide the character with an "authenticating existence outside the confines of plot" (175), the stories can be used for conventional, misinformed notions of womanhood in which "women are contested and affirmed at the same time" (176). *Oth* in particular illustrates how "the double-edged effect of images of woman is acted out." Iago, Brabantio, Cassio, Roderigo, and Othello express "conflicting meanings" of who Desdemona is; these images are imposed on her and become the "contest over the truth of Desdemona's sexuality" (180). The "iconic, exemplary" power of Desdemona on stage contrasts with the Desdemona fantasized through Iago's misogyny and Othello's language. The male fantasy of "female duplicity" arbitrarily becomes the only truth. In Act 5.2, Desdemona as the sacrificial victim and the betrayer is the recipient of violence and reverence associated with pornography. A powerful force for truth, Desdemona, unlike Iago and Othello, "needs no narrative of her own" (181). The same "contradiction between visual and verbal signs" is found in *WT* where Leontes's "version of events" is colored by his images and male anxiety and thus contrasts with Hermione's stage presence as a mother. In Leontes's twisted syllogism, "Hermione, chaste or false, cannot be Hermione; she must be representative, exemplary ... " (183). Denying the signs of her innocence, Leontes demonstrates that a woman's identity can be sullied by the biased cultural expectations of all women.

427. Neely, Carol Thomas. "Constructing the Subject: Feminist Practice and the New Renaissance Discourses." *English Literary Renaissance* 18 (1988): 5-18.

New theoretical discourses–new historicist, cultural materialist (the two together best labeled "cult-historicists" [12]), Lacanian, and deconstructive–reproduce patriarchy by marginalizing or erasing women. The texts of new historicism are "male, upper class, hierarchal, and prescriptive" (8), and by concentrating on power and politics they subordinate women. Materialist criticism devotes few studies to women–see *Shakespeare and the Question of Theory* (item 303)–and yet even the study by McLuskie (item 295) argues that women have no way to enter the literary text. Hence, it is "hard to know how the materialist feminist critic is to proceed" (10). Though feminist critics share many of the goals of "Derridean deconstructionism, [and] Lacanian psychoanalysis," such as undoing hierarchies and binary opposition and challenging phallocentric cultures, these discourses "in their constitution of linguistic subjects appropriate women to dematerialize them" (10). Rose (item 307) and Vickers (item 313), for example, collapse gender differences. In Vickers, the "female signifier metamorphoses into the male signified" (11). Waller (item 349) similarly erases both gender and history. Feminism must read over texts profiting from new theoretical discourses without being marginalized by them. A recent anthology, *Rewriting the Renaissance* (item 333), and articles by Jardine (item 377), Newman (item 387), and Kahn (item 378) illustrate how feminist criticism of Shakespeare can successfully read the plays within the "contexts of social history, biography, women's history, and women writers" (16).

428. Noling, Kim H. "Grubbing Up the Stock: Dramatizing Queens in *Henry VIII." Shakespeare Quarterly* 39 (1988): 291-306.

In *H8*, Shakespeare endorses the historical monarch's "expedient use of queens" as the means of obtaining a male heir. The "most theatrically powerful queen" in the play, Katharine resists Henry's attempts to nullify her. Shakespeare enlarges her stature through strong, emphatic staging. For her first entrance she takes center stage beside Henry, and during her trial scene she crosses to stand beside Henry, thus upstaging her judges. Shakespeare also increases Katharine's theatrical force by developing her subjectivity. Defining herself through her speeches, she expresses "a succession of attitudes, including confidence in her integrity, defiance, alienation, indignation, and bitter regret" (295). Her strength, however, is balanced by the characterizations of the other queens. With Anne, Shakespeare "ultimately re-affirms Henry's valuing of a queen according to her ability to produce a suitable heir" (298). She is distanced by limited exposure and by failure to express or assert her will. Anne is defined more by other characters' determinations of her. By the end of the play she is completely supplanted by the stage presence of the infant Elizabeth. The daughter fulfills Henry's patriarchal need for an heir because she will become the "maiden Phoenix" whose "ashes new create another heir,/As great in admiration as herself" (Act 5.5.40-42). Although a girl child, she is the means, through "her legitimizing of James I," of restoring the throne to patriarchal monarchy.

429. Rabkin, Gerald. "Shakespeare Our Ideologist." *Modern Language Studies* 18 (1988): 3-22. Esp. "The Turn of the Shrew," 16-18.

New political and theoretical criticisms of Shakespeare are exemplified by the work included in such anthologies as *Alternative Shakespeares* (item 282); *Shakespeare and the Question of Theory* (item 303); and *Shakespeare Reproduced* (item 376).

Discussing Shakespeare's plays, feminists often debate questions
of theory and are aware of the advantages and limitations of
aligning their political goals with Marxism. In debating the politics
of Shakespeare, "the most privileged patriarch of all" (16),
feminists attack simplistic readings of the plays dividing characters
and issues into masculine and feminine. "A frequent theme in
feminist essays...is the theoretical inadequacy of feminist criticism
which approaches Shakespeare from a humanist, essentialist
perspective" (17). Seeing feminism as a "project for social change,"
McLuskie (item 295) "challenges liberal feminism's understanding
of the material circumstances which produce gender values" (17).
Similarly, Belsey's "radical methodology" (item 275) opposes a
"fixed grid of gender," arguing for the pluralization of meaning of
Shakespeare's works.

430. Reynolds, Peter. *As You Like It: A Dramatic Commentary*.
     London: Penguin Books, 1988. Esp. Chapter Four: "A Feminist
     Text," 80-100.

Interpretations of a romantic love affair between a female
Rosalind and a male Orlando distort the idea of marriage and
women in Shakespeare's times. The Rosalind/Ganymede "spoken
text is almost entirely masculine" (85). Shakespeare's audience
would have been aware of the gender of the actor playing the
"woman"; Ganymede/Rosalind, like Viola/Cesario, is not
"exclusively female" but "inseparable from the actor with distinct
and recognizable male qualities" (83). Unlike a woman,
Rosalind/Ganymede is a teacher and Orlando's "equal or better"
(85), one man speaking to another man. The homoerotic
implications in the roles actually "parody romantic wooing" (88).
Reflecting Shakespeare's patriarchal views and fears of female
sexuality, *AYL* "sounds dire warnings about the dangers of
uncontrollable pre-marital desire" (91). At court Celia is the
dominant figure in the women's relationship; her "verbal skills
seem to be more a product of class than gender" (95). But in the
forest, Rosalind is in charge showing a "transformation of the
previous female relationship to one between individuals of
different sex" (97). When Rosalind appears as herself at the end
of *AYL*, she departs from the fantasy world of Arcadia where "you

may go about in disguise and pretend to be a man" for the more natural world of man/woman "as opposed to an unnatural one (man and man)" (99).

431. Rose, Mary Beth. *The Expense of Spirit: Love and Sexuality in English Renaissance Drama.* Cornell UP, 1988. Esp. 35-42 (*Ado*; *LLL*; *MND*); 131-56 (*Oth*); and 178-86 (romances).

By celebrating marriage, Elizabethan romantic comedy symbolizes the ongoing life of society. Before the Renaissance, sexual love was considered out of the question as a basis for marriage. Celibacy was the highest state of being. During the Renaissance, thanks to the Puritan theologians, "conjugal loyalty and affection replaced celibacy as the officially idealized pattern of sexual conduct" (17) and for the state a way to legitimatize patriarchy. Shakespeare presents the silliness of the vow of celibacy in *LLL*. The absurd oath is broken immediately, rejecting the courtly love syndrome as sterile, shallow, and static. In *MND*, conflict arises between individual choice and forced marriage. The lovers think they are asserting their individuality, but the lack of differentiation among them and the mix-up in the forest signify both their lack of uniqueness and the arbitrary quality of their choices. Achieving the sense of irony "enjoyed by the audience" of *MND*, Beatrice and Benedict in *Ado* become "humbly aware that in seeming to lose their identities, they have in fact gained self-knowledge" (39). Romantic comedy helped to form "female dignity and autonomy" (42) through marriage thus leading to a more harmonious society.

In *Oth*, "tragedy participates in the dissolution of a prior system of meaning" (98). The martial feats of an earlier tragedy of action, symbolized by Othello, clash with the new private heroics of marriage represented by Desdemona. These new heroics of marriage, though, are a "failed achievement" (131) because *Oth*, revealing a dual mentality at work, "simultaneously exalts and degrades women." The heroics of marriage "dissolved from its own unresolved contradictions" (131). Othello's "relationship to the state, forged through public service, is also personal and intimate, in that it permeates every aspect of his life and identity" (132). He cannot assimilate his life as a married man into his view of himself as a public servant. Because of this inability, Othello is susceptible to Iago's wily assertions that love leads to adultery. Harshly separating public life from private life, Othello thereby associates desire with fear, sin, and death. Desire for him subverts his identity, and so he feels justified executing Desdemona in his role as a public servant. "Freedom for Othello, therefore, would seem to lie in a commitment to the heroics of marriage, yet he is unable adequately to make the leap from the hierarchies of the heroism of action to the analogies of the heroism of marriage" (140). Because of this "erotic ambivalence," Othello must be disqualified as "a protagonist in the heroics of marriage" (142).

In contrast to Othello, Desdemona's definition of marriage combines the mental and the physical. She is the "heroine of marriage," especially in the senate scene where she selects her own husband in opposition to parental authority. But while this scene shows that marriage for Desdemona is an adventure it also undermines her own claims. Her "predicament can be located in the contradictory terms in which female identity is constructed in the heroics of marriage" (148). Shakespeare's diffusing "female heroism between" Desdemona and Emilia establishes "significant implications ... for assessing the tragic representation of sexuality" (155).

The "heroics of marriage" lie behind the construction of the romances as well.

Reviews: *Queen's Quarterly* 97 (1990): 154; Helms, Lorraine, *Theatre Journal* 41 (1989): 416; Jordan, C., *Renaissance Quarterly* 43 (1990): 223-26; Peake, R.H., *Choice* 26 (1989): 1331; Slade, Giles, *Huntington Library Quarterly* 53 (1990): 243-47; Stockton, Sharon, *Genre* 22 (1989): 197-201.

432. Rubinstein, Frankie. "Persistent Sexual Symbolism: Shakespeare and Freud." *Literature and Psychology* 34 (1988): 1-26.

Shakespeare's sexual puns anticipate by three hundred years Freud's dream symbols. As Freud was to do, Shakespeare links the face and its parts (eyes, lips, cheeks, ears) as "a surrogate for the pubic-anal area" (2). Ears could symbolize the vagina, and the eye could represent the vagina as well as the male member. In *H5* a "serious conceit on the eye exploits its bawdy innuendo as the male symbol of power and potency, and the mistaken idea that manhood can be measured by 'balls' and 'gun-stones'" (4). The emphasis on blindness suggests man's folly in the pursuit of his desires as well as emasculation. Architectural elements also symbolize the private parts of the body. Doors can stand for women's lips. Portia, whose sexual language is purposely excessive, has a name that means doors, and suitors knock at her portals to gain access to her fortune (11). Her Belmont is a temple which, as Freud indicates, in "dreams, churches, and chapels represent women's genitals" (10). Stairs, ladders, rising/falling imagery, and falling off a pear tree also connote the sexual as Act 2 of *RJ* attests. Though "boxes, chests, ovens, apples, and pears" are traditionally "female symbols in Shakespeare as in dream language," it would be "hasty" to see these concave shapes as always referring to the female. They can be masculine, too, referring to "men's buttocks and testicles" (16). Apples and pears are penises in *RJ* and *AC*.

433. Shaffer, Brian W. "'To Manage Private and Domestic Quarrels': Shakespeare's *Othello* and the Genre of Elizabethan Domestic Tragedy." *Iowa State Journal of Research* 62 (1988): 443-57.

Oth shares much in common with Elizabethan domestic tragedies *Arden of Feversham, A Warning for Fair Women,* and *A Woman Killed with Kindness*. Like these plays, *Oth* is concerned with jealousy, adultery, and the idea of woman; like them structurally, it moves from marriage to "disintegration" to punishment and death. Yet while the conventions of domestic tragedy inform *Oth*, Shakespeare violates and subverts a "number of its 'comfortable' assumptions." Most significantly, he "renders more complex and problematic than do the other playwrights the issues of women and epistemology" (450). There is no unfaithful wife in *Oth*. Othello's supposed punishment of Desdemona becomes the crime itself; and the didacticism of Elizabethan domestic tragedy is engulfed by irony. The popular notion that women are morally inferior to men is exploded in *Oth* which shows that it is "the men not the women who cheat, murder, and are deceived–who bring about the tragedy" (453). Breaking sexual stereotypes as well as "generic expectations," Shakespeare gives

Emilia far more insight about "the question of women and the world around her" than the women in domestic tragedy–Alice Arden, Anne Sanders, or Anne Frankford. By providing Othello with ocular proof based on sexual stereotypes and misleading stories, Iago gives the Moor a new form of knowledge supposedly founded on hard facts. Yet Othello's internal faith is wiped away by external doubt. In *Oth* a "parody of Baconian method *and* incorrect assumptions about women come together" (454).

434. Singh, Sarup. *The Double Standard in Shakespeare and Related Essays: Changing Status of Women in 16th and 17th Century England.* Delhi: Konark, 1988.

Chapter One focuses on "The Debate on Chastity." The Renaissance, as other patriarchal eras, prescribed a double standard for sexual behavior for men and women. Female chastity was imperative to the moral and social structure of civilization. Women's natures, however, were generally viewed as lascivious; "hence a rigorous cultural conditioning of girls [was] necessary in order to produce virtuous wives" (4). Women, who were brought up under rigid restrictions, had to rely on male family members to help preserve their chastity. The Puritans elevated the status of marriage by attacking the male exploitation of women. However, while they advocated both male and female chastity, the Puritans nonetheless regarded adultery (sex involving a married woman) as a more serious offense than fornication (sex involving a married man). Elizabethan laws reinforced the idea of woman as property, first her parents' then her husband's. Many Puritans believed the only way to ensure marital fidelity for both sexes was to promote marriages based on compatibility.

In Chapter Two on *"Othello* and Others," a happy marriage is an ideal to be sought. Shakespeare's plays endorse the attitude of some of his contemporaries that adultery resulted from arranged marriages and that compatible marriages encouraged chastity. Shakespeare's male protagonists are often as chaste as his female. In Shakespeare, lecherous men are either comic or pitiable. In spite of his apparent understanding of women, however, Shakespeare applies a double standard to the sexes. "Indeed [men] have a tendency to denigrate the female sex and to treat as property even the women they profess to love" (28). Men are especially proprietorial about women's sexual behavior. Even Shakespeare's most independent women accept wifely obedience as their chief duty. Rosalind, Katharine, and Portia all submit to their husbands. The most important area of obedience was chastity. Wifely chastity was thought, in general, to be a class attribute: Desdemona cannot envision a faithless wife; Emilia can. When Emilia attacks the double standard, she is not speaking for Shakespeare, who "no where takes the view that it is man's conduct which is responsible for women's conduct" (37). Shakespeare's attitudes toward male chastity in marriage are often ambivalent. In *Lear*, Gloucester accepts his illegitimate son and raises him with his legitimate one. The bastard is a result of "sport," not sin. However, Edmund's evil reflects the Puritanical equation of bastardy with baseness. No good can come of male infidelity. Shakespeare has no such ambivalence toward female adultery. "Shakespeare's men clearly claim the *right* to kill their wives in the event of a lapse on their part or indeed even in the event of a strong enough suspicion" (44). It is indicative of the double standard that no one questions this right. The husband is blamed only for being mistaken about his wife's virtue. In *CE*, Shakespeare presents a case where the wife, Adriana, suspects her husband, Antipholus, of adultery. She is portrayed as a jealous nag who drives her husband away with her accusations. Her suspicions are false, but so are Othello's and Posthumus's whose jealousy is nonetheless accepted.

Chapter Three surveys "The Humanists."

Chapter Four deals with "The Seventeenth Century." In the late 16th and early 17th centuries education for women emphasized accomplishments over learning. While Shakespeare's women reflect this emphasis on social graces, he is also influenced by Puritan ideas of the work ethic. His young heroines have generally been trained by tutors–as Bianca is–or, in Miranda's case, by her father. In none of his plays does Shakespeare portray women's education as a corrupting influence.

Chapters Five and Six deal with "The Double Standard in Restoration Comedy."

Reviews: *Reference & Research Book News* 5 (Apr. 1990): 29; Koreth, A. *Yearly Review* [U of Delhi] 2 (Dec. 1988).

435. Slights, William E. "The Changeling in *A Dream*." *Studies in English Literature, 1500-1900* 28 (1988): 259-72.

A traditional reading of *MND* arguing that women's passions are controlled by men's intellect through the harmony of marriage does not explain the complex indeterminacy found in the text. This indeterminacy is best illustrated in the conflicting and competing views of the changeling boy; for Titania he is a sign of "sorority and pregnancy"; for Oberon, a symbol of "wifely insubordination." The boy is one of "three childish faces of love" (with Cupid and Puck), and he "represents no uniform or fixed approach to the meaning of love" (266). Like the weather, he is a source of "conflicting evidence" (265). Shakespeare certainly does not endorse marriage as "a patriarchal triumph over female waywardness"; in fact, love is presented as a series of "uncontrollable, carnavalesque impulses" (267) that the patriarchs Theseus and Egeus are powerless to contain or suppress. Shakespeare ignores male respectability, does not limit reason to men (whose main acts are to make war and to hunt), and shows that though women are taught to "acknowledge ... male superiority in a patrilineal-patrological culture" (267), they do not. Titania does not really give up the boy. The fact that the true source of vitality for Shakespeare is not found in princes' courts but in the marginal world further proves that the "male rules of power break down often with ... extremely amusing results" (268). "The real forces celebrated in the play would seem to be not marital restraint, chastity, or even, perhaps, constancy, but natural sexual impulses and radically unstable sense perceptions" (269).

436. Snyder, Susan. "*All's Well That Ends Well* and Shakespeare's Helens: Text and Subtext, Subject and Object." *English Literary Renaissance* 18 (1988): 66-77.

Helena's shifts between "assertion and self ab-negation" (67) are reflected in gaps–disjunctions, indirections, silences–in the text of *AWW*. These gaps point to the problems Helena experiences as the aggressive subject desiring her lover rather than being the (typically feminine) object of his desire. Unlike Rosalind or Portia, Helena is "highly unusual among Shakespeare's comic

heroines" (70) in initiating the wooing. *MND* provides a "subtext"
for *AWW*; the "conflicts" in this earlier comedy remain "half
submerged" in the later problem play (76). Male corrections of
female behavior are more directly expressed in *MND*.
Shakespeare links the Helenas of these two plays by a name that
recalls Helen of Troy, a woman who (like Venus) actively pursued
her man. Both Helenas venture "into alien territory" for their
men. Illustrating the "radical reversal of male and female" (44) in
AWW, Helena switches roles in the Daphne/Apollo story by
chasing Bertram and then feeling guilt and shame. But while
Oberon ends Helena's subversive initiation of wooing in *MND*,
forcing her and Titania under patriarchal control, Helena in *AWW*
persists in being the desiring subject; she "acts as her own
Oberon" (75). Two possible interpretations make Helena's
subversive behavior less intimidating. The "safer" one is to see her
deeds as dictated by providence; "Helena's purpose must be God's
purpose" (76). The "riskier" reading emphasizes the strong bonds
between Helena and the other women. This feminist
interpretation underscores the "female integrity of self" (76) and
reinstitutes the type of female friendship that Helena loses in
MND.

437. Thompson, Ann. "'The Warrant of Womanhood': Shakespeare
      and Feminist Criticism." In *The Shakespeare Myth*. Ed. Graham
      Holderness. Manchester: Manchester UP, 1988. 74-88.

A survey of feminist criticism of Shakespeare reveals how
influential and productive it has been during the 1980s. While
feminists such as Elizabeth Abel disallow feminist analysis of
male-written texts, many other feminists want to avoid the
isolationism and irresponsibility of gynocriticism that neglects
Shakespeare. At the worst, feminism risks being "naive and
unproblematic" by not going beyond "old-fashioned character
study" (77). Apologists who see Shakespeare as a proto-feminist
have effectively challenged masculine critical views that women
characters should be seen through male characters. As Dash
shows (item 152), male producers and directors have stereotyped
and marginalized women, too. But feminists must recognize that
women characters are "restricted by patriarchal structures that

dominate their lives" (77). Arguing for mutuality in the plays, apologist Novy (item 262) "makes the best of these situations." In shedding light on Shakespeare's problematic characters such as Cressida, Kate, or Cleopatra, feminist criticism can "diminish" or "destroy" traditional pleasures readers have had, and in emphasizing the "victim-status of women" producers can adopt feminist readings. Studies of social history by Dusinberre (item 6) and Belsey (item 275) relate marriage and women to changes in religious and political thought. McLuskie (item 295) and others study disrupting theatre conventions associated with cross-dressing. Psychoanalytic readings such as Showalter's of Ophelia (item 308) can be extended to the "Cordelia myth"; and Rose (item 307) usefully considers gender in relationship to "author's motivation, the audience or reader's responses, and to the latent structures of literary texts themselves" (83). Adelman (item 274) and Kahn (item 160) write about male characters from a feminist/psychoanalytic perspective. While French (item 155) sees the plays as a debate between male and female principles, Jardine (item 224) deplores this "essentialist" tradition. Feminist criticism of Shakespeare proves that there are many ways to see the plays and that women reading the plays can provide fresh, keen insights. Feminists should not privilege the tragedies but turn to the early plays and histories. Feminist studies of Shakespeare must not be ghettoized but be seen as a "major new perspective that must eventually inform *all* readings" (84).

438. Traub, Valerie. "Jewels, Statues, and Corpses: Containment of Female Erotic Power in Shakespeare's Plays." *Shakespeare Studies* 20 (1988): 215-238.

Hamlet, Laertes, Othello, Brabantio, and Leontes exhibit masculine anxiety about uncontrollable female sexuality and inevitable inconstancy. The erotic is chaos; stasis is security. Victims of male sexual dualism, women are seen as angels or whores but feared to be whores all along. To contain female eroticism and assuage male anxiety, Shakespeare's men use a strategy of containment, metaphorically displacing "their own desire for stasis" with the women they love and fear (216). In *Ham*, where sex is equated with disease, Gertrude can be safe only by living a chaste marriage, according to the Ghost whose revenge is "sexually sadistic." Similarly, Ophelia, who as a woman is contaminated by Gertrude's sin, can reclaim "sexual desirability only as a dead, perpetual virgin" (219). When her body is suitably "fetishized" (220) in the grave, Ophelia fulfills the male ideal of chastity. Hamlet and Laertes's fight in the graveyard symbolizes their "sexual possession" of her. In *Oth,* woman's constancy is seen as "the very foundation" of marriage. Like Hamlet, Othello believes "women's sex should be locked up" (223) and links sexual gratification with death. Murdering Desdemona and objectifying her as a jewel (Act 5.2.343) enables Othello to impose stasis on his wife, idealize her, and sanctify himself as a priest. "Othello may safely sexualize Desdemona only posthumously ... " (227). *WT* does not necessarily "amend the tragic vision of *Ham* and *Oth*" (228) or offer a victory for feminine ideals. Even though Hermione is united with Leontes, he uses the same strategies of containment that characterized their earlier relationship. Being transformed into a statue reveals that Hermione is "metaphorically contained and psychically disarmed" (230). Since the tragedies and romances are filtered through male anxieties that vilify female erotic power, Shakespeare "perpetuates defensive structures of dominance instituted by men" (232).

439. Wexler, Joyce. "A Wife Lost and/or Found." *The Upstart Crow* 8 (1988): 106-17.

Informed by Derrida's "strategy of reversing and displacing [the] polarities" of (male/female), feminist criticism can challenge traditional interpretations based on hero-dominated texts. For Derrida the text is undecidable, embracing alternative readings in which women's silence is powerful while man's phallocentric attempt to seek meaning in language is impossible. The hymen, a symbol of undecidability of meaning, is female and voiceless. The discovery of Hermione in *WT* precisely "fits Derrida's description of the hymen" (114). Because of his phallocentric drive, Leontes relies on words and so argues that "false words produce false heirs" (109). Yet women's truthfulness represented by their silence punctures his quest for meaning. Seeking the constant, Leontes distrusts anyone who plays multiple roles, as do his daughter and Autolycus who "provides a comic parallel to Perdita" (113). Hermione's reappearance is "the culminating scene" for all the "interpretive contexts" and embodies the logical contraries at the heart of Derrida's view of the undecidable text. "Hermione on her pedestal is statue and woman, art and nature, trick and miracle, aged and resurrected" (114). All these alternatives ("and/or") are possible simultaneously. Though customarily regarded as a "happy ever-after ending," the reunion of Leontes and Hermione "need not be staged as a reconciliation" (116), since Hermione greets Leontes only perfunctorily, speaks only to her daughter for whom she kept herself alive, and has no other character to "sanction" such a reconciliation. The ending of *WT* can offer "religious affirmation or a psychological portrait of Leontes"; the play can express both "the wish for forgiveness and the impossibility of receiving it." Leontes might be ignored in his foolish rambling, unaware of the permanent consequences of his sins, while the women reap the fruits of a mother-daughter bond.

AUTHOR INDEX

This index contains two types of numbers. Those in italics, appearing first, refer to page numbers in the introduction; those numbers following in Roman type refer to entry numbers in the bibliography.

PLAY/POEM INDEX

This index contains two types of numbers. Those in italics, appearing first, refer to page numbers in the introduction; those numbers following in Roman type refer to entry numbers in the bibliography.

SUBJECT INDEX

This index contains two types of numbers. Those in italics, appearing first, refer to page numbers in the introduction; those numbers following in Roman type refer to entry numbers in the bibliography.

Made in the USA
Coppell, TX
17 March 2022

75110172R00240